绍兴市高等教育重点教材

德英双语汽车教程

**Deutsch-English
Kraftfahrzeugtechnik
German-English
Automotive Engineering**

浙江越秀外国语学院西方语言学院组编
主编　张建强　张杰
参编　冀婷婷　裘媛平　周芳蓉
　　　冯　晞　骆超群　龚　曦

机械工业出版社

本教程的编写参考了大量国外汽车专业文献，全书分为汽车技术篇、制造技术篇和新技术篇，每篇有10个部分，每课均有一篇德文课文和一篇英文课文，后面还附有相关问题。书后附有课文的参考译文。本书内容涉及汽车构造、汽车总成、汽车技术、机械加工、汽车生产等各方面，既适用于教学，也适合广大工程技术人员及德语、英语爱好者自学使用。

图书在版编目（CIP）数据

德英双语汽车教程 / 张建强，张杰主编 . —北京：机械工业出版社，2019.9
绍兴市高等教育重点教材
ISBN 978-7-111-64421-7

Ⅰ. ①德⋯ Ⅱ. ①张⋯ ②张⋯ Ⅲ. ①汽车工程 – 英语 – 高等学校 – 教材 ②汽车工程 – 德语 – 高等学校 – 教材 Ⅳ. ①U46

中国版本图书馆 CIP 数据核字（2019）第 286741 号

机械工业出版社（北京市百万庄大街22号 邮政编码100037）
策划编辑：孙　鹏　责任编辑：孙　鹏
责任校对：肖　琳　封面设计：鞠　杨
责任印制：常天培
北京虎彩文化传播有限公司印刷
2020年1月第1版第1次印刷
184mm×260mm・18.5印张・419千字
标准书号：ISBN 978-7-111-64421-7
定价：79.90元

电话服务　　　　　网络服务
客服电话：010-88361066　机 工 官 网：www.cmpbook.com
　　　　　010-88379833　机 工 官 博：weibo.com/cmp1952
　　　　　010-68326294　金 书 网：www.golden-book.com
封底无防伪标均为盗版　机工教育服务网：www.cmpedu.com

前言
■ Vorwort
■ Foreword

汽车工业是我国的重要产业之一，中国汽车工业在发展过程中借鉴了大量德国及美国等国家汽车工业的先进技术。自改革开放以来，世界主要汽车大国的企业纷纷进入中国，以独资及合资的方式在中国建立了许多汽车制造企业。这些企业在日常运行中需要大量既懂汽车行业相关知识又懂德语及英语的专业人才。据了解，浙江省在这方面也对德语/英语应用型人才有很大的需求。为了满足市场的需求以及培养应用型外语人才的需要，我们组织编写了《德英双语汽车教程》。

自20世纪80年代以来，国内已出版了众多专业外语读本，并结合各个专业出版了一些按学科分类的科技外语读本和教材，但是作为汽车专业的德英双语读物或教材却一直是个空白。

本书的编写正是为了满足广大读者的这一迫切需要。本书的编写参考了大量国外汽车专业文献，全书分为3篇，分别为汽车技术篇、制造技术篇及新技术篇，每篇10个部分，共计30个部分，内容涵盖汽车主要组成部件、汽车及其零部件的制造工艺以及近年来在汽车上应用的新技术，每课由一篇文章及课后复习题构成，课文分为德文课文和英文课文，课文后还附有与本课内容相关的参考译文。

本书既适用于教学，也适合广大汽车行业工程技术人员及外语爱好者自学使用。

本书由浙江越秀外国语学院西方语言学院组织编写，由曾经在汽车行业从事近40年翻译工作的张建强老师和张杰博士主持编写，冯晞博士、裘媛平、冀婷婷、骆超群、周芳蓉老师以及龚曦老师参加了本书的编写工作。

本书的立项得到对外经贸大学陈建平教授的大力支持，在此表示感谢。

浙江吉利汽车控股公司资深副总裁、浙江越秀外国语学院客座教授张爱群女士对本书进行了指导，在此表示感谢。

由于编者能力有限，在编写过程中难免出现这样那样的问题，欢迎批评指正。希望本书能给读者提供切实有效的帮助，欢迎读者对本书提出建议。

目录

■ Inhaltsverzeichnis
■ Contents

Vorwort 前言
Foreword

Kapitel 1　Automobiltechnologie　汽车技术篇
Chapter 1　Technology of Automobile　汽车技术篇

Teil 1　Grundlagen des Automobils　汽车基础	**2**
Part 1　Basis for Automobile　汽车基础	**2**
Text 1　Entwicklung des Kraftfahrzeuges汽车发展史（德文）	2
Text 2　Evolution of the motor vehicle汽车发展史（英文）	7
Teil 2　Verbrennungsmotor　内燃机	**12**
Part 2　Engine　发动机	**12**
Text 1　Verbrennungsmotor内燃机（德文）	12
Text 2　Engine 发动机（英文）	15
Teil 3　Verbrennungsmotorblock　内燃机缸体	**18**
Part 3　Engine block　内燃机缸体	**18**
Text 1　Zylinder气缸体（德文）	18
Text 2　Engine block发动机缸体（英文）	22
Teil 4　Getriebe　变速器	**29**
Part 4　Variable-speed gearbox　变速器	**29**
Text 1　Getriebe变速器（德文）	29
Text 2　Variable-speed gearbox变速器（英文）	33
Teil 5　Kraftübertragungssystem　传动系统	**40**
Part 5　Drivetrain　传动系统	**40**
Text 1　Kraftübertragungssystem传动系统（德文）	40
Text 2　Drivetrain 传动系统（英文）	42
Teil 6　Lenkung　转向系统	**47**
Part 6　Steering　转向系统	**47**
Text 1　Lenkung 转向系统（德文）	47
Text 2　Steering gear转向器（英文）	53

| Teil 7 | Bremssystem | 制动系统 | 60 |
| Part 7 | Brakesystem | 制动系统 | 60 |

    Text 1   Bremse 制动器（德文）   60

    Text 2   Drum brake 鼓式制动系统（英文）   64

| Teil 8 | Fahrwerk | 底盘系统 | 74 |
| Part 8 | Chassis | 底盘系统 | 74 |

    Text1   Fahrwerk, Fahrgestell und Radaufhängung 底盘、车架与悬架（德文）   74

    Text 2   Chassis 底盘系统（英文）   81

| Teil 9 | Karosserie | 车身 | 86 |
| Part 9 | Vehicle body | 车身 | 86 |

    Text1   Karosserie 车身（德文）   86

    Text 2   Vehicle body 车身（英文）   89

| Teil 10 | Elektrisches System | 电气系统 | 96 |
| Part 10 | Electric System | 电气系统 | 96 |

    Text 1   Elektrische Anlage 汽车电器（德文）   96

    Text 2   Electric System 电气系统（英文）   99

2. Kapitel 2　Fertigungstechnik　制造技术篇
Chapter2　Production engineering　制造技术篇

| Teil 1 | Fertigungstechnik | 制造工艺 | 106 |
| Part 1 | Production engineering | 制造工艺 | 106 |

    Text 1   Fertigungstechnik 制造工艺（德文）   106

    Text 2   Production engineering 制造工艺（英文）   109

| Teil 2 | Umformen | 成型技术 | 115 |
| Part 2 | Forming | 成型技术 | 115 |

    Text 1   Umformen 成型技术（德文）   115

    Text 2   Forming 成型技术（英文）   120

| Teil 3 | Gießtechnik | 铸造技术 | 127 |
| Part 3 | Casting | 铸造技术 | 127 |

    Text 1   Gießtechnik 铸造技术（德文）   127

    Text 2   Casting 铸造技术（英文）   130

Teil 4	**Schmieden 锻造技术**	**135**
Part 4	**Forming 锻造技术**	**135**
Text 1	Schmieden锻造技术（德文）	135
Text 2	Forming锻造技术（英文）	137
Teil 5	**Trennen durch Spanen 切削加工**	**141**
Part 5	**Cutting and shaping with machine tools 切削加工**	**141**
Text 1	Trennen durch Spanen切削加工（德文）	141
Text 2	Cutting and shaping with machine tools切削加工（英文）	145
Teil 6	**Drehen 车削**	**151**
Part 6	**Turning 车削**	**151**
Text 1	Drehen车削（德文）	151
Text 2	Turning车削（英文）	154
Teil 7	**Fräsen und Bohren 铣削和钻削**	**158**
Part 7	**Milling and Drilling 铣削和钻削**	**158**
Text 1	Fräsen und Bohren铣削和钻削（德文）	158
Text 2	Milling and Drilling铣削和钻削（英文）	162
Teil 8	**Schweiβen 焊接技术**	**167**
Part 8	**Welding 焊接技术**	**167**
Text 1	Schweiβen焊接技术（德文）	167
Text 2	Metal-arc welding金属焊接（英文）	170
Teil 9	**Fahrzeuglackierung 汽车涂装技术**	**178**
Part 9	**Vehicle paintwork 汽车涂装技术**	**178**
Text 1	Fahrzeuglackierung汽车涂装（德文）	178
Text 2	Vehicle paintwork汽车涂装（英文）	182
Teil 10	**Arbeitssicherheit 劳动安全**	**193**
Part 10	**Working-Safety 劳动安全**	**193**
Text 1	Arbeitssicherheit und Unfallverhütung劳动安全与事故防护（德文）	193
Text 2	Working-Safety劳动安全（英文）	197

Kapitel 3　Neue Technologie　新技术篇
Chapter 3　New Technology　新技术篇

Teil 1　Benzineinspritzung　汽油直喷　　　　　　　　　　　　　　202
Part 1　LH–Motronic　汽油直喷　　　　　　　　　　　　　　　　202
　　Text 1　Benzineinspritzung汽油直喷（德文）　　　　　　　　　202
　　Text 2　LH-Motronic 汽油喷射（英文）　　　　　　　　　　　207
Teil 2　Elektronische Dieselregelung (EDC)　柴油机电子调节系统　216
Part 2　Injection systems for diesel engines　柴油机喷射系统　　 216
　　Text 1　Elektronische Dieselregelung（EDC）
　　　　　　柴油机电子调节系统（德文）　　　　　　　　　　　216
　　Text 2　Injection systems for diesel engines柴油机喷射系统（英文）　220
Teil 3　Katalysator　废气催化净化技术　　　　　　　　　　　　　225
Part 3　Catalyst　废气催化净化技术　　　　　　　　　　　　　　225
　　Text 1　Katalysator催化器（德文）　　　　　　　　　　　　　225
　　Text 2　Catalyst 催化器（英文）　　　　　　　　　　　　　　227
Teil 4　Hybridantriebe　混合动力驱动技术　　　　　　　　　　　231
Part 4　Hybrid drive systems　混合动力驱动系统　　　　　　　　　231
　　Text 1　Hybridantriebe混合动力驱动(德文)　　　　　　　　　 231
　　Text 2　Hybrid drive systems混合动力驱动系统（英文）　　　　234
Teil 5　Erdgasantrieb　天然气驱动技术　　　　　　　　　　　　　239
Part 5　Natural gas drives　天然气驱动技术　　　　　　　　　　　239
　　Text 1　Erdgasantrieb天然气驱动技术（德文）　　　　　　　　239
　　Text 2　Natural gas drives天然气驱动技术（英文）　　　　　　241
Teil 6　Brennstoffzelle　燃料电池技术　　　　　　　　　　　　　244
Part 6　Drives with fuel cells　燃料电池驱动　　　　　　　　　　244
　　Text 1　Wasserstoffantrieb - Brennstoffzelle氢燃料电池驱动装置
　　　　　　（德文）　　　　　　　　　　　　　　　　　　　　244
　　Text 2　Drives with fuel cells燃料电池驱动（英文）　　　　　　247
Teil 7　Elektrische Fensterheber　电动车窗　　　　　　　　　　　251
Part 7　Comfort and convenience systems　舒适与便捷系统　　　　251
　　Text 1　Elektrische Fensterheber 电动车窗（德文）　　　　　　251
　　Text 2　Comfort and convenience systems舒适与便捷系统（英文）　253

Teil 8　Navigationssystem　导航系统　　　　　　　　　　　　256
Part 8　Navigation system　导航系统　　　　　　　　　　　　256
　　Text 1　Navigationssystem导航系统（德文）　　　　　　　256
　　Text 2　Navigation system导航系统（英文）　　　　　　　259
Teil 9　Zentralverriegelung　中央控制门锁系统　　　　　　　264
Part 9　Central locking system　中央控制门锁系统　　　　　264
　　Text 1　Zentralverriegelung中央控制门锁系统（德文）　　264
　　Text 2　Central locking system中央控制门锁系统（英文）　270
Teil 10　Diebstahlschutzsystem　汽车防盗系统　　　　　　　276
Part 10　Anti-theft alarm system (ATA)　汽车防盗系统　　　276
　　Text 1　Diebstahlschutzsystem汽车防盗系统（德文）　　　276
　　Text 2　Anti-theft alarm system (ATA)汽车防盗系统（英文）　282

Kapitel 1
Automobiltechnologie

汽车技术篇

Chapter 1
Technology of Automobile

汽车技术篇

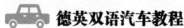

Teil 1　Grundlagen des Automobils　汽车基础
Part 1　Basis for Automobile　汽车基础

学习目标

【知识目标】

1. 了解汽车发展史及汽车的主要结构并掌握与汽车发展史和汽车结构、分类等相关的德语、英语专业术语、单词和词汇。

2. 掌握有关汽车主要结构的德英双语表达方法。

【能力目标】

1. 能对汽车历史及汽车总体结构的各大总成进行中、德、英语互译。

2. 能进行与汽车大体构造相关的德语、英语资料的阅读和翻译。

3. 能在汽车实物上标识出相应汽车结构的德语、英语单词和词汇。

Text 1　Entwicklung des Kraftfahrzeuges汽车发展史（德文）

◇1860　Der Franzose Lenoir baut den ersten lauffähigen, mit Leuchtgas betriebenen Verbrennungsmotor. Wirkungsgrad etwa 3%.

◇1867　Otto und Langen zeigen auf der Pariser Weltausstellung einen verbesserten Verbrennungsmotor. Wirkungsgrad etwa 9%.

◇1876　Otto baut den ersten Gasmotor mit Verdichtung in Viertakt-Arbeitsweise. Fast gleichzeitig baut der Engländer Clerk den ersten Zweitaktmotor mit Gasbetrieb.

◇1883　Daimler und Maybach entwickeln den ersten schnelllaufenden Viertakt-Benzinmotor mit Glührohrzündung.

◇1885　Erstes motorgetriebenes Zweirad von Daimler. Erster Dreiradkraftwagen von Benz (1886 patentiert) (Bild 1).

◇1886　Erste Vierradkutsche mit Benzinmotor von Daimler.

Kapitel 1   Automobiltechnologie // Chapter 1   Technology of Automobile

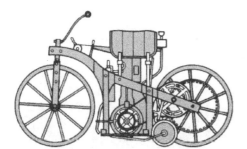

Daimler Motorrad, 1885
1 Zylinder, Bohrung 58 mm
Hub 100 mm, 0.26 1
0.37kW bei 600min^{-1}, 12km/h

Benz Patent–Motorwagen, 1886
1 Zylinder, Bohrung 91.4 mm
Hub 150 mm, 0.99 1
0.66kW bei 400min^{-1}, 15km/h

Bild: Daimler Motorrad und Benz Motorwagen

◇1887   Bosch erfindet die Abreißzündung.

◇1889   Der Engländer Dunlop stellt erstmals pneumatische Reifen her.

◇1893   Maybach erfindet den Spritzdüsenvergaser.

◇1893   Der Amerikaner Ford baut sein erstes Automobil und Diesel lässt sein Arbeitsverfahren für Schwerölmotoren mit Selbstzündung patentieren.

◇1897   MAN stellt ersten betriebsfähigen Dieselmotor her.

◇1897   Erstes Elektromobil von Lohner-Porsche (Bild 2).

◇1899   Fiatwerke in Turin gegründet.

◇1913   Einführung der Fließbandfertigung durch Ford. Produktion der Tin-Lizzy (T- Modell).

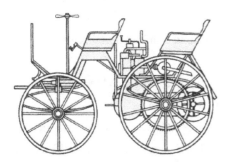
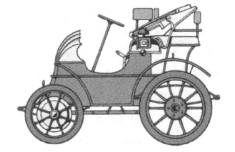

Daimler Motorwagen, 1886
1 Zylinder, Bohrung 70 mm
Hub 120 mm, 0.46 1
0.8kW bei 600min^{-1}, 18km/h

Elektromobil, 1897
System Lohner–Porsche
Transmissionsloser Antrieb
mit Radnaben–Elektromotor

Bild: Daimler Motorwagen und 1. Elektromobil

◇ 1916　Bayerische Motorenwerke gegründet.

◇ 1923　Erste Lastkraftwagen mit Dieselmotoren von Benz – MAN (Bild 3).

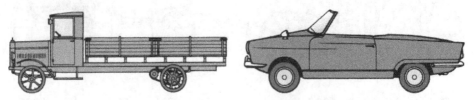

Benz–MAN Lastkraftwagen, 5 K 3
1.Diesel–LKW, 1923

NSU–Spider mit Wankelmotor,
1963, 500 cm^3, 37 kW bei
6000min^{-1}, 153km/h

Bild: 1. Lastkraftwagen mit Dieselmotor
　　　2. Pkw mit Wankelmotor

◇ 1936　Daimler-Benz baut serienmäßig Pkw mit Dieselmotoren.

◇ 1938　Gründung des VW-Werkes in Wolfsburg.

◇ 1949　Erster Niederquerschnittreifen und erster Stahlgürtelreifen von Michelin.

◇ 1950　Erste Gasturbine im Kraftfahrzeug durch Rover in England.

◇ 1953　Erste Automobilwerke (FAW) in China gegründet.

◇ 1954　NSU-Wankel baut den Kreiskolbenmotor (Bild 3).

◇ 1966　Elektronisch gesteuerte Benzineinspritzung (D-Jetronic) von Bosch für Serien-Fahrzeuge.

◇ 1970　Sicherheitsgurte für Fahrer und Beifahrer.

◇ 1978　Das Anti-Blockiersystem (ABS) wird bei Pkw-Bremsen eingebaut.

◇ 1984　Einführung von Airbag und Gurtstraffer.

◇ 1985　Einführung von geregelten Katalysatoren (Lamdasonde) für bleifreies Benzin.

◇ 1997　Elektronische Fahrwerk-Regelsysteme.

◇ 1999　Bi-Xenon-Licht (Bosch, D), schlüsselloser Fahrzeugzugang (Mercedes).

◇ 2000　EOBD für Ottomotor, Euro 3 für Pkw-Dieselmotoren.

◇ 2010　Dr. Li Jun, Leiter R&D Center der China FAW AG, wurde für die Amtszeit.

◇ 2012 bis 2014 zum Präsidenten der FISITA gewählt. Chinesische Automobilfirma Geely hat schwedische Firma Volvo angekauft.

Einteilung und Aufbau der Kraftfahrzeuge

Einteilung

Straßenfahrzeuge sind alle Fahrzeuge, die zum Betrieb auf der Straße vorgesehen sind und nicht an Gleise gebunden sind (Bild 1). Sie werden in zwei Gruppen eingeteilt, die Kraftfahrzeuge und die Anhängefahrzeuge. Kraftfahrzeuge besitzen immer einen maschinellen Antrieb.

Zweispurige Kraftfahrzeuge

Kraftwagen gelten als zwei- oder mehrspurige Kraftfahrzeuge. Dazu zählen.

Bild: Übersicht Straßenfahrzeuge

– **Personenkraftwagen (Pkw).** Sie sind hauptsächlich zum Transport von Personen, deren Gepäck oder von Gütern bestimmt. Sie können auch Anhänger ziehen. Die Zahl der Sitzplätze ist einschließlich Fahrer auf 9 beschränkt.

– **Nutzkraftwagen (Nkw).** Sie sind zum Transport von Personen, Gütern und zum Ziehen von Anhängefahrzeugen bestimmt. Personenkraftwagen sind keine Nutzkraftwagen.

Einspurige Kraftfahrzeuge

Krafträder sind einspurige Kraftfahrzeuge mit 2 Rädern. Sie können einen Beiwagen mitführen, wobei die Eigenschaft als Kraftrad erhalten bleibt, wenn das Leergewicht von 400 kg nicht überschritten wird. Auch das Ziehen eines Anhängers ist möglich.

– **Motorräder.** Sie sind mit festen Fahrzeugteilen (Kraftstoffbehälter, Motor) im Kniebereich und mit Fußrasten ausgestattet.

– **Motorroller.** Keine festen Teile im Kniebereich, die Füße stehen auf einem Bodenblech.

– **Fahrräder mit Hilfsmotor.** Sie haben Merkmale von Fahrrädern, z.B. Tretkurbeln (Moped, Mofa).

Aufbau

Ein Kraftfahrzeug besteht aus Baugruppen und deren einzelnen Bauteilen.

Die Festlegung der Baugruppen und die Zuordnung von Baugruppen zueinander ist nicht genormt. So kann z. B. der Motor als eigene Baugruppe gelten, oder er wird als Unterbaugruppe dem

Treibwerk zugeordnet.

Eine in diesem Buch vorgenommene Möglichkeit ist die Einteilung in die 4 Haupt- Baugruppen Motor, Kraftübertragung, Fahrwerk und elektrische Anlage. Die Zuordnung der Baugruppen und Bauteile ist im Bild 2 dargestellt.

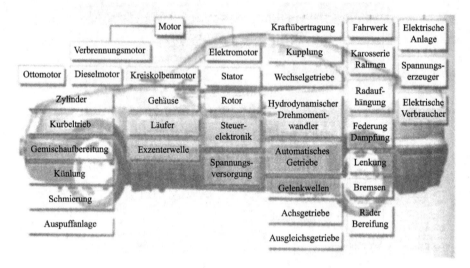

Bild: Aufbau eines Kraftzeuges

Neue Wörter

das	Kraftfahrzeug	汽车	das	Zweirad	二轮车
die	Entwicklung	发展、开发	der	Dreiradkraftwagen	三轮车
der	Wirkungsgrad	效率	das	Patent	专利
das	Motorrad	摩托车	die	Vierradkutsche	四轮车
der	Zylinder	气缸		erfinden	发明
die	Bohrung	缸孔	die	Abreißzündung	火花塞点火
der	Hub	行程		pneumatische Reifen	充气轮胎
der	Gasmotor	燃气发动机	der	Spritzdüsenvergaser	喷雾汽化器
die	Verdichtung	密封	das	System	系统
die	Viertakt-Arbeitsweise	四冲程工作方式	das	Elektromobil	电动车
der	Zweitaktmotor	二冲程发动机	das	Automobil	汽车
	schnelllaufend	快速运转的	der	Diesel	柴油机
der	Benzinmotor	汽油发动机	das	Arbeitsverfahren	工作方式
die	Glürohrzündung	预热塞点火	der	Schweröelmotor	重油发动机
	motorgetrieben	发动机驱动的	die	Selbstzündung	自燃

Kapitel 1　Automobiltechnologie // Chapter 1　Technology of Automobile

	patentieren	申请专利
	betriebsfähig	运转的
der	Dieselmotor	柴油发动机
die	Fliessbandfertigung	流水线制造
die	Produktion	生产、产品
das	Modell	型号，模型
der	Lastkraftwagen	载货汽车
	serienmässig	批量
	PKW	乘用车
der	Niederquerschnittreifen	低断面轮胎
der	Stahlgürtelreifen	钢带轮胎
die	Gasturbine	汽轮机
der	Kreiskolbenmotor	旋转活塞发动机
der	Wankelmotor	汪克尔发动机
der	Sicherheitsgurt	安全带
der	Fahrer	驾驶人
der	Beifahrer	前排乘员
das	Anti-Blokiersystem (ABS)	防抱死制动系统
	bremsen	制动
der	Airbag	气囊
der	Gurtstraffer	安全带张紧器
der	geregelte Katalysator (Lamdasonde)	可调节的催化器
	bleifrei	无铅
das	Benzin	汽油
das	Fahrwerk-Regelsystem	底盘可调节系统
	betriebener Verbrennungsmotor mit Leuchtgas	用煤气驱动的内燃机
	elektronische gesteuerte Benzineinspritzung (D-Jetronic)	电控汽油喷射

Text 2　Evolution of the motor vehicle 汽车发展史（英文）

◇1860　The Frenchman Lenoir constructs the first internal-combustion engine. Thermal efficiency is in the 3%.

◇1867　Otto und Langen display an improved internal-combustion engine. Thermal efficiency is in the 9%.

◇1876　Otto builds the first gas-powered engine to utilise the four-stroke compression cycle. At virtually the same time Clerk constructs the first gas-powered two stroke engine in England.

◇1883　Daimler and Maybach develop the first high speed four-cycle petrol engine using a hot tube ignition system.

◇1885　The first automobile from Benz (patented in 1886). First self-propelled motorcycle from Daimler.

◇1886　First four wheeled motor carriage with petrol engine from Daimler.

◇1887　Bosch invents the magneto ignition.

◇1889　Dunlop in England produces the first pneumatic tyres.

◇1893　Maybach invents the spray-nozzle carburettor. Diesel patents his design for a heavy oilburning powerplant employing the self-ignition concept.

◇1897　MAN presents the first workable diesel engine.

◇1897　First Electromobile from Lohner-Porsche.

◇1913　Ford introduces the production-line to automotive manufacturing. Production of the Tin Lizzy (Model T).

◇1916　The Bayerian Motor Works are founded.

◇1923　First motor lorry powered by a diesel engine produced by Benz-MAN.

◇1936　Daimler-Benz inaugurates series-production of passenger cars propelled by diesel engine.

◇1938　The VW- Works founded in Wolfsburg.

◇1949　First low-profile tyre and first steel-belted radial tyre produced by Michelin.

◇1953　The First Automobile Work (FAW) founded in China.

◇1954　NSU-Wankel constructs the rotary engine .

◇1966　Electronic fuel injection (D-Jetronic) for standard production vehicles produced by Bosch.

◇1970　Seatbelts for driver and front passengers.

◇1978　Mercedes Benz installs the first Antilock Braking System (ABS) in vehicles.

◇1984　Debut of the airbag and seatbelt tensioning system.

◇1997　Electronic suspension control systems (ESP).

◇1999　Bi-Xenon-Licht (Bosch, D).

◇2000　Parking assistance, distance warning systems, lane change assistance.

◇2010　Dr. Li Jun, Director of R&D Center China FAW Co. will become President of FISITA in Years from 2012 to 2014. Chinese private Automobile Company Geely acquiring schwede Automobile Company Volvo.

Motor vehicle classifications

Road vehicles is a category comprising all vehicles designed for road use, as operation on tracks or rails.

There are basically two vehicle classes: motor vehicles and trailers. Motor vehicles always possess an integral mechanical propulsion system.

Dual-track vehicles

Motor vehicles with more than two wheels can be found in dual-track and multiple-track versions. These include:

Passenger cars. These are primarily intended for use in transporting people, as well as their luggage and other small cargo. They can also be used to pull trailers. The number of seats, including that of the driver, is restricted to nine.

Commercial vehicles. These are designed to transport people and cargo and for pulling trailers. Passenger cars are not classified as commercial vehicles.

Kapitel 1 Automobiltechnologie // Chapter 1 Technology of Automobile

Single-track vehicles

Motorcycles are single-track vehicles with 2 wheels. A sidecar may be attached to the motorcycle, which remains classified as such provided that the unladen weight of the combination does not exceed 400 kg. A motorcycle can also be employed to pull a trailer. Single-track vehicles include:

Motorcycles. These are equipped with permanent, fixed-location components (fuel tank, engine) located adjacent to the knees as well as footrests.

Motor scooters. Since the operator's feet rest on a floor board, there are no fixed components at knee level on these vehicles.

Bicycles with auxiliary motors. These vehicles share the same salient features as bicycles, e.g. pedals (mopeds, motorised bicycles, etc.).

New Words

evolution	发展、开发	car	轿车
efficiency	效率	low-profile tyre	低断面轮胎
motorcycle	摩托车	steel-belted radial tyre	钢子午线轮胎
stroke	行程	rotary engine	旋转活塞发动机
gas-powered engine	燃气发动机	seatbelt	安全带
compression	压缩	driver	驾驶人
four-stroke	四冲程	front passengers	前排乘员
two-stroke	二冲程	Antilock Breaking System (ABS)	防抱死制动系统
petrol engine	汽油发动机		
ignition	点火	breaking	制动
four wheeled motor carriage	四轮车	airbag	气囊
magneto ignition	磁电机点火	seatbelt tensioning system	安全带张紧器系统
pneumatic tyre	充气轮胎	electronic fuel injection (D-Jetronic)	电子燃油喷射
spray-nozzle carburettor	喷雾汽化器		
system	系统	hot tube ignition	热管点火
electromobile	电动车	Electronic suspension control system (ESP)	电子悬架控制系统
automobile	汽车		
diesel	柴油	motor vehicles	机动车
self-ignition	自燃	trailer	挂车、拖车
diesel engine	柴油发动机	integral mechanical propulsion system	一体式动力装置
production-line	流水线		
production	生产	dual-track	双轨的
model	型号、模型	sidecar	边车、挎斗
series-production	批量生产	motor scooter	小型踏板摩托车

课文参考译文

汽车发展史

◇1860年，法国人雷诺（Lenoir）制造了第一台完全可以实用的内燃发动机。这台发动机使用民用煤气作为燃料，热效率为3%左右。

◇1867年，奥托（Otto)和朗恩（Langen）在巴黎国际博览会展示了一台改进型的内燃机，其热效率约为9%。

◇1876年，奥托制造了第一台利用四冲程工作循环的燃气发动机。同年，克拉克（Clerk）在英格兰制造了第一台二冲程燃气轮机。

◇1883年，戴姆勒（Daimler）和迈巴赫（Maybach）研制出第一台利用热管点火系统点火的高速四冲程汽油发动机。

◇1885年，戴姆勒制造了第一台自推进两轮机动车。本茨（Benz）制造了第一台自推进三轮车（1886年获得专利）。

◇1886年，戴姆勒制造了第一台装有汽油发动机的四轮汽车。

◇1887年，博世（Bosch）发明了磁电机点火系统。

◇1889年，邓禄普（Dunlop）在英国生产了第一批充气轮胎。

◇1893年，迈巴赫发明了喷嘴式化油器。

◇1893年，狄塞尔（Diesel）利用自点火概念设计了燃烧柴油的发动机，并申请了专利。

◇1897年，德国曼（MAN）公司推出了第一台实用的柴油机。

◇1897年，罗纳尔-保时捷（Lohner-Porsche）生产了第一台电动汽车。

◇1899年，菲亚特（Fiat）汽车制造厂在意大利的都灵诞生。

◇1913年，福特（Ford）将生产线引入汽车制造过程，开始生产廉价的小汽车——福特T型车，到1925年，每天有9109辆汽车从生产线上下线。

◇1916年，巴伐利亚汽车制造厂（BMW）成立。

◇1923年，本茨-曼（Benz-MAN）公司制造了第一辆由柴油发动机驱动的载货汽车。

◇1936年，戴姆勒-本茨开始成批生产由柴油机驱动的乘用车。

◇1938年，大众（Volkswagen)汽车制造厂在德国沃尔夫斯堡成立。

◇1949年，米其林（Michelin)公司生产了第一只扁平轮胎和第一只钢丝带束子午线轮胎。

◇1950年，第一台作为汽车动力装置的燃气轮机在英国罗孚（Rover）公司下线。

◇1953年，中国第一汽车制造厂（FAW）建厂。

◇1954年，纳苏-汪克尔（NUS-Wankel）发动机厂制造出转子发动机。

◇1966年，博世生产的电子燃油喷射系统（D-Jetronic）成为批量生产的汽车标准配置。

◇1970年，汽车开始配备驾驶人和前排乘员的座椅安全带。

◇1978年，ABS（防抱死制动系统）在乘用车上开始应用。
◇1984年，安全气囊和座椅安全带张紧器开始应用。
◇1985年，与闭环混合气控制系统联合工作、用于无铅汽油的催化转化器问世。
◇1997年，电子悬架控制系统投入使用。
◇2000年，EOBD用于汽油发动机，同年柴油发动机开始应用欧Ⅲ法规。
◇2010年，中国一汽技术中心主任李骏博士当选为2012—2014年度国际汽车工程师协会（FISITA）轮值主席。同年，中国私营汽车企业吉利控股公司收购了世界上知名的汽车企业——瑞典沃尔沃汽车公司。

汽车构造与分类

道路或公路上行驶的车辆是为在道路上使用而设计的机动车和挂车，它不同于在赛道或轨道上行驶的车辆。道路车辆又可分为许多种类。

道路车辆主要分为两类：机动车和挂车。机动车总是装有一体式动力装置。

1. 双轨迹车辆

具有两个以上车轮的车辆属于双轨迹或多轨迹车辆。这一类车辆包括：

1）乘用车。在其设计和技术特性上主要用于载运乘客及其随身行李和/或临时物品的汽车，包括驾驶人座位在内最多不超过9个座位。它也可牵引一辆挂车。

2）商用车。商用车是指在设计和技术特性上用于运送人员和货物的汽车，并且可以牵引挂车。

2. 单轨迹车辆

摩托车是具有两个车轮的单轨迹车辆。摩托车可以附加一个挎斗，但摩托车与挎斗组合后的自身质量不能超过400kg。摩托车也可用来拖带挂车。单轨迹车辆包括：

1）普通摩托车。这种摩托车装有永久性的、位置固定的部件（燃油箱、发动机），这些部件位于驾驶人的膝部，以及脚踏板的附近。

2）小型踏板摩托车。由于驾驶人的脚放在底板上，因此，这种摩托车在膝部的高度位置没有固定部件。

3）助力自行车。这种车辆具有与普通自行车一样的特点，如脚踏板、窄轮胎等，但与普通自行车相比，增加了辅助动力装置。

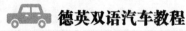

Teil 2　Verbrennungsmotor　内燃机
Part 2　Engine　发动机

【知识目标】

1. 掌握与内燃机结构、分类、运行原理等相关的专业术语、单词和词汇。
2. 掌握内燃机主要结构的德文、英文表达方法。

【能力目标】

1. 能对内燃机总体结构的各大总成进行中、德、英文互译。
2. 能进行与内燃机大体构造相关的德语、英语资料的阅读和翻译。
3. 能在内燃机实物上标识出相应结构的德语、英语单词和词汇。

Text 1　Verbrennungsmotor 内燃机（德文）

Einteilung der Verbrennungsmotoren

Nach Gemischbildung und Zündung

　– **Ottomotoren.** Sie werden vorzugsweise mit Benzin und äußerer, aber auch mit innerer Gemischbildung betrieben. Die Verbrennung wird durch Fremdzündung (Zündkerze) eingeleitet.

　– **Dieselmotoren.** Sie haben innere Gemischbildung und werden mit Dieselkraftstoff betreiben. Die Verbrennung im Zylinder wird durch Selbstzüdung ausgelöst.

Nach der Arbeitsweise

　– **Viertaktmotoren.** Sie haben einen geschlossenen (getrennten) Gaswechsel und benötigen für ein Arbeitsspiel 4 Kolbenhübe bzw. 2 Kurbelwellenumdrehungen.

　– **Zweitaktmotoren.** Sie haben einen offenen Gaswechsel und benötigen für ein Arbeitsspiel 2 Kolbenhübe bzw. eine Kurbelwellenumdrehung.

Nach der Zylinderanordnung

　– Reihenmotoren　　　– Boxermotoren
　– V-Motoren　　　　　– VR-Motoren

Nach der Kolbenbewegung

- **Hubkolbenmotoren**
- **Kreiskolbenmotoren**

Nach der Kühlung

- **Flüssigkeitsgekühlte Motoren**
- **Luftgekühlte Motoren**

Otto-Viertaktmotor

Aufbau und Arbeitsweise

Aufbau

Der Otto-Viertaktmotor besteht im wesentlichen aus 4 Baugruppen und zusätzlichen Hilfseinrichtungen:

- **Motorgehäuse**

    Zylinderkopfhaube, Zylinderkopf, Zylinder, Kurbelgehäuse, Ölwanne

- **Kurbeltrieb**

    Kolben, Pleuelstange, Kurbelwelle

- **Motorsteuerung**

    Ventile, Ventilfedern, Kipphebel, Kipphebelwelle, Nockenwelle, Steuerräder, Steuerkette oder Zahnriemen

- **Gemischbildungsanlage**

    Einspritzanlage oder Vergaser, Ansaugrohr

- **Hilfseinrichtungen**

    Zündanlage, Motorschmierung, Motorkühlung, Auspuffanlage.

4 Takte Arbeitsweise

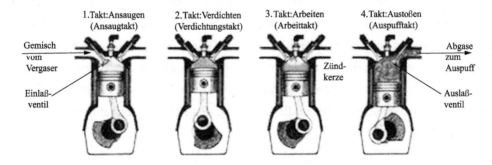

Die 4 Takte des Arbeitsspieles sind: Ansaugen, Verdichten, Arbeiten und Ausstoßen. Ein Arbeitsspiel läuft in 2 Kurbelwellenumdrehungen ab (720 ° Kurbelwinkel).

1. Takt-Ansaugen

Beim Abwärtsgehen des Kolbens entsteht infolge der Raumvergrößerung im Zylinder eine Druckdifferenz von -0,1 bar bis -0,3 bar gegenüber dem Außendruck. Da der Druck außerhalb des Motors größer ist als im Zylinder, wird Luft in das Ansaugsystem gedrückt. Das zündfähige Kraftstoff-Luft-Gemisch wird entweder im Ansaugkanal oder direkt im Zyinder durch Einspritzen von Kraftstoff gebildet. Um möglichst viel Ansaugluft oder Kraftstoff-Luft-Gemisch in den Zylinder zu bekommen, öffnet das Einlassventil (EV) schon bis zu 45°KW vor dem oberen Totpunkt (OT) und schließt erst 35° KW bis 90° KW nach dem unteren Totpunkt (UT).

2. Takt-Verdichten

Beim Aufwärtsgehen des Kolbens wird das Kraftstoff-Luft-Gemisch auf den 7. bis 12. Teil des ursprünglichen Zylinderraumes verdichtet. Dabei erwärmt sich das Gas auf 400℃ bis 500℃. Da sich das Gas bei der hohen Temperatur nicht ausdehnen kann, steigt der Verdichtungsenddruck bis auf 18 bar an. Die Verdichtung des Kraftstoff-Luft-Gemisches fördert die weitere Vergasung des Kraftstoffes und die innige Vermischung mit der Luft. Dabei wird die Verbrennung so vorbereitet, dass sie im 3. Takt, dem Arbeitstakt, sehr rasch und vollkommen ablaufen kann. Während des Verdichtungstaktes sind Einlassventile und Auslassventile (AV) geschlossen.

3. Takt-Arbeiten

Die Verbrennung wird durch das Überspringen des Zündfunkens an den Elektroden der Zündkerze eingeleitet. Die Zeitspanne vom Überspringen des Funkens bis zur vollen Entwicklung der Flammenfront beträgt etwa 1/1000 Sekunde bei einer Verbrennungsgeschwindigkeit von 20m/s. Aus diesem Grund muss der Zündfunke je nach Motordrehzahl 0°KW bis etwa 40°KW vor OT überspringen, damit der nötige Verbrennungshöchstdruck von 30 bar bis 60 bar kurz nach OT (4° KW ⋯ 10° KW) zur Verfügung steht. Die Expansion der bis 2500℃ heißen Gase treibt den Kolben zum UT, die Wärmeenergie wird in mechabische Energie umgewandelt.

4. Takt-Ausstoßen

Das Auslassventil öffnet schon 40°KW bis etwa 90°KW vor UT, dadurch wird die Abgasausströmung begüstigt und der Kurbeltrieb entlastet. Durch den am Ende des Arbeitstaktes noch vorhandenen Druck von 3 bar bis 5 bar puffen die bis zu 900°C heißen Abgase mit Schallgeschwindigkeit aus dem Zylinder. Der Abgasrest wird beim Aufwärtsgehen des Kolbens mit einem Staudruck von etwa 0,2 bar ausgestoßen. Um das Abströmen der Abgase zu begünstigen, schließt das Auslassventil erst nach OT, während sich das Einlassventil beteits öffnet. Diese Überschneidung der Ventilzeiten fördert die Entleerung und Kühlung des Verbrennungsraumes und verbessert die Füllung.

Neue Wörter

das Ansaugen	进气	das Ausstoßen	排气
das Verdichten	压缩	die Kurbelwelle	曲轴
das Arbeiten	做功	das Kolben	活塞

der	Zylinder	气缸	das	Zünden	点火
das	Kraftstoff-Luft-Gemisch	可燃混合气	die	Zündfunke	火花
das	Einspritzen	喷射	die	Elektrode	电极
der	obere Totpunkt	上止点	die	Zündkerze	火花塞
der	untere Totpunkt	下止点	die	Geschwindigkeit	速度
die	Expansion	膨胀	das	Abströmen	排出
das	Vergasen	汽化			

Text 2 Engine 发动机（英文）

Operating Principle of Spark-ignition Engine

The four strokes of the power cycle are induction, compression, combustion and exhaust. One power cycle takes place in two crankshaft revolutions (720° crank angle).

1st stroke-Induction

As the piston moves down the cylinder, the increased volume in the cylinder causes a pressure differential of - 0.1 bar to - 0.3 bar compared with the external pressure. Since the pressure outside the engine is greater than that inside the cylinder, air is forced into the induction system. The ignitable fuel-air mixture is formed either in the intake port or directly in the cylinder through the injection of fuel. In order to admit as much intake air or fuel-air mixture as possible into the cylinder, the inlet valve (IV) opens at up to 45° CA before top dead centre (TDC) and closes only at 35°CA to 90°CA after bottom dead centre (BDC).

2nd stroke-Compression

As the piston moves up the cylinder, the fuel-air mixture is compressed to a 7th to a 12th of the original cylinder volume. In the case of direct injection, pure air is compressed in the lower torque and speed range (up to approx. 3,000 rpm). The fuel is injected shortly before ignition. The gas heats to 400℃ to 500℃. Because it cannot expand at the high temperature, the final compression pressure increases up to 18 bar. The high pressure encourages further carburation of the fuel and its internal mixture with the air. This enables combustion to take place quickly and completely in the 3rd stroke. The inlet and exhaust valves are closed during the compression stroke.

3rd stroke-Combustion

Combustion is initiated by an ignition spark jumping across the electrodes of the spark plug. The length of time between the jumping of the spark and the complete development of the flame front is approx. 1/1,000 second at a combustion velocity of 20 m/s. For this reason, the ignition spark must jump across at 0° to approx. 40° before TDC, depending on the engine speed, so that the necessary maximum combustion pressure of 30 bar to 60 bar is available shortly after TDC (4°CA to 10°CA). The expansion of the gases heated up to 2,500℃ forces the piston to bottom dead centre and thermal energy is converted into mechanical energy.

4th stroke-Exhaust

The exhaust valve opens at 40° to approx. 90° before BDC; this encourages the discharge of the exhaust gases and relieves the load on the crankshaft drive. The pressure of 3 bar to 5 bar still available at the end of the power stroke causes the exhaust gases heated up to 900℃ to be expelled from the cylinder at the speed of sound. As the piston moves up the cylinder, the remaining exhaust gas is discharged at a dynamic pressure of roughly 0.2 bar. To encourage the exhaust gases to be discharged, the exhaust valve closes only after TDC while the inlet valve is already open. This overlapping of the valve times encourages the draining and cooling of the combustion chamber and improves cylinder charge.

New Words

induction	进气	bottom dead centre	下止点
compression	压缩	expand	膨胀
combustion	燃烧	carburation	汽化
exhaust	排气	ignition	点火
crank	曲轴	spark	火花
piston	活塞	electrode	电极
cylinder	气缸	spark plug	火花塞
fuel-air mixture	可燃混合气	velocity	速度
injection	喷射	discharge	释放
top dead centre	上止点	drain	排出

课文参考译文

内燃机

点燃式发动机工作循环的四个行程包括进气、压缩、做功和排气。完成一个工作循环需要曲轴转两圈（720°曲轴转角）。

（1）第一个行程（进气行程）

随着活塞在气缸中的向下移动，气缸中容积增加，从而使气缸内的压力比外部压力低10~30kPa。因为发动机外面的压力高于气缸内的压力，所以空气被迫进入进气系统。可燃混合气或者在进气道形成，或者借助于燃油喷射，在气缸内直接形成。为了让尽可能多的空气或空气与燃油的混合气进入气缸，进气门（IV）在上止点（TDC）前最多可达45°曲轴转角（CA）时就已经开启，而在下止点（BDC）后35°～90°才能关闭。

（2）第二个行程（压缩行程）

随着活塞在气缸中的向上移动，气缸内的混合气被压缩为原来气缸容积的1/12～1/7。在直接喷射的情况下，空气被压缩，并在TDC之前不远处开始喷油。缸内的气体温度升高到400～500℃。由于在此高温下气体无法膨胀，因而最后压力将升高到1.8MPa。此高压促进了燃油的进一步汽化，以及燃油蒸气与空气的进一步混合，从而使燃烧在第三个行程中能够快速而彻底地进行。在压缩行程期间，进气门、排气门均处于关闭状态。

（3）第三个行程（做功行程）

点燃混合气的火花跳过火花塞电极，从而开始了燃烧过程。在燃烧速度为20m/s时，从跳火到火焰前锋的完全形成，所需时间约为1/1000s。为此，根据发动机转速的不同，必须在TDC之前0°～40°时进行跳火，这样才能在TDC之后的很短时间内（4°～10°曲轴转角）获得需要的3～6MPa的最高燃烧压力。温度高达2500℃的燃气的膨胀迫使活塞向下移向下止点（BDC）。这样，热能转变成机械能。

（4）第四个行程（排气行程）

在BDC之前大约40°～90°时，排气门开启。这将有利于废气的排出和减小加在曲轴上的负荷。在做功行程终了时，气缸内仍有300～500kPa的压力，这就导致温度高达900℃的废气以声速从气缸向外排出。随着活塞向上运动，剩余废气就以20kPa左右的动态压力排出。为使排气彻底，排气门只能在TDC之后关闭，而此时进气门已经开启。这种气门开启时间的重叠现象有利于减少燃烧室内的残余废气，并有利于燃烧室的冷却，从而提高了充气效率。

Teil 3　Verbrennungsmotorblock　内燃机缸体
Part 3　Engine block　内燃机缸体

【知识目标】
1. 掌握与内燃机缸体结构、分类、运行原理等相关的专业术语、单词和词汇。
2. 掌握内燃机缸体主要结构的德文和英文表达方法。

【能力目标】
1. 能对内燃机缸体总体结构总成进行中、德、英互译。
2. 能进行与内燃机缸体大体构造相关的德语、英语资料的阅读和翻译。
3. 能在内燃机缸体实物上标识出相应结构的德语、英语单词和词汇。

Text 1　Zylinder气缸体（德文）

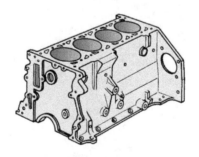

Aufgaben und Beanspruchungen

Aufgaben

– Zusammen mit dem Kolben den Verbrennungsraum bilden

– hohen Verbrennungsdrücken standhalten

– aufgenommene Wärme rasch an das Kühlmittel abführen

– der Zylinder dient außerdem der Führung des Kolbens.

Beanspruchungen

– Hohe Verbrennungsdrücke und Temperaturen

- große Wärmespannungen durch schnelle Temperaturwechsel
- Verschleiß der Zylinderlaufban durch Kolbenreibung und Verbrennungsrückstände
- unvergaster Kraftstoff wächst beim Kaltstart den Schmierfilm von der Zylinderwand ab.

Eigenschaften der Werkstoffe. Sie ergeben sich aus den Beanspruchungen:
- Große Festigkeit und Formsteifigkeit
- gute Wärmeleitung, geringe Wärmedehnung
- für die Zylinderlauffläche: große Verschleißfestigkeit und gute Gleiteigenschaft.

Zylinderbauarten

Flüssigkeitsgekühlte Zylinder

Die Zylinder flüssiggekühlter Motoren sind meist zu einem Block zusammengefasst. Der doppelwandige Zylinderblock wird von Kühlkanälen durchzogen; die Kühlflüssigkeit wird im unteren Bereich durch die Wasserpumpe zugeführt, kühlt die Zylinderwandungen und fließt durch Durchflusskanäle in den Zylinderkopf. Meist werden Zylinderblock und Kurbelgehäuseoberteil in einem Stück gegossen. Man nennt diese besonders steife Bauform Zylinderkurbelgehäuse. Bei den meisten Motoren mit Flüssigkeitskühlung wird das Zylinderkurbelgehäuse aus Gusseisen mit Lamellengraphit gegossen.

Neben guter Steifigkeit und Festigkeit, gutem Gleit- und Verschleißverhalten hat es geringe Wärmedehnung und gute Geräuschdämpfung. Besondere Maßnahmen zur Verbesserung der Zylinderlaufbahn sind meist nicht erforderlich.

Zunehmend werden Zylinderkurbelgehäuse auch als Al-Legierungen gegossen, vor allem wegen der geringen Dichte und der guten Wärmeleitfähigkeit. Zur Verbesserung der Formsteifigkeit sind sie meist zusätzlich verrippt. Die Verschleißeigenschaften der Zylinderlaufbahnen von Al-Zylinerkurbelgehäusen müssen durch besondere Herstellungsverfahren verbessert werden oder es werden Zylinderlaufbuchsen eingesetzt.

Closed-Deck-Ausführung. Die Dichtfläche des Zylinderkurbelgehäuses zum Zylinderkopf hin ist um die Zylinderbohrungen herum weitgehend geschlossen, nur die Bohrungen und Kanäle für Drucköl und Ölrücklauf, für Kühlflüssigkeit und evtl. für die Kurbelgehäuseentlüftung sind vorhanden. Zylinderkurbelgehäuse aus Gusseisen mit Lamellengraphit sind fast ausschließlich in dieser Bauweise hergestellt. Zylinderkurbelgehäuse aus AlSi-Legierungen (z.B. für ALUSIL-Zylinder) werden in dieser Bauweise im Kokillenguss bzw. Niederdruckguss hergestellt.

Open-Deck-Ausführung. Der Wassermantel um die Zylinderbohrungen herum ist zum Zylinderkopf hin offen. Dadurch ist es gießtechnisch möglich, Zylinderblöcke mit Zylinderlaufflächen nach dem LOKASIL-Konzept im Druckgussverfahren zu fertigen. Die geringere Steifigkeit von Zylinderblöcken in Open-Deck-Ausführung erfordert Metall-Zylinderkopfdichtungen statt Weichstoff-Zylinderkopfdichtungen. Metall-Zylinderkopfdichtunge ermöglichen wegen ihrem geringen Setzverhalten eine niedrige Vorspannkraft der Zylinderkopfverschraubung. Dadurch werden Zylinderverzug und Deckplattenverformung reduziert.

Zylinderlaufbuchsen

Zylinderlaufbuchsen aus hochwertigem, feinkörnigen Gusseisen (Schleuderguss) werden in Zylinderblöcke aus Gusseisen oder aus Al-Legierung eingezogen. Da sie verschleißfester sind als die Zylinderlaufbahnen gusseiserner Zylinderblöcke, haben sie eine lange Lebensdauer. Man unterscheidet nasse und trockene Zylinderlaufbuchsen.

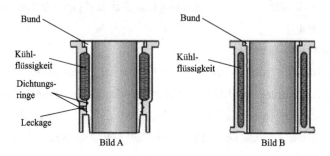

Nasse Zylinderlaufbuchsen werden von der Kühlflüssigkeit direkt umspült, dadurch ergibt sich eine gute Kühlwirkung. Sie können einzeln ausgewechselt werden; auch ist nur eine Kolbengröße erforderlich. Der Zylinderblock ist jedoch nicht so steif und verzieht sich leichter. Die Laufbuchsen haben am oberen Ende einen Bund; gegen das Kurbelgehäuse müssen sie durch Dichtungsringe sorgfältig abgedichtet werden, da sonst Kühlflüssigkeit ins Kurbelgehäuse gelangt.

Trockene Zylinderlaufbuchsen kommen nicht mit der Kühlflüssigkeit in Berührung. Der Wärmeübergang auf das Kühlmittel ist daher nicht so gut wie bei nassen Zylinderlaufbuchsen. Trockene Zylinderlaufbuchsen werden mit Schiebesitz oder mit Festsitz als dünnwandige Buchsen in den Zylinderblock eingesetzt. Laufbuchsen mit Schiebesitz werden vor dem Einbau fertigbearbeitet. Laufbuchsen mit Festsitz werden mit vorgebohrter Zylinderbohrung in den Zylinderblock eingepresst. Danach werden sie feingebohrt und gehont.

Luftgekühlte Zylinder

Luftgekühlte Zylinder sind zur Vergrößerung der Mantelfläche und damit zur Verbesserung der Kühlwirkung mit Kühlrippen versehen. Sie werden als einzeln stehende Rippenzylinder mit dem Kurbelgehäuse verschraubt.

Luftgekühlte Zylinder werden überwiegend aus Al-Legierungen gegossen, dabei kann die Recyclingrate bis zu 90% betragen. Die Gleit- und Verschleißeigenschaften der Zylinderlaufbahnen müssen wie bei flüssigkeitsgekühlten Zylindern aus Al-Legierungen durch besondere Herstellungsverfahren verbessert werden.

Kapitel 1　Automobiltechnologie // Chapter 1　Technology of Automobile

Zylinderlaufbahnen von Al-Zylindern

Eisen-Aluminium-Verbundgussverfahren (Alfin-Verfahren). Die Laufbuchsen aus Gusseisen mit Lamellengraphit werden mit einer Schicht aus Eisenaluminium ($FeAl_3$) überzogen und danach mit der AlSi-Legierung für den Rippenzylinder umgossen. Durch die Alfin-Zwischenschicht wird eine innige Verbindung mit guter Wärmeleitung zwischen der gusseisenen Laufbuchse und der AlSi-Legierung des Rippenzylinders erzielt.

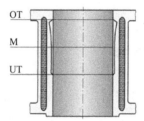

ALUSIL-Verfahren. Für das ALUSIL-Verfahren wird der Zylinderblock aus einer Al-Legierung mit hohem Silicium-Anteil meist im Kokillenguss oder Zylinderlaufbahn wird durch elektrochemisches Ätzen oder durch Läppen das weiche Aluminium um die Silicium-Kristalle herum abgetragen. Die hervorstehenden harten Si-Kristalle bilden eine verschleißfeste Trägerlaufbahn für Kolben und Kolbenringe. Zur Verminderung des Kolbenverschleißes werden meist Ferrocoat-Kolben verwendet.

NIKASIL-Verfahren. Die Zylinderlaufbahn aus Al-Si-Legierung wird galvanisch beschichtet mit einer verschleißfesten Schicht aus Nickel mit eingelagerten Siliciumkarbid-Kristallen.

LOKALSIL-Verfahren. Für die Zylinderbohrungen werden Formkörper aus Silicium mit einem keramischen Bindemittel als Hohlzylinder hergestellt. Die Formkörper sind hochporös, sie werden als sogenannte Preforms, vorgewärmt auf etwa 700℃, in die Gussform eingesetzt. In einem speziellen Druckgussverfahren (Squeeze Casting), bei dem der Druck in der Schmelze nach dem Füllen der Form auf etwa 700 bar gesteigert wird, werden die Performs von der Al-Legierung durchdrungen und die Poren ausgefüllt. Als Al-Legierung kann eine kostengünstige Sekundärlegierung (Recycling-Al) mit geringerem Si-Anteil verwendet werden. Die notwendige Silicium-Anreicherung im Bereich der Zylinderlaufbahnen wird durch die Preforms gewährleistet. Durch mehrstufiges Honen werden die Siliciumkristalle reliefartig freigelegt, wodurch eine verschleißfeste Zylinderlaufbahn entsteht. In LOKALSIL-Zylindern werden meist Ferrocoat-Kolben verwendet.

WIEDERHOLUNGSFRAGEN

1. Welche Aufgaben hat Zylinder?

2. Welchen Beanspruchungen ist Zylinder ausgesetzt?

3. Welche Eigenschaften soll der Zylinder bzw. die Zylinderlaufbahn haben?

4. Welcher Unterschied besteht zwischen nassen und trockenen Zylinderlaufbuchsen?

5. Welche Vor- und Nachteile haben Zylinder aus Leichtmetalllegierungen?

Neue Wörter

das	Kurbelgehäuse	曲轴箱	die	Zylinderlaufbuchse	气缸套
der	Zylinder	气缸	die	Al-Legierung	铝合金
der	Zylinderkopf	气缸盖	die	Kühlflüssigkeit	冷却液
der	Verbrennungsraum	燃烧室	das	Dichtungsring	密封圈
der	Motorzylinderblock	发动机气缸体	die	nasse Zylinderlaufbuchse	湿式气缸套
das	Gußeisen mit Lamellengraphit	片状石墨铸铁	die	trockene Zylinderlaufbuchse	干式气缸套
die	Legierung	合金	die	Bohrung	承孔
die	Steifigkeit	刚度		honen	研磨
das	Lager	轴承	der	luftgekühlte Zylinder	风冷式气缸
die	Zylinderbohrung	缸筒	die	Schicht	层
	verschleißfest	耐磨的	das	Silikon	硅
das	Wassermantel	水套	der	Kokillenguß	金属型铸造
der	Weichstoff	软材料	der	Niederdruckguß	低压铸造
das	geringe Setzverhalten	低沉降	die	Korrosion	腐蚀
die	Schraube	螺栓	das	Schmieröl	润滑油
die	Verformung	变形	das	Nickel	镍

Text 2　Engine block 发动机缸体（英文）

Engine blocks of liquid-cooled engines consist of a crankcase upper half and the cylinder block and are cast as a single unit.

The following materials are used:

• **Flake-graphite and cast iron (grey cast iron).** As well as good rigidity and strength and good sliding and wear performance, it has low thermal expansion and good noise damping.

- **Vermicular-graphite cast iron.** As the casting cools, the graphite precipitates not in the form of lamellas but rather in a vermicular form. The notch effect between the structure crystals is lower than with cast iron, thereby greatly increasing strength and rigidity. This facilitates higher internal cylinder pressures using the same wall thickness or weight savings with thinner wall thickness.
- **Al alloys.** Of particular benefit is the low density in comparison with grey cast iron and good thermal conductivity. The engine blocks are also finned in order to improve inherent stability. The wear properties of the cylinder barrels must be improved by means of special production processes; alternatively cylinder liners are used.

Crankcase

The crankcase houses the crankshaft.

Since high forces and torque act on the crankshaft, the crankcase must exhibit high strength and inherent stability.

Design. The crankcase is usually divided at the height of the crankshaft bearings. The crankcase upper half contains the bearing seats for the crankshaft. The bearing caps are secured from below with bolts. The advantage of this arrangement is that the crankshaft or individual pistons can be easily removed.

In engines producing high torques, bed plates are used instead of individual bearing shells. This is a plate-shaped component joining all engine bearing shells to one another. This interconnection provides the crankcase with greater rigidity.

The crankcase lower half is designed as an oil pan and is bolted oil-tight to the crankcase upper half.

Cylinder block

The cylinders of liquid-cooled engines are usually combined to form a single block.

Stresses
- High combustion pressures and temperatures
- High thermal stresses due to rapid temperature changes
- Cylinder barrel subject to wear due to piston friction and combustion residues.
- Increased friction during cold starting, uncarburated fuel washes lubricant layer off the cylinder.

Material requirements:
- Good heat conductivity
- High wear resistance
- Good sliding properties for the cylinder face.

Design: The double-walled cylinder block is traversed by cooling channels. Coolant is supplied by the water pump, it cools the cylinder walls and flows through ducts into the cylinder head.

There are different structural types:

Open deck cylinder block.

The water jacket around the cylinder bores is open to the cylinder head. This makes it technically possible to produce cylinder blocks with cylinder faces in accordance with the LOKASIL concept in the die-casting process. The lower rigidity of open-deck cylinder blocks calls for metal instead of soft-material cylinder head gaskets. Because of their low setting behaviour, they provide a low initial force for the cylinder heat bolt connection. In turn, this reduces cylinder distortion and deck deformation.

Closed deck cylinder block.

The sealing surface of the engine block to the cylinder head is closed up to the cooling/oil ducts. This design is used almost exclusively for cast iron; for SISi alloys (e.g. ALUSIL cylinders) these cylinder blocks are manufactured in gravity die-casting or in low-pressure casting.

Cylinder block with cylinder liners. Superior quality, close-grained cast iron (centrifugal) cylinder liners are inserted into cast iron or aluminium-alloy cylinder blocks. They have a long service life, since they are more resistant to wear than the cylinder liners of cast iron cylinder blocks.

Two different types are used: wet and dry cylinder liners.

Wet cylinder liners. Coolant flows directly around liners of this type, thereby providing a good cooling effect. Wet liners can be replaced individually. However, the cylinder block is not as rigid and is distorted more easily.

Liners of this type feature a flange at their top end. They must be sealed against the crankcase by sealing rings, since otherwise coolant will get into the crankcase.

Dry cylinder liners. These are slip fit or press fit as thin-walled liners into the cylinder block. Since they do not come into contact with the coolant, the transfer of heat to the coolant is not as good as with wet liners. Cylinder liners with a slip fit are finish-machined prior to installation. Liners with a press fit installation are pressed with a predrilled cylinder bore into the cylinder block. They are then fine-bored and honed.

Air-cooled cylinders

Air-cooled cylinders are provided with cooling fins to increase the size of the surface area and thereby improve the cooling effect. They are bolted to the crankcase in the form of individually positioned finned cylinders.

Air-cooled cylinders are cast predominantly from aluminium (Al) alloys.

Cylinder barrels

Since aluminium cylinder barrels do not meet sliding and wear characteristics requirements, they must be improved using special manufacturing methods. Otherwise cylinder liners are cast-in.

Iron-aluminium composite casting process (Alfin process). The liners of flake-graphite cast iron are coated on the outside with a layer of iron aluminium ($FeAl_3$) and then cast in with the AlSi alloy for the finned cylinder. The Alfin intermediate layer establishes a connection with good heat conduction between the cast-iron liner and the AlSi alloy of the finned cylinder.

ALUSIL process. The cylinder block is cast from an Al alloy with a high silicon content (up to 18%) in gravity die-casting or low-pressure casting. In order for the silicon crystals to be formed primarily on the cylinder faces, the cores which form the casting mould on the cylinders are cooled. After honing, the soft aluminium is removed around the silicon crystals by electrochemical etching. This creates a wear-resistant carrier barrel for piston and piston rings with spaces for the lubricating oil. Usually, ferrocoated pistons are used in order to reduce piston wear.

NIKASIL process. The cylinder barrel of AlSi alloy is galvanically coated with a wear-resistant layer of nickel with intercalated silicon-carbide crystals.

LOKASIL process. Silicon crystals are placed on the cylinder barrel with the aid of form bodies, also known as preforms. Preforms are highly porous and are made up of silicon crystals which are sintered with water glass (silicates dissolved in water). They are manufactured as hollow cylinders and inserted at that point in the casting mould where the face is located. In a special die-casting process, known as squeeze casting, the Al alloy is pressed slowly with low pressure from below into the vertical casting mould.

The preforms must be preheated to 300℃ during insertion so that the Al alloy cannot cool down during penetration and in the process solidify before it has completely penetrated the preforms. Finally, the pressure is increased from 120 bar to 500 bar to close all the pores and eliminate air inclusions. Multistage honing is used to expose the silicon crystals in relief form, which in turn results in a wear-resistant cylinder barrel. Ferrocoated pistons are usually used in LOKASIL cylinders.

PTWA process (Plasma Transferred Wire Arc). Here a running layer is thermally applied to the AlSi alloy of the cylinder. Within the interior of the cylinder bore iron-carbon wires are guided to a plasma generator. An arc melts the wires into metal droplets which are then sprayed at high speed onto the cylinder wall using a gas flow. A nano-crystalline iron coating approx. 0.3 mm thick forms on the cylinder wall. The coating has a porosity of approx. 2% which serves to retain oil volume. Consequently, fine machining of the surface area suffices as a finishing operation. The result is a surface that is smooth as glass with low friction coefficients and limited wear.

New Words

crankcase	曲轴箱	flake-graphite and cast iron	片状石墨铸铁
cylinder	气缸	grey cast iron	灰铸铁
cylinder head	气缸盖	vermicular-graphite cast iron	蠕墨铸铁
combustion chamber	燃烧室	alloy	合金
engine block	发动机气缸体	rigidity	刚度

notch effect	刻痕效应	bore	承孔
bearing	轴承	hone	研磨
cylinder barrel	缸筒	air-cooled cylinder	风冷式气缸
resistance	耐磨性	alloy	合金
water jacket	水套	layer	层
soft-material	软材料	silicon	硅
low setting	低沉降	gravity die-casting	金属型铸造
bolt	螺栓	low-pressure casting	低压铸造
distortion	变形	electrochemical	电化学
ducts	孔道	etching	蚀刻
cylinder liner	气缸套	lubricating oil	润滑油
aluminium-alloy	铝合金	ferrocoate	镀铁
coolant	冷却液	nickel	镍
sealing ring	密封圈	silicon-carbide crystal	碳化硅晶体
wet cylinder liners	湿式气缸套	hollow	空心
dry cylinder liners	干式气缸套	dissolve	溶解

课文参考译文

发动机气缸体

水冷式发动机的气缸由气缸体和曲轴箱上体铸成一个零件。其铸造材料有：

1）片状石墨铸铁（灰铸铁）这种材料具有良好的刚度和强度，以及良好的滑动性和耐磨性，所以它具有低的热膨胀系数，以及良好的吸声性能。

2）蠕墨铸铁当铸件冷却时，石墨不是以薄片的形式析出，而是以蠕虫形析出。结构晶格之间的刻痕效应减轻，因而增加了强度和刚度。这样，就能用较小的壁厚（减小质量）承受更高的缸内压力，提高了性能。

3）铝合金与灰铸铁相比，这种材料密度低，且传热性好。发动机气缸体上制有散热片，改善了稳定性。气缸的磨损特性必须经过特种生产工艺加以改善，即采用气缸套。

曲轴箱

曲轴箱用来容纳曲轴，有时也用来容纳凸轮轴。气缸固定在曲轴箱上。

曲轴箱通常在曲轴轴承的高度分开。曲轴箱上半体上有曲轴轴承座。轴承盖用螺栓从下面向上固定。这种布置的优点是曲轴拆卸容易。曲轴箱下半体设计成油底壳,它与上半体之间没有密封,以防漏油,并用螺栓固定到上半体上。

曲轴箱一般用铸铁制造,但在风冷发动机上则用铝合金制造。

气缸类型

水冷式发动机的气缸通常组合在一起,形成一个气缸体。

1. 功用
1)与气缸盖一起形成燃烧室。
2)气缸对活塞运动起导向作用。

2. 工作条件
1)高的燃烧压力和燃烧温度。
2)由于温度快速变化,热应力大。
3)由于活塞的摩擦和燃烧残留物,气缸筒会磨损。
4)未汽化燃料将润滑油从气缸上冲刷掉,冷起动期间磨损增加。

3. 材料特性
1)高强度,稳定性好。
2)良好的传热性。
3)受热膨胀量小。
4)高的耐磨性。
5)气缸表面具有良好的滑动性。

上平面封闭式气缸体的上平面在气缸孔周围全面封闭,只留下冷却液通过的孔道。这种结构几乎只应用于铸铁气缸体。应用AlSi合金(例如ALUSIL气缸)的气缸体用金属型压铸或低压铸造。

上平面敞开式气缸体周围的水套在对着气缸盖的方向是敞开的。这就使得使用压铸工艺来生产具有气缸端面的气缸体从技术上成为可能。上平面敞开式气缸体的刚度较小,这就需要使用金属气缸垫来代替软材料气缸垫。由于这样的气缸垫具有低沉降特性,气缸盖连接螺栓的初始拉力小。这还会减小气缸盖的变形和气缸体上平面的变形。

气缸套

组织致密的优质铸铁(离心铸造)气缸套被压入铸铁气缸体或铝合金气缸体。这样的气缸套比铸铁气缸体的气缸孔更耐磨,因此使用寿命长。

目前使用的气缸套有两种:湿式气缸套和干式气缸套。

（1）湿式气缸套。冷却液直接在这种气缸套的周围流动，因此冷却效果好。湿式气缸套可以一个一个地更换。不过，气缸体的刚度较差，容易变形。这种气缸套在顶端带有一个凸缘。气缸套与曲轴箱之间必须通过密封圈密封，否则，冷却液就会进入曲轴箱。

（2）干式气缸套。这种薄壁气缸套用过渡配合或使用过盈配合镶入气缸体内。由于这些气缸套并不与冷却液接触，因此，与冷却液之间的热传递不如湿式气缸套那么好。采用过渡配合的气缸套安装前要经过精加工。采用过盈配合时，气缸体上预先制有气缸套承孔，气缸套被压入气缸体。然后，对气缸套进行精镗和衍磨。

风冷式气缸

风冷式发动机的气缸外面制有散热片，增加了表面尺寸，因而改善了冷却效果。这些气缸固定到曲轴箱上，各气缸相互独立，呈现为带有散热片的立式结构型式。

风冷式发动机气缸主要用铝（Al）合金铸造而成。因为这样的气缸套滑动性和耐磨性较差，所以，像用铝合金制造的水冷式发动机气缸套一样，必须采取专门措施，即将气缸套铸入，如采用专用铸造工艺。

气缸体的缸筒

（1）ALUSIL工艺是用具有高含硅质量分数（高达18%）的Al合金，用金属型铸造或低压铸造制造气缸体的工艺。为了在气缸表面上能够形成硅晶体，形成气缸铸模的型芯必须得到冷却。衍磨后，用电化学腐蚀的方法将硅晶体周围的软质铝去掉。这就形成了一个可存留机油的耐磨的活塞和活塞环导向管。为了减轻活塞磨损，大多采用了镀铁活塞。

（2）NIKASIL工艺用电镀的方法，在Al合金气缸筒上涂覆加有碳化硅晶体的镍耐磨层。

（3）LOKASIL工艺借助于成型体，将硅施覆于气缸筒。预型坯呈多孔性结构，并由与水玻璃（溶解在水中的硅酸盐）一起烧结的硅晶体制成。将预型坯制成空心气缸，再将空心气缸插到铸模中，并使其进入端面定位的位置。在特种压铸工艺（叫作挤压铸造）中，Al合金在低压下慢慢地从下面压入垂直铸模中。在预型坯气缸插入期间，必须将预型坯预热到300℃，这样在渗透期间和固化过程中，在完全渗透预型坯之前，Al合金才不会冷下来。最后，应将压力从12MPa提高到50MPa，以使所有的微孔封闭，并消除夹杂空气的现象。使用多级衍磨，就能使硅像浮雕一样暴露出来，从而形成耐磨的气缸筒。大多数镀铁活塞都用在LOKASIL气缸中。

Teil 4　Getriebe　变速器
Part 4　Variable-speed gearbox　变速器

学习目标

【知识目标】
1. 掌握与变速器结构、分类、运行原理等相关的专业术语、单词和词汇。
2. 掌握变速器主要结构的德文和英文表达方法。

【能力目标】
1. 能对变速器总体结构的各大总成进行中、德、英互译。
2. 能进行与变速器大体构造相关的德语和英语资料的阅读和翻译。
3. 能在变速器实物上标识出相应结构的德语和英语单词和词汇。

Text 1　Getriebe变速器（德文）

Das Wechselgetriebe ist im Antiebsstrang zwischen Kupplung und Achsgetriebe angeordnet und übersetzt Motordrehmoment und Motordrehzahl.

Aufgaben

– Motordrehzahl wandeln
– Motordrehmoment wandeln und übertragen

- Leerlauf des Motors bei stehendem Fahrzeug ermöglichen
- Umkehr des Drehsinns für Rückwärtsfahrt ermöglichen.

Jeder Verbrennungsmotor arbeitet zwischen einer Mindest- und Höchstdrehzahl und kann in diesem leistungsfähigen Drehzahlbereich nur ein begrenztes Drehmoment abgeben.

Die ohne Wechselgetriebe und Achsgetriebe erreichbaren Belastungs- und Geschwindigkeitsbereiche werden durch die Leistung des Motors begrenzt. Deshalb müssen Motordrehzahl und Motordrehmoment durch die Übersetzungen des Wechselgetriebes und Achsgetriebes gewandelt werden können.

Durch die Wandlung stellen sich an den Antriebsrädern Drehzahlen und Drehmomente ein, die den gewünschten Fahrgeschwindigkeiten bei ausreichend hohen Antriebsmomenten bzw. Zugkräften entsprechen.

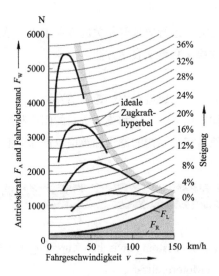

Bild: Getriebeausgangskennlinien

Getriebeausgangskennlinien (Bild). Soll ein Fahrzeug aus dem Stand beschleunigt werden oder große Steigungen befahren können, ist eine hohe Zugkraft bzw. ein hohes Antriebsdrehmoment erforderlich. Dies ist durch eine entsprechende Übersetzung ins Langsame möglich.

Wird z.B. im 1. Gang das Drehmoment durch das Wechselgetriebe um das 3,45-fache erhöht, vermindert sich die Drehzahl um den gleichen Faktor. Ist z. B. der 5. Gang geschaltet, so wird das Ausgangsdrehmoment um den Faktor 0,81 kleiner und die Drehzahl entsprechend höher.

Um beim Gangwechsel einen möglichst geringen Zugkraftverlust zu haben, sollen sich die Getriebeausgangskennlinien der Zugkrafthyperbel annähern. Dies ist ein Maß für die Güte eines Getriebes.

Drehmoment-Drehzahlwandlung. Bei einer Zahnradpaarung wirkt am größeren Zahnrad (größerer Hebelarm, mehr Zähne) immer das größere Drehmoment.

Das Hebelverhältnis entspricht dem Verhältnis der Zähnezahl des getriebenen Zahnrades zum treibenden Zahnrad.

Es wird **Übersetzungsverhältnis *i*** genannt.

Ist das treibende Zahnrad kleiner als das getriebene, wird das Drehmoment um das Übersetzungsverhältnis größer und die Drehzahl entsprechend gesenkt.

Ist das treibende Zahnrad größer als das getriebene, wird das Drehmoment um das Übersetzungsverhältnis kleiner und die Drehzahl entsprechend erhöht.

Durch ein Zwischenrad wird der Drehsinn geändert, jedoch nicht die Übersetzung.

Bei einer Zahnradpaarung bewirkt eine

– Drehmomenterhöhung eine Drehzahlabsenkung

– Drehmomentabsenkung eine Drehzahlerhöhung.

Leerlaufstellung. Sie bewirkt die Unterbrechung des Kraftflusses im Wechselgetriebe.

Umkehr des Drehsinns. Die Straßenverkehrs-Zulassungs-Ordnung schreibt vor, dass Kraftfahrzeuge mit mehr als 400 kg zulässigem Gesamtgewicht eine Einrichtung für die Umkehr des Drehsinns zum Rückwärtsfahren besitzen.

Bauarten von handgeschalteten Wechselgetrieben (Schaltgetrieben)

Man unterscheidet nach dem Verlauf des Kraftflusses im Getriebe

– gleichachsige Schaltgetriebe

– ungleichachsige Schaltgetriebe

nach der Anzahl der Wellen im Getriebe

– 2-Wellen-Schaltgetriebe (= ungleichachsig)

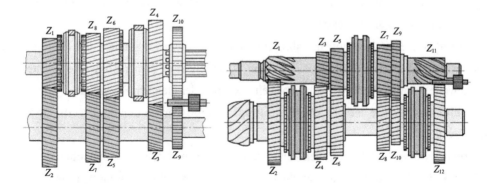

– 3-Wellen-Schaltgetriebe (= gleichachsig)

nach den Bauteilen, die die Losräder (Schalträder) mit ihren Wellen drehfest verbinden

– Schaltmuffengetriebe

– Schaltklauengetriebe

nach der Synchronisierung

– synchronisierte Schaltgetriebe

– unsynchronisierte Schaltgetriebe.

Schaltmuffengetriebe

Der Kraftfluss zwischen Schaltrad (Losrad) und Getriebewelle wird über eine Schaltmuffe hergestellt, die über einen Synchronkörper drehfest mit der Welle verbunden ist.

Alle Zahnradpaarungen für die Vorwärtsgänge sind ständig miteinander im Eingriff.

Dies ist nur möglich, wenn bei jeder nicht geschalteten Zahnradpaarung ein Zahnrad (Losrad) frei auf der Welle drehbar ist.

Schaltvorgang. Es wird jeweils eine Schaltmuffe so versschoben, dass das entsprechende Losrad (Schaltrad) drehfest mit der Welle verbunden wird. Dabei werden die Innenklauen der Schaltmuffe über die Schaltverzahnung des Schaltrades geschoben.

Ungleichachsige Schaltmuffengetriebe

Sie werden in Fahrzeugen mit quer zur Fahrtrichtung eingebautem Frontmotor und Vorderradantrieb oder Heckmotor und Hinterradantrieb verwendet und auch als „2-Wellengetriebe" bezeichnet (Antriebswelle, Hauptwelle).

Antriebswelle und Hauptwelle liegen auf verschiedenen (ungleichen) Fluchtlinien. Beim dargestellten Getriebe ist der Motor quer eingebaut. Die Übersetzung wird in allen Gängen über je eine Zahnradpaarung erreicht.

Auf der Antriebswelle sitzen die treibenden Zahnräder Z_1, Z_3, Z_5, Z_7, Z_9, Z_{11}. Auf der Hauptwelle sitzen die getriebenen Zahnräder Z_2, Z_4, Z_6, Z_8, Z_{10}, Z_{12}.

Wird z.B. der 3. Gang geschaltet, so wird die Schaltmuffe S_2 nach links verschoben.

Der Kraftfluss verläuft von der Antriebswelle über die Schaltmuffe S_2 auf die Schaltverzahnung von Z_5 und über die Zähne von Z_5 auf das Zahnrad Z_6 und von hier über die Hauptwelle zum Abtrieb.

Gleichachsige Schaltmuffengetriebe

Sie werden in Fahrzeuge mit in Fahrtrichtung eingebautem Frontmotor und Hinterradantrieb eingebaut und auch als „3-Wellen-getriebe" bezeichnet (Antriebswelle, Hauptwelle, Vorgelegewelle). Antriebswelle und Abtriebswelle liegen in der gleichen Fluchtlinie.

Antriebswelle. Sie ist mit der Kupplungsscheibe verbunden und treibt über Z_1 die Vorgelegewelle.

Vorgelegewelle. Sie bildet mit den Zahnrädern Z_3, Z_5, Z_7 und Z_9 einen Zahnradblock.

Hauptwelle. Sie ist zugleich Abtriebswelle und wird über die Schaltmuffen drehfest mit den Losrädern Z_2, Z_4, Z_6, Z_8, Z_{10} verbunden.

Zum Schalten der Gänge werden die Schaltmuffen S_1, S_2 und S_3 nach links oder rechts verschoben. Dadurch wird jeweils ein Schaltrad (Losrad) drehfest mit der Hauptwelle verbunden.

Die Übersetzungen i_G der einzelnen Gänge werden, außer im direkten Gang (4. Gang), jeweils über zwei Zahnradpaarungen erreicht.

Dabei ist immer die durch die Zahnräder Z_1 und Z_2 gebildete Teilübersetzung, die auch

„konstante" genannt wird, wirksam.

Im 3. Gang wird die Schaftmuffe S_1 nach rechts verschoben und dadurch die Antriebswelle drehfest mit der Hauptwelle verbunden.

Hier erfolgen eine Drehmomenterhöhung und eine Drehzahländerung ins Langsame.

Neue Wörter

das	Kraftwagengetriebe	汽车变速器	das	Umlaufgetriebe	循环传动装置
das	Wechselgetriebe	手动变速器	das	Planetengetriebe	行星传动机构
das	Schaltgetriebe	换档变速装置	das	Klauengetriebe	爪形传动器
der	Kennungswandler	变矩器	das	Synchrongetriebe	同步器
die	Fahrgeschwindigkeit	运行速度	die	Schaltmuffe	换档滑套
die	Leistung	功率	die	Sperrsynchronisierung	棘轮同步
der	Drehzahlbereich	转速范围		stufenlos	无级的
das	Zahnradgetriebe	齿轮传动机构	der	Keilriemen	V带
die	Übersetzung	传动比	die	Riemenscheibe	带轮
der	Gang	档位	die	Fliehkraftgewichte	离心力配重块
die	Vorgelegewelle	副轴	die	Gaspedalstellung	加速踏板位置
die	Getriebehauptwelle	传动主轴		axial	轴向的
der	Rückwärtsgang	倒档	der	Kraftfluss	力流
das	Gruppengetriebe	联动传动装置		hydrodynamisch	液体动力学的

Text 2 Variable-speed gearbox 变速器（英文）

The Variable-speed gearbox is situated in the drivetrain of a motor vehicle between the clutch and the final drive and converts engine torques and engine speeds.

Functions

- Converts and transmits engine torque
- Converts engine speed
- Facilitates engine idling while the vehicle is stationary
- Facilitates reversal of the direction of rotation for reversing.

Every internal-combustion engine operates between a minimum speed and a maximum speed and can only output a limited torque within this powerful speed range.

The speed range between maximum engine torque and maximum engine power is known as the elastic range.

The torques and speeds output by the engine within the powerful speed range are converted so that they can be utilised for driving a motor vehicle.

The desired drive speeds and torques are achieved at the drive wheels by the different transmission stages in the gearbox via an intermediate final drive.

Torque and speed conversion

This is effected in variable-speed gearboxes with the aid of gear wheels.

In the case of a gear wheel pair, the greater torque and the lesser speed always act on the larger gear wheel (larger lever arm, more teeth).

The leverage ratio r_2/r_1 corresponds to the ratio of the numbers of teeth Z_2 of the driven gear wheel to the driving gear wheel Z_1 or to the ratio of the driving speed n_1 to the driven speed n_2.

This ratio is known as the gear ratio i or transmission ratio and expresses the degree of torque and speed conversion.

A transmission ratio $i > 1$ results in a torque increase and a speed decrease, while a transmission ratio $i < 1$ results in a torque decrease and a speed increase.

Gearbox output curves

Different gear ratios achieve different output torques and output speeds. The gearbox output curves are plotted from the results.

The curve points are calculated from the values of the engine torque curve and the gearbox gear ratios.

Torque hyperbola. The gearbox output torques needed to propel a vehicle are plotted against the gearbox output speeds.

For example, a high drive torque is needed to accelerate a vehicle from a standstill. This is made possible, for example, by the gear ratio of 1st gear. The gearbox output curves should approach the torque hyperbola in order to achieve as low a torque loss as possible during the gear change. This is a feature of the favourable stepping of a gearbox.

Traction-force hyperbola. If instead of the output torques the traction forces are plotted against the driving speed, a traction-force hyperbola is obtained as the vehicle's driving chart.

Idle position

This effects the interruption of the power flow.

Reversal of direction of rotation

The German Road Traffic Licensing Regulations require motor vehicle with a permissible total weight of more than 400 kg to be equipped with a facility for reversing the direction of rotation in order to reverse/back up the vehicles.

This rotation reversal is achieved with an idler gear, and has no effect on the transmission ratio.

Manual variable-speed gearbox

Gearboxes of this type are differentiated according to:

the progression of the power flow in the gearbox:
- identical shaft manual gearbox
- non-identical shaft manual gearbox

the installation position in the vehicle:
- longitudinal gearbox (= identical shaft)
- transverse gearbox (= non-identical shaft)

the components which non-rotatably connect the shift gear wheels (idler gears) with their shafts:
- selector sleeve gearbox
- shift dog gearbox

Selector sleeve gearbox

The power flow between the shift gear wheel (idler gear wheel) and the gearbox shaft is established via a selector sleeve, which is non-rotatably connected for example via a synchromesh body to the gearbox shaft.

All the gear wheel pairs for the forward gears have helical teeth and constantly mesh with each other. This is only possible if for each non-shifted gear wheel pair one gear wheel is freely rotatable as an idler gear on the shaft.

Gearshift process. A selector sleeve is displaced in such a way that corresponding shift gear wheel (idler gear) is non-rotatably connected to that shaft. Here the inner dogs of the selector sleeve are displaced via the shift teeth of the shift gear wheel.

Non-identical shaft selector sleeve gearbox

In non-identical shaft gearboxes, the gear ratios are achieved by means of one gear wheel pair in each case.

Gearboxes of these types are used, for example, in vehicles with engines mounted transversally to the direction of travel. The input and output shafts lie on different (unequal) planes. The output shaft is also known as the main shaft.

Example (gearshift, 3rd gear): Selector sleeve S_2 is displaced to the left to the shift teeth of shift gear wheel Z_5.

Power flow, 3rd gear: Input shaft → synchromesh body → selector sleeve S_2 → shift teeth of Z_5 → gear wheel Z_5 → gear wheel Z_6 → output shaft.

6-speed manual gearbox short design

This is a non-identical-shaft gearbox and is used for transverse installation in front-wheel and all-wheel drives.

Design:
- 1 input shaft In with 5 gear wheels (fixed gears).
- 2 output shafts Out1 and Out2 with shift gear wheels and 2 output gear wheels Z_{out1}, Z_{out2}, which act or a common final drive spur gear.

- 4 selector sleeves S_1 through S_4, 2 on each output shaft.

Gear wheels: Z_1, Z_3, Z_5, Z_7, Z_9 are mounted as fixed gear wheels on the input shaft In.

Shift gear wheels: Z_2, Z_4, Z_6, Z_8 for 1st to 4th gears are mounted as idler gear wheels on output shaft Out1.

The shift gear wheels Z_{10}, Z_{12}, Z_{16} for 5th, 6th and R (reverse) gears are mounted on output shaft Out2.

Selector sleeves: S_1, S_2, S_3 and S_4 for the forward gears establish the torque-proof connection of the shift gear wheels with output shafts Out1 and Out2.

Identical shaft selector-sleeve gearbox

In identical shaft gearboxes, the input and output shafts are mounted in the same plane.

Gearboxes of this type are used in vehicles with front engines and rear-wheel drives installed in the direction of travel and are known as "3-shaft gearboxes" (input shaft, countershaft, output shaft).

Input shaft. This is connected with the clutch disc and drives the countershaft via Z_1.

Countershaft. Together with gear wheels Z_2, Z_3, Z_5, Z_7, Z_9 and Z_{11}, this forms a cluster gear.

Output shaft (main shaft). Shift gear wheels (idler gears) are mounted on this shaft.

Selector sleeves S_1, S_2 and S_3 are displaced to the left or right to shift the gears. In this way, one shift gear wheel (idler gear) in each case is non-rotatably connected to the output shaft via the synchromesh body.

The gear ratios i_G of the individual gears are, except in the direct gear, achieved in each case by means of two gear wheel pairs. The gear wheel pair Z_1/Z_2 is always effective here.

Direct gear (4th gear): Selector sleeve S_1 is displaced to the left and the input shaft is non-rotatably connected to the input shaft. There is no torque or speed change here.

New Words

drivetrain	传动系统	transmission ratio	变速比
variable-speed gearbox	变速器	torque hyperbola	转矩双曲线
clutch	离合器	traction-force hyperbola	牵引力双曲线
torque	转矩	idle position	怠速位置
convert	改变	reversal of direction of rotation	倒档齿轮
reversal	反转	rotation	转动
elastic range	弹性范围	manual	手动
gear wheel	齿轮	identical shaft manual gearbox	同轴手动变速器
leverage ratio	杠杆比	non-identical shaft manual gearbox	
gear ratio	档位比		非同轴手动变速器

Kapitel 1　Automobiltechnologie // Chapter 1　Technology of Automobile

longitudinal gearbox	纵向变速器	identical shaft selector sleeve gearbox	同轴接合套式变速器
transverse gearbox	横向变速器	non-identical shaft selector sleeve gearbox	非同轴接合套式变速器
selector sleeve gearbox	接合套变速器	input shaft	输入轴
shift dog gearbox	接合齿变速器	output shaft	输出轴
shift gear wheel	换档齿轮	countershaft	中间轴
gearbox shaft	齿轮轴	direct gear	直接档
selector sleeve	接合套		

课文参考译文

变速器

变速器位于汽车传动系统的离合器与主减速器之间，它能够传递和改变发动机传来的转矩和转速。

功用

1）改变和传递来自发动机的转矩。
2）改变来自发动机的转速。
3）当汽车停驶时，便于发动机怠速。
4）实现反向转动，以便倒车。

每一种内燃机都在最小转速与最大转速之间工作，而且在其高转速范围内只能输出有限的转矩。

最大发动机转矩与最大发动机功率之间的转速范围叫作弹性范围。

发动机在有效的转速范围内输出的转矩和转速需进行改变，以便用来驱动汽车。

驱动轮上理想的驱动速度和转矩是通讨变速器在不同档位变换，并经主减速器传递后获得的。

转矩-转速变换

转矩与转速的变换是由变速器不同档位齿轮的啮合实现的。

就不同档位的齿轮副来说，较大的转矩和较小的转速总是发生在较大的齿轮上（较长的杠杆臂，较多的齿数）。

杠杆比r_2/r_1等于从动齿轮齿数Z_2与主动齿轮齿数Z_1之比，或等于主动轮转速n_1与从动轮转速n_2之比。

上述之比叫作档位比或变速比i，它表示了转矩与转速变换的程度。

变速比$i>1$导致了转矩增大和转速下降，而变速比$i<1$的结果是转矩下降和转速升高。

变速器输出特性曲线

不同的变速比获得不同的输出转矩和输出转速。变速器输出曲线就是根据其转速绘制的转矩变化曲线。曲线上各个点是根据发动机转矩曲线的值和变速器的变速比计算得出的。

1）转矩双曲线表达的是变速器输出的驱动汽车所需要的转矩相对于变速器输出转速的关系。例如，汽车由静止开始加速时需要大的驱动转矩。此时，1档的变速比能够满足这一需要。变速器输出曲线应接近转矩双曲线，以便在换档过程中获得尽可能低的转矩损失。这是变速器良好换档性能的表现。

2）牵引力双曲线。如果不采用转矩，而是将牵引力相对于汽车车速的关系绘制成曲线，则可获得牵引力双曲线。

3）急速位置。急速位置时切断动力传递。

4）倒档齿轮。德国道路交通法规要求允许总质量大于400kg的汽车装有反向传动齿轮，以便汽车倒车。变速器通常采用倒档惰轮实现反方向传动。

手动变速器

手动变速器可按照以下因素分类。

1. 按照变速器中动力传递的路线

1）同轴手动变速器。

2）非同轴手动变速器。

2. 按照汽车上的安装位置

1）纵向变速器（即同轴手动变速器）。

2）横向变速器（即非同轴手动变速器）。

3. 按照换档齿轮(惰轮)与齿轮轴的连接部件

1）接合套变速器。

2）接合齿变速器。

接合套式手动变速器

换档齿轮（惰轮）与齿轮轴之间的动力传递是经过接合套实现的，接合套经花键与齿轮轴连接。

前进档的所有传动齿轮都是斜齿轮，并且是常啮合齿轮。这样只能是每一对固定的常啮合齿轮副中的一个齿轮空套在轴上，可以自由转动。

换档过程中使接合套移动，将接合套的接合齿移向换档齿轮的换档齿，使相应的换档齿轮（空套在轴上的齿轮）与轴连接，能够传递转矩。

1. 非同轴接合套式手动变速器

在非同轴变速器中，每一档位情况下的变速比都是通过一对齿轮副获得的。

这种形式的变速器被用于发动机横置（相对于汽车运行方向）的汽车上。输入轴和输出轴位于不同的平面上。输出轴也叫作主轴。

例如，换入3档时，接合套S_2被向左移动到换档齿轮Z_5上。此时动力传递路线为：输入轴→同步器花键毂→接合套S_2→换档齿轮Z_5的接合齿→换档齿轮Z_5→档位齿轮Z_6→输出轴。

短型6档手动变速器

这种变速器属于非同轴手动变速器,它被横向安装在前轮驱动或全轮驱动的汽车上。其基本结构如下:

1)1根输入轴In上装有3个齿轮(固定齿轮)。

2)两根输出轴Out1和Out2上装有换档齿轮和两个输出齿轮Z_{out1}和Z_{out2},这两个输出齿轮均与普通的主减速器的圆柱齿轮相啮合。

3)4个接合套S_1、S_2、S_3、S_4,每一输出轴上各装两个。

档位齿轮Z_1、Z_3、Z_5、Z_7、Z_9以固定的形式装在输入轴In上。1~4档用的换档齿轮Z_2、Z_4、Z_6、Z_8以惰轮形式被安装在输出轴Out1上。5档、6档和R档(倒档)用的换档齿轮Z_{10}、Z_{16}安装在输出轴Out2上。用于前进档的接合套S_1、S_2、S_3和S_4实现换档齿轮与输出轴Out1和Out2的连接。

2. 同轴接合套式手动变速器

在同轴接合套式手动变速器中,输入轴和输出轴被安装在同一平面上。

同轴接合套式手动变速器用于前置发动机后轮驱动的汽车,采用纵向(沿汽车行驶方向)布置。这种变速器被叫作3轴变速器(输入轴、中间轴、输出轴)。

1)输入轴。输入轴与离合器从动盘连接,并通过Z_1驱动中间轴。中间轴上装有齿轮Z_2、Z_3、Z_5、Z_7、Z_9和Z_{11},从而形成了一组齿轮。

2)输出轴。输出轴(主轴)上装有换档齿轮(惰轮)Z_4、Z_6、Z_8、Z_{10}、Z_{12}。接合套S_1、S_2、S_3被向左或向右移动与换档齿轮接合进行换档。每次进行换档操作时,都有一个换档齿轮(惰轮)通过同步器的花键毂与输出轴相接合。

除直接档外,每一档位的变速比 i_G 都是通过两对齿轮副获得的。其中,齿轮副Z_1/Z_2总是参与工作。

3)直接档(4档)。接合套S_1被向左移动,输入轴与输出轴直接连接。这种情况下转矩或转速都不改变。

Teil 5　Kraftübertragungssystem　传动系统
Part 5　Drivetrain　传动系统

【知识目标】

1. 掌握与传动系统结构、分类、运行原理等相关的专业术语、单词和词汇。

2. 掌握传动系统主要结构的德文、英文表达方法。

【能力目标】

1. 能对传动系统总体结构的各大总成进行中、德、英互译。

2. 能进行与传动系统大体构造相关的德英双语资料的阅读和翻译。

3. 能在传动系统实物上标识出相应结构的德语、英语单词和词汇。

Text 1　Kraftübertragungssystem传动系统（德文）

Gelenkwelle, Achswelle, Gelenke

Aufgaben

- Drehmomentübertragen
- Winkeländerungen ermöglichen
- Längenänderungen (axiale Verschiebungen) zulassen
- Drehschwingungen dämpfen.

Das vom Wechselgetriebe gewandelte Drehmoment wird auf das Achsgetriebe und die Antriebsräder übertragen.

Hinterachsantrieb mit Frontmotor. Der Kraftfluss verläuft im Antriebsstrang von Wechselgetriebe über die Gelenkwelle (Kardanwelle) zum Achsgetriebe und weiter über die Achswellen und Gleichlaufgelenke zu den Antriebsrädern.

Vorderradantrieb mit Frontmotor und Hinterradantrieb mit Heckmotor. Die Drehmomentübertragung erfolgt vom Wechselgetriebe über Achsgetriebe, Gleichlaufgelenke, Achswellen zu den Antriebsrädern.

Wechselgetriebe und Achsgetriebe sind in einem Gehäuse untergebracht; es ist keine

Gelenkwelle (Kardanwelle) erforderlich.

Gelenkwellen

Sie sind bei Fahrzeugen mit Frontmotor und Hinterantrieb zwischen Wechselgetriebe und hinterem Achsgetriebe angeordnet.

Gelenkwelle bestehen aus dem Gelenkwellenrohr mit Schiebenstück und Kreuzgelenken.

Ist bei Fahrzeug mit Einzelradaufhängung zwischen Wechselgetriebe und Achsgetriebe ein großer Abstand zu überwinden, so wird eine zweiteilige Gelenkwelle verwendet und durch ein Zwischenlager abgestützt.

Um zwischen Wechselgetriebe und Achsgetriebe einen Achsversatz zu ermöglichen, werden z. B. Trockengelenke und Kreuzgelenke eingebaut.

Zwischenlager. Hier ist die geteilte Gelenkwelle elastisch gelagert.

Das Zwischenlager ist durch einen Lagerbock am Fahrzeugboden befestigt. Es enthält ein Kugerlager, das in Gummi eingebettet ist.

Durch die Teilung der Gelenkwelle wird ein schwingungsarmer und ruhiger Lauf erreicht und Dröhnungsgeräusche vermieden.

Achswelle

Sie sind im Antriebsstrang zwischen Achsgetriebe und Antriebsrädern angeordnet und werden auch als Antriebswellen bezeichnet.

Achswellen bestehen aus dem Achswellenrohr und den Gleichlaufgelenken.

Gelenke

Man verwendet

- Kreuzgelenk   – Scheibengelenk
- Kugelgelenk   – Tripodegelenk

Kreuzgelenk. Die Gelenkgabeln sind durch die im Zapfenkreuz angeordneten Gelenkzapfen gelenkig miteinander verbunden. Die Gelenkzapfen sind in den Gelenkgabeln meist in vollgekapselten Naderlagern wartungsfrei gelagert.

In Kraftfahrzeugen werden Kreuzgelenk für Beugungswinkel bis 8° angewendet.

Sonderausführungen, z. B. für Nebenantriebe, lassen größere Beugungswinkel zu.

Scheibengelenke. Scheibengelenke sind elastische Gelenke, die nicht geschmiert werden müssen und nur geringe Beugungswinkel und Längeänderungen zulassen. Sie werden im Antriebsstrang hauptsächlich als elastische Glieder eingebaut, um auftretende Vibrationen und Geräusche zu dämpfen. Zum Einsatz kommen sie bei Fahrzeugen, deren Achsgetriebe fest mit dem Aufbau oder Rahmen verbunden sind.

Kugelgelenke. Kugelgelenke ermöglichen Beugungswinkel bis 47°.Sie lassen keine axiale Verschiebungen zu.

Sie bestehen aus Kugelstern, Kugelschale, Kugelkäfig.

Kugelschale und Kugelstern haben gekrümmte Laufbahnen, auf denen die Kugeln laufen.

Tripodegelenke. Tripodegelenke ermöglichen Beugungswinkel bis 26° und axiale Verschiebungen bis 55 mm.

Tripodegelenke können bei Einzelradaufhängung sowohl bei angetriebenen Vorderachsen (Vorderradantrieb) als auch bei angetriebenen Hinterachsen (Hinterradantrieb) verwendet werden.

Der Tripodestern ist immer der Achsgetriebe zugekehrt.

Wiederholungsfragen

1. Welche Aufgaben haben Gelenkwellen?
2. Welche Arten von Gelenken werden im Fahrzeugbau verwendet?
3. Welche Beugungswinkel sind bei den verschiedenen Gelenken zulässig?
4. Wie verhalten sich die Drehgeschwindigkeiten bei einem gebeugten Kreuzgelenk?
5. Wie unterscheiden sich Gleichlauf-Festgelenke und Gleichlauf-Verschiebegelenke?

Neue Wörter

das	Kraftübertragungssystem	传动系统	das	Kugerlager	球轴承
die	Gelenkwelle	传动轴	das	Gummi	橡胶
die	Achswelle	半轴	der	Gelenkgabel	万向节叉
die	Gelenke	万向节	das	Naderlager	滚针轴承
der	Hinterradantrieb	后轮驱动	das	Kreuzgelenk	十字轴式万向节
das	Achsgetriebe	主减速器	das	Scheibengelenk	滑动式等速万向节
das	Gelenkwellenrohr	轴管	das	Tripodegelenk	三销轴式万向节
das	Schiebenstück	滑动节	das	Kugelgelenk	球笼式万向节
die	Einzelradaufhängung	独立悬架	der	Kugelstern	星形球座
das	Zwischenlager	中间支承	die	Kugelschale	桶形球壳
die	elastische Scheibe	挠性盘	das	Kugelkäfig	球笼
die	Vibration	振动	die	Kugel	钢球
der	Lagerbock	轴承座			

Text 2   Drivetrain 传动系统（英文）

Propeller shafts, drive shafts, joints

Functions

- Transmit torques
- Facilitate angular variations
- Permit linear variations (axial displacement)

- Damp torsional vibrations.

The torque converted by the variable-speed gearbox is transmitted to the final drive and the drive wheels.

Example of rear-wheel drive with front engine:

The power flow progresses in the drivetrain from the variable-spccd gearbox via the propeller shaft (cardan shaft) to the final drive and onward via the axle shafts and constant-velocity joints to the drive wheels.

Example of front-wheel drive with front engine and rear-wheel drive with rear engine:

The power flow progresses in the drivetrain from the variable-speed gearbox via the final drive, constant velocity joints and drive shafts to the drive wheels.

No cardan shaft is required here.

The variable-speed gearbox and the final drive are accommodated in a single housing.

Propeller shafts

In vehicles with front engines and rear-wheel drives, these are situated between the variable-speed gearbox and the final drive in the vehicle longitudinal direction.

Propeller shafts consist of a shaft tube with slide and joints, e.g. two universal joints.

If in vehicle with independent suspension a large distance has to be covered between the variable-speed gearbox and the final drive, a two-piece propeller shaft is used which is supported by an intermediate mount.

Universal joints are deployed to facilitate an axis offset between the variable-speed gearbox and the final drive. The flexible discs serve to damp vibrations.

Intermediate mount. The split propeller shaft is resiliently supported here.

The intermediate mount is secured to the vehicle floor by means of a bearing pedestal. It contains a ball bearing which is embedded in rubber.

The separation of the propeller shaft results in low-vibration, quiet running and eliminates droning noises.

Drive shafts (axle shafts)

These are arranged in the drivetrain between the final drive and the drive wheels.

The drive shafts can be equipped at the final drive end, for example, with a tripod joint and at the wheel end with a ball joint.

Joints

The following are used: Universal joints

- Flexible discs
- Ball joints
- Tripod joints
- Double joints

In motor vehicle universal joints are used for diffraction angles up to 8°.

Special designs, e.g. for power takeoff units, permit greater diffraction angles.

Flexible discs. Flexible discs are resilient, maintenance-free joints. They permit only small diffraction angles and linear variations. They are installed in the drivetrain primarily as flexible elements for damping vibrations and noises. Flexible discs are used in vehicles whose final drives are permanently connected with the body or frame.

Ball joints. These consist of the ball star, ball shell, ball cage and balls.

The ball shell and ball star have curved tracks on which the balls run.

Ball joints permit diffraction angles up to 38° in their normal version and up to 47° in their special version. They do not permit any axial displacement.

Tripod joints. These can be used in the case of independent suspension both on powered front axles (front-wheel drive) and on powered rear axles (rear-wheel drive).

Tripod joints permit diffraction angles up to 26° and axial displacement up to 55 mm.

The tripod star is always turned towards the final drive end.

Universal joints. The link forks/yokes are flexibly connected with each other by the joint bolts arranged in the spider. The joint bolts are usually mounted in the link forks in fully encapsulated needle bearing (therefore requiring no maintenance).

REVIEW QUESTIONS

1. What are the functions of propeller shafts?
2. Into which categories are joints subdivided?
3. Which constant velocity joints are used in vehicle manufacturing?
4. What is the function of the slide of a propeller shaft?
5. What are the functions of flexible discs?

New Words

drivetrain	传动系统	vibration	振动
propeller shaft	传动轴	bearing pedestal	轴承座
drive shaft	半轴	ball bearing	球轴承
joint	万向节	rubber	橡胶
rear-wheel drive	后轮驱动	link fork	万向节叉
final drive	主减速器	joint bolt	轴销
shaft tube	轴管	encapsulate	密封，封装
slide	滑动节	needle bearing	滚针轴承
independent suspension	独立悬架	constant velocity	等速
intermediate mount	中间支承	sliding constant velocity joint	滑动式等速万向节
flexible disc	挠性盘	tripod joint	三销轴式万向节

Kapitel 1　Automobiltechnologie // Chapter 1　Technology of Automobile

diffraction angles	交角	ball star	星形球座
axial displacement	轴向伸缩	ball shell	桶形球壳
pot joint	伸缩型球笼式万向节	ball cage	球笼
fixed constant velocity joint	固定式等速万向节	ball	钢球
ball joint	球笼式万向节		

课文参考译文

传动系统

传动轴、半轴和万向节

功能

1）传递转矩。

2）适应传动方向的角度变化。

3）允许传动部件的轴向位移。

由变速器变换的转矩通过万向传动装置传递给主减速器和驱动车轮。

前置发动机后轮驱动的万向传动装置举例如下：

传动系统中的动力传递是从变速器经传动轴（万向节轴）到主减速器，然后经万向节和半轴传给驱动车轮。

前置发动机前轮驱动和后置发动机后轮驱动的万向传动装置举例如下：

传动系统中的动力传递是从变速器经主减速器、万向节和半轴传给驱动车轮。这种传动系统不需要传动轴。变速器和主减速器被装在一个壳体中。

传动轴

在前置发动机后轮驱动的汽车上，传动轴沿汽车的纵向位于变速器和主减速器之间。传动轴由轴管、滑动节、万向节组成。

如果在具有独立悬架的汽车上，必须跨越变速器与主减速器之间较大的距离，则通常采用两段式传动轴，并利用中间支承对其进行支撑。

万向节的作用是使变速器与主减速器之间的传动轴便于轴线偏斜，即改变动力的传递角度。挠性盘用来减小振动。

中间支承

断开式传动轴被弹性地支撑在中间支承上。中间支承通过轴承座固定在汽车底板上。它由球轴承组成，球轴承被嵌入在橡胶垫中。

传动轴分段的好处是振动小，运转平静，消除了嗡嗡的噪声。

半轴

半轴被布置在传动系统的主减速器与驱动车轮之间。半轴在主减速器侧装有三销轴式万向节，而在驱动车轮侧装有球笼式万向节。

万向节

汽车传动系统通常使用以下几种万向节：

1）挠性盘式万向节。

2）三销轴式万向节。

3）十字轴式万向节。

4）球笼形万向节。

挠性盘式万向节

挠性盘式万向节具有弹性，无须维护。这种万向节只允许小的两轴交角和轴向伸缩。它们安装在传动系统中，主要是作为弹性元件，以减小振动和噪声。挠性盘式万向节用于主减速器与车身或车架永久连接的汽车上。

三销轴式万向节。

这种万向节可以用于独立悬架汽车的前半轴（前轮驱动）或后半轴（后轮驱动）上。

三销轴式万向节可以允许输入轴和输出轴的交角达到26°，允许的轴向伸缩达到55mm。该种万向节的三销轴总是朝向主减速器一端。

十字轴式万向节

万向节叉通过十字轴上的轴销被挠性地相互连接在一起。轴销通常采用完全密封的滚针轴承安装在万向节叉中，因而不需要进行维护。在汽车上，十字轴式万向节可以使两轴的交角达到8°。在专门的结构中，例如作为动力输出装置，可以允许更大的交角。

当十字轴式万向节在两轴以一定交角工作时，则在输出轴上会产生不均匀的转动。

球笼式万向节

球笼式万向节可允许两轴交角达到47°。但不允许任何的轴向伸缩。

这种万向节由星形球座、桶形球壳、球笼和钢球组成。桶形球壳和星形球座具有曲线球道，钢球在其中滚动。

Teil 6　Lenkung　转向系统
Part 6　Steering　转向系统

【知识目标】
1. 掌握与转向系统结构、分类、运行原理等相关的专业术语、单词和词汇。
2. 掌握转向系统主要结构的德英文表达方法。

【能力目标】
1. 能对转向系统总体结构的各大总成进行中、德、英互译。
2. 能进行与转向系统大体构造相关的德语、英语资料的阅读和翻译。
3. 能在转向系统实物上标识出相应结构的德语、英语单词和词汇。

Text 1　Lenkung 转向系统（德文）

Mit der Lenkung kann die Fahrtrichtung eines Fahrzeugs willkürlich beeinflusst und können bei Geradeausfahrt äußere Störeinflüsse kompensiert werden. Die Lenkung besteht im Allgemeinen aus: Lenkrad, Lenkspindel, Lenkgetriebe, Lenkstockhebel, Spurstange, Lenkschubstangen und Lenkhebeln an den Rädern.

Im Lenkgetriebe wird die Drehbewegung des Lenkrads in die Drehung der Lenkwelle oder axiale Bewegung einer Zahnstange umgeformt und zweckmäßig übersetzt.

Formen des Lenkgetriebes

Zahnstangenlenkung

Ritzel mit Zahnstangeist besonders einfach. Untersetzungist beschränkt, daes durch Lenkrad und Ritzelhalbmesser gegebenist, keine Dämpfung von Fahrbahnstoßen, oft Einbauschwierigkeiten.

Rollenzahnlenkung besteht aus Lenkschnecke und wälzgelagertem Ritzelsegment.

Rollenfingerlenkung hat einen im Lenkstock wälzgelagerten kegellgen Finger, der in einem trapezförmigen Gewindegang der Lenkschnecke geführt wird.

Beide Lenkungen bauen relativ klein, haben gute Wirkungsgrade mit ausreichender Dämpfung und erlauben eine Progression der Übersetzung (Bendix Varialenkung).

Kugelmutterlenkung

Hier ist die Lenkschnecke als Schraube ausgebildet, deren Kraftschluss mit der Lenkmutter über rollende Kugeln erfolgt. Die Kugeln verlassen am Ende den Gewindegang und kehren über ein Rückführrohr wieder an den Anfang zurück. Die Axialbewegung der Lenkmutter wird in die Drehbewegung der Lenkwelle über Zahnstange oder Hebel mit Kugelzapfen überführt. Besonders guter Wirkungsgrad mit guter Spielfreiheit.

Lenkgestänge

Aufgaben

– Übertragung der vom Lenkgetriebe erzeugten Lenkbewegung auf die Vorderräder

– Führung der Räder in einer bestimmten Spurstellung zueinander.

Hauptteile

Spurstange(n), Spurstangengelenke, Spurstangenhebel, evtl. Zwischenhebel und Lenkstange.

Starre Vorderachse. Bei Nkw werden als Lenkgetriebe meist Kugelumlauf- Lenkgetriebe verwendet. Vom Lenkstockhebel des Lenkgetriebes wird die Bewegung über die Lenkstange auf Zwischenhebel und Spurhebel (Spurstangenhebel) übertragen. Dieser ist durch ein Spurstangengelenk mit der einteiligen Spurstange und dem Spurhebel der anderen Achsseite verbunden.

Einzelradaufhängung. Die gelenkten Räder können sich unabhängig voneinander auf und ab bewegen. Dabei ändert sich der Abstand zwischen den Spurhebeln, was bei Verwendung einer einteiligen (ungeteilten) Spurstange zu Spuränderungen führen würde. Die Lenkgestänge für Einzelradaufhängung haben deshalb geteilte Spurstangen (zwei- oder dreiteilige Spurstangen).

Die meist verwendeten Zahnstangen-Lenkgetriebe besitzen zweiteilige Spurstangen.

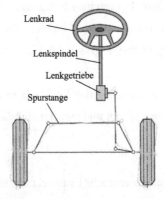

Bild: Hauptteile der Lenkung

Lenkgetriebe

Aufgaben

– Umwandlung der Drehbewegung des Lenkrads in ein Schwenken des Lenkstockhebels bzw. ein Verschieben der Zahnstange

– Vergrößerung (Übersetzung) des durch Handkraft erzeugten Drehmomentes am Lenkrad.

Die Übersetzung im Lenkgetriebe muss so ausgelegt sein, dass die maximale Betätigungskraft am Lenkrad z.B. 250 N nicht übersteigt. Sie beträgt bei Personenkraftwagen bis etwa $i=19$, bei Nutzkraftwagen bis etwa $i=36$.

Bei Personenkraftwagen werden heute fast ausschließlich Zahnstangen-Lenkgetriebe verwendet.

Aufbau

Ein Ritzel, das im Lenkgehäuse gelagert ist und auf der Lenkspindel sitzt, greift über eine Schrägverzahnung in die Verzahnung der Zahnstange ein. Die Zahnstange wird in Büchsen geführt und ständig über ein Druckstück durch Tellerfedern fast spielfrei an das Ritzel gedrückt.

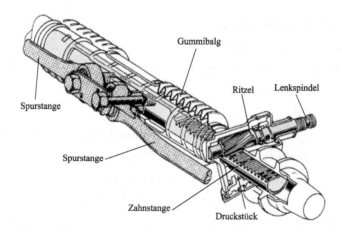

Bild: Zahnstangen-Lenkgetriebe

Wirkungsweise

Dreht man am Lenkrad, so wird die Zahnstange durch die Drehbewegung des Ritzels axial verschoben und schwenkt über Spurstangen und Spurhebel die Räder.

Zahnstangen-Lenkgetriebe zeichnen sich durch direkte Übersetzung, leichte Rückstellung und flache Bauweise aus.

Neben der konstanten Übersetzung im Lenkgetriebe gibt es auch die variable Übersetzung.

Variable Übersetzung

Bei rein mechanischen Lenkgetrieben ohne hydraulische Servowirkung wird die Übersetzung so ausgelegt, dass die Lenkung im Bereich kleiner Ausschläge direkter wirkt als bei großen Ausschlägen. Dies wird erreicht, indem die Zahnstange unterschiedliche Zahnteilungen erhält. Im Mittenbereich ist die Zahnteilung (Anstand von Zahn zu Zahn) größer als im Außenbereich.

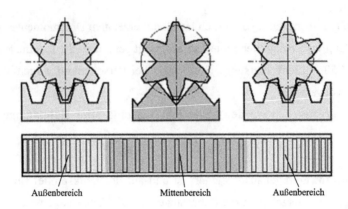

Bild: variable Übersetzung

Vorteile der variablen Übersetzung:
- Direkte Lenkung für schnelle Geradeausfahrt,
- geringerer Kraftaufwand beim Einparken.

Zahnstangen-Hydrolenkung

Aufbau

Die Zahnstangen-Hydrolenkung besteht aus dem mechanischen Zahnstangen-Lenkgetriebe, dem integrierten hydraulischen Arbeitszylinder, dem Steuerventil und der Flügelzellenpumpe. Der Antrieb zu den Spurstangen ist zweiseitig als Seitenabtrieb ausgeführt.

Das Gehäuse, in dem die Zahnstange untergebracht ist, bildet den Arbeitszylinder, der durch einen Kolben in zwei Arbeitsräume unterteilt wird. Als Steuerventil werden Drehschieberventile oder Drehkolbenventile verwendet.

Der Drehstab ist durch 2 Stifte an einem Ende mit der Steuerbüchse und dem Antriebsritzel, am anderen Ende mit der Lenkspindel und dem Drehschieber drehfest verbunden.

Drehschieber und Steuerbüchse bilden das Drehschieberventil. Sie besitzen auf ihren Mantelflächen Steuernuten. Die Nuten der Steuerbüchse münden in Gehäusekanälen, die zu den beiden Arbeitsräumen, zur Flügelzellenpumpe und zum Vorratsbehälter führen.

Wirkungsweise

Wird das Lenkrad eingeschlagen, so wird die manuell aufgebrachte Lenkkraft über den Drehstab auf das Antriebsritzel übertragen. Dabei wird der Drehstab entsprechend der Gegenkraft auf Torsion beansprucht und geringfügig verdreht. Dies bewirkt ein Verdrehen des Drehschiebers gegenüber der ihn umschließenden Steuerbüchse. Dadurch werden die Stellungen der Steuernuten zueinander verändert. Die Einlassschlitze (P) werden für den Drucköl-Zulauf geöffnet. Das von der Flügelzellenpumpe kommende Drucköl fließt durch die Einlassschlitze (P) in die untere Radialnut der Steuerbüchse und wird in den entsprechenden Arbeitsraum geleitet.

Der Flüssigkeitsdruck wirkt entweder auf die rechte oder linke Seite des Arbeitskolbens und erzeugt hier die hydraulische Unterstützungskraft. Sie wirkt zusätzlich zu der vom Ritzel mechanisch auf die Zahnstange übertragenen Lenkkraft.

Wird das Lenkrad nicht mehr weiter verdreht, so gehen Drehstab und Drehschieberventil in die Neutralstellung zurück. Die Steuerschlitze zu den Arbeitsräumen werden geschlossen, die für den Rücklauf (T) sind geöffnet.

Das Öl fließt von der Pumpe über das Steuerventil zurück zum Vorratsbehälter.

Servotronic

Sie ist eine elektronisch gesteuerte Hydrolenkung, bei der die hydraulischen Unterstützungskräfte ausschließlich von der Fahrgeschwindigkeit beeinflusst werden.

Bei geringer Fahrgeschwindigkeit wirkt die volle Unterstützungskraft der Hydrolenkung. Mit zunehmender Fahrgeschwindigkeit wird diese Unterstützungskraft geringer, die Lenkung wird direkter.

Bauteile(Bild): Elektronischer Tachometer, Steuergerät, elektro-hydraulischer Wandler, Hydrolenkung, Druckölpumpe, Ölbehälter.

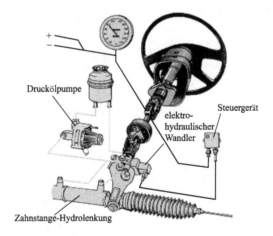

Wirkungsweise. Bei Geschwindigkeiten unter 20 km/h bleibt das vom Steuergerät beeinflusste Magnetventil geschlossen.

Wird z.B. bei Rechtsteinschlag, die Lenkspiel im Uhrzeigersinn gedreht, so wird der rechte Ventilkolben nach unten gedrückt. Das Drucköl strömt sowohl in den rechten Arbeitsraum als auch über das Rückwirkungsraum und über die beiden Drosseln in den linken Rückwirkungsraum. Das Rückschlagventil ist dabei geschlossen. In beiden Rückwirkungsräumen herrschen gleiche Drücke. Deshalb entsteht kein Rückwirkungsmoment auf den Drehstab, der volle Unterstützungsdruck wird wirksam. Das Lenkrad kann leicht gedreht werden.

Fahren mit hoher Geschwindigkeit. Das Magnetventil ist ganz geöffnet. Das Drucköl fließt vom rechten Arbeitsraum über das rechte Rückschlagventil, die Drossel und das Magnetventil zum Rücklauf. Der rechte Rückwirkungsraum ist durch die Drosselwirkung der Drossel mit höherem Druck beaufschlagt als der linke fast drucklose Rückwirkungsraum. Dadurch entsteht ein linksdrehendes Rückwirkungsmoment auf die Lenkspindel, das die Ventilkolben in die Neutrallage zurückdreht. Es kann kein Unterstützungsdruck für die Hydrolenkung aufgebaut werden, die Lenkung erfordert vom Fahrer mehr Lenkkraft und ist dadurch direkter.

Elektrische Servolenkung

Die für die Servowirkung benötigte Unterstützungskraft wird von einem Elektromotor erzeugt, der von der Starterbatterie bei Bedarf mit elektrischer Energie versorgt wird.

Die Komponenten des elektrisch unterstützen Lenksystems (Electrical Power Steering = EPS) sind im Systembild dargestellt.

Wiederholungsfragen

1. Welche Aufgaben hat die Lenkung?
2. Welche Merkmale besitzt die Drehschemellenkung, wo wird sie verwendet?
3. Wie verläuft die Lenkdrehachse bei den Rädern einer Achsschenkellenkung?
4. Erklären Sie das Abrollen der Vorderräder einer Achsschenkellenkung?
5. Wie wird das Lenktrapez gebildet?

Neue Wörter

die	Lenkung	转向	die	Grundforderung	基本要求
die	Fahrtrichtung	行驶方向	die	Spurstange	转向横拉杆
der	Fahrzeug	汽车	die	Zwischenhebel	中间杠杆
die	Geradefahrt	直线行驶	das	Lenkverhalten	转向特性
das	Lenkgetriebe	转向器	die	Vorspur	前束
die	Drehung	旋转，转动		vorhanden	现有的，现存的
die	Bewegung	运动	der	Schräglaufwinkel	偏驶角
die	Zahnstangenlenkung	齿轮齿条式转向器	der	Nachlauf	主销后倾
das	Ritzel	小齿轮	das	Übersteuern	过调
die	Fahrbahn	路面	die	Ursache	理由，原因
der	Einbau	安装		zunehmen	增加，增长
	einbauen	安装，装配	die	Ausnutzung	利用，使用
der	Lenkstock	转向柱	die	Hilfskraftlenkung	助力转向
	kegelig	锥形的		entsprechend	相应地
die	Wirkung	作用，效果		entsprechen	符合
	wirken	发生作用	der	Arbeitskolben	工作活塞
die	Lenkschnecke	转向蜗杆	der	Öldruck	油压

beeinflussen	影响	die Lenkspindel		转向轴
kompensieren	补偿	die Dämpfung		阻尼
kompensiert	补偿的，平衡的	der Gewindegang		螺距

Text 2　Steering gear转向器（英文）

Basic principles of steering

The main steering components in the motor vehicle are:

- Steering wheel
- Steering gear
- Tie rod
- Steering shaft
- Tie rod end.

Steering makes it possible to turn (pivot) the front wheels at different angles. In addition, steering amplifies the torque generated manually at the steering wheel.

Designs

- Fifth wheel (swinging beam) steering
- Ackermann steering.

Fifth wheel steering

This design involves steering by swivelling a rigid axle, usually the front axle. A pin or pivoted bogie (also fifth wheel) makes it possible to pivot the axle connection to the vehicle. In the case of trailers, the steering force is transferred across the drawbar.

Features. In the case of fifth wheel steering the tilting angle of the trailer is at its maximum, thus increasing its instability. The radius of the turn is less due to the larger steering angle, resulting in good manoeuvrability.

Ackermann steering

Unlike fifth wheel steering, in Ackermann steering each wheel pivots around its own axis. The axis is formed by the connection of the upper and lower mounting points of the wheel suspension or by the longitudinal connection of the kingpins. Ackermann steering is used on all dual-track motor vehicles. When the wheels are turned about the steering axis, the contact patch remains almost the same size.

Rolling motion of the wheels when cornering. To ensure that the wheels roll smoothly when cornering, each steered wheel has to turn according to the radius of the turn.

Since on dual-track vehicles, the wheels on the inside of a curve follow a smaller radius of the turn than those on the outside of a curve (toe difference angle), they must be turned at a greater angle.

Ackermann principle. The wheels must be turned such that the projected centre lines of the steering knuckle of the wheels on the inside and the outside of the turn meet the projected line of the rear axle. The circular trajectories covered by the front and rear wheels then have a common centre point.

Steering trapezoid

The steering trapezoid allows the front wheels to turn at different angles.

This is formed by the tie rod, the two tie-rod arms and the line through the two steering axles when the wheels are set to the straight-ahead position.

Steering gear

Functions

• Translates the rotational movement of the steering wheel to a steering angle at the steered wheels

• provides precise steering of the vehicle in all driving situations.

Regulations require that the steering gear transmission ratio be designed such that the max. force at the steering wheel without power assistance does not exceed 150 N for M1 category vehicles (PC with 4 wheels), for instance. For N1 category vehicles (commercial vehicles with 4 wheels used to transport goods, 3.5 t perm. gross weight), the max. force is 200 N.

The ratio is up to $i=19$ on passenger cars and up to $i=36$ on commercial vehicles.

Rack-and-pinion steering is used on almost all passenger cars today, whereas commercial vehicles generally use recirculating ball steering.

Rack-and-pinion steering gear (mechanical)

Design. A pinion fitted in the steering gear housing engages with the rack by way of helical teeth. The rack is guided in bushes and is continuously pressed against the pinion by a disc spring under the thrust member.

Operating principle. The rack-and-pinion steering gear set converts the rotational motion of the steering wheel into a linear motion compatible with the tie rod.

Design types. Constant or variable ratio mechanical steering gear systems are available. In the case of the constant ratio system, the tooth pitch is the same over the whole rack. The variable ratio steering gear is designed so that the steering in the middle is more direct (smaller steering wheel angle).

Power assisted steering systems

Power assisted steering systems amplify the steering force of the driver.

The following systems are available:

• Hydraulically assisted, e.g. rack-and-pinion or recirculating ball steering

• Electro-hydraulically assisted, e.g. Servotronic

• Electrically assisted, e.g. Servolectric and superimposed steering (active steering).

Hydraulic rack-and-pinion steering

Design. This consists of the following:
- Mechanical rack-and-pinion steering gear
- Torsion bar with rotary valve
- Hydraulic fluid pump, reservoir and lines.

Operating principle. When the steering wheel is turned, the steering force applied manually is transferred via the torsion bar to the drive pinion. This causes the torsion bar to twist, making the rotary valve turn in relation to the control bushing surrounding it. The hydraulic fluid pressure acts on either the right-hand or the left-hand side of the working plunger and generates the hydraulic assisting force here. It acts in addition to the steering force transferred mechanically from the pinion to the rack.

Electro-hydraulic power steering (Servotronic)

Servotronic® is an electronically controlled hydraulic rack-and-pinion steering system. Steering assistance is dependent on driving speed.

Design. This consists of the following:
- Hydraulic rack-and-pinion steering mechanism
- Electronic control unit (ECU) and electronic speedometer
- Electro-hydraulic converter with torsion bar and rotary valve
- Hydraulic fluid lines, pump and reservoir.

Operating principle. The basic hydraulic operation of Servotronic is similar to the operation of a hydraulic rack-and-pinion steering system. The speed signal output by the electronic speedometer is analysed in the ECU and converted to an electrical signal, which drives the electro-hydraulic converter.

Electronic control unit (ECU) and electronic speedometer. The ECU receives the vehicle speed data from the electronic speedometer. The steering wheel torque and the pressure in the steering system are regulated depending on this speed by activating the electro-hydraulic converter.

Electro-hydraulic converter. At high speeds, the assisting torque is reduced to allow for more direct steering. At low speeds, the goal is to increase the assisting torque to allow for a wider steering angle while applying less steering force.

Steering power assistance. The reaction piston is connected to the torsion bar in the rotary valve. When the steering wheel is turned, the reaction piston rotates with the torsion bar. Fluid flows through the opening of the control notch into the relevant side of the ram chamber. The fluid pressure is controlled by a solenoid valve according to the degree of power assistance desired. In order for the rack to move, the discharge area is opened in the ram chamber on the opposite side. This allows the hydraulic fluid to flow to the fluid reservoir. Different forces act on the right and left sides of the rack piston.

Self-centring. If the steering wheel is returned to the straight-ahead position, differing forces no longer act on the rack piston. Assistance is not provided for setting the wheels straight. The fluid pressure regulated by the solenoid valve acts on the reaction piston to make self-centring easier. This causes the lower piston to torque via a ball and sloped cylinder walls.

Straight-ahead travel. The ball and sloped cylinder walls prevent relative motion between the pressurised reaction and lower pistons.

Fluid pump. This may be a vane-type pump, generating hydraulic pressure up to 125 bar. The delivery rate is 11 to 15 cm^3 per rotation.

New Words

steering	转向	steering knuckle	转向节
steering wheel	转向盘	circular trajectories	圆轨迹
steering gear	转向器	steering trapezoid	转向梯形
tie rod	横拉杆臂，转向梯形臂	rotational movement	转动
steering shaft	转向轴	transmission ratio	传动比
tie rod end	横拉杆	rack-and-pinion steering	齿轮齿条式转向器
swinging beam	摆臂式转向机构	helical teeth	螺旋齿齿轮
Ackermann steering	阿克曼式转向机构	rack	齿条
rigid axle	刚性轴	disc spring	盘式弹簧
trailer	挂车	hydraulically	液压地
longitudinal connection	轴向连接线	servotronic	电子伺服助力
dual-track	双轨迹	torsion bar	扭力杆
kingpin	主销	rotary valve	转阀
rolling motion	滚动	hydraulic fluid pump	液压泵
radius	半径	disc spring	盘式弹簧
curve	弧线		

课文参考译文

转向的基本原理

汽车转向系统的主要部件如下：
① 转向盘。

② 转向器。
③ 横拉杆臂（转向梯形臂）。
④ 转向轴。
⑤ 横拉杆。

1. 转向系统的功能
① 使前轮转向（回转）。
② 允许产生不同的转向角。
③ 增加驾驶人手动转向所产生的转矩。

2. 基本结构
① 摆臂式转向机构。
② 阿克曼式转向机构。

摆臂式转向机构

当转向节上的车轮转向时，它们绕着共同的旋转轴线（转向主销轴线）产生枢轴式转动。采用摆臂式转向机构的汽车，由于转向时不转动区域尺寸的减小，汽车倾斜的趋势增加。摆臂式转向机构用于双车桥挂车。它具有良好的机动性。

阿克曼式转向机构

这种转向机构中，每一车轮都绕着自己的旋转轴线（转向主销轴线）做枢轴式转动。转向主销轴线是通过连接车轮悬架的上部和下部支承点形成的，或通过主销的轴向连接线形成的。阿克曼式转向机构用于所有的双轨迹汽车。当车轮绕着其转向主销轴线转动时，不转动区域的尺寸几乎保持不变。

1. 转弯时车轮的滚动
为了使车轮在转弯时能完全地滚动，每一转向轮必须转动到与转向半径相适应的角度。小的转弯半径比大的转弯半径需要更大的车轮转角。

由于双轨迹汽车转弯内侧的车轮比外侧车轮的转弯半径更小，因此，内侧车轮必须比外侧车轮转至更大的角度。

不同的转向限制是由转向梯形实现的。

2. 阿克曼式转向机构的工作原理
车轮必须被转动至转弯内侧和外侧车轮的转向节投影中心线与后桥的投影中心线相交。因此，前轮和后轮行驶的圆轨迹应有一个共同的中心点。

3. 转向梯形
转向梯形是在前轮处于直线向前的位置时，由横拉杆、两个转向梯形臂和通过两个转向节（前轴）的连线组成的几何图形。

转向梯形允许前轮以不同的角度摆动，转向的内车轮比外车轮摆动的角度更大。

转向器

1. 功能
1）将转向盘的转动转变成齿条移动和/或转向摇臂的摆动。

2）增大手动转向所产生的转矩。

转向器传动比的设计必须保证转向盘上最大的力不超过限值，如M1类汽车，不超过200N。乘用车转向器传动比达到$i=19$，商用车的约可达到$i=36$。

现在，几乎所有的乘用车都使用齿轮齿条式转向器，而商用车一般使用循环球式转向器。

2. 齿轮齿条式转向器（机械式）

（1）基本结构　装在转向器壳中的小齿轮为转向轴上的一个部件，该齿轮以弧齿与齿条啮合。齿条由导向套导向并通过推力元件和盘式弹簧一直被压靠在小齿轮上，以消除间隙。

（2）工作原理　转动转向盘时，小齿轮转动，带动齿条轴向移动，从而通过横拉杆、转向节臂和转向节使车轮做枢轴式摆动。

齿轮齿条式转向器具有直接传动比和扁平设计、结构简单等特点。

1）恒定传动比。整个齿条的齿距相等。

2）可变传动比。对没有液压辅助的机械式齿轮齿条式转向器来说，传动比的设计保证了在较小偏离范围（中间区域）的转向比在较大偏离范围的外部区域能有更直接的效果。

（3）可变传动比的优点　具有可变传动比的机械式齿轮齿条式转向器具有以下优点：

1）高速直线行驶时具有更好的直线控制能力。

2）对大的转向角度，如驶入停车场时，比其他转向器需要的转向力小。

转向系统的类型

转向系统通常分为以下几种类型：

1）液压辅助转向系统，如齿轮齿条式和循环球式动力转向系统。

2）电-液辅助转向系统（伺服效应），如电子伺服助力和主动转向系统。

3）电动辅助转向系统，如电子伺服助力和主动转向系统。

液压齿轮齿条式转向系统

1. 基本结构

液压齿轮齿条式转向系统由以下部件组成：

1）机械式齿轮齿条转向器。

2）具有柱塞的液压工作缸。

3）作为控制阀的转子滑动阀。

4）液压泵、限压阀、储液罐。

齿条由齿轮驱动，齿条产生的驱动力通过两端输出，施加到横拉杆上。齿条的壳体构成了液压工作缸。工作缸被柱塞分成两个工作室。转子滑动阀或转动柱塞阀被用作控制阀。扭力杆的一端由两个销与控制套和主动小齿轮连接，而另一端与转向轴和转子滑动阀刚性连接。

转子滑动阀由转子滑动件和控制套组成。它们在其横向表面上具有控制槽。控制套上的控制槽通向壳体槽然后通向两个栓塞室，输送给叶片泵。最后流入储液罐。

2. 工作原理

当转向轮摆动时，手动施加的转向力通过扭力杆被传递到主动小齿轮。同时，扭力杆在一定比例反作用力的作用下被稍微扭转。这就引起了转子滑动阀相对于围绕着它的控制套转动，从而改变了控制槽相互之间的位置。用以供给压力油的进油口被打开，来自液压泵的压力油通过进油口流入到控制套上较低的径向槽，并经过通道流入相关的柱塞室。

液压力既作用在工作缸柱塞的右边，也作用在它的左侧，并在这里产生液压辅助转向力。它被附加在由小齿轮机械式传递给齿条的转向力上。

如果转向盘不再继续转动，那么，扭力杆和转子滑动阀返回到中间位置。通向柱塞室的出口被关闭，用于回流的出口被打开。压力油从液压泵经过控制阀返回到储液罐。

电-液助力转向系统

这种伺服系统是电子控制的齿轮齿条式转向系统，该系统的液压辅助力受行驶速度的影响。

汽车低速行驶时，齿轮齿条转向的全部液压辅助力都发挥作用。随着行驶速度的增加，液压辅助力减小。

1.基本结构

系统部件包括：

① 电子车速表。

② 液压齿轮齿条转向器。

③ 电-液转换器。

④ ECU。

⑤ 储液罐。

⑥ 液压泵。

2. 工作原理

车速低于20km/h时，ECU控制的电磁阀保持关闭。随着速度的增加，电磁阀逐步打开。

1）低速时右转向。如果转向轴被顺时针转动，则右阀柱塞被扭力杆和装在它上面的扭转杠杆向下推动，使压力油流入到柱塞室，作用在工作缸柱塞上，因而帮助增加转向力。与此同时，液压油通过单向阀流入到油腔。

2）高速时右转向。此时电磁阀完全打开，压力油从柱塞室经过打开的单向阀、节流阀和打开的电磁阀流入到回油管。由于液压油在打开的单向阀中流动和节流阀的节流作用，一个油腔中的压力大于另一个油腔的压力。这个压力推动柱塞中的杠杆向上移动，从而在扭力杆和转向轴上产生一个反作用转矩。这样，使转向助力减小，驾驶人必须施加较大的转向力才能转动车轮，因此，高速时使汽车有更好的直线控制能力。

在电动助力转向系统中，转向助力是由电子控制的电动机产生的。电动机只在需要时被接通。

工作原理

驾驶人施加的转向转矩通过具有转矩传感器的扭力杆进行测量，此外，车速由车速传感器测量。这两种信号被传给ECU。ECU利用储存的程序模型计算需要的转矩及其力的传递方向，并将相关的输出信号传送给电动机，由电动机产生辅助转矩。该转矩通过蜗轮蜗杆副传递，并经转向轴传递到齿轮齿条转向器。

Teil 7　Bremssystem　制动系统
Part 7　Brakesystem　制动系统

【知识目标】
1. 掌握与制动系统结构、分类、运行原理等相关的专业术语、单词和词汇。
2. 掌握制动系统主要结构的德文、英文表达方法。

【能力目标】
1. 能对制动系统总体结构的各大总成进行中、德、英互译。
2. 能进行与制动系统大体构造相关的德语、英语资料的阅读和翻译。
3. 能在制动系统实物上标识出相应结构的德语、英语单词和词汇。

Text 1　Bremse 制动器（德文）

Bremsen dienen bei einem Kraftfahrzeug zum Verzögern, zum Abbremsen bis zum Stillstand und zum Sichern gegen Wegrollen. Beim Bremsen wird Bewegungsenergie in Wärme umgewandelt.

Bremsanlagen

Betriebsbremsanlage (BBA). Sie soll, wenn erforderlich, die Geschwindigkeit des Fahrzeugs verringern, unter Umständen ist zum Stillstand. Das Fahrzeug soll dabei seine Spur beibehalten. Die Betriebsbremse wird stufenlos mit dem Fuß betätigt (Fußbremse) und wirkt auf alle Räder.

Hilfsbremsanlage (HBA). Sie soll bei Störungen der Betriebsbremsanlage deren Aufgaben, eventuell mit verminderter Wirkung, erfüllen. Es muss keine unabhängige dritte Bremse sein, sondern es genügt der intakte Kreis einer zweikreisigen Betriebsbremsanlage oder eine abstufbare Feststellbremsanlage.

Feststellbremsanlage (FBA). Sie soll ein haltendes oder abgestelltes Fahrzeug gegen Wegrollen, auch bei geneigter Fahrbahn, sichern. Ihre Bauteile müssen aus Sicherheitsgründen eine mechanische Verbindung (Gestänge, Seilzug) haben. Sie wird meist durch einen Handhebel (Handbremse) oder ein Fußpedal abstufbar betätigt. Sie wirkt auf die Räder nur einer Achse.

Dauerbremsanlage (DBA). Sie soll bei Talfahrt die Geschwindigkeit des Fahrzeugs auf einem vorgeschriebenen Wert halten (Dritte Bremse).

Antiblockiersystem (ABS). Es besteht aus den Bauteilen einer Betriebsbremsanlage, die während des Bremsens selbsttätig den Schlupf der Räder überwacht. Mit Hilfe ihrer Signale werden die Bremskräfte an den Rädern geregelt.

Aufbau einer Bremsanlage

Eine Bremsanlage besteht aus

– Energieversorgungseinrichtung

– Betätigungseinrichtung

– Übertragungseinrichtung

– eventuell Zusatzeinrichtung für Anhängefahrzeuge, z.B. Anhängersteuerein-Richtung

– Feststellbremse

– Betriebsbremse

– eventuell Bremskraftregelung wie z.B. ABS

– Radbremse an Vorderachse und Hinterachse.

Duo-Servo-Bremse. Bei ihr wird die Selbstverstärkung der auflaufenden Bremsbacke zur Anpressung der zweiten auch auflaufenden Bremsbacke ausgenützt. Das Stützlager ist schwimmend. Die Abstützung erfolgt am doppelt wirkenden Radzylinder. Die Bremswirkung ist bei Vorwärts- und Rückwärtsfahrt gleich. Sie dient häufig als Feststellbremse in Topfscheiben. Anstelle des Radzylinders tritt dann ein seilzugbetätigtes Spreizschloss.

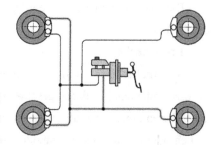

Bild: Duo-Servo-Bremse

Spannvorrichtungen

Sie sollen beim Bremsen die Bremsbacken spannen bzw. spreizen und an die Bremstrommel anpressen. Man verwendet bei hydraulischen Bremsen meist Radzylinder. Bei mechanisch betätigten Feststellbremsen Spannhebel oder Spreizschloss.

Radzylinder. Man unterscheidet doppelt wirkende Radzylinder mit zwei Kolben und einfach wirkende Radzylinder mit nur einem Kolben. Im Radzylinder wirkt der im Hauptzylinder erzeugte Druck auf die Kolben und erzeugt die Spannkraft. Ihre Kolben sind durch Gummimanschetten (Nutringmanschetten, selten Topfmanschetten) abgedichtet. Staubkappen verhindern das Eindringen von Schmutz. Auf der Rückseite des Radzylinders befinden sich Gewindebohrungen für seine Befestigung am Bremsträger und für den Anschluss der Bremsleitung. An der höchsten Anschluss der Bremsleitung. An der höchsten Stelle ist ein Entlüftungsventil eingeschraubt.

Spannvorrichtungen für die Feststellbremse. Sie werden meist an den Trommelbremsen der Hinterachse zusätzlich eingebaut. Durch Seilzug und Spannhebel können die Bremsbacken zur Betätigung der Feststellbremse unabhängig von der hydraulischen Bremse gespreizt werden.

Bremstrommel

Eigenschaften

– Große Verschleißfestigkeit.

– Formsteifigkeit.

– gute Wärmeleitung.

Werkstoff

– Meist Gusseisen.

– Temperguss.

– Gusseisen mit Kugelgraphit.

– Stahlguss.

– Verbundguss von Leichtmetall mit Gusseisen.

Die Bremstrommel muss zentrisch und schlagfrei laufen. Die Bremsfläche ist feingedreht oder geschliffen.

Bremsbacken

Sie erhalten ihre Steifigkeit durch ein T-Profil und werden aus einer Leichtmetalllegierung gegossen oder aus Stahlblech geschweißt. An einem Ende haben sie eine Anlagefläche für den meist geschlitzten Druckbolzen des Radzylinders. Das andere Ende ist in einem Bolzen gelagert oder es liegt gleitend am festen Stützlager an. Die Backen können sich so in der Trommel zentrieren. Sie liegen besser an und die Belagabnutzung wird gleichmäßiger.

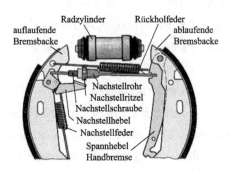

Bild:Bremsscheibe

Scheibenbremse

Es werden vornehmlich Teilscheibenbremsen verwendet. Sie können mit einem Festsattel oder einem Faustsattel versehen sein. Im Bremssattel, der nur einen kleinen Teil der Bremsscheibe umspannt, sind Bremskolben untergebracht. Diese drücken beim Bremsen die Beläge gegen die Bremsscheibe.

Eigenschaften

– Keine Selbstverstärkung wegen der ebenen Bremsflächen. Dies erfordert größere Anpresskräfte, daher sind Bremszylinder mit größerem Durchmesser (40 mm bis 50 mm)als bei den Radzylindern der Trommelbremse und Bremskraftverstärker erforderlich.

– kaum Schiefziehen und die Bremskraft lässt sich gut dosieren, da durch die fehlende Selbstverstärkung und die nur geringen Reibungszahl-Änderungen kaum Bremskraftschwankungen auftreten.

– gute Kühlung, wenig Fading, obwohl wegen der kleinen Bremsflächen und der großen Anpresskräfte örtlich höhere Temperaturen auftreten können.

– starker Belagverschleiß durch die hohen Anpresskräfte.

– Wartung und Belagwechsel einfach.

– selbsttätige Nachstellung des Lüftspiels.

– Bremswirkung unabhängig von der Fahrtrichtung.

– gute Selbstreinigung durch die Fliehkraft.

– Neigung zur Dampfblasenbildung, weil die Bremskolben dicht am Bremsbelag anliegen.

– Feststellbremse relativ aufwendig anzuordnen. Es werden häufig Trommelbremsen an der Hinterachse verwendet oder in der Topfscheibe sitzt eine Trommelbremse als Feststellbremse.

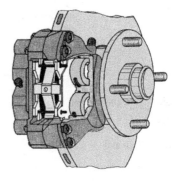

Bild:Anti-Blockier-System

Anti-Blockier-System

Anti-Blockier-System (ABS), auch Automatische-Blockier-Verhinderer (ABV) genannt, werden in hydraulischen Bremsanlagen und Druckluftbremsanlagen zur Bremskraftregelung verwendet.

Aufgabe

Beim Bremsen den Bremsdruck eines Rades entsprechend seiner Haftfähigkeit auf der Fahrbahn so regeln, dass ein Blockieren des Rades verhindert wird.

Nur rollende Räder sind lenkbar und können Seitenführungskräfte übertragen.

Vorteile

– Seitenführungskräfte und Fahrstabilität bleiben erhalten, wodurch die Schleudergefahr verringert wird.

– Fahrzeug bleibt lenkbar, dadurch kann man Hindernissen ausweichen.

– Erreichen eines optimalen Bremsweges auf normalen Straßen (kein Sand und Schnee).

– „Bremsplatten" an den Reifen werden verhindert, da kein Rad blockiert. Die Reifen werden geschont.

Aufbau

Ein ABS besteht aus folgenden Komponenten:

– Radsensoren (Drehzahlfühler) mit Impulsringen.

– Elektronisches Steuergerät.

– Magnetventile.

Die Magnetventile werden vom elektronischen Steuergerät in drei Regelphasen Druckaufbau, Druckhalten und Druckabbau geschaltet. Sie verhindern ein Blockieren der Räder.

WIEDERHOLUNGSFRAGEN

1. Wozu dienen Bremsen?

2. Welche Arten von Bremsanlagen unterscheidet man nach der Verwendung?

3. Erklären Sie den Aufbau einer Bremsanlage.

4. Welche Bremsanlagen sind in den Fahrzeugklassen M und N vorgeschrieben?

5.Wie unterscheidet man die Bremsanlagen nach der Betätigung ?

Neue Wörter

die	Trommelbremse	鼓式制动器		das	Kugelgraphit	球状石墨
fest		紧紧地		die	Leichtmetalllegierung	轻质合金
die	Radnabe	车轮毂		die	Scheibenbremse	盘式制动器
die	Radzylinder	制动轮缸		der	Festsattel	固定钳
der	Handhebel	拉杆		der	Faustsattel	浮钳式制动器
die	Selbstverstärkung	自增力		die	Anpresskraft	压紧力
die	Duo servo bremse	双伺服制动器		der	Durchmesser	直径
die	führende Bremsbacke	领蹄		der	Bremskolben	制动活塞
die	auflaufende Bremsbacke	从蹄		der	Hauptzylinder	制动主缸
der	Stützpunkt	支点		die	Primärmanschette	主密封皮碗
die	Staubkappe	防尘罩		das	Zentralventil	中心阀
die	Wärmeleitung	热传导性		der	Tandem- Hauptzylinder	串联式主缸
das	Kugelgraphit	灰铸铁		der	Ausfall	故障
das	Temperguss	可锻铸铁		der	Bremskreis	制动回路

Text 2   Drum brake 鼓式制动系统（英文）

Drum brakes today are predominantly used as brakes for rear wheels of passenger cars or in commercial vehicles.

Structure and operating principle

The brake drum fits snugly on the wheel hub. The brake shoes and the components which generate the application force are found on the brake anchor plate. The brake anchor plate is fixed to the wheel suspension. When braking occurs, the brake shoes and their pads are pressed against the brake drum by the clamping fixture, thus generating the friction required. The application force can be created hydraulically by the wheel brake cylinder (service brake) or mechanically by the control cable and the tension lever, expander lever or brake shoe expander (parking brake).

Features:

- Self-reinforcement.
- Dirt-proof design.
- Parking brake easier to use.
- Long idle time to brake pads.

- Pad replacement and maintenance is costly and time-consuming.
- Poor heat dissipation.
- Tendency towards fading.

Designs

According to the actuation methods and brake shoe supports, a distinction can be made between the following:

- Simplex brakes.
- Duo-servo brakes.

Simplex brake. This brake has one overrun and one trailing brake shoe. To tension the brake shoes, a double-acting wheel brake cylinder, brake shoe expander, S cam, expanding wedge or expander lever can be used. Each brake shoe has a fixed pivot or fulcrum point, such as a support bearing.

Simplex brakes have the same effect when driving forwards as they do when reversing but have only reduced self-reinforcement. The pad wear on the overrun brake shoe is greater. A parking brake is easy to use.

Duo-servo brake. The self-reinforcement of the overrun brake shoe is used to press down the second overrun brake shoe. The support bearing is floating. The support is provided by the double-acting wheel brake cylinder. The braking action is the same when driving forwards or reversing. It is often used as a parking brake in cup washers. A control-cable-actuated brake shoe expander is then used in place of a wheel brake cylinder.

Self-reinforcement. The friction creates torque which pulls the overrun brake shoe into the drum and strengthens the braking effect. This reinforcement is expressed by the brake coefficient. The pressing force on the trailing brake shoe is then reduced.

Fading. This is an abatement of the braking effect caused by overheating, e.g. during long braking. The friction coefficient in the pad decreases at high temperatures or high sliding speeds. The brake drum can also become deformed to a conical shape, because the heat supply to the wheel hub is more efficiently carried off. The brake area then becomes smaller.

Clamping fixtures

These are intended to tension or expand the brake shoes and press them onto the brake drum. Wheel brake cylinders are normally used with hydraulic brakes. With mechanically operated parking brakes, a tensioning lever or a brake shoe expander is used.

Wheel brake cylinder

In the double-acting wheel brake cylinder, the pressure generated in the master cylinder acts on the plungers and generates an application force. The plungers are sealed by rubber sleeves. Dust caps prevent dirt from entering. On the back of the wheel brake cylinder are threaded bore holes which fasten it to the brake anchor plate and the brake line connection. A bleeder valve is screwed in at the highest point.

Brake drum

Features:

- High wear resistance.
- Inherent stability.
- Good heat conductivity.

Materials:

- Cast iron with flake graphite.
- Malleable cast iron.
- Cast iron with nodular graphite.
- Cast steel.
- Combined casting of light alloy and cast iron.

The brake drum must run centrally and free from runout. The brake area is finely spun or ground.

Brake shoes

Brake shoes maintain their rigidity due to a T-section and are cast from a light metal alloy or welded from pressed steel. At one end they have a bearing surface for the mostly slotted pressure pins on the wheel brake cylinder. A bolt is fitted at the other end, or the end of the shoe is flush with the fixed support bearing. The shoes can therefore be centred in the drum. They fit better and the pad wear is more even.

Adjusting components

The clearance between the brake pad and the brake drum is increased by the brake pad wear. This also increases the pedal idle travel. The brakes must therefore be adjusted on a regular basis, either by hand or using an automatic adjusting component.

Disc brake

Disc brakes are designed as a fixed calliper or floating calliper brake. The brake plungers are located in the brake calliper. They press the pads against the brake disc when the vehicle is braked.

Features:

- No self-reinforcement due to the even brake areas. This requires greater downforces and therefore brake cylinders whose diameters (40 mm to 50 mm) are larger than the diameters of the wheel brake cylinders in the drum brake and additional brake boosters are required.
- Good metering of the braking force, because the absence of self-reinforcement and the minor changes in friction coefficient ensure that hardly any fluctuations occur in the braking.
- Efficient cooling.
- Low tendency towards fading.
- Higher brake pad wear due to the high downforces.

- Easy maintenance and pad replacement.
- Automatic adjustment of clearance.
- More heat generated by the brake fluid, since the pads fir tightly on the brake plungers; danger of vapour bubbles.
- Improved heat dissipation duo to internal ventilation of the brake discs.
- Low tendency to fade when brake discs are perforated or slotted.
- More effort required to use the parking brake.

Designs

Fixed calliper disc brake. Two- and four-cylinder fixed calliper disc brakes are normally used.

The fixed brake cylinder backplate (fixed calliper) is bolted onto the wheel suspension. This backplate grips the brake disc like pliers. It consists of one two-piece housing. Each housing section contains brake cylinders which are situated opposite each other in pairs. They contain the brake plungers with sealing ring, protective cap and clamping ring. The brake cylinders are linked by channels. The bleeder valve sits on top of the housing.

When the vehicle ist braked, the brake cylinder plungers press against the brake pads. The brake pads are then pushed against the brake disc on both sides.

Plunger reset

A rectangular rubber sealing ring used to seal the plunger is located in a groove in the brake cylinder. The inner diameter of the sealing ring is somewhat smaller than the plunger diameter. It therefore encompasses the plunger with its pretension.

The braking movement of the plunger deforms the sealing ring elastically due to its static friction and the plunger stroke. When the pressure drops in the brake fluid, the sealing ring returns to its starting shape or position. This also removes the plunger from the clearance of about 0.15 mm and releases the brake disc. This is only possible with complete pressure reduction in the wire system and ease of movement of the plunger and pads.

Expander spring. It fits the brake pads onto the plungers and thus prevents the pads from knocking and chattering.

Floating calliper disc brake

This consists of two main components, the bracket and the housing or floating calliper and has the following features:

- Low weight.
- Small size.
- Good heat dissipation.
- Large pad surfaces.
- Takes up less space.
- Reduced, tendency toward vapour-bubble formation, as only one or two of the brake cylinders

are on the bracket side.

- Maintenance-free housing versions, therefore not sensitive to dirt and corrosion.

Bracket. The bracket is fixed to the wheel suspension. The housing is fitted within the bracket. Floating calliper disc brakes with various guides are used, such as:

- guide teeth.
- guide pins.
- guide pins and guide teeth combined.
- guide pins with retractable floating calliper.

Floating calliper disc brake with guide teeth

Bracket. The bracket has two teeth on each side.

Housing. The housing is kept in the bracket by the guide teeth which fit into its semicircular grooves, thus enabling it to slide back and forth.

Guide spring. The guide spring presses the housing onto the bracket teeth to prevent clattering noises from occurring.

Floating calliper disc brake with guide pins

This brake has two guide pins bolted onto the housing on the cylinder side of the bracket. The bracket has two bore holes which contain sliding inserts made of Teflon, for example. The housing is kept in these bore holes by the guide pins and can slide back and forth.

Braking. The plunger in the housing presses the inner brake pad against the brake disc once the clearance has been overcome. The reaction force pushes the housing in the opposite direction. The plunger in the housing now also presses the outer brake pad against the brake disc once the additional clearance has been overcome. Both brake pads are pushed against the brake disc with the same amount of force.

The guide teeth support the inner pad directly, the outer pad is supported against the housing by peripheral force.

If guide pins are used, both brake pads are supported on the housing. When the brake is released, the return forces of the sealing ring restore the clearance with the support of the expander spring.

Brake disc

The brake disc is normally disc-shaped and is made of cast iron, malleable cast iron or cast steel. In race cars, this disc can also be made of composite materials reinforced with carbon fibres or ceramic carbon.

Internally ventilated brake discs. These discs are used when the brakes are subject to very high loads. They contain radially mounted air ducts which are designed such that a fan effect is produce during revolutions. This produces a more efficient cooling effect. Sometimes, the brake are even contains bore holes and possibly also oval-shaped grooves. This ensures that water is drained away more rapidly if the brake is applied when the discs are wet. The brakes respond evenly and the risk of fading is low. At the same time, the bore holes also bring about a reduction in weight.

REVIEW QUESTIONS

1. What are brakes for?
2. Which types of brake systems can be distinguished according to their method of use?
3. Explain the structure of a hydraulic brake system.
4. Which brake systems are specified in vehicle classes M and N?
5. How can brake systems be distinguished according to their mode of operation?

New Words

drum brake	鼓式制动器	bleeder valve	放气阀
snugly	紧紧地	heat conductivity	热传导性
wheel hub	车轮毂	cast iron with flake graphite	灰铸铁
brake anchor	制动底板	malleable cast iron	可锻铸铁
brake cylinder	制动轮缸	nodular graphite	球状石墨
tension lever	拉杆	light alloy	轻质合金
expander lever	凸轮推杆	adjusting component	调整部件
self-reinforcement	自行增强制动力	disc brake	盘式制动器
dirt-proof	防尘保护	fixed calliper	固定钳
idle time	闲置时间	floating calliper brake	浮钳式制动器
heat dissipation	散热	downforce	压紧力
duo-servo brake	双伺服制动器	diameter	直径
overrun	领蹄	fluctuation	波动
trailing brake shoe	从蹄	plunger	活塞
fixed pivot	固定枢轴	rectangular rubber sealing ring	矩形橡胶密封圈
fulcrum point	支点	expander spring	张开弹簧
fading	制动衰减	floating calliper disc brake	浮钳盘式制动器
abatement	效果降低	bracket	支架
sliding speed	打滑速度	guide pins	导向销
conical shape	锥形	internally ventilated brake discs	内通风式制动盘
clamping fixture	促动装置		

课文参考译文

制动器

鼓式制动器

鼓式制动器主要用于乘用车或商用车的后轮制动。

1. 基本结构和工作原理

制动鼓紧紧地装在车轮毂上。制动蹄和产生制动促动力的部件装在制动底板上。制动底板被固定在车轮悬架上。汽车制动时，制动蹄和制动摩擦片由张紧装置压紧在制动鼓上，从而产生制动所需要的摩擦力。制动促动力可以通过液压传动的方式由制动轮缸（从动缸）传递，也可以通过控制拉索和拉杆、凸轮推杆，或制动蹄张开装置（驻车制动器）机械式传递。

2. 主要特点

① 自行增强制动力。

② 具有防尘保护。

③ 容易使用驻车制动。

④ 较长的制动摩擦片闲置时间。

⑤ 摩擦片更换和维护费用高，工时长。

⑥ 散热不良。

⑦ 有衰减倾向。

3. 结构类型

根据促动方法和制动蹄支承方式，鼓式制动器可分为以下两种类型：

① 简单式制动器。

② 双伺服制动器。

（1）简单非平衡式制动器。这种制动器具有一个领蹄和一个从蹄。为使制动蹄张开，采用了一个双作用制动轮缸、制动蹄张开装置、S形凸轮、张开楔形块或凸轮推杆。每一制动蹄都有一个固定枢轴或支点，如支承销。

当汽车向前行驶时，简单式制动器具有与倒车时相同的效果，只不过向前行驶时具有较小的自行增力，这种增力由制动系数C表示。领蹄的制动摩擦片磨损较大。这种制动器的驻车制动器容易使用。

（2）双向自动增力式制动器。这种制动器领蹄的自增力被用来压在第二领蹄上。支承销为浮动式。制动蹄的支承是由双作用制动轮缸提供的。当汽车向前行驶和倒车时具有相同的制动效果。这种制动器通常用作带杯形衬垫的驻车制动器，控制拉索拉动制动蹄张开装置代替了制动轮缸。

自行增力：制动摩擦片与制动鼓之间的摩擦力产生转矩，该转矩拉动领蹄压紧制动鼓，从而增强制动效果。而在从蹄上的压力会被减小。

制动衰减：制动衰减是指因过热（如长时间制动）引起的制动效果降低。在制动器高温时，或较高的打滑速度时，摩擦片的摩擦系数下降。制动鼓也可能会因为传递到轮毂上的热量会很快散发而变成锥形，从而使制动鼓的制动区域变小。

4. 促动装置

促动装置的作用是张开制动蹄并将它们压紧在制动鼓上。液压制动器通常采用制动轮缸来促动制动蹄。在机械操纵的驻车制动器上，采用了拉杆或制动蹄张开装置来促动制动蹄。

5. 制动轮缸

在双作用制动轮缸中，来自主缸的压力作用在两个活塞上，并产生促动力。活塞由橡胶套密封。防尘罩防止灰尘进入。

在制动轮缸的后面有螺纹孔，用来将轮缸固定到制动底板上和制动管的接头上。放气阀通过螺纹旋入在缸体的最高点。

6. 制动鼓

（1）制动鼓的特点

1）较高的耐磨性。

2）固有的稳定性。

3）良好的热传导性。

（2）制动鼓的材料

1）灰铸铁。

2）可锻铸铁。

3）球墨铸铁。

4）铸钢。

5）轻质合金和铸铁的混合铸件。

制动鼓必须以其中心转动并且无圆跳动。制动鼓的摩擦面应进行精加工或磨削。

7. 制动蹄

制动蹄采用T形截面而保持其刚性，它由轻金属合金铸造，或由冲压钢焊接而成。在其一端，制有支承面以便与制动轮缸上的带槽的顶杆相接触。制动蹄的另一端装有一螺栓销支承，或制动蹄端头与固定支承销齐平，因而制动蹄能够与制动鼓同轴。制动蹄安装得越好，摩擦片磨损得越均匀。

8. 调整部件

制动摩擦片和制动鼓之间的间隙会因摩擦片的磨损而增加。该间隙的增加也会使制动踏板的自由行程增大。因此，制动蹄必须定期进行调整。调整的方法或者为手工调整，或由自动调整部件自行调整。

盘式制动器

盘式制动器被设计成固定钳或浮钳式制动器。制动轮缸活塞装在制动钳上。汽车制动时，活塞将摩擦块压向制动盘。

（1）主要特点

1）因这种制动器具有均匀的制动摩擦面积，因此，无自增力功能。盘式制动器需要更大的压紧力，因而需要的制动轮缸直径（40~50mm）大于鼓式制动器的轮缸直径，而且需要采用额外的制动助力器。

2）制动力易于测量，因为没有自行增力，而且摩擦系数变化较小，保证了制动过程中制动力几乎没有任何波动。

3）有效的冷却性能。

4）较低的制动力衰减。

5）因为压紧力较大，所以制动摩擦块磨损大。

6）易于维护和更换摩擦块。

7）制动盘与摩擦块之间的间隙自动调整。

8）制动液产生的热量较多，因为摩擦块在制动活塞上装得较紧。有产生气泡的危险。

9）驻车制动需要的力较大。

（2）基本结构

1）固定钳盘式制动器汽车通常采用2缸和4缸固定钳盘式制动器。

固定式制动轮缸底板（固定钳）用螺栓固定在车轮悬架上。该底板（固定钳）在制动时就像钳子一样夹紧制动盘。底板由一个两件式壳体组成，每一壳体部件都具有制动轮缸，它们相互对置地安装在制动钳上。制动轮缸中装有制动活塞，活塞上具有密封环、保护罩和锁环。各制动轮缸之间通过油道连通。放气阀位于缸体的顶部。

当汽车制动时，制动轮缸活塞压向摩擦块，因此，使摩擦块从制动盘两侧将其夹紧。

2）活塞的复位。用来密封活塞的矩形橡胶密封圈装在制动轮缸的一个槽中。密封圈的内径比活塞直径小一些，因而它以一定的预紧力套装在活塞上。

汽车制动时，活塞的制动运动使密封圈因其静摩擦和活塞行程而弹性变形。当制动液的压力下降时，密封圈恢复到其开始的形状和位置。这也使活塞撤离出约0.15mm的间隙，并松开了制动盘。这只有在管路系统中压力完全减小并且活塞和摩擦块自由移动时才是可能的。

3）张开弹簧。该弹簧使制动摩擦块靠紧在活塞上，从而防止摩擦块敲击和颤动。

（3）浮钳盘式制动器

浮钳盘式制动器由两个主要部件组成，即制动盘支架和壳体或浮动钳。这种制动器有以下特点：

1）重量轻。

2）尺寸小。

3）散热好。

4）摩擦块面积大。

5）占用空间小。

6）产生气泡的倾向小，因为只有一个或两个制动轮缸被装在支架侧面。

7）壳体免维护，因而不易受灰尘和腐蚀的影响。

制动钳支架固定在车轮悬架上，壳体被装在支架里，浮钳盘式制动器采用了各种导向部件，如：

1）导向齿。

2）导向销。

3）导向销与导向齿的结合。

4）具有可伸缩浮动钳的导向销。

（4）具有导向设计的浮钳盘式制动钳。

1）支架。支架的每一侧面都有两个齿。

2）壳体。壳体由导向齿保持在支架中，导向齿被装在壳体的半圆槽中，因而使壳体能前后滑动。

3）导向弹簧。导向弹簧将壳体压在支架齿上，以防发出"咔嗒"声。

4）具有导向销的浮钳盘式制动器。这种制动器具有两个导向销，导向销用螺栓固定在支架的制动缸侧的壳体上。支架有两个孔，孔中装有由Teflon（特氟龙，即聚四氟乙烯）制成的滑块。壳体由导向销保持在这些孔中，并且能前后滑动。

汽车制动时，壳体中的活塞在消除间隙后，将内制动摩擦块压紧在制动盘上，反作用力以相反的方向推动壳体。此时，壳体中的活塞在消除额外间隙后也将外摩擦块压紧在制盘上。两个制动摩擦块以相同大小的力压靠在制动盘上。

导向齿直接支承内制动摩擦块，外摩擦块被切向力顶靠在壳体上。

如果使用导向销，两个制动摩擦块都被顶靠在壳体上。当解除制动时，在张开弹簧的帮助下，密封圈的反弹力使摩擦块与制动盘之间的间隙恢复。

1）制动盘。制动盘为圆盘形，并且由铸铁、可锻铸铁或铸钢制成。在赛车上，制动盘也可能由加入碳纤维或陶瓷材料的复合材料制成。

2）内通风式制动盘。当制动器经常受到非常大的制动力时，则需使用内通风式制动盘。这种制动盘装有径向空气通道，它们能在转动时产生风扇的作用。有的情况下，制动摩擦面上甚至也有一些孔，并且也可能有椭圆形槽。这就保证了在制动盘湿的情况下进行制动时，能使水更迅速地排出。制动器能均匀地制动，而且衰减的危险较低。同时，制动盘上的孔也使其质量减小。

Teil 8　Fahrwerk　底盘系统
Part 8　Chassis　底盘系统

【知识目标】
1. 掌握与底盘系统结构、分类、运行原理等相关的专业术语、单词和词汇。
2. 掌握底盘系统主要结构的德文和英文表达方法。

【能力目标】
1. 能对底盘系统总体结构的各大总成进行中、德、英互译。
2. 能进行与底盘系统大体构造相关的德语、英语资料的阅读和翻译。
3. 能在底盘系统实物上标识出相应结构的德语、英语单词和词汇。

Text1　Fahrwerk, Fahrgestell und Radaufhängung 底盘、车架与悬架（德文）

Das Fahrgestell setzt sich aus dem Fahrwerk und dem darauf montierten Triebwerk zusammen.

Fahrwerk

Zum Fahrwerk gehören: das Hauptrüst des Fahrzeugs(Rahmen). Die bereiften Räder, die Radaufhängung (Achsen), die Federung, die Bremsanlage und die Lenkung.

Der verwindungssteife, vielfach aus zwei durch Quer und Diagonalstreben verschweißten oder vernieteten Längsträgern bestehende Rahmen bildet das tragende Gerüst für den Aufbau. Bei manchen Personenkraftwagen und Omnibussen ist der eigentliche Rahmen, jedoch nur noch teilweise oder überhaupt nicht mehr vorhanden. Hier ist die Karosserie selbsttragend ausgeführt, oder Triebwerksteile sind mit als tragende Elemente verwendet (vielfach im Schlepperbau).

Die Räder der Kraftfahrzeuge (Radnabe, Radkörper oder Speichen und Felge) werden bei den Einspurfahrzeugen (Mofa, Moped, Motorroller, Motorrad) ausschließlich als Speichenräder, bei Kraftwagen vorwiegend als Scheibenräder ausgeführt. Obwohl die Speichenräder gegenüber den Scheibenrädern den Vorteil geringeren Gewichts (kleinere ungefederte Masse) und besserer Abführung der im Reifen durch Walkarbeit entstehenden Wärme haben, werden sie im Kraftwagenbau wegen der höheren Herstellungskosten fast nur bei Sport und bei Rennwagen verwendet.

Auf der Felge des Rades sitzt die aus dem eigentlichen Reifen, dem Luftschlauch und dem Wulst oder Felgenband bestehende oder auch schlauchlos ausgeführte Bereifung. Sie stellt das elastische Bindeglied zwischen Fahrzeug und Fahrbahn dar und muss neben guten Federungseigenschaften (weicher, großvolumiger Reifen), hoher Abriebfestigkeit und geräuscharmcm Lauf ein griffiges, rutschfestes und selbstreinigendes Profil der Lauffläche aufweisen. Diese Reifenprofile werden in den verschiedensten Ausführungsformen hergestellt und sind teilweise besonderen Erfordernissen speziell angepasst; es gibt grobstollige Geländereifen, grobprofilierte M+S Reifen (Matsch und Schnee Reifen)mit weitgehender Feinprofilierung der Stollen, sogenannte Sportreifen für hohe Fahrgeschwindigkeiten u.a.. Um die Reifentemperatur niedrig zu halten, haben Rennreifen dünnwandige Reifenwände und außerdem eine besonders dünne Lauffläche (Protektor); dadurch bleiben die Fliehkräfte niedrig und das Ablösen der Lauffläche kann auch bei hohen Fahrgeschwindigkeiten verhindert werden.

Verwendet werden allgemein großvolumige Reifen, deren Luftfüllung das Fahrzeug trägt und kleine Fahrbahnstöße schluckt. Der Luftdruck im Schlauch oder im schlauchlosen Reifen beträgt je nach Radlast bei

Krafträdern	etwa 1,0 bis 2,0 atü
PKW mit Ballonreifen	etwa 1,25 bis 2,5 atü
PKW mit Superballonreifen	etwa 1,1 bis 1,8 atü
LKW mit Rieseluftreifen	etwa 4,0 bis 6,0 atü

Hierbei steigt mit wachsendem Luftdruck, die Tragfähigkeit, während die Federungseigenschaften naturgemäß abnehmen. Ein zu niedriger Reifenluftdruck führt durch Walken zu starker Erwärmung des Reifens und zu größerem Verschleiß.

Über die Federung stützt sich der Rahmen bzw. der Aufbau gegen die Radachsen ab. Dadurch wird die Beanspruchung der gefederten Teile durch Fahrbahnstoße verringert und so die Fahrbequemlichkeit der Insassen erhöht.

Die durch geeignete Federung erzielte bessere Bodenhaftung der Räder ergibt außerdem günstigere Fahreigenschaften. Die wichtigsten Federungselemente sind Blatt Schrauben und Drehstabfedern (Torsionsstäbe), jedoch dienen auch Gummi und Luft als federndes Glied.

Alle die Bauteile, die Kräfte zwischen Rad und Aufbau übertragen oder der Radführung dienen zählen zur Radaufhängung, so die Federungselemente, die Quer-und Längslenker und die verschiedenen Arten von Achsen. Die früher allgemein übliche Starrachse durch federndes Rad das andere gleichen Achse beeinflusste, ist im PKW- Bau und vielfach im Omnibusbau der unabhängigen Radaufhängung (Einzelradaufhängung) gewichen. Es sind zu unterscheiden: Pendelachse, Schwingachse mit Radführung durch Quer-oder Längslenker, Radführung in Hülsen (Teleskopführung).

Zur Dämpfung der durch Fahrbahnstöße angeregten Schwingbewegungen des Wagenkörpers sind zwischen diesem und der Radführung mechanische (selten) oder hydraulische Stoßdämpfer eingebaut. Einer Neigung des Aufbaus bei Kurvenfahrt wird durch Versteifung der kurvenäußeren Federung mit Stabilisatoren entgegengewirkt. Die Bremsvorrichtung soll als Feststellbremse das abgestellte wegrollende abgestellten Fahrzeugs verhindern, als Beharrungsbremse eine unerwünschte Geschwindigkeitserhöhung bei Talfahrt ausschließen und als Verzögerungsbremse ein Herabsetzen der Fahrgeschwindigkeit ermöglichen. Allgemein gebräuchlich sind mechanisch, oder pneumatisch betätigte Innenbacken-, seltener (bei Sportfahrzeugen) Scheibenbremsen an allen Rädern (Allradbremse).

Zur Änderung der Fahrtrichtung wird bei Kraftwagen ausschließlich die Achsschenkellenkung, bei Anhängern auch die Drehschemellenkung verwendet. Gelenkt werden die Vorderräder, und nur bei einigen Sonderkraftwagen, die besonders wendig sein müssen, werden zusätzlich noch die Hinterräder gelenkt (Allradlenkung).

Radaufhängen haben die Aufgabe, eine Verbindung zwischen Fahrzeugaufbau und Rädern herzustellen. Sie müssen hohe statische Kräfte (Zuladung) und dynamische Kräfte (Antriebs-, Brems- und Seitenkräfte) aufnehmen.

Die Radgeometrie soll sich beim Durchfedern der Achsen wenig oder in der gewünschten Weise ändern, um hohe Fahrsicherheit und Komfort bei geringem Reifenverschleiß zu erreichen. Man unterscheidet

- Starrachsen
- Einzelradaufhängung
- Halbstarrachsen

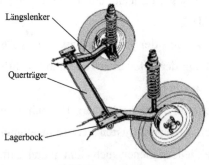

Bild: Starrachse

Starrachse

Beide Räder sind durch eine starre Achse miteinander verbunden und gegen die Karosserie abgefedert.

Bei der Starrachse tritt bei gleichmäßigem Ein- und Ausfedern keine Änderung von Spur und Sturz ein, was den Reifenabrieb vermindert.

Beim Überfahren eines einseitigen Hindernisses wird jeweils die ganze Achse schräggestellt und der Sturz der Räder verändert.

Starrachse mit integriertem Antrieb. Hier sind Achsantrieb mit Ausgleichsgetriebe und Achswellen in einem Gehäuse untergebracht. Dadurch ergibt sich eine verhältnismäßig große ungefederte Masse, wodurch Fahrkomfort und Fahrsicherheit vermindert werden. Bei Nutzfahrzeugen erfolgt die Befestigung am Rahmen oder an der Karosserie am einfachsten durch Blattfedern. Diese übernehmen Radführung und Federung. Bei Verwendung von Schraubenfedern oder Luftfedern werden die Radkräfte durch Schubstreben (Längslenker), die Seitenkräfte durch eine Querstrebe (Panhardstab) übertragen.

Durch Verwendung mehrere Längslenker kann das Eintauchen beim Bremsen und das Absinken des Hecks beim Beschleunigen vermindert werden.

Starrachse mit getrenntem Antrieb (De Dion- Achse). Um die großen ungefederten Massen der angetriebenen Achse zu vermeiden, wird der Achsantrieb von der Achse getrennt und am Aufbau befestigt. Die Kraftübertragung erfolgt über Gelenkwellen mit je 2 homokinetischen Gelenken mit zusätzlichem Längenausgleich. Die Seitenführung der starren Hinterachse kann durch ein Wattgestänge oder einen Panhardstab, die Längsführung durch Schubstreben erfolgen.

Starrachse als Lenkachse. Sie besteht meist aus einem vergüteten Schmiedestück mit T-förmigem Querschnitt. Zur Aufnahme der Achsschenkel ist eine Faust- Faustachse- oder eine Gabel- Gabelachse – angeschmiedet.

Halbstarrachsen

Dabei sind die Räder durch Achsträger starr miteinander verbunden. Durch die Elastizität der Achsträger ist eine gewisse unabhängige Bewegung der Räder zueinander möglich.

Sie werden häufig als Hinterachse bei Fahrzeugen mit Vorderradantrieb verwendet. Die ungefederten Massen sind gering.

Halbstarrachsen verhalten sich bei gleichmäßigem Einfedern wie Einzelradaufhängungen.

Verbundlenkerachse. Die Hinterräder sind an Längslenkern aufgehängt, die mit einem Querträger aus Federstahl verschweißt sind. Der Querträger selbst ist mit Gummi-Metall- Lagern an der Karosserie angeschraubt. Federn beide Räder gleichmäßig ein, so wird der ganze Achskörper in den Lagern gleichmäßig geschwenkt. Federt nur ein Rad ein, so wird der Querträger in sich verdreht und wirkt wie ein Stabilisator. Es treten keine Spur- und Sturzänderungen auf.

Koppellenkerachse. Zwei Längslenker sind mit einem Achsträger aus torsionsweichem U-Stahl zusammengeschweißt. Die Schweißstelle liegt nicht wie bei der Verbundlenkerachse am Ende, sondern etwa in der Mitte der Längslenker. Bei wechselseitigem Einfedern stellt sich deshalb der Achsträger schräg und wirkt hinsichtlich des Sturzverhaltens der Räder wie eine Schräglenkerachse.

Einzelradaufhängung

Bei der Einzelradaufhängung kann die Masse der ungefederten Teile klein gehalten werden. Beim Ein- oder Ausfedern beeinflussen sich die Räder gegenseitig nicht.

Vorderräder werden an Doppelquerlenkern, Längslenkern, Mc Pherson- Achsen aufgehängt, Hinterräder an Längslenkern und Schräglenkern. Für aufwendige Vorder- und Hinterradaufhängung setzen sich Mehrlenkerachsen durch.

Radaufhängung an ungleichlangen Querlenkern. Bei der Aufhängung der Räder an zwei übereinanderliegenden, Querlenkern (Doppelquerlenkerachse) ist der obere Querlenker immer kürzer als der untere. Beim Ein- und Ausfedern ergeben sich ein negativer Sturz und eine geringe Spuränderung, wodurch die Kurvenstabilität verbessert wird.

Gleichlange Querlenker (Parallelogrammform). Beim Einfedern ändert sich der Sturz nicht, jedoch tritt eine Spuränderung auf.

Querlenker sind meist als Dreieckslenker ausgeführt, um die Steifheit in der Fahrtrichtung zu erhöhen. Sie sind am Fahrgestell mit zwei Lagern befestigt.

Radaufhängung mit Federbein und Querlenker (McPherson- Achse). Die Mc Pherson - Achse ist aus der Doppelquerlenkerachse entstanden. Der obere Querlenker wurde durch ein Schwingungsdämpferrohr, an dem ein Achsschenkel befestigt ist, ersetzt. Die Kolbenstange des Dämpfers ist am Fahrzeugaufbau in einem elastischen Gummilager befestigt. Zwischen diesem Befestigungspunkt und dem Federteller am Dämpferrohr befindet sich eine Schraubenfeder. Wegen der großen Brems-, Beschleunigungs- und Seitenführungskräfte sind Kolbenstange und Kolbenstangenführung besonders kräftig ausgeführt.

Radaufhängung an Längslenkern. Sie eignet sich besonders bei Fahrzeugen mit Frontantrieb, da der Kofferraumboden zwischen den Hinterrädern tiefer gelegt werden kann. Bei waagrecht liegender Lenkerdrehachse ändern sich Spurweite, Vorspur und Sturz beim Ein -und Ausfedern der Räder nicht.

Um Geräusche und Schwingungen besser von der Karosserie fernhalten zu können, werden Lenker nicht direkt an der Karosserie befestigt, sondern an einem Fahrschemel. Der Fahrschemel besteht aus 2 Aufnahmearmen, die mit einem Querrohr verbunden sind. Er wird über 4 Gummilager mit der Karosserie verschraubt, wobei der vorderen Gummilager als Hydrolager ausgebildet sind. Die beiden Längslenker sind über Kegelrollenlager am Fahrschemel befestigt. Um Spuränderungen durch die bei Kurvenfahrt auftretenden Seitenkräfte zu minimieren, ist der Längslenker mit einem Zuganker versehen. Beide zusammen bilden ein Gelenkviereck.

Radaufhängung an Schräglenkern. Schräglenkerachsen bestehen aus 2 Dreieckslenkern, bei denen die Drehachse der beiden Anlenklager schräg zur Querachse des Fahrzeuges ($\alpha = 10°$bis$20°$) und horizontal oder leicht zur Fahrzeugmitte geneigt (β) verläuft.

Die Spur- und Sturzänderungen beim Ein- und Ausfedern sind von dem Schräglenker abhängig. Vergrößert man die Winkel α und β, so bekommen die Räder beim Einfedern stärkeren negativen Sturz, wodurch sich die Seitenführungskraft bei Kurvenfahrt erhöht.

Bei dieser Radaufhängung ergeben sich beim Ein- und Ausfedern Längenänderungen an den

Antriebswellen, wodurch auf jeder Seite 2 Gelenke mit je einem Längenausgleich nötig werden.

Verläuft die Drehachse unter einem Winkel $α = 45°$ und trifft in der Verlängerung auf das Gelenk der Antriebswelle, so kann die Antriebswelle ebenfalls um die Drehachse schwingen. Dadurch ist nur ein Gelenk ohne Längenausgleich erforderlich.

Mehrlenkerachsen. Alle bisherigen Radaufhängungen lassen aufgrund der Fahrt unerwünschte Lenkbewegungen zu. Lenkbewegungen entstehen, wenn Kräfte auf das Rad einwirken und es aus der Fahrtrichtung um einen Lenkwinkel in Richtung Vorspur oder Nachspur bewegen. Dies kann, z.B. bei Seitenwind, zu erheblichen Kursabweichungen des Fahrzeuges führen.

Da durch die Antriebskraft entstandene Lenkwinkel dargestellt. Während der hintere Stablenker auf Zug beansprucht wird und sich durch die elastische Aufhängung etwas verlängert, wird der vordere Stablenker auf Druck beansprucht, was zu einer geringen Verkürzung führt. Dadurch wird das Rad aus der Fahrtrichtung heraus gedreht (elastischer Lenkfehler).

Zusätzlich zur Abfederung von Straßenunebenheiten müssen Radaufhängungen die Kurvenneigung abstützen, sowie einen guten Geradeauslauf ermöglichen, indem unerwünschte Radbewegungen weitgehend ausgeschaltet werden.

Art und Wirkung von Kräften auf die Räder:

– Antriebskräfte wirken in Radmitte in Fahrzeuglängsrichtung und drehen das Rad in Richtung Vorspur.

– Bremskräfte wirken in der Mitte des Reifen-Latsches in Fahrzeuglängsrichtung und drehen das Rad in Richtung Nachspur.

– Seitenkräfte wirken knapp hinter der Mitte des Reifen-Latsches quer zur Fahrzeuglängsachse. Bei kurvenfahrt wird das kurvenäußere Rad in Richtung Nachspur gelenkt, was die Kurvensicherheit vermindert.

Raumlenkerachse. Sie gleicht elastische Lenkfehler aus. Entwickelt wurde sie aus der Doppelquerlenkerachse mit Stabilisator; die ursprünglich starr verbundenen Lenker sind in 5 einzelne Stablenker aufgelöst worden, die in genau festgelegter Position zueinander im Raum liegen und das Rad führen. Der Schnittpunkt der Lenkermittellinien liegt außerhalb der Rad-Mittelebene, so dass das Rad z.B. bei Einfluss von Antriebskräften gerade so viel nach außen lenkt (M_2), wie durch den elastischen Fehler nach innen gelenkt wird(M_1).

Wankzentrum und Wankachse

Bei Kurvenfahrt neigt sich ein Fahrzeug aufgrund der Fliehkraft nach außen. Die Kurvenneigung ist abhängig von Fahrgeschwindigkeit, Kurvenradius, Fahrzeugmasse, Federung, Schwerpunktlage und Wankzentrum.

Wankzentrum (Momentanzentrum). Es ist der Punkt, um den die durch Federn mit dem Fahrwerk verbundene Karosserie unter dem Einfluss einer Seitenkraft kippt. Momentan bedeutet, dass sich dieser Punkt nur für einen Augenblick in dieser Lage befindet. Bis zum Beginn einer angreifenden Seitenkraft befindet er sich in Fahrzeugmitte. Bei allen parallel geführten Rädern (Längslenker, gleichlange Querlenker) ist das Wankzentrum in der Fahrbahnebene, bei ungleich langen Querlenkern wandert es beim Einfedern etwas. Bei Starrachsen liegt es in Höhe des Anlenkpunktes der Feder an der Achse.

Je höher das Wankzentrum liegt, desto geringer wird de Abstand zum Schwerpunkt des Fahrzeuges, d.h. der Hebelarm an dem die Fliehkraft angreift wird kleiner, die Seitenneigung nimmt ab. Nachteilig wirkt sich aber die größere Spurweitenänderung mit unruhigem Geradeauslauf aus. Die Verbindungslinie durch die Wankzentren von Vorder- und Hinterachse ergibt die Wankachse (Rollachse). Ihr Abstand zum Schwerpunkt bestimmt die Seitenneigung der Karosserie.

WIEDERHOLUNGSFRAGEN

1. Welche Vor- und Nachteile haben Starrachsen?
2. Was versteht man unter Halbstarrachsen?
3. Nennen Sie die wichtigsten Arten von Halbstarrachsen und Einzelradaufhängung?
4. Welchen Vorteil hat die Radaufhängung an Doppelquerlenkern?
5. Was ist ein Fahrschemel?

Neue Wörter

der	Rahmen	车架	die	Anhängerkupplung	挂车连轴器
die	Radaufhängung	悬架	der	Hinderbock	后弹簧座
das	Gerüst	构架	die	Felge	轮缘
der	Schlepperbau	拖拉机制造	die	Halbfeder	半簧
die	Radnabe	轮毂	die	Zusatzfeder	附加弹簧
der	Radkörper	轮体	die	Gelenkwelle	传动轴
das	Fahrwerk	行驶机构	der	Trittbretthalter	脚踏板支架
das	Fahrgestell	车架、底盘	die	Wechselgetriebe	换档变速器
der	Bremsschlauch	制动软管	die	Lichtmaschine	照明
das	Kühlluftgeblase	风扇	die	Vorderfeder	前悬架弹簧
der	Luftfilter	空气滤清器	das	Abdeckbleck	盖板
der	Handbremshebel	制动操纵杆	die	Abschleppkupplung	拖钩
das	Kraftstoffbehälter	油箱	die	Stoßstange	保险杠
der	Schalthebel	操纵杆	die	Speiche	轮幅
das	Lenkrad	转向轮	das	Einspurfahrzeug	单轨车辆
der	Bremsseilzug	制动拉杆	das	Speichenrad	有轮辐的车轮
das	Ausgleichgetriebe	差速器	die	Abführung	放出（空气蒸气），导出
die	Hinterachse	后桥			

Text 2 Chassis 底盘系统（英文）

The chassis of a motor vehicle includes:

- Steering
- Wheel suspension
- Suspension
- Wheels and tyres
- Brakes

These assemblies are responsible for driving dynamics, comfort and safety.

Driving dynamics

Driving dynamics is the effect of forces and motion on the vehicle.

Different forces influence driving dynamics:

- Forces acting along the longitudinal axis: motive force, braking force, friction force.
- Forces acting along the transverse axis: centrifugal force, crosswind force, lateral force.
- Forces acting along the vertical axis: wheel load, forces created by jolts from uneven road surfaces.

Three different types of movement come into play:

Movement around the vertical axis

This rotational motion of the vehicle about its vertical axis (yaw axis) is called yawing. The yaw velocity is measured by yaw sensors on vehicles with ESP.

Movement around the transverse axis

This rotational movement of a vehicle is called pitching.

Movement around the longitudinal axis

The tilting movement around the longitudinal axis is called rolling.

Drivability

Drivability is affected by the following:

- The location of the centre of gravity, driving axis, roll axis, roll centre.
- The type of drive and the mounting location of the drivetrain components.
- The wheel suspension and the wheel positions.
- The suspension and the oscillation damping.
- The wheel control systems, such as ABS, TCS, EBD, BAS, ESP, ABC, AAS, drive select, etc.

Axis of symmetry. This runs in vehicle longitudinal direction through the centre of the front and rear axles.

Geometrical driving axis. This is formed by the position of the rear wheels and is the bisector of the toe in angle of the rear wheels. It affects the directional stability of the vehicle.

Wheel offset angle

Wheel offset occurs when the wheels of one axle are offset against each other towards the front or towards the rear.

The wheel offset angle is the angular deviation of the connecting line of the wheel contact points to a line that runs 90° to the axis of symmetry. The wheel offset angle is positive when the right wheel hub mounting surface is offset toward the front and is negative when it is offset towards the rear.

The wheel offset is the measurement used to determine the angular alignment of an axle.

Roll centre

This is the point (W) on an imaginary perpendicular to the centre of the axle, about which the vehicle body rotates due to the action of lateral forces.

Roll axis

This is formed by connecting the roll centres of front axle (W_F) and rear axle (W_R). It usually slopes down towards the front of the vehicle. The closer the centre of gravity S lies to the roll axis, the less the vehicle leans when cornering.

Wheel slip angle

Wheel slip angle α is the angle between the steering angle and the wheel's or vehicle's direction of travel.

A lateral force (e.g. wind, centrifugal force) acting on a rolling vehicle results in lateral forces acting on all four tyre contact patches. If the steering is not corrected, the vehicle will change its direction of travel.

Attitude angle

The attitude angle is the angle between the vehicle's direction of travel within its centre of gravity and the vehicle's longitudinal axis.

This relates to the whole vehicle.

Self-steering effect

To assess drivability, standard driving manoeuvres are performed (e.g. steady-state turn, ISO slalom test or evasive manoeuvre) and the self-steering effect of a motor vehicle is determined.

Up to the cornering limit speed, the adhesion between tyres and road surface is adequate for establishing the lateral forces required.

If the cornering limit speed is exceeded, lateral slip occurs at the front or rear wheels or at all wheels.

A distinction is drawn between:

• Understeering. Understeering occurs when the steering angle is greater than that required for the turn. The vehicle shifts outward over the front wheels (FA wheel slip angle is greater than the RA wheel slip angle).

• Oversteering. Oversteering occurs when the steering angle is less than that required for the turn. The rear of the vehicle starts skidding (FA wheel slip angle is less than the RA wheel slip angle).

• Neutral drivability. The wheel slip angle of the front and rear wheels is the same. The vehicle drifts evenly on all the wheels.

The aim is for neutral or slightly understeered drivability. In the case of sports vehicles, some oversteering is desirable.

Review questions

1. What are the three types of movement around a vehicle's three spatial axes called?
2. What impact does the wheel slip angle have on drivability?
3. Explain the terms understeer, oversteer and neutral drivability.

New Words

chassis	底盘	axis of symmetry	侧倾中心
friction force	摩擦力	wheel slip angle	车轮打滑角
centrifugal force	离心力	attitude angle	偏位角
crosswind force	风力	understeering	转向不足
lateral force	侧向力	oversteering	转向过度
oscillation damping	减振装置	neutral drivability	中性操纵性能

课文参考译文

汽车底盘系统

汽车底盘包括：
①车轮悬架。
②悬架系统。
③车轮和轮胎。
④转向系统。
⑤制动系统。
它们负责汽车的动态特性和路面安全性。

操纵动态特性
动态特性是指汽车被驱动时，对汽车产生影响的作用力和由此产生的汽车运动。

汽车行驶时，在力的作用下绕着纵向轴线、横向轴线和垂直轴线产生运动。影响汽车的作用力可以分为以下几种：

1）沿纵向轴线作用的力：驱动力、制动力、摩擦力。
2）沿横向轴线作用的力：离心力、风力、侧向力。
3）沿垂直轴线作用的力：车轮负荷、路面颠簸产生的力。
由各种力一起作用产生的运动表现了汽车的操纵性能。
影响操纵性能的因素有：
1）重心、侧倾中心、侧倾轴线、驱动轴线的位置。
2）驱动布置形式和动力装置的支承位置。
3）车轮悬架和车轮位置。
4）悬架系统和减振装置。
5）车轮控制系统，如ABS、TCS、ES。

（1）侧倾中心（瞬时中心）。这是想象的至车桥中心的垂线上的点（W），汽车车身由于侧向力F_s而围绕这一点转动。从前向后看时，汽车车桥的侧倾中心位于汽车的中心。其高度取决于车轮悬架。

（2）侧倾轴线。侧倾轴线是通过连接前桥侧倾中心W_F和后桥侧倾中心W_R形成的。它通常朝汽车前方而向下倾斜，因为前轮悬架上的侧倾中心比后轮悬架上的侧倾中心低。重心S的位置越靠近侧倾轴线，则在转弯时，汽车倾斜得越少。

（3）对称轴线。对称轴线以纵向通过前桥和后桥中心。

（4）几何驱动轴线。该轴线是由后轮位置形成的，它是后轮前束角的平分线。车轮偏距是两个后轮向前相互靠近（+）或向后相互靠近（-）而偏斜的角度。

（5）车轮打滑角。如果汽车运行中偶然遇到侧向干扰因素（如风力、离心力），那么，侧向力F_s作用在所有4个车轮的轮胎接触面上。如果不修正转向的话，在侧向力作用下，车轮行驶的方向会发生改变，它们将以与原始方向成夹角α的方向行驶。

车轮打滑角是车轮平面与车轮实际运动方向之间的夹角。

（6）偏位角。偏位角与整个汽车有关。偏位角是行驶方向（汽车运动方向）与汽车纵向轴线之间的夹角。

（7）自转向效应。为评价操纵性能，采用标准的驾驶操作，如进行稳定状态的转向，并且测定汽车的自转向效应。

在低于转向规定的限速时，轮胎与路面之间的附着力足以建立稳定转向需要的横向力。

如果车速较高时转弯，则前轮或后轮，或所有车轮将会产生打滑现象，使汽车产生自转向效应。这种效应被区分为：

1）转向不足。前轮的车轮打滑角大于后轮的车轮打滑角。汽车试图以大于相应前轮应有的转向半径进行转向，因而整个前轮向外偏离。

2）转向过度。后轮的车轮打滑角大于前轮的车轮打滑角。汽车试图以小于前轮应有的转向半径进行转向，因而汽车后轮开始侧滑。

3）中性操纵性能。前轮和后轮的车轮打滑角相等。汽车的所有车轮都均匀地轻微滑移。

不同驱动布置形式的汽车对转向的影响如下：

1）前轮驱动汽车趋向于转向不足。

2）后轮驱动汽车趋向于转向过度。

3）全轮驱动汽车趋向于中性操纵性能。

最好的目标是实现中性操纵性能或稍微转向不足（运动型汽车除外）。

汽车偏航是指汽车绕着其垂直轴线（偏航轴线）的旋转运动。在具有ESP的汽车上，偏航速度是通过偏航传感器测量的。

侧倾是指汽车绕着其侧倾轴线的旋转运动。

前倾（俯仰）是指汽车绕着其横向轴线的旋转运动。

Teil 9　Karosserie　车身
Part 9　Vehicle body　车身

【知识目标】
1. 掌握与结构、分类、运行原理等相关的专业术语、单词和词汇。
2. 掌握主要结构的德文和英文表达方法。

【能力目标】
1. 能对总体结构的各大总成进行中、德、英互译。
2. 能进行与大体构造相关的德语、英语资料的阅读和翻译。
3. 能在实物上标识出相应结构的德语、英语单词和词汇。

Text1　Karosserie车身（德文）

Unter dem Fahrzeugaufbau versteht man die zum Fahrwerk gehörende Tragkonstruktion, an dem die einzelnen Teilsätze wie Motor, Lenkung, Federung, Achsen usw. befestigt sind.

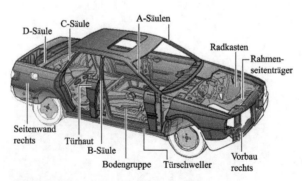

Selbsttragende Karosserie eines personenkraftwagens

Karosseriebauformen. Man unterscheidet z.B. im Pkw- Bereich zwischen
　– Limousine.　　　　　　　– Kombi.

- Kabrio-Limousine.
- Coupé.
- Pullman – Limousine.
- Kabriolett.
- Mehrzweck-PKW.
- Spezial-Pkw, z.B. Wohnmobil.

Karosseriebauweisen. Bezüglich des Fahrzeugaufbaus wird unterschieden in
- getrennte Bauweise.
- mittragende Bauweise.
- selbsttragende Bauweise.

Getrennte Bauweise

Dabei wird der Fahrzeugaufbau einen Rahmen montiert. Die weiteren Fahrwerks ebenfalls am Rahmen befestigt. Diese Bauweise findet aufgrund ihrer Flexibilität heute fast ausschließlich im Nutzkraftfahrzeugbau, bei Geländewagen und im Anhängerbau Anwendung.

Als Rahmenbauform wird überwiegend der Leiterrahmen verwendet. Zwei Längsträger sind dabei mit mehreren Querträgern(Traversen) vernietet, verschraubt oder verschweißt. Die verwendeten Stahlträger mit offenem Profil(U-Profil, L- Profil) oder geschlossenem Profil(Rund-, Rechteckprofil) ergeben einen Rahmen mit großer Biegesteifigkeit, großer Verwindungselastizität und hoher Tragkraft.

Mittragende Bauweise

Meist werden dabei ein Vorder- und ein Hinterrahmen mit einer im mittleren Teil selbsttragenden Karosserie verschraubt.

Selbsttragende Bauweise

Die selbsttragende Bauweise wird bei Personenkraftwagen und bei Omnibussen verwendet.

Bei Personenkraftwagen wird der Rahmen durch eine Bodengruppe ersetzt, die neben den tragenden Teilen wie Motorträger, Längsträger, Querträger auch Kofferraumboden und Radkästen enthält.

Durch weitere mit der Bodengruppe verschweißten Blechteile wie A-, B-, C-, D-Säulen, Dachrahmen, Dach, Kotflügel und eingeklebte Front- und Heckscheiben ergibt sich eine selbsttragende Karosserie in Schalenbauweise. Dabei wird die Karosserie durch Sicken, Absetzungen, geschlossene Profile und Außenflächen stabilisiert.

Neben der Schalenbauweise findet auch die Gerippebauweise Anwendung.

Gerippebauweise. Sie wird häufig auch als Gitterrahmenbauweise bezeichnet. Ein fachwerkartiges Stabsystem bildet dabei die primär tragende Funktion der Karosserie. Die Außenflächen können mittragende Funktion haben. Diese Bauweise wird z.B. bei Pkw-Konstruktionen mit Aluminiumkarosserie verwendet. Verschieden geformte Strangpress – und Aluminiumblechprofile bilden dabei die Rahmenstruktur, die durch Gussknoten an hoch beanspruchten Stellen verbunden werden.

Bei Reparaturen an selbsttragenden Karosserien sind die Herstellervorschriften genau einzuhalten. Durch Verwendung falscher Materialien, falscher Reparaturmethoden, durch Hinzufügen oder Weglassen von Bauteilen wird die Stabilität der Karosserie verändert und damit die Fahrzeugsicherheit bei Unfällen vermindert.

Werkstoffe im Karosseriebau

Als Werkstoffe werden vorwiegend Stahlbleche, verzinkte Stahlblech, Aluminiumbleche, sowie Profile aus diesen Werkstoffen und Kunststoffe verwendet.

Stahlblech

Selbsttragende Fahrzeugkarosserien werden überwiegend aus höherfesten und hochfesten Stahlblechformteilen hergestellt. Höherfeste Karosseriebleche haben eine Streckgrenze bis ca.400 N/mm^2 liegt. Die Blechdicken variieren von 0,5 mm bis zu 2 mm. Blechzuschnitte unterschiedlicher Festigkeit und Dicke (Tailored Blanks) werden entsprechend der Anforderungen zu Platinen (= komplettes Karosserieteil, z.B. Seitenteil) verschweißt.

Rückverformen höherfester Stahlbleche. Sie lassen sich schwerer Rückverformen und haben ein stärkeres Rückfederverhalten. Beim Übergang vom normalfestem Stahlblech zum höherfestem Stahlblech können beim Rückverformen zusätzliche Verankerungen an den normalfesten Stahlblechen erforderlich werden, um eventuelle unterwünschte Verformungen zu vermeiden.

Neue Wörter

die	Limousine	高级轿车	das	Gerippe	筋，骨架，框架
der	Kombi	客货两用车	der	Gitter	散热器格栅，点阵，
das	Kabrio	软篷敞篷轿车			光栅，栅极
die	Pullman-Limousine	四门六窗中排座	das	Aluminium	铝
		可折叠式轿车，普尔曼	das	Strangpressprofil	挤压型材，挤压形状
		加长高级轿车	der	Guß	铸品，铸件；浇铸
	montieren	装配，安装			铸造；生铁，铸铁
die	Flexibilität	柔性，柔韧性，灵活性，		hinzufügen	附加，添加
		可弯曲度，伸缩性		verzinken	给...镀锌
der	Kofferraum	行李舱	die	Streckgrenze	屈服点，弹性极限
der	Kotflügel	汽车挡泥板，翼子板	der	Übergang	过渡
die	Schalenbauweise	车身承载式外壳	die	Verformung	变形
		结构方式		ventuell	也许发生的，可能发生的

Text 2　Vehicle body车身（英文）

Vehicle body/bodywork

The vehicle body serves to protect occupants and contents against environmental influences and in the event of accidents. It also assumes the function of supporting the chassis and drive assemblies as well as carrying the occupants and payload.

Body shapes. The following different shapes may be used for example for passenger vehicles:

- Saloon/ sedan.
- Coupé.
- (Stretch) limousine vehicle.
- Convertible.
- Estate/station wagon.
- Convertible saloon/ sedan.
- Multipurpose passenger.
- Special passenger vehicle, e.g. camper van.

Body constructions. The following different construction may be used:

- Separate construction.
- Partially self-supporting construction.
- Self-supporting construction.

Separate construction

With this construction, the vehicle body is mounted on a frame. The further chassis groups, such axles, steering etc., are also mounted on the frame. Because of its flexibility, this construction is used almost exclusively in the manufacture of commercial vehicles, offroad vehicles and trailers.

The main body shape used here is the ladder-type frame. Here, two side members are riveted, bolted or welded to several cross-members. The steel members used with open sections (U-sections, L-[angle] sections) or closes sections (round or box sections) produce a frame with great flexural strength, great torsional elasticity and high carrying force.

Partially self-supporting construction

A partially self-supporting construction generally uses front and rear frame bolted into the self-supporting body in the centre section. When compared with the self-supporting construction, it is possible to implement different body framing variants more easily.

Self-supporting construction

The self-supporting construction is used in passenger cars and buses/coaches.

In passenger cars the frame is replaced by a floor assembly, which, in addition to the supporting components such as engine bearers, side members and cross-members, also contains the luggage-compartment floor and wheel houses.

Further sheet-metal panels welded to the floor assembly, such as A-, B-, C- and D-pillars, roof frame, roof and wings/fenders, and bonded windscreen and rear window produce a self-supporting, monocoque-construction body. In this case, the body is stabilised by beads, reliefs, closed sections and outer surfaces.

Carcass construction is used as well as monocoque construction.

Carcass construction. This is often also referred to as space frame construction. A latticework-like rod system performs the main supporting function of the body. The outer surfaces can have a co-supporting function. This construction is used, for example, in passenger car designs with aluminium bodies. Here, the frame structure is formed by differently shaped extruded and sheet aluminium sections which are joined at highly stressed points by cast plates.

It is essential to follow the manufacturer's instructions to the letter when making repairs to self-supporting bodies. Using incorrect materials and incorrect repair methods and adding or omitting components alters the stability of the body, reducing vehicle safety in the event of accidents.

Materials in body making

The materials predominantly used are sheet-steel plates, galvanised sheet-steel plates, sheet aluminium plates, sections of these materials, and plastics.

Sheet-steel plate

Self-supporting vehicle bodies are primarily manufactured from high-strength and super-high-strength steel-plate preforms. High-strength body panels have a yield point of approximately 400 N/mm^2, whereas normal body panels have a yield point of 120 N/mm^2 to 180 N/mm^2. Plate's thicknesses vary from 0.5 mm to 2 mm.

Tailored blanks. These are sheet-metal blanks of different strengths and thicknesses. They are welded according to requirements to plates (= complete body component e.g. side section).

Reforming high-strength sheet-steel plates. These are reformed with greater difficulty and have a stronger resilience. In the transition from normal-tensile to high-strength sheet-steel plates, normal-tensile sheet-steel plates require additional braces during reforming in order to avoid unwanted deformations.

High-strength sheet-steel plates must not be straightened hot, since they already lose more than 50% of their strength starting from a temperature of 400 °C.

Reforming normal-tensile sheet-steel plates

These should normally be reformed cold. If, however, there is a risk of cracking, they may be heated up to a maximum temperature of 700 °C.

Super-high-strength sheet-steel plates

These have a yield point of 400N/mm^2 to 1,300 N/mm^2. They should not be reformed either cold or hot. Depending on the manufacturer, they are used for example in the A- and B-pillar areas and help to significantly stiffen the body while keeping the weight low.

In order to avoid the application of heat during a repair, adhesive bonding in connection with rivets is frequently used for joining.

Galvanised sheet steel

Body panels can be galvanised for reasons of corrosion protection. Floor panels are hot-dip-galvanised. Electrogalvanising, due to the surface quality, is used on panels for the body outer skin.

Aluminium

Aluminium is only used as an alloy in body making (alloying constituents are primarily silicon and magnesium). The following manufacturing processes are used on aluminium body components, depending on their shape and stress:

- Pressing, e.g. roof skin, bonnet/hood, wing/fender.
- Extruding, e.g. space frame.
- Pressure diecasting, e.g. spring-strut mount, cast plate.

Whereas pressed parts and extruded sections can be partially repaired by reforming, this is not possible with pressure diecastings.

Properties. Aluminium alloys begin to lose strength significantly when subjects to temperatures starting from approx. 180°C. If they come into contact with other materials, e.g. steel, electrochemical corrosion will occur if an electrolyte is present. The surface of aluminium forms a tight oxide layer with high electrical resistance. Aluminium must therefore not be welded with standard workshop resistance spot welding equipment. Al alloys can be welded to good effect with TIG or MIG inert gas welding processes (inert gas: 100% argon or argon-helium mixture).

Workshop notes

- Due to potential contact corrosion:
  – do not use machining tools for aluminium bodies on other metals,
  – use only special-steel wire brushes,
  – when using different joining techniques, e.g. bolting, riveting, use only the connecting elements approved by the manufacturer.
- In order to eliminate strength losses, do not heat body components to temperatures in excess of 120°C when straightening.
- Welding and straightening tasks may only be carried out by specially trained personnel.
- Because of the risk of cracking due to electrochemical reactions, do not tin sheet-aluminium plates.
- Due to the risks to health and the danger of explosion, draw off or extract Al grinding dust immediately.

Aluminium-steel mixed construction

With this construction, the vehicle front end made of Al alloys, for example, is joined in the area of A-pillars to the steel body. Because of the possibility of electrochemical corrosion between aluminium and steel, insulating adhesive fillings are used between the abutting parts.

Plastic

Plastics are used in body making for the following reasons:

- Low specific weight and thus significant weight savings.

- Corrosion resistance.
- Extensive freedom of shaping.
- Not susceptible to shocks.
- Manufacture of components without reworking.
- When damaged, they can be repaired at low cost with the appropriate knowledge.

Repairing plastic

Plastic parts can be repaired by welding, laminating or gluing with two-component repair materials.

Welding. This process can only be used on thermoplastics, such as PA, PC, PE, PP, ABS, PMMA.

Laminating. Here, holes for example are repaired with hardeners with the aid of glass-fibre mats (GFRP)and resin (polyester resin; epoxy resin). The area of damage must be bevelled in such a way that a connection can be established between each glass-fibre mat layer and the original part. If necessary, a reinforcing layer should be applied to the area of damage prior to lamination.

Gluing with two-component repair materials. Depending on the repair material used, holes, cracks and scratches can be repaired without knowing the type of plastic to be repaired. The base is established for example by a two-component polyurethane glue in a twin cartridge mixed in the correct proportions via a forced mixing tube. The glue is applied to the cleaned and prepared area of damage. The glued area can then be heated with a radiant heater. This makes it harden more quickly. The repaired area can then be further treated by grinding and painting.

New Words

drive assemblies	传动系统总成	reforming high-strength sheot-steel plate	高抗拉强度薄钢板的整形
offroad vehicle	越野汽车		
ladder-type frame	梯形车架	normal-tensile	正常抗拉强度
riveted	用铆钉固定	galvanised sheet steel	镀锌钢板
bolted	螺栓固定	zinc/dust paint	磁粉防锈漆
welded	焊接	overlapping areas	重叠区域
flexural strength	抗弯强度	aluminium	铝
torsional elasticity	扭转弹性	silicon	硅
floor assembly	底板总成	magnesium	镁
pillar	柱	bonnet hood	发动机罩
a latticework-like rod system	格子状的杆系	extruding	挤压
sheet-steel plate	薄钢板	spring-strut mount	悬架弹簧滑柱座
tailored blanks	拼焊板	laminating	叠压

Kapitel 1　Automobiltechnologie // Chapter 1　TECHNOLOGY of Automobile

课文参考译文

汽车车身

汽车车身和车身部件

汽车车身的作用是保护乘员和货物免受环境的影响和意外事故的伤害。它也具有支撑底盘和传动系统总成，以及承载乘员和货物载荷的功能。

1. 车身的形状

乘用车通常采用以下几种不同形状的车身。

1）普通轿车车身。

2）活动顶篷厢式车车身。

3）双门轿车车身。

4）大型豪华轿车车身。

5）专用乘用车，如厢式房车车身。

6）旅行车车身。

7）活动顶篷轿车车身。

8）多用途车车身。

2. 车身结构

乘用车车身结构主要有以下几种不同形式：

1）独立式结构。

2）部分自支承结构。

3）自支承结构（承载式车身）。

独立式结构车身

采用这种结构的汽车车身被安装在车架上。一些底盘系统，如车桥、转向系统等也被安装在车架上。由于其良好的灵活性，因此，几乎所有的商用汽车、越野汽车和拖挂车制造商均采用这种结构。

这种结构的主车身形状是梯形车架。它的两根边梁（纵向梁）用铆钉、螺栓固定或焊接在多根横梁上。钢质边梁和横梁采用开口式截面（U形或L形截面）或封闭式截面（圆形或箱形截面），这些形式的截面会使钢梁具有大的抗弯强度、扭转弹性和高的抗载荷能力。

部分自支承结构车身

在这种车身形式中，自支承部件承担着除车架外总支承功能的一部分。与自支承结构车身相比，部分自支承车身能够更容易地实现不同车架的变换。

自支承结构车身

自支承结构（承载式）车身被用于乘用车和公共汽车或大客车。在乘用车上，车架被一个底板总成代替。该底板除了支承诸如发动机支座、纵梁和横梁外，它还包含行李舱底板和车轮罩。

还有一些金属板件被焊接在底板总成上，如A、B、C、D柱，车顶架、车顶板和翼子板，以及粘结的风窗玻璃和后车窗。这些部件也产生支承作用，它们与底板一起形成承载式车身结构。在这种情况下，车身通过卷边、凹凸、封闭截面和外面板获得稳定。车身骨架也被用作承载式车身结构。

车身骨架

车身骨架通常也被称作空间构架。格子状的杆系承担着车身的主要支承功能。外面板也能产生联合支承作用。这种结构通常被用于乘用车的铝质车身上。其骨架结构是由不同形状的挤压件和铝板件构成的，并在其高应力点处采用铸造件连接。

对自支承车身进行修理时，必须严格遵守制造商的说明和要求。使用不正确的材料和不正确的方法，或添加和减少车身部件都会改变车身的稳定性，从而降低汽车在意外事故中的安全性。

车身材料及其应用

汽车车身使用的材料主要有薄钢板、镀锌薄钢板、薄铝板、合金板和塑料等。

1. 薄钢板

自支承车身主要由超高抗拉强度和高抗拉强度钢板的预成型材料制作。超高抗拉强度车身钢板的屈服点约为400N/mm^{2}以上，而通常的车身钢板的屈服点为120~180N/mm^2。钢板的厚度为0.5~2mm。

2. 拼焊板

拼焊板是由不同强度和厚度的薄金属板经裁剪而成的车身坯板。它们根据需要被焊接成车身板（成为完整的车身部件，如车身侧板等）。

3. 高抗拉强度薄钢板的整形

高抗拉强度薄钢板的整形具有较大的难度，它们具有较高的弹性。在正常抗拉强度薄钢板向高抗拉强度薄钢板过渡的地方，整形过程中应在正常抗拉强度薄钢板上施加额外的支撑，以免产生不希望的变形。

高抗拉强度薄钢板一定不要加热矫正，因为它们会在400℃时失去其50%的强度。

4. 正常抗拉强度薄钢板的整形

正常抗拉强度薄钢板的整形通常应在冷态下进行。然而，如果冷态整形存在开裂的危险，也可以将其加热至700℃左右进行整形。

5. 超高抗拉强度薄钢板的整形

超高抗拉强度薄钢板的屈服点大约为400~950N/mm^2。这种钢板既不能冷态整形，也不能热态整形。根据制造商的说明，它们可以用于A、B柱区域，能在保持较小质量的同时，有助于显著地增加车身的强度。

为了在维修时尽可能保持热的利用，通常使用MIG（熔化极惰性气体保护焊）对这种钢板进行焊接。

6. 镀锌钢板

车身板可以被镀锌以防止腐蚀，底板通常进行热浸镀锌。为获得更好的表面质量，通常对车身外表面板采用电镀锌。

7. 铝板

在车身制造中，铝只以合金的形式使用（铝合金的添加成分主要是硅和镁）。铝车身部件根据其形状和承受的应力，通常采用以下制造程序：

1）冲压，如车顶面板、发动机罩、翼子板。

2）挤压，如空间骨架板。

3）压力铸造，如悬架弹簧滑柱座、铸制板等。

尽管冲压件和挤压件可以通过整形进行部分修复，但对压力铸造件是不可能进行整形修复的。

铝板的特性是当它遭遇到180℃以上的温度时，铝合金的强度开始明显下降。如果铝合金与其他金属（例如钢）接触，且存在电解质时，则会发生电化学腐蚀。铝的表面会形成具有高电阻的致密氧化层。因此，焊接铝合金时一定不要使用标准的车间接触点焊设备。利用TIG（钨极电弧惰性气体保护焊）或MIG（熔化极惰性气体保护焊）可以对铝合金进行有效地焊接。惰性气体为100%的氩气或氩氦混合气。

8. 铝钢混合结构

在A柱区域，利用铝钢混合结构将铝合金制作的汽车前端连接到钢板车身上。由于铝和钢之间存在电化学腐蚀的可能性，因此，在邻接的部件之间应施加绝缘粘合剂填充物。

9. 塑料

塑料被用于车身部件的原因如下：

1）密度较低，因而明显减小了质量。

2）抗腐蚀。

3）成形的自由度大。

4）不易受冲击的影响。

5）部件制造后不需继续加工。

6）损坏后，需要较低的成本和适当的知识即可修复。

在车身部件中，使用塑料的一些区域如下。

10. 塑料部件的维修

塑料部件可以通过焊接、叠压，或采用两种成分的维修材料进行粘结修复。

1）焊接。这种方法只能用于热塑性塑料，如PA、PC、PE、PP、ABS、ABS/PC。

2）叠压。塑料部件的孔通常利用固化剂借助于玻璃纤维垫（GFRP）和树脂（聚酯树脂或环氧树脂）以叠压的方法进行修复。损坏的区域必须被切成斜角，以便每一层玻璃纤维垫与被修部件之间增加接触。如果需要的话，必须在叠压之前为损坏的区域提供加强层。

3）胶粘。根据胶粘时使用的维修材料，孔、裂纹和擦伤不需识别拟修理的塑料种类即可进行维修。胶粘的基本方法通常是采用装在两个管中的两种成分的聚氨酯胶，它们通过压力混合管以正确的比例进行混合。将这种胶涂抹在经清洁和打磨的损坏区域。完成胶粘后，应采用发光热源对胶粘区域进行加热，以使其更迅速地固化。然后，对修复的区域进行打磨和喷涂。

Teil 10　Elektrisches System　电气系统
Part 10　Electric System　电气系统

【知识目标】
1. 掌握与电气系统结构、分类、运行原理等相关的专业术语、单词和词汇。
2. 掌握电气系统主要结构的德文、英文表达方法。

【能力目标】
1. 能对电气系统总体结构进行中、德、英互译。
2. 能进行与电气系统大体构造相关的德语、英语资料的阅读和翻译。
3. 能在电气系统实物上标识出相应结构的德语、英语单词和词汇。

Text 1　Elektrische Anlage汽车电器（德文）

Sie ist zur Versorgung der elektrischen Anlage im Kraftfahrzeug mit elektrischer Energie nötig. Diese wird bei stehendem Motor einer Batterie entnommen. Bei laufendem Motor wird ein Generator angetrieben, der die Verbraucher mit elektrischer Energie versorgt und gleichzeitig die Batterie auflädt.

Spannungserzeuger

Starterbatterien

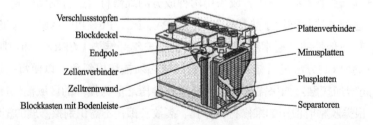

Bild: Starterbatterie

Aufbau. Eine Zelle ist die kleinste Einheit aus den positiven und negativen Plattenblöcken, den Scheidern und den für den Zusammenbau und Anschluss erforderlichen Teilen. Mittels der Zellenverbinder werden bei 6 V-Starterbatterien drei, bei 12 V-Starterbatterien sechs Zellen in Reihenschaltung in einem Blockkasten miteinander verbunden.

Elektrochemische Vorgänge

Geladener Zustand. Die aktive Masse der positiven Platten bestent aus braunem Bleidioxid (PbO_2), die der negativen Platten aus grauem Blei (Pb). Der Elektrolyt ist verdünnte Schwefelsäure (H_2SO_4) mit einer Dichte von $\delta = 1{,}28 g/cm^3$.

Entladevorgang. Das braune Bleidioxid der Plusplatten und das graue Blei (Pb) der Minusplatten wird in weißes Bleisulfat ($PbSO_4$) umgewandelt. Dabei wird Schwerfelsäure (H_2SO_4) umgesetzt. Es entsteht Wasser (H_2O). Die Säuredichte verringert sich.

$$PbO_2 + 2H_2SO_4 + Pb \rightarrow PbSO_4 + 2H_2O + PbSO_4$$

Ladevorgang. Das weiße Bleisulfat ($PbSO_4$) der Plusplatten wird in braunes Bleidioxid (PbO_2), das der Minusplatten in graues Blei (Pb) umgewandelt. Dabei wird Wasser (H_2O) umgesetzt. Es entsteht Schwefelsäute (H_2SO_4). Die Säuredichte vergrößert sich.

$$PbSO_4 + 2 H_2O + PbSO_4 \rightarrow PbO_2 + 2H_2SO_4 + Pb$$

Formieren. Beim Herstellungsprozess werden die aktiven Massen der Plus- und Minusplatten durch einen elektrochemischen Prozess in den geladenen Zustand versetzt. Bei der Inbetriebnahme muss noch Schwefelsäule mit einer Dichte von 1,28 g/cm^3 eingefüllt werden. Nach einer Einwirkzeit von etwa 20 Minuten ist die Starterbatterie betriebsbereit.

Selbstentladung. Sie erfolgt im Inneren der Batterie, ohne dass der äußere Stromkreis geschlossen ist. Wärme, Verunreinigungen des Elektrolyten und Kriechströme beschleunigen den Vorgang. Bei +15 ℃ ist eine vollgeladene Starterbatterie nach etwa 4 Monaten, bei +40 ℃ etwa nach zwei Wochen entladen.

Generatoren

Drehstromgeneratoren

Der Bedarf an elektrischer Energie hat bei modernen Kraftfahrzeugen stark zugenommen. In den 50er Jahren betrug die durchschnittliche Leistung eines Gleichstromgenerators 150 W bis 180 W.

Mit der Ablösung des Gleichstromgenerators durch den Drehstromgenerator waren nur bei kleiner Bauweise und geringem Gewicht Generatoren herstellbar, die einen elektrischen Leistungsbedarf zwischen 400W und 1600 W abdecken konnten.

Mit zunehmendem Einzug der Elektronik in die Kraftfahrzeugtechnik wurden viele Steuerungs- und Regelungsaufgaben nicht mehr mechanisch, sondern durch elektrisch angetriebener Lüfter, elektrisch betätigte Einsprizventile, Katalysatorheizung, Fenster- und Spiegelbeheizung.

Ein weiterer Bedarf an elektrischer Energie wurde durch den Einzug der Komfortelektronik hervorgerufen, z.B. Klimaanlagen mit bis zu 10 Elektromotoren, Sitzheizung und Standheizung.

Eine neue Generation von Drehstromgeneratoren für Personenkraftwagen kann Leistungen von etwa 1600 W abgeben, dies entspricht bei 14 V-Generatoren einem Strom von etwa 120 A. Um die bei diesen Strömen im Generator entstehende Verlustwärme abführen zu können, wurden Generatoren entwickelt, die an den Kühlmittelkreislauf angeschlossen werden.

Die Erzeugung der elektrischen Energie im Kraftfahrzeug erfordert zusätzlichen Kraftstoff. Gibt ein Generator eine Stunde lang eine Leistung von 1600W ab, so verbraucht er zur Erzeugung dieser Energie etwa 0,8 L Ottokraftstoff.

Aufgaben

Während des Betriebes des Kraftfahrzeuges die

– elektrischen Verbraucher mit Energie zu versorgen.

– Starterbatterie zu laden.

Eigenschaften

– Hohe Leistung bei kleiner Bauweise und geringem Gewicht (kleines Leistungsgewicht).

– Leistungsabgabe schon bei Motorleerlauf möglich, dadurch frühzeitiger Ladebeginn der Starterbatterie.

– verschleißarm, dadurch geringer Wartungsaufwand und lange Lebensdauer.

– der Ladestrom wird feststehenden Klemmen entnommen, über Schleifkohlen und Schleifringe fließt nur ein kleiner Erregerstrom.

– bei Verwendung eines entsprechenden Lüfterrades ist er drehrichtungsunabhängig.

– die Plusdioden verhindern den Stromfluss von der Starterbatterie in den Generator.

– Einsatz einfacher und billiger elektronischer Regler möglich.

– Kein Überlastungsschutz für den Generator erforderlich.

Neue Wörter

der	Generator	发电机	die	Starterbatterie	起动机蓄电池
der	Regulator	电压调节器	die	Elektrodeplate	极板
die	Batterie	蓄电池	die	Elektrolyte	电解液
der	Spannungserzeuger	发电机	das	Bleidioxid	二氧化铅
der	Drehstromgenerator	三相交流发电机	das	Bleisulfat	硫酸铅
die	elektronische Zündung	电子控制点火	die	Schwefelsäule	硫酸
die	Einsprizung	燃油喷射	das	Spannung	电压
die	Standheizung	辅助加热	die	Terminalspannung	端电压

Kapitel 1 Automobiltechnologie // Chapter 1 Technology of Automobile

Text 2 Electric System 电气系统（英文）

Power supply

To reliably supply the motor vehicle's electrical systems with electrical power, a system consisting of a voltage generator, voltage regulator and a charge accumulator is used.

With the engine running, the alternator supplies die vehicle electrical system with electrical energy and charges the battery. The alternator generates a three-phase current which is rectified and supplies the electrical consumers.

The vehicle electrical system is supplied with power by the battery when the engine is idling or, where necessary, switched off. The battery also supplies all of the power required for the starting procedure.

The demand for electrical energy has increased greatly in motor vehicles. The alternator currently satisfies a demand for electrical power of up to approximately 2,000 W.

This demand results from increasing electronic regulations as well as safety and comfort and convenience electronics, such as:

- electronic ignition and fuel-injection systems,
- self-monitoring,
- seat and auxiliary heating.
- window and mirror heating.
- electrically driven fans.
- air conditioning systems with up to 10 electric motors.
- ABS and ESP.

The average efficiency of an alternator in a motor vehicle is approximately 60%. If it outputs power of 2,000 W for an hour under these conditions, it consumes approximately 1 litre of fuel to generate this power.

Starter battery

The starter battery supplies and stores the energy for the electrical systems in a motor vehicle. Since it can be recharged, it is also referred to as an accumulator.

Design

Battery cell. The starter battery consists of several cells. A cell consists of the positive and negative lead plates. To avoid contact and short circuiting, they are separated by separators. To enable a high current to flow, the plate surface must be large. Therefore, the cells are equipped with as many thin electrode plates as possible. The cells are grouped into blocks. One cell provides a nominal voltage of 2 volts. Series connection of the cells results in 6 or 12 volts, depending on the number of cells.

Electrolyte. This fills the space between the lead plates and the separator. The electrolyte reservoir is located above the plate groups. Beneath the plates, there is a sludge compartment that collects the lead that breaks away.

Housing. The cells are enclosed in a block box. The battery is closed with the block cover, which contains the drain and filler plugs. To enable the battery to be fixed to the vehicle body, a guide rail is cast on the side at the bottom.

Absolutely maintenance-free starter battery

It is tightly sealed and does not require the acid level to be topped up. A battery tilt angle of 70 degrees is permissible.

These batteries do not have a filler plug and are stored full. The lead lattice plates contain calcium instead of antimony, which significantly reduces self-discharge and water consumption. This means that the electrolyte supply via the plates lasts for the entire service life of the battery and the batteries are suitable for vehicles with long periods out of use. The batteries only have ventilation openings which allow a tilt angle through a safety labyrinth system. The state of charge can no longer be determined via an electrolyte density test. Therefore, many of these batteries have integrated control displays that give information on the charge state of the starter battery; for example:

- green: OK .
- grey: recharge (check) .
- white: charge.

Heavy duty batteries

These are batteries with a high service life, which have an extremely high vibration and cycle resistance.

Separators with a glass fibre mat support the positive plate and reduce erosion. Securing with cast resin or plastic prevents loosening of the plate blocks. These batteries are particularly suitable for construction machines.

Batteries with bonded electrolyte

This type of battery is completely fail-safe and can be fitted in any position. It has an increased cycle resistance and allows complete discharging.

The electrolyte is no longer liquid. It can be bonded into gel or in fibres. The distance between the positive and negative plates is smaller, which reduces the internal resistance. A chemical reaction prevents gassing through an internal oxygen recombination. That is the gases are converted back into water within the cell. Features include:.

- Very low self-discharge.
- Compact construction concept, since there is no electrolyte reservoir.
- Higher short-circuit current.
- A safety valve opens if battery is overcharged.

These batteries are suitable for vehicles with long periods out of use and can also be used as general purpose batteries. A distinction is made between gel and glass-mat battery technology.

Gel batteries. With these, the electrolyte is bonded into a fixed multi-component gel. Adding silica to the sulphuric acid results in a gel-type material in which the electrochemical reaction takes place.

Glass-mat technology. With this design, intermediate layers of glass-fibre fleece surround and bind the acid. The capillary attraction and the wetting cause the electrolyte liquid to be absorbed into the networked microfibres (AGM, Absorbent Glass Mat). At the same time, the layers act as the separator and exert an equal and high contact pressure on the plate surface. The active material is thus bound solidly between the fleece. This prevents the active materials from breaking away and at the same time improves the stability through the support measures. In a special design construction, the lead plates and the glass-fibre fleece are wound up. This leads to a further increase in the packing density.

Battery sensor

This enables a permanently high state of battery charge thanks to regulation of the charging voltage depending on temperature and charge state.

A small control unit integrated in the battery sensor determines the optimum charge voltage reference value from the currently measured battery temperature and the state of charge. To calculate the battery state of charge (SoC), the charging and discharging current, terminal voltage and electrolyte temperature are recorded and saved in every operating status of the vehicle.

The sensor is integrated in the terminal slot of the battery negative line.

REVIEW QUESTIONS

1. What are the processes involved when charging or discharging a starter battery?
2. What is the electrolyte density in a fully charged or fully discharged starter battery?
3. What are the most important specifications of a starter battery?
4. What is the cold test current and how is it defined?
5. Why must the charging voltage always be below the gassing voltage?

New Words

voltage generator	发电机	auxiliary heating	辅助加热
voltage regulator	电压调节器	starter battery	起动型蓄电池
charge accumulator	蓄电池	electrodeplate	极板
alternator	交流发电机	electrolyte	电解液
three-phase current	三相交流电	brown lead dioxide	二氧化铅
electronic Ignition	电子控制点火	grey lead	纯铅
fuel-injection	燃油喷射	white lead sulphate	白色的硫酸铅

steady-state voltage	开路电压	glass-mat	玻璃纤维
terminal voltage	端电压	filler plug	加液孔
ageing process	老化	jump starting with booster cable	跨接起动
contamination	杂质	boost charging	快速充电
cell short circuit	单格电池短路	trickle charging	小电流充电
sulphation	硫化	resistance characteristic	电阻特性
cyclic discharging	循环放电	constant voltage characteristic	恒压特性
maintenance-free starter battery	免维护蓄电池	constant current characteristic	恒流特性
heavy duty	重载	detonating gas	爆炸性气体
gel battery	胶体电解质蓄电池		

课文参考译文

电源与汽车电气系统

为了保证汽车电气系统电源供给可靠，汽车上使用了包括发电机、电压调节器和蓄电池的电源系统。

随着发动机的运转，发电机为汽车电气系统提供电源并对蓄电池充电。交流发电机发出的是三相交流电，经整流后供给用电设备。

当发动机怠速运转或不工作时，汽车电气系统由蓄电池供电。发动机起动过程也是由蓄电池供电。

现代汽车对电能的需求日渐增加，当前常用的发电机能够供给的电能约为2kW。这些需求主要缘于电子调节装置，以及安全和舒适性方面的电子装置的增加。这些电子装置包括：

1）电子控制点火和燃油喷射系统。

2）自监测系统。

3）座椅和辅助加热。

4）车窗和后视镜加热。

5）电动风扇。

6）空调系统，其电动机可达10个。

7）ABS（防抱死制动系统），ESP（电子稳定程序）。

汽车发电机的平均效率约为60%，如果发电机的输出功率为2kW，那么每1h发出这些电能需要消耗约1L汽油。

起动机蓄电池

起动机蓄电池为汽车电气系统提供和储存电能，由于它可以充电，因此也被称为二次电池。

(1) 蓄电池的结构由以下部分组成

1) 单格电池。起动机蓄电池由多个单格电池组成,单格电池由正、负极板组成。为了防止正、负极板接触短路,用隔板将其隔开。为了保证蓄电池能够提供较大电流,蓄电池必须有较大的极板表面积,因此单格电池应有尽可能薄而多的极板。许多单格电池组装成一个蓄电池,一个单格电池提供2V的额定电压,将单格电池串联起来就可以形成6V或12V的蓄电池,这取决于单格电池的数量。

2) 电解液。电解液充入蓄电池极板与隔板之间的空间,电解液的液位应高于极板组,极板的下方有一个空间可以积存从极板上脱落的活性物质。

3) 壳体。单格电池被封装在蓄电池壳体内,蓄电池盖上有加液孔盖将蓄电池密封。为了保证蓄电池可靠地固定在车身上,蓄电池底座边缘有安装导轨。

4) 极柱。极柱用于将蓄电池电压与汽车的电气系统连接。极柱上标有"+"和"−",为了避免混淆,正极柱的直径大于负极柱。

(2) 新型蓄电池

1) 免维护蓄电池(符合欧洲标准)。蓄电池的加液孔可以注入电解液,并且可以添加蒸馏水以调整电解液液位。铅蓄电池极板的铅栅架中含有锑,作用是增加栅架的强度。但锑会导致蓄电池自放电,并在充电时产生气体,因此使水的消耗增加。对于新蓄电池,采用干储存的方式,要使用时加入质量分数为37%的硫酸,静置20min以上就可以使用。

在正常情况下,免维护蓄电池在两年内不需要添加蒸馏水。

2) 完全免维护蓄电池。完全免维护蓄电池没有加液孔,新蓄电池已经加注了电解液。极板铅栅架中的锑被钙代替,这可以大大降低自放电和水的消耗。这意味着蓄电池内的电解液可以使用至达到蓄电池的使用寿命。完全免维护蓄电池适合于长时间不使用的汽车。完全免维护蓄电池只有很小的通气孔,由于通气孔采取迷宫通道,因此允许蓄电池倾斜较大角度。蓄电池的充电程度不再通过测试电解液的密度确定,因此这种蓄电池许多都采用集成控制显示装置,显示蓄电池的充电程度,例如:

① 绿色:代表良好。

② 灰色:代表需要充电(检查)。

③ 白色:代表需要更换。

完全免维护蓄电池是严密密封的,它不需要调整电解液的液位。蓄电池可以允许倾斜70°。

3) 重载蓄电池。重载蓄电池使用玻璃纤维垫支承正极板,可起到缓冲击和耐腐蚀的作用。极板采用树脂或塑料固定以防松动。这种蓄电池特别适合用于工程机械。

重载蓄电池使用寿命长,耐振动和循环放电。

4) 胶体电解质蓄电池。这种蓄电池的电解质不再是液体而是胶体,正负极板之间的距离更小,从而减小了蓄电池的内阻。内部的化学反应通过使氧结合而防止产生气体,即在蓄电池内气体重新转化成水。胶体电解质蓄电池具有以下特性:

① 自放电很少。
② 由于不需要存储电解液，所以结构紧凑。
③ 短路电流大。
④ 如果蓄电池过充电，安全阀可以打开。

胶体电解质蓄电池即使完全放倒也是安全的，它可以安装在任何位置。胶体电解质蓄电池耐循环放电并允许深度放电。

胶体电解质蓄电池适合于长时间停止使用的汽车，也可以用作普通用途蓄电池。

① 胶体电解质蓄电池。电解质由多种成分混合而成的胶体构成，将二氧化硅加到硫酸中就形成了胶体电解质，化学反应可以在这种胶体内进行。

② 玻璃纤维技术。玻璃纤维网中间隔层的周围是酸，它的毛细作用以及吸湿性会将电解液吸入网状微纤维。同时隔层起到隔板的作用，并对极板表面施加相等的、很高的接触压力。活性物质被固定在玻璃纤维网之间，可以防止活性物质脱落，同时通过支承措施改进其稳定性。还可以用玻璃纤维网将极板套装起来，这样可以使蓄电池的体积更加紧凑。

（3）蓄电池传感器

蓄电池控制单元与蓄电池传感器集成在一起，控制单元根据传感器检测的蓄电池当前温度和充电状态，确定最佳的充电电压参考值。要计算蓄电池的充电状态，应记录和储存在汽车各种工况下蓄电池的充、放电电流，端电压和电解液温度。

蓄电池传感器可以检测蓄电池的温度和充电状态，依此对充电电压进行控制，从而保证蓄电池总是处于较高的充电程度。

Kapitel 2
Fertigungstechnik

制造技术篇

Chapter 2
Production engineering

制造技术篇

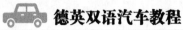

Teil 1　Fertigungstechnik　制造工艺
Part 1　Production engineering　制造工艺

学习目标

【知识目标】
1. 掌握与制造工艺、分类、工艺原理等相关的专业术语、单词和词汇。
2. 掌握制造工艺主要专业技术的德文、英文表达方法。

【能力目标】
1. 能对与制造工艺相关的专业技术进行中、德、英互译。
2. 能进行与制造工艺相关的德、英语专业技术资料的阅读和翻译。
3. 能在相关制造工艺图示上标识出相应的德语、英语单词和词汇。

Text 1　Fertigungstechnik制造工艺（德文）

Fertigungstechnik

Fertigungstechnische und wirtschaftliche Überlegungen bestimmen die Fertigungsverfahren, die Fertigungsabläufe und Arbeitsgänge bei der Fertigung und Bearbeitung von Werkstücken.

In der Fertigung sind alle Arbeitsvorgänge zusammengefasst, die ein Werkstück vom Rohzustand in einen planmäßig bestimmten Fertigzustand überführen. Das Werkstück befindet sich vor jedem Arbeitsvorgang im Ausgangszustand, danach im Endzugstand.

Mit unterschiedlichen Fertigungsverfahren kann ein für die Herstellung eines Werkstückes erforderlicher Werkstoffzusammenhalt erst geschaffen oder, wenn schon vorhanden, vermindert oder vermehrt werden oder die Form eines Werkstückes oder die Stoffeigenschaften von Werkstoffen verändert werden.

Hauptgruppen von Fertigungsverfahren

Die Fertigungsverfahren werden in 6 Hauptgruppen eingeteilt.

Bei den einzelnen Fertigungsverfahren können Zusammenhalt (Stoffeigenschaft) und Form des Werkstoffes geschaffen, geändert, beibehalten, vermehrt oder vermindert werden.

-Zusammenhalt schaffen bedeutet, dass formlose Stoffe, z.B. Pulver, Flüssigkeiten in geometrisch bestimmte feste Körper urgeformt werden, z.B. durch Pressen, Sintren, Gießen.

– Zusammenhalt beibehalten heißt, dass ein bereits geformtes Teil oder Werkstück bei der Fertigung umgeformt wird, z.B. durch Biegen.

– Zusammenhalt vermindern heißt, dass Werkstoffe oder Werkstückteile in der geometrischen Form getrennt werden, z.B. durch Sägen.

– Zusammenhalt vermehren heißt, dass Werkstück oder Werkstoffe hinzugefügt werden, z.B. durch Schrauben, Auftragschweißen.

Gliederung der Hauptgruppen

Urformen

Beim Urformen wird aus formlosem Stoff ein fester Körper mit einer bestimmten Form gefertigt. Die Formgebung kann abgeschlossen sein oder eine Vorstufe für weitere Fertigungsverfahren ergeben.

Der Zusammenhalt wird geschaffen aus dem

– flüssigen Zustand, z.B. durch Gießen.

– teigigen oder plastischen Zustand, z.B. durch Extrudieren (Verdrängen), Spritzgießen.

– pulverfömigen oder körnigen Zustand, z.B. durch Pressen und Erwärmen beim Sintern.

– ionisierten Zustand durch elektrolytisches Abscheiden, z.B. durch Galvanoplastik.

Umformen

Beim Umformen werden die Masse und der Zusammenhalt eines Stoffes beibehalten. Die Form eines festen Körpers (Rohling) wird durch plastisches (bildsames) Umformen verändert durch

– Druckumformen, z.B. Freiformschmieden, Gesenkformen, Walzen.

– Zugdruckumformen, z.B. Tiefziehen, Durchziehen, Drücken.

– Zugumformen, z.B. Längen, Weiten, Tiefen.

– Biegeumformen, z.B. Abkanten, Gesenkbiegen.

– Schubumformen, z.B. Verschieben, Verdrehen.

Trennen

Beim Trennen wird die Form eines festen Körpers geändert. Dabei wird der Zusammenhalt eines Stoffes örtlich aufgehoben durch

– Zerteilen, z.B. Beißschneiden, Scherschneiden, Reißen, Brechen.

– Spanen mit geometrisch bestimmten Schneiden, z.B. Meißeln, oder mit geometrisch unbestimmten Schneiden, z.B. Schleifen.

– Abtragen, z.B. Brennschneiden (thermisches Abtragen), Erodieren.

– Zerlegen und Entleeren, z.B. Abschrauben, Auskeilen, Auspressen.

– Reinigen, z.B. Bürsten, Waschen, Entfetten, Beizen.

– Evakuieren, z.B. Auspumpen von Gasen aus Glühlampen.

Fügen

Beim Fügen werden Werkstücke verbunden durch

– Zusammensetzen, z.B. Auflegen, Einhängen, Einrenken.

– An- und Einpressen, z.B. Schrauben, Klemmen, Verspannen.

– Schweißen, z.B. Schmelzschweißen, Pressschweißen.

– Umformen, z.B. Bördeln, Falzen, Quetschen, Nieten.

– Löten, z.B. Weichlöten, Hartlöten.

– Kleben, z.B. Nasskleben, Kontaktkeben, Reaktionskleben.

Beschichen

Beim Beschichten wird ein formloser Stoff als festhafende Schicht auf ein Werkstück aufgebracht aus dem

– gas- oder dampfförmigen Zustand, z.B. Aufdampfen.

– flüssigen oder pastenförmigen Zustand, z.B. Auftragsschweißen.

– ionisierten Zustand, z.B. Galvanisieren (chemisches Abscheiden).

– festen oder körnigen Zustand, z.B. Wirbelsintern.

Stoffeigenschaftändern

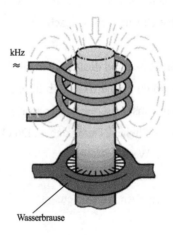

Bild:Stoffeigenschaftändern

Beim Umlagern, Aussondern oder Einbringen von Stoffteilchen werden Stoffeigenschaften von festen Stoffen geändert durch

– Umlagern von Stoffteilchen, z.B. Härten , Anlassen.

– Aussondern von Stoffteilchen, z.B. Entkohlen.

– Einbringen von Stoffteilchen, z.B. Aufkohlen, Nitrieren.

制造技术篇

Kapitel 2 Fertigungstechnik // Chapter 2 Production engineering

Neue Wörter

das	Werkstück	工件		drehen	车削
der	Zusammenhalt	聚合，内聚性		bohren	钻削
die	Eigenschaft	特性	das	Brennschneiden	气割
	sintern	烧结	die	Korrosion	腐蚀
	gießen	铸造		demontieren	拆卸
	biegen	弯曲		schrauben	拧开螺纹
	sägen	用锯切割		pressen	压出
	schrauben	用螺栓固定		entfetten	脱脂，去油污
	auftragschweißen	堆焊		montieren	装配
	extrudieren	挤压成型		einbauen	安装
	spritzgießen	注射成型		klemmen	夹持固定
	verdrängen	扩张成型		nieten	铆接
	körnig	颗粒（或微粒）状的		schweissen	焊接
	ionisiert	离子化的		löten	钎焊
	electrolytisch	电解沉积		kupferschweißen	铜焊
die	Galvanoplastik	电镀成型	der	Auftrag	涂覆
	fest	紧压的	das	Schutzgasschweissen	惰性气体保护焊
	druckformen	轧制成型		elektrolytische oder chemische	
	gesenkformen	冲模成型		Beshichtung	电解或化学沉积涂覆
	tiefziehen	深冲成型		schleifen	磨削
	zugumformen	张拉成型		thermalspraying	热喷涂
das	Abkanten	去棱角，卷边		härten	淬火
das	Scherschneiden	剪切		anlassen	退火
	Falzen	翻边		entkohlen	脱碳
das	Quetschen	挤压成型		galvanisieren	电镀
	schneiden	切割	die	Aufkohlung	渗碳
	scheren	剪切		nitrieren	渗氮

Text 2 Production engineering制造工艺（英文）

Manufacturing and economic considerations determine the manufacturing processes, sequences and oparations associated with the manufacturing and machining of workpieces.

With different manufacturing processes, the material cohesion required for the manufacture of a

109

workpiece can first be created or, if it already exists, be reduced or increased. The shape or form of a workpiece or the properties of materials can be changed.

Main categories of manufacturing processes

Manufacturing processes are divided into six main categories.

In the individual manufacturing processes the cohesion (property) and shape of the material can be created, changed, retained, increased or reduced.

• **Creating cohesion** involves creatively forming formless substances or materials, e.g. powders, liquids, into geometrically defined solid bodies, such as by pressing, sintering, casting.

• **Retaining cohesion** involves reforming an already formed part or workpiece during manufacture, such as by bending.

• **Reducing cohesion** involves separating the material or the workpiece part (s) into its/their geometrical shape, e.g. by sawing.

• **Increasing cohesion** involves adding workpieces or materials, such as by screwing, bolting, deposit welding.

Subdivision of main categories

Creative forming

In the case of creative forming, a solid body with a defined shape is manufactured from a formless substance or material.

The forming process can be a completed operation in itself or a preliminary stage for further manufacturing processes.

Cohesion is created from the:

- liquid state, e.g. by casting,
- paste-like or plastic state, e.g. by extruding (displacing), injection moulding,
- powdery or granular state, e.g. by pressing and heating during sintering, or the
- ionised state by electrolytic depositing, e.g. by electroforming.

Forming

In the case of forming, the mass and cohesion of a material are retained. The shape of a solid body (blank) is changed by plastic forming such as by:

- forming under compressive conditions, e.g. rolling, die forming,
- forming under combination of tensile and compressive conditions, e.g. deep-drawing, compression,
- forming under tensile conditions, e.g. widening, extending, stretch forming,
- forming under bending conditions, e.g. edge folding, bending, or
- forming under shearing conditions, e.g. twisting, displacing.

Separating

In the case of separating, the shape of a solid body is changed. Here, the cohesion of a material

is locally eliminated by:
- severing, e.g. cropping, parting, breaking,
- machining-cutting, e.g. turning, grinding, drilling,
- removing, e.g. flame-cutting, eroding,
- disassembling, e.g. unscrewing, pressing out, or
- cleaning, e.g. brushing, washing, degreasing.

Joining

In the case of joining, workpieces are connected by:
- assembling, e.g. laying on, hanging,
- pressing on and in, e.g. screwing, bolting, clamping,
- forming, e.g, riveting, clinching,
- welding, e.g. inert-gas-shielded welding,
- soldering, e.g. soft-soldering, hard-soldering (brazing), or
- bonding, e.g. cold-bonding, two-component bonding.

Coating

In the case of coating, a formless substance or material is applied as an adherent layer to a Workpiece. Coatings may be applied:
- in a liquid or paste-like form, e.g. spray-painting, deposit welding.
- in a solid or powdery form, e.g. thermal spraying.
- by electrolytic or chemical depositing, e.g. electroplating.
- in a solid or granular form, e.g. whirl Sintering.

Changing the property of a material

In the case of ageing, segregation or introduction of material particles, the material properties of solid bodies are changed by:
- rearrangement of material particles, e.g. hardening, annealing.
- segregation of material particles, e.g. decarburising.
- introduction of material particles, e.g. carburising, nitriding.

REVIEW QUESTIONS

1. What are the main categories of production engineering?
2. Which manufacturing processes change the shape of a workpiece?
3. Which manufacturing processes create material cohesion?
4. Name processes which change the properties of a material.

New Words

workpiece	工件	flame-cutting	火焰切割
cohesion	聚合，内聚性	eroding	腐蚀
property	特性	disassembling	拆卸
sintering	烧结	unscrewing	拧开螺纹
casting	铸造	pressing out	压出
bending	弯曲	degreasing	脱脂，去油污
sawing	用锯切割	assembling	装配
screwing	用螺纹连接	laying on	安装
bolting	用螺栓固定	clamping	夹持固定
depositwelding	堆焊	riveting	铆接
extruding	挤压成型	widening	展宽成型
injectionmoulding	注射成型	clinching	冲铆连接
extending	扩张成型	welding	焊接
granular	颗粒（或微粒）状的	soldering`	钎焊
ionised	离子化的	brazing	铜焊
electrolyticdepositing	电解沉积	coating	涂覆
electroforming	电铸成型	inert-gas-shielded welding	惰性气体保护焊
compressive	紧压的	electrolytic or chemical depositing	电解沉积或化学沉积涂覆
rolling	轧制成型		
dieforming	冲模成型	grinding	磨削
tensile	张力的，拉力的，抗张的	thermalspraying	热喷涂
deep-drawing	深冲成型	whirl sintering	回转热压结
stretchforming	张拉成型	ageing	改质
edgefolding	卷边	segregation	偏析
shearing	剪切	hardening	淬火
twisting	扭转成型	annealing	退火
displacing	挤压成型	decarburising	脱碳
eliminate	消除、根除、除去	adherent	黏着的
severing	切割	electroplating	电镀
cropping	剪切	carburising	渗碳
turning	车削	nitriding	渗氮
drilling	钻削		

Kapitel 2　Fertigungstechnik // Chapter 2　Production engineering

课文参考译文

制造工艺

制造技术条件和经济条件决定了工件的制造和加工采用什么制造工艺、操作顺序和工序。

使用不同的制造工艺，可以先形成制造工件所需要的材料聚合，或者如果已经存在聚合，可将聚合物料增大或减小；可以改变工件的外形和材料的特性。

制造工艺的主要类型

制造工艺可以分为以下几种主要类型。

在这些制造工艺中，可以创新、改变、保持、增大或减小材料的聚合和形状。

创新聚合。创新聚合是通过用压制、烧结、铸造等方法，将一些无形的物质或材料（例如粉末、液体），创造性地构建成几何形状确定的实体。

保持聚合。保持聚合是已经成型的零件或工件在生产过程中的再成形（例如弯曲）。

减小聚合。减小聚合是将具有一定几何形状的材料或工件通过某种方法（如用锯切割）分割开。

增加聚合。增加聚合是指通过螺纹连接、螺钉固定、堆焊等方法，来增加工件或材料。

制造工艺的详细分类

1. 创新成型

在创新成型的工艺中，具有一定形状的实体是由一种无形的物质或材料制成的。这种成型工艺本身可以是一个完整的工艺，或者是另一个制造工艺的前期阶段。

使用下述方法可使物质或材料形成实体：

液态利用铸造等方法。

膏状或塑性状态利用挤压成型、注射成型等方法。

粉末或颗粒状态利用压制和烧结加热的方法。

离子化状态利用电镀（如电铸成型）的方法。

2. 成型

成型是材料的质量和聚合情况保持不变，而实体（坯件）的形状通过塑性变形而改变的工艺，如：

在压缩条件下成型，如轧制成型、冲模成型。

在拉压组合条件下成型，如深冲成型、冲压成型。

在拉伸条件下成型，如展宽成型、扩张成型、张拉成型。

在弯曲条件下成型，如卷边、弯曲。

在剪切条件下成型，如扭转成型、挤压成型。

3. 分离

分离是指可以改变实体的形状的工艺。这样，在局部消除了材料的聚合，所用的方法有：

切割，如剪切、斩断和轧碎。

机械切削，如车削、磨削、钻削。

去除，如火焰切割、腐蚀。

解体，如拆卸螺纹连接、压出。

清洗，如刷洗、冲洗和脱脂。

4. 连接

连接是用下述方法将工件连接起来的成形工艺：

装配，如安装、悬挂。

压上或压入，如用螺钉固定，用螺栓固定，夹持固定。

成形，如铆钉铆接，冲铆连接。

焊接，如惰性气体保护焊。

钎焊，如软钎焊，硬钎焊（铜焊）。

5. 涂覆

涂覆是将一种将无形的物质或材料作为粘附层涂到工件表面上的工艺。涂覆包括：

液体或膏状物涂覆，如喷漆、堆焊。

固体或粉末状物涂覆，如热喷涂。

电解沉积或化学沉积涂覆，如电镀。

固态或颗粒物涂覆，如回转热压结。

6. 改变材料特性

在改质、偏析或引入材料颗粒的情况下，通过一系列方法使实体的材料特性发生变化：

材料颗粒的重新排列，如淬火、退火。

材料颗粒的偏析，如脱碳。

材料颗粒的引入，如渗碳、渗氮。

制造技术篇

Kapitel 2　Fertigungstechnik // Chapter 2　Production engineering

Teil 2　Umformen　成型技术
Part 2　Forming　成型技术

【知识目标】
1. 掌握与成型技术原理等相关的专业术语、单词和词汇。
2. 掌握成型技术主要知识的德文、英文表达方法。

【能力目标】
1. 能对成型技术进行中、德、英互译。
2. 能进行与成型技术相关的德语、英语资料的阅读和翻译。
3. 能在零件实物上标识出相应结构的德语、英语单词和词汇。

Text 1　Umformen成型技术（德文）

Umformen ist ein Fertigungsverfahren, bei dem ein plastisch verformbarer fester Körper durch Einwirkung äußerer Kräfte eine neue Form erhält.

Voraussetzung für jedes Umformen ist die plastische Verformbarkeit des Werkstoffes. Durch Einwirkung von äußeren Kräften wird das Werkstück elastisch, bei höherer Belastung plastisch verformt. Die Masse und der Zusammenhalt des Werkstoffes bleiben dabei erhalten, die Form wird jedoch geändert, d.h. umgeformt.

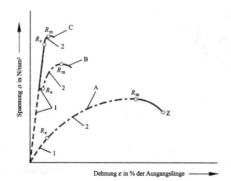

Bild：Umformbereich im Spannung- Dehnung – Diagramm

Das Umformen erfolgt in einem Bereich über der Streckgrenze R_e und unterhalb der Zugfestigkeit R_m. Dabei tritt eine Gefügeveränderung ein, es wird verformt. Beim Erwärmen des umgeformten Werkstücks bildet sich bei der – für jeden Werkstoff charakteristischen– Rekristallisationstemperatur ein neues unverformtes Gefüge. Dadurch werden die Spannungen im Werkstück vermindert.

Warmumformen erfolgt oberhalb der Rekristallisationstempratur. Durch Gefügeneubildung werden Spannungen im Werkstück vermindert. Mit steigender Temperatur nimmt die Festigkeit ab, Dehnung und Verformbarkeit nehmen zu, die Umformkräfte werden kleiner.

Kaltumformen erfolgt unterhalb der Rekristallisationstemperatur, es erfolgt also keine Gefügeneubildung. Durch die teilweise großen Gefügeveränderungen ergibt sich eine Erhöhung der Festigkeit und eine Verminderung der Dehnung (Kaltverfestigung). Die Gefahr einer Rissbildung nimmt zu.

Vorteile des Umformens

– Verbesserung der Werkstoffeigenschaften, weil der Faserverlauf erhalten bleibt und dadurch die Kerbwirkung verringert wird.

– die Festigkeit kann sich beim Kaltumformen wesentlich erhöhen.

– verlustarme Werkstoffverarbeitung, da die Rohteile häufig den Fertigteilen angenähert sind, wenig Abfall.

– kürzere Festigungszeiten gegenüber der spanenden Formgebung.

– Möglichkeit zur Herstellung einbaufertiger Teile mit hoher Oberflächengüte und kleinen Maßtoleranzen.

Einteilung der Umformverfahren

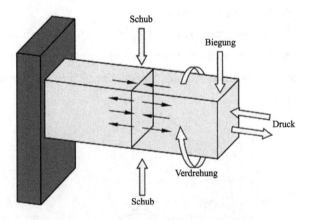

Bild : Beanspruchungen im Werkstückquerschnitt

Die Einteilung kann erfolgen nach der Temperatur (Kalt-, Warmumformen), nach der Werkstückform (Massiv-, Blechumformen) und nach der Beanspruchungsart beim Umformen.

Nach der Beanspruchung des Werkstückquerschnittes unterscheidet man:

– Biegumformen, z.B. Abkanten, Bördeln, Sicken, Profilieren.

– Zugdruckumformen, z.B. Tiefziehen, Drücken, Durchziehen.

– Zugumformen, z.B. Streckrichten.

– Schubumformen, wobei zwei benachbarte Querschnitte des Werkstückes durch die Schubbeanspruchung gegeneinander parallel (Verschieben) oder in einem Winkel zueinander (Verdrehen) verschoben werden.

– Druckumformen, z.B. Freiformen (Schmieden), Walzen.

Biegeumformen

Biegeumformen (Biegen) ist das Umformen eines festen Körpers, wobei der plastische Zustand im Wesentlichen durch eine Biegebeanspruchung hervorgerufen wird.

Voraussetzung für das Biegen:

– Werkstoff muss ausreichend dehnbar sein.

– Elastizitätsgrenze des Werkstoffes muss überschritten werden.

– Bruchgrenze des Werkstoffes darf nicht erreicht werden.

Beim Biegen soll keine wesentliche Veränderung des Werkstückquerschnittes eintreten. Der Zusammenhalt des Werkstoffes bleibt erhalten, nur ein Teil des Werkstückes, die Biegezone, wird verformt.

Biegevorgang

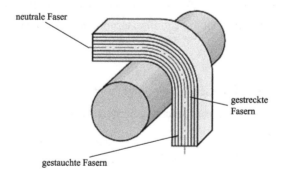

Bild : Faserverlauf beim Biegen

Beim Biegen eines Werkstücks werden äußeren Fasern gestreckt (Zugbeanspruchung), die inneren gestaucht (Druckbeanspruchung). Zwischen beiden befindet sich eine spannungslose, neutrale Faser, deren Länge unverändert bleibt. In Nähe der neutralen Faser ist die Verformung elastisch. Dadurch federt das Werkstück geringfügig zurück. Diese Rückfederung ist beim Biegen zu berücksichtigen. Beim Biegen von Blech ist wegen Rissgefahr auf die Walzrichtung zu achten.

Die Biegekraft ist abhängig von:

– Dehnbarkeit des Werkstoffes.

- Biegeradius.
- Temperatur des Werkstoffes.
- Größe und Form des Biegequerschnittes.
- Lage der Biegeachse.

Biegeverfahren

- Gesenkbiegen. Das Werkstück wird mit einem Stempel in das Biegegesenk gedrückt.
- Schwenkbiegen mit der Biegemaschine.
- Abkanten ergibt einen kleinen Biegeradius.
- Rundbiegen mittels Biegwalzen ergibt großen Biegradius.
- Bördeln dient zum Umbiegen eines Randes an Blechen.
- Sicken bewirken eine Blechversteifung z.B. in Wellblechen.
- Profilieren. Blechstreifen erhalten beim Walzen ihre Profile.

Biegen von Rohren

Beim Biegen von Rohren und anderen Hohlprofilen liegen in den meist dünnwandigen Profilen die gestreckte Zone (Zugbeanspruchung) und die gestauchte Zone (Druckbeanspruchung) sehr nahe beieinander. Durch die Verringerung des Werkstückquerschnitts kann es leicht zum Einknicken kommen. Rohre lassen sich kalt biegen, wenn sie mit trockenem Sand, Kolophonium, Blei oder einer Schraubenfeder satt ausgefüllt werden. Die Enden werden mit Holzstopfen verschlossen. Der Biegeradius soll nicht kleiner als der dreifache Rohrdurchmesser sein. Bei längsgeschweißten Roren muss die Naht immer in die neutrale Zone gelegt werden, da sie sonst aufplatzt. Durch die seitliche Abstützung der Rohre in der Biegevorrichtung entfällt das zeitraubende Ausfüllen der Rohre für den Biegevorgang.

Zugdruckumformen

Beim Zugdruckumformen werden feste Körper umgeformt, wobei der plastische Zustand durch eine zusammengesetzte Zug- und Druckbeanspruchung herbeigeführt wird.

Zugdruckumformverfahren

- Druckziehen, z.B. Drahtziehen durch eine Ziehdüse.
- Drücken, z.B. Drücken über eine rotierende Form.
- Tiefziehen.

Tiefziehen

Tiefziehen ist das Zugdruckformen eines ebenen oder bereits vorgeformten Blechzuschnittes in einem oder mehreren Arbeitsgängen ohne beabsichtigte Veränderung der Blechdicke.

Voraussetzung für Tiefziehen ist ein fließfähiger Werkstoff wie z.B. Tiefziehblech, CuZn-(Messing) und Aluminiumbleche. Durch Tiefziehen werden Karosserie-, Fahrgestellt- und Rahmenteile hergestellt.

Das Tiefziehwerzeug besteht aus dem Ziehstempel, Niederhalter, Ziehring und Auswerfer.

Tiefziehvorgang

Der ebene Blechzuschnitt(Ronde) wird auf den Ziehring gelegt. Dann drückt der Niederhalter auf die Ronde und klemmt sie zwischen Niederhalter und Ziehring fest. Danach zieht der Ziehstempel die Ronde in die Öffnung des Ziehrings, wobei der Werkstoff in Richtung Ziehringkante fließt. Die Umformkraft beansprucht den Werkstoff auf Zug und Druck. Der Niederhalter glättet die anfangs entstehenden Falten, wobei der überschüssige Werkstoff durch Stauchen in die Wandung des Ziehteils einfließen muss. Bei großer Ziehtiefe wird der Flansch verringert und verschwindet beim vollständigen Durchzug der Ronde. Nach Beendigung des Ziehvorganges geht der Ziehstempel zurück. Das durchgezogene Werkstück federt etwas aus und wird am Ziehring abgestreift. Bei Ziehteilen mit Flansch dient der Niederhalter als Abstreifer, der erst nach dem Ziehstempel nach oben geht und das Werkstück freigibt. Meist sind mehrere Züge zur Fertigstellung eines Ziehteiles notwendig.

Beim Tiefziehen wird durch Schmierstoffe die Reibung zwischen Blech und Ziehwerkzeug verringert, wodurch Werkzeugverschleiß und Werkstoffbeanspruchung vermindert werden.

Zugumformen

Zugumformen ist das Umformen eines festen Körpers, wobei der plastische Zustand hauptsächlich durch eine ein- oder mehrachsige Zugbeanspruchung herbeigeführt wird.

Beim Streckziehen (Zugumformen) wird der Blechzuschnitt fest eingespannt. Die Zugvorrichtung bewirkt die Verformung des Bleches durch Zugbeanspruchung. Durch Streckziehen werden Blechformteile mit großen Abmessungen und Krümmungen hergestellt, z.B. Beplankungen für Fahrzeuge und Omnibusaufbauten.

Druckumformen

Druckumformen ist das Umformen eines festen Körpers, wobei der plastische Zustand durch Druckkräfte hervorgerufen wird.

Zum Druckumformen gehören das

– Walzen. Zwischen sich stetig oder schrittweise drehenden Walzen werden Profile, Bleche, Rohre, Drähte hergestellt.

– Eindrücken. Dabei dringt das Werkzeug nur an einzelnen Stellen in die Oberfläche des Werkstückes ein, z.B. Anreißen.

– Durchdrücken. Beim Strangpressen werden erwärmte Werkstoffe durch eine Matrize gedrückt und zu Profilen geformt. Beim Fließpressen werden Werkstoff mittels Stempe und Matrize zu voll- oder Hohlkörpern gepresst.

WIEDERHOLUNGSFRAGEN

1. Was versteht man unter Umformen?
2. Welche Umformverfahren gibt es?
3. Welche Vorteile bietet das Umformen?

4. Welche Voraussetzungen müssen für das Biegen vorhanden sein?

5. Wie läuft ein Tiefziehvorgang ab?

Neue Wörter

die	Voraussetzung	前提，必备条件		das	Streckrichten	拉力校平，扭转成型
die	Streckgrenze	屈服点		das	Schmieden	锻造成型
die	Zugfestigkeit	抗拉强度		das	Walzen	辊压成型
die	Rekristallisation	再结晶		die	Elastizitätsgrenze	弹性极限
die	Dehnung	伸长		die	Bruchgrenze	断裂极限
die	Verformbarkeit	变形性			gestreckt	被拉长
die	Rißbildung	开裂			verstärken	被加厚
die	Kerbwirkung	缺口效应			zurückfedern	弹回
die	verlustarme Werkstoffverarbeitung	低损耗材料加工		die	Elastizität	弹性
				der	Faserverlauf	纹路，花样，纤维表面走向
die	Maßtoleranz	尺寸公差				
das	Massivumformen	块料成型		die	neutrale Faser	中性纤维
das	Blechpressen	板材冲压成型		das	Gesenkbiegen	模锻弯曲
das	Abkanten	去棱角，边缘折叠		das	Ziehwerkzeug	拉拨模，冲模
das	Bördeln	翻边		das	Biegegesenk	弯曲模，压弯模
das	Sicken	轧制波纹		die	Biegemaschine	压弯机
das	Profilieren	整形		das	Bördeln	边缘折叠
das	Tiefziehen	深拉		das	Drahtziehen	拉丝
das	Durchziehen	韧化拉平				

Text 2　Forming成型技术（英文）

Forming is a manufacturing process in which a plastically deformable, solid body acquires a new shape through the influence of external forces.

The prerequisite for each instance of forming is the plastic deformability of the material in question. As a result of the influence of external forces, the workpiece is subject to elastic deformation and, with higher forces, to plastic deformation. The mass and cohesion of the material are retained in the process, but the shape is changed, i.e. reformed.

Forming takes place in a range above yield point R_e and below tensile strength R_m. This involves a structural change, and deformation takes place. When the formed workpiece is heated, a new undeformed structure is created at the recrystallisation temperature characteristic for each material.

This reduces the stresses in the workpiece.

Hot forming occurs above the recrystallisation temperature. The new structural formation reduces stresses in the workpiece. As the temperature rises, strength decreases, elongation and deformability increase, and the forming forces become smaller.

Cold forming occurs below the recrystallisation temperature, therefore there is no new structural formation. The partially great structural changes give rise to increased strength and reduced elongation (strain-hardening). The risk of cracking increases.

Advantage of a formed part:
- Fibre orientation is retained and therefore the notch effect is reduced.
- Strength can be increased considerably during cold forming.
- Low-loss material processing since the unmachined parts are frequently closer to the finished parts, little waste.
- Shorter production time compared with metal-cutting forming.
- Possibility of manufacturing parts ready for installation with high surface quality and small dimensional tolerances.

Subdivision of forming processes

The processes can be subdivided according to the:
- temperature (cold, hot forming).
- workpiece shape (massive forming, pressing).
- type of stress during forming.

The following different processes are available according to the stressing of the workpiece cross-section:
- **Forming under bending conditions,** e.g. edge folding, bordering, beading, profiling.
- **Forming under combination of tensile and compressive conditions,** e.g. deep-drawing.
- **Forming under tensile conditions,** e.g. patent flattening.
- **Forming under shearing conditions,** e,g, twisting.
- **Forming under compressive conditions,** e.g. forging, rolling.

Forming under bending conditions

Forming under bending conditions (bending) is the forming of a solid body where the plastic state of the cross-section is primarily brought about by bending stress.

Prerequisites for bending:
- Material must be sufficiently extensible.
- Limit of elasticity of material must be exceeded.
- Breaking limit of material must not be reached.

During bending, a change to the workpiece cross-section occurs at the bending point. Specific bending radii must therefore not be undershot. The cohesion of the material is retained; only a part of the workpiece, the bending zone, is deformed.

Bending operation

When a workpiece is bent, the outer fibres are stretched (tensile stress) while the inner fibres are upset (compressive stress). Between the outer and inner fibres is a stress-free, neutral fibre, the length of which remains unchanged.

The deformation is elastic in the vicinity of the neutral fibre. This allows the workpiece to spring back slightly. This resilience must be taken into consideration during bending. When bending sheet metal, it is important to pay attention to the grain due to the danger of cracking.

The bending force is dependent on:
- Extensibility and temperature of the material.
- Bending radius.
- Size and shape of the bending cross-section.
- Position of the bending or neutral axis.

Bending processes
- **Swage bending.** The workpiece is pressed with a punch into the bending swage.
- **Bending with** bending press.
- **Edge folding** produces a small bending radius.
- **Rounding** with bending rollers produces a large bending radius.
- **Bordering** serves to bend an edge on sheet metal.
- **Beading** stiffens a metal plate.
- **Profiling.** Metal strips are given their profiles during rolling.

Bending pipes

When bending brake lines and tubing, the thinwalled profiles are stretched on one side (tensile stress) and compressed on the other (compressive stress). Due to the small diameters of the profiles, both stress types are close to one another; consequently, buckling can result from the changes in the material cross-sections.

Therefore, bending tools and pipe-bending apparatuses should be used when bending brakelines and smelt pipes. The bending radius should not be less than three times the pipe diameter.

In the case of lengthwise welded pipes, the seam must always be located in the neutral zone to prevent splitting. A coil spring or sand can be used to fill pipes with a larger diameter to avoid buckling during the bending process.

Forming under combination of tensile and compressive conditions

Forming under a combination of tensile and compressive conditions involves workpieces being formed simultaneously by tensile and compressive forces.

Following are the different processes:
- Deep-drawing, e.g. of body sheets.

- Compressing, e.g. compressing by means of a rotating shape.
- Stripping, e.g. pipes, profiles, wire drawing.

Deep-drawing

Deep-drawing is the forming under a combination of tensile and compressive conditions of a circular blank in one or more operations. The thickness of the metal remains roughly the same in the process.

Free-flowing materials such as deep-drawing sheet steel (e.g. DC 03) and aluminium sheets are used for deep-drawing. Body sections are manufactured.

Deep-drawing process

The flat circular blank is placed on the drawing die and clamped in place by the blank holder. The drawing punch is now pressed downwards and draws the circular blank over the drawing edge into the opening of the drawing die. The material is subjected by the forming force to tensile and compressive stress. The blank holder presses the metal plate onto the drawing die, thus preventing the formation of wrinkles. The width of the drawing gap is slightly larger than the thickness of the metal plate. Lubricants reduce friction between the metal plate and the drawing die. When the deep-drawing process is finished, the upward-moving drawing punch releases the workpiece.

New Words

prerequisite	前提，必备条件	deep-drawing	深拉
yield point	屈服点	patent flattening	韧化拉平
tensile strength	抗拉强度	twisting	扭转成型
recrystallisation	再结晶	forging	锻造成型
elongation	伸长	rolling	辊压成型
deformability	变形性	limit of elasticity	弹性极限
cracking	开裂	breaking limit	断裂极限
notch	缺口	radii	半径（复数）
low-loss material processing	低损耗材料加工	undershot	低于，未达到
unmachined	未加工的	stretch	被拉长
dimensional tolerance	几何公差	upset	被加厚
massiveforming	块料成型	vicinity	邻近地区
pressing	板材冲压成型	spring back	弹回
edgefolding	边缘折叠	resilience	弹性
bordering	翻边	grain	外纤维表面
beading	轧制波纹	extensibility	可扩展性
profiling	整形	neutral axis	中性轴

swage bending	模锻弯曲	lengthwise welded pipe	纵向焊管
punch	冲模	seam	接缝
bending swage	型模	simultaneously	同时
bending press	压弯机	stripping	拉丝
edge folding	边缘折叠	drawing die	拉丝模
rounding	大弧弯曲	blank holder	压边圈
stiffen	使僵硬，使挺直	drawing edge	拉丝模边缘
brake line	制动管路	wrinkle	皱纹
buckling	屈曲	friction	摩擦
apparatuse	设备		

课文参考译文

成型技术

成型是通过外力的影响使可塑性变形的实体获得新的形状所用的制造工艺。

每种成型情况的前提都是上面说的材料具有塑性变形能力。在外力的作用下，工件首先发生弹性变形，然后在更大的作用力下，将会出现塑性变形。在此过程中，工件材料的质量和聚合情况保持不变，但是形状发生变化，也就是再成型。

成型发生在拉应力高于屈服点R_e而低于抗拉强度R_m的范围内。在这期间，材料组织发生变化，并出现畸变。当对变形的工件进行加热时，在每种材料的再结晶温度时就会形成一种新的无畸变的组织结构。这样就会减小工件内的应力。

热成型。这是在高于再结晶温度条件下进行的成型。新的组织的形成减小了工件内的应力。随着温度的升高，强度下降，伸长率和可变形能力增加，因而成型力减小。

冷成型。这是在低于再结晶温度条件下进行的成型。因而，没有形成新的组织。局部会出现大的组织变化，提高了强度，降低了伸长率（应变硬化），出现裂纹的可能性增加。

1. 成型的优点

纤维走向得以保留，因而降低了缺口效应。

在冷成型期间，能明显提高强度。

由于未加工的坯件常常与成品零件很接近，所以材料处理的去除量小，很少浪费。

与金属切削成形相比，生产时间缩短。

可以制造表面质量高且尺寸公差小、可直接安装的零件。

2. 成型工艺的分类

成型工艺可以根据温度（冷成型、热成型）、坯件外形（块料成型、板材冲压成型）、成型期间应力类型来分类。

根据坯件横断面的应力的不同，可以将成型分为下面几种：

弯曲条件下的成型，例如折叠、翻边、轧制波纹、整形等。

拉、压组合条件的成型，例如深拉。

拉伸条件下的成型，例如韧化拉平。

剪切条件下的成型，例如扭转成型。

压缩条件下的成型，例如锻造成型、辊压成型。

弯曲条件下的成型

弯曲条件下的成型是在弯曲应力作用下处于塑性状态的实体的成型。

1. 弯曲成型的必要条件

材料必须具有良好的延展性。

必须超过材料的弹性极限。

不得达到材料的断裂极限。

在弯曲期间，材料的弯曲点处的工件横断面会发生变化。因此，弯曲半径所处的位置必须正确。材料的聚合得到保持，只有工件的一部分（弯曲区）发生变形。

2. 弯曲成型的操作

当弯曲工件时，外层的纤维被拉长而变薄（拉应力），而内层的纤维受压缩而加厚。内、外层纤维中间是无应力的中性层，其长度保持不变。

靠近中性层的纤维发生弹性变形。因此，工件会出现轻微的弹复现象。在弯曲期间，必须考虑这种弹复。当弯曲板材时，由于存在开裂的危险，所以一定要留意外纤维层表面。

弯曲力的大小取决于材料的延展能力、弯曲半径、弯曲的横断面大小和形状、弯曲的部位和中性层的位置。

3. 弯曲方法

型模弯曲。这种方法是将工件用冲模冲压进弯曲型模中。

用压弯机弯曲。

折边就是形成一个小的弯曲半径。

大弧弯曲是用弯曲滚轮形成一个大的弯曲半径。

翻边用于弯曲板材边缘。

轧制波纹能提高金属板的刚度。

整形能使金属带在辊压之后具有一定的轮廓。

4. 弯管

当弯曲管件和其他空心坯件（大部分为薄壁件）时，拉伸区（受拉应力）和压缩区（受压应力）相互之间靠得非常近。当坯件的横断面缩小时，坯件可能很容易变皱。

当将管件内充满干沙或装入一个螺旋弹簧时，就可以对这些管件进行冷态弯曲。操作时，要将管口密封。弯曲半径不应小于三倍的管径。

对于纵向焊接管，应总是将接缝置于中性区上，否则，管件将会裂开。沿着横向将管件支撑在弯曲设备上就不需要在弯曲之前往管内填充干沙，节省了时间。

拉、压组合条件下进行的成型

拉、压组合条件下的成型是指在拉伸和压缩作用力同时作用的情况下对工件进行的成型。

这种成型有下述不同的方法：

深拉，例如车身板件的深拉。

压缩，例如借助于旋转成型机进行压缩成型。

拉丝。

1. 深拉

深拉是一个圆形坯件在拉伸和压缩组合条件下进行的一次或多次成型。在此过程中，金属胚件的厚度大致保持不变。

例如深拉钢板（如DC 03）和铝板这样的可塑性材料适用于深拉。车身部件就是用深拉工艺制造的。

2. 深拉过程

将圆形平坯件放在凹模上，并用压边圈夹持在适当的位置上。凸模向下冲压，从而将覆盖在凹模边缘上的圆形坯件拉入凹模孔中。在成型力作用下，坯件受到拉应力和压应力作用。压边圈将钢板坯件压紧在凹模上，从而防止了坯件起皱变形。凸、凹模间隙比坯件板材的厚度略大。润滑剂减小了板材与凹模之间的摩擦。当深拉过程完成后，凸模向上运动，工件从凹模中脱离。

Kapitel 2　Fertigungstechnik // Chapter 2　Production engineering

Teil 3　Gießtechnik　铸造技术
Part 3　Casting　铸造技术

学习目标

【知识目标】
1. 掌握与铸造技术原理等相关的专业术语、单词和词汇。
2. 掌握铸造技术主要知识的德文、英文表达方法。

【能力目标】
1. 能对铸造技术进行中、德、英互译。
2. 能进行与铸造技术相关的德语、英语资料的阅读和翻译。
3. 能在铸件实物上标识出相应结构的德语、英语单词和词汇。

Text 1　Gießtechnik 铸造技术（德文）

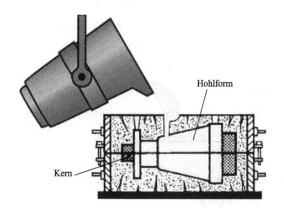

Giessen

Beim Giessen wird geschmolzenes Metall in eine Form gegossen(Tab.1). Die Schmelze füllt die Hohlräume der Form aus. Nach Erstarren der Schmelze ist die Urform eines Werkstücks geschaffen.

Tab.1 Übersicht über Form-und Giessverfahren

Giessen in verlorene Formen mit Schwerkraft	Giessen in Schwerkraft	Dauerformen mit Druck	Zentrifugalkraft
Dauermodelle	Ohne Modelle	Ohne Modelle	Ohne Modelle
Handformen	Kokillenguss Strangguss	Druckgiessen	Schleudergiessen
Maskenformen			
Verlorene Modelle		Kaltkammerverfahren	Horizontal-Schleuderguss
Feingiessen		Warmkammerverfahren	Vertikal-Schleuderguss
Vollformgiessen			

Giessen mit Dauermodell in verlorener Sandform

Zur Herstellung verlorener Formen werden Modelle verwendet. Das Modell benötigt man zum Einformen der Aussenkontur des Werkstücks. Unter verlorener Form versteht man eine Giessform, die nach einem Giessvorgang unbrauchbar geworden ist. Giessmetalle ziehen sich beim Abkühlen zusammen, sie „schwinden ". Das Modell wird deshalb grösser hergestellt (0.5%...2%) als das Gussstück.

Um in einem Gussstück einen Hohlraum zu erhalten, muss in die Form ein Kern eingelegt werden. Der Kern dient zur Erstellung der Innenkontur. Er ist nach dem Giessvorgang unbrauchbar (verloren).

Zum Einformen des zweiteiligen Modells werden untere Modellhälfte und Unterkasten auf das Modellbrett gelegt und mit Formstoff (Formsand) aufgefüllt. Dieser wird durch Stampfen verdichtet. Nach Umdrehen des Unterkasten wird der Oberkasten aufgesetzt. Nach Aufsetzen der oberen Modellhälfte werden Modele für Einguss und Speiser gelegt, Formstoff eingefüllt und festgestampft. Nach Abheben des Oberkasten werden beide Modellhälften und Modellteile entnommen. Danach werden Abschnitte und Lauf in den Formstoff eingeschnitten und der Kern eingelegt. Beim Zusammensetzen von Ober-und Unterkasten entsteht ein Hohlraum, der der Form des Werkstückses entspricht.

Das Füllen der Form erfolgt durch den Einguss. Speiser lassen beim Füllen die Luft entweichen. Durch die grossen Speiserquerschnitte kann beim Abkühlen flüssiges Metall in das erstarrende Werkstück nachfliessen, dadurch werden Schwindungshohlräume (Lunker) vermieden. Nach dem Abkühlen wird die Form zerstört und das Gussstück entnommen.

Druckgiessen

Beim Druckgiessen wird Metall in flüssigem oder teigigem Zustand unter hohem Druck schnell in eine Dauerform (Stahlform) gedrückt.

Nichteisen-Schwermetalllegierungen, z. B. Feinzink-Gusslegierungen und Leichtmetalllegierungen, z. B. Aluminiu-oder Magnesium-Gusslegierungen, werden vielfach durch Druckgiessen vergossen. Die Giessdrück betragen je nach Verfahren 100 bar...2500 bar.

Beim Druckgiessen im Warmkammerverfahren befindet sich die Druckkammer in der Schmelze, beim Kaltkammerverfahren wird die Schmelze von ausserhalb in die Druckkammer gefüllt.

Vorteile des Druckgiessens.

– Abgüsse mit größer Massgnauigkeit.

– Herstellung von Fertigteilen möglich, da Bohrungen und Gewinde eingegossen werden können. Nur Grate und Einguss entfernen.

Feingiessen (Modellausschmelzverfahren)

Feingiessen ist ein Giessen mit verlorenen (ausgeschmolzenen) Modellen in einer verlorenen einteiligen Form.

Nach einem Mustermodell werden Modele aus einem niedrig schmelzenden Wachs oder Kunststoff gefertigt und zu einer „Modelltraube " zusammengesetzt.Die „Modelltraube " wird mehrmalig in einen Keramikbrei getaucht, mit Keramikpulver bestreut und danach getrocknet. Zur Erhöhung der Festigkeit wird die Giessform (Keramikschale) bei etwa 1000°C gebrannt. Die Modele schmelzen dabei aus und bilden die Hohlräume zum Ausgiessen.

Vorteile des Feingiessens

– Fast alle Werkstoffe vergiessbar, auch schwer zerspanbare Metalle.

– für kleinste Teile und geringe Wandstärke geeignet.

– sehr hohe Massgenauigkeit und hohe Oberflächengüte,gratfrei.

– Giessen von Fertigteile möglich, Nacharbeiten nur an Passflächen.

– Herstellung komplizierter Teile mit Hinterschneidungen möglich .

Schleudergiessen

Die Schmelze wird in eine schnell umlaufende Dauerform (Kokille) gegossen und durch die Zentrifugalkraft an die Innenwände der Form geschleudert, wo sie erstarrt.

Horizontal-Schleudergiessen dient vor allem zur Erzeugung von Hohlkörpern, z. B. Rohre, Kolbenringe, Ringträger.

Vertikal-Schleudergiessen dient zur Herstellung niedriger Werkstücke, z. B. Zahnräder, Riemenscheiben.

Vorteile des Schleudergiessens

– Fliehkraft bewirkt verdichtetes Gefüge und höhere Festigkeit.

– Gefüge ist frei von Gasblasen, Lunkern und Verunreinigungen, die eine geringere Dichte als die Schmelze haben.

Kokillenguss

Die Schmelze wird in Metalldauerformen (Kokillen) gegossen, wobei die Füllung durch Schwerkraft erfolgt.

WIEDERHOLUNGSFRAGEN

1.Was versteht man unter Giessen?

2.Welche Giessverfahren unterscheidet man?

3. Welche Vorteile bietet das Feingiessen?
4. Welche Vorteile bietet das Druckgiessen?
5. Welche Vorteile bietet das Schleudergiessen?

Neue Wörter

	schmelzen	融化，熔化	der	Steiger	冒口
die	Form	模具，模型	der	Zulauf	横浇道
der	Hohlraum	腔，洞	das	Druckgießen	压力铸造
die	Modelle	模样	die	Bohrung	孔
die	Sandform	砂模	die	Gewinde	螺纹
der	Kontur	轮廓，周线	die	Grate	脊
	zusammenziehen	收缩，缩小	das	Feingießen	熔模铸造
die	Kurbelwelle	曲轴	die	einteilige Form	单件式铸型
der	Motorblock	发动机缸体		tauchen	浸，泡
der	Formkern	型芯	das	Korbenring	活塞环
die	Modellhälfte	半分模样	das	Turbinerad	涡轮
der	Oberkasten	上型箱	das	Schleudergießen	离心铸造
der	Unterkasten	下型箱		umlaufen	旋转
der	Formsand	型砂	die	Zylingderbuchse	气缸套
der	Auslauf	浇口	das	Zahnrad	齿轮

Text 2 Casting 铸造技术（英文）

Casting involves pouring a molten metal into a mould. The melting mass fills the cavities in the mould. The original shape of the workpiece is created once the melting mass has solidified.

Casting with permanent pattern in broken sand mould

Patterns are used to produce broken moulds. The pattern serves to mould the outside contour of the workpiece. A broken mould is a casting mould which is rendered unusable after casting. Since casting metals contract as they cool, the pattern must be made approx. 0.5% to 2% bigger than the casting. Applications include: engine block made of cast iron EN-GJL-200, crankshaft made of nodular cast iron EN-GJS-700-2.

A core must be inserted into the mould in order to obtain a cavity. In order to cast the two-part Pattern, the lower pattern half and the bottom box are filled with moulding sand. The sand is compressed by tamping. The top box is placed on top of the bottom box after the latter has been turned over. Then patterns are inserted for the funnel and feeders and the moulding sand is added and tamped. When the top box is lifted off, both pattern halves and pattern parts are removed. Chamfers and a runner are then cut into the moulding sand and the core is inserted. Joining the top and bottom boxes together creates a cavity which corresponds to the shape of the workpiece.

The mould is filled through the funnel. Feeders allow air to escape during the filling process. The large feeder cross-sections enable liquid metal to continue flowing into the solidifying workpiece during cooling, thus preventing blowholes. After cooling, the mould is destroyed and the casting removed.

Pressure die-casting

Pressure die-casting involves forcing metal swiftly in a liquid or paste-like state at high pressure into a permanent mould (steel mould).

Non-ferrous heavy-metal alloys (e.g. throttle valve housings made of zinc casting alloys) and light-metal alloys (e.g. forged pistons and rims as well as housings made of aluminium or magnesium casting alloys) are often manufactured by means of pressure die-casting.

Advantages of pressure die-casting:
- Castings with maximum dimensional accuracy.
- Manufacture of finished parts possible because bores and threads can be cast. Only burrs and the funnel need to be removed.

Investment casting (pattern melt-out process)

Investment casting is a casting process with broken (melted-out) patterns in a broken, one-part mould.

Patterns are manufactured from wax or plastic based on a sample and are combined into a pattern nest. The pattern nest is immersed repeatedly into a ceramic paste, covered with ceramic powder and then dried. The casting mould is burned in order to increase strength. The patterns melt out in the process and form blowholes for pouring in. Applications include: piston rings, turbine wheels.

Advantages of investment casting:
- Virtually all materials can be cast, even metals which are difficult to machine.
- Good for the smallest parts and low wall thicknesses.
- Very high dimensional accuracy.
- High surface quality, without burrs.
- Casting of finished parts possible, subsequent machining on locating surfaces only.
- Manufacture of complicated parts possible.

Centrifugal casting

The melting mass is cast into a permanent mould (casting die) rotating at high speed and thrown by centrifugal force against the inner walls of the mould, where it solidifies.

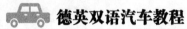

Horizontal centrifugal casting. Used to manufacture liners and piston rings, for example.

Vertical centrifugal casting. Used to manufacture flat components such as gear wheels and pulleys.

Advantages of centrifugal casting:

• Centrifugal force brings about a compressed structure of increased strength compared with casting with gravitational force.

• Structure is free of pinholes, blowholes and contaminants which have a lower density than the melting mass.

Gravity die-casting

The melting mass is cast by gravity into permanent metal moulds (casting dies).

Compared with sand casting, the casting die produces increased surface quality. Heat dissipation can be specifically influenced. Thus, for example, when a camshaft is being cast, inserted casting dies at the subsequent bearings can effect such a rapid removal of heat that the surface is hardened. Applications: rims, gear wheels, etc.

New Words

melt	融化，熔化	chamfer	倒角
mould	模具，模型	runner	横浇道
cavity	腔，洞	cross-section	横截面
pattern	模样	blowhole	通气孔
brokensandmould	易碎的砂模	pressure die-casting	压力铸造
contour	轮廓，周线	bore	镗孔
contract	收缩，缩小	thread	螺纹
crankshaft	曲轴	burr	毛边
engine block	发动机缸体	investmentcasting	熔模铸造
nodular cast iron	球墨铸铁	one-part mould	单件式铸型
core	型芯	immerse	浸，泡
two-part Pattern	半分模样	pistonring	活塞环
tamp	捣固	turbinewheel	涡轮
topbox	上砂箱	centrifugalcasting	离心铸造
bottombox	下砂箱	rotate	旋转
mouldingsand	型砂	liner	气缸套
funnel	浇口	gearwheel	齿轮
feeder	冒口		

制造技术篇

Kapitel 2　Fertigungstechnik // Chapter 2　Production engineering

课文参考译文

铸造

在铸造过程中，将熔化的金属注入一个铸型中。这些熔化的金属会充满铸型的空腔。在熔化的金属固化后，就会形成工件的初始形状。

使用永久模的砂型铸造

模样用于制作砂型。这些模样用于模制工件的外形。砂型是一种铸造后不可再用的铸型。由于铸造金属会随着冷却而收缩，所以模样必须比铸件大约0.5%~2%。应用举例：发动机气缸体用铸铁EN-GJL-200铸造而成，曲轴用球墨铸铁EN-GJS-700-2铸造而成。

必须将型芯插入铸型中，才能获得型腔。为了铸造半分模样，下半模样和下砂箱要填满型砂，并将型砂捣实。然后将其翻过来，上面再合上上砂箱。然后，为模样插上浇口和冒口，并且填充型砂并捣实。当提起上砂箱后，便可取出两半模样和模样零件。然后在型砂上切出倒角和横浇道，插入型芯。将上、下砂箱扣合在一起，从而形成与工件外形相同的型腔。

通过浇口注入液态金属。在浇注过程中，冒口能使空气逸出。冒口横截面较大，从而在冷却过程中，仍可使液态金属慢慢地流回到正在固化的工件上。冷却之后，打碎铸型，取出铸件。

压力铸造

压力铸造是在高压下迫使液态或膏状金属快速充入永久铸型（钢质铸型）中的一种铸造方法。

有色重金属合金零件（如用锌合金铸造而成的节气门体）和轻金属合金零件（如模锻活塞和轮辋，以及用铝合金或镁合金铸造的壳体类零件）常常用压力铸造来生产。

压力铸造的优点：

铸件的尺寸精度最高。

由于孔和螺纹都可以铸造出来，所以可能制造出不需其他加工的零件，只需去毛刺和浇口即可。

熔模铸造

熔模铸造是使用熔化（熔化后冒出）模样和一个易碎的单件式铸型进行铸造的一种铸造方法。

按照样本，用蜡或塑料制成模样，并将模样组合成模样组。将模样反复浸入陶瓷膏中，再撒上陶瓷粉并干燥。烧制铸型，以便提高强度。在这个过程中，模样熔化，从而形成型腔孔。熔模铸造的应用举例：活塞环、涡轮等。

熔模铸造的优点：

实际上所有的材料，甚至包括难加工的金属，都可以用于熔模铸造。

可用于制造最小的零件和壁厚很薄的零件。

铸造的尺寸精度非常高。

铸件表面质量高，无毛边。

可以铸造成品件，仅需要对局部表面进行后续加工。

可以制造复杂零件。

离心铸造

将熔化的金属倒入高速旋转的永久铸型中，这些金属会因离心力被抛向铸型的内壁上，并在那里凝固。

水平离心铸造。这种方法可用于制造气缸套和活塞环。

垂直离心铸造。这种方法用于制造像齿轮和带轮这样的扁平形的零件。

离心铸造的优点：

与采用重力铸造相比，离心力产生压缩作用，所以离心铸造提高了铸件的强度。

铸件结构内无销孔、通气孔和杂质（因为杂质的密度比熔化的金属小）。

金属型铸造

将熔化的金属在重力的作用下流入永久铸型中。

与砂型铸造相比，永久铸型会使铸件表面质量提高。可以对散热进行专门的干预，例如，在铸造凸轮轴时，在后面的轴承处嵌入铸型就能使铸件快速冷却，从而产生表面硬化效应。金属型铸造的应用举例：轮辋、齿轮等。

制造技术篇

Kapitel 2　Fertigungstechnik // Chapter 2　Production engineering

Teil 4　Schmieden　锻造技术
Part 4　Forming　锻造技术

【知识目标】
1. 掌握与锻造技术相关的专业术语、单词和词汇。
2. 掌握锻造技术的德文、英文表达方法。

【能力目标】
1. 能对锻造技术专业方面进行中、德、英互译。
2. 能进行与锻造技术相关的德语、英语资料的阅读和翻译。
3. 能在锻造机械实物上标识出相应结构的德语、英语单词和词汇。

Text 1　Schmieden锻造技术（德文）

Freiformen und Gesenkformen

Schmieden ist Druckumformen von warmen Metallen im plastischen Zustand.Beim Schmieden formt man Werkstücke meist in glühendem Zustand durch Schlag oder Druck spanlos um. Durch Stauchen und Strecken des Werkstoffes wird sein Gefüge geändert. Geschmiedete Werkstücke haben einen zusammenhängenden Faserverlauf. Das dichte Gefüge und der beanspruchungsgerechte Faserverlauf gewährleisten die hohe Festigkeit und Belasbarkeit von Schmiedestücke.

Schmiedbarkeit der Werkstoffe

Die wichtigsten schmiedbaren Metalle sind Stahl, Aluminium und seine Legierungen, Kupfer, CuZn-und CuSn-Legierungen. Gusseisen ist nicht schmiedebar, weil es beim Erwärmen nicht knetbar wird. Mit zunehmenden Kohlenstoffgehalt und höhere Legierungsbestandteilen nimmt die Dehnung und damit die Schmiedebarkeit der Stähle ab. Je geringer der Kohlenstoffgehalt eines unlegierten Stahles ist, desto höher muss die Schmiedetemperatur sein. Die Schmiedebarkeit von Werkstoffen ist auch abhängig von der Anfangs-und Endschmiedetemperaturen, die nicht über-bzw. Unterschritten werden dürfen. Beim Formen im Bereich der angegebenen Temperaturn wird das Gefüge dicht und fein und die Festigkeit hoch. Erwärmt man über die Anfangstemperatur hinaus und hält das Werkstück längere Zeit auf diese Temperatur, wird der Stahl überhitzt. Überhitzter Stahl ist grobkörnig und spröde.

Freiformen

Beim Freiformen kann der Werkstoff zwischen den Wirkflächen von Amboss und Hammer bzw. Presse frei verdrängt werden.

Freiformen kann erfolgen durch

– Stauchen, eine verringerung der Höhe bei gleichzeitiger Querschnittvergrösserung der erwärmten Werkstückzone.

– Abzeten, Schmieden eines scharfkantigen Absatzes.

– Recken(Strecken), eine Verlängerung des Werkstücks bei gleichzeitiger Querschnittverminderung.

Schmiedewerkzeuge

Das Schmieden von Hand geschieht vorwiegend auf dem Amboss . Ambosshilfswerkzeuge werden in die Löcher im Amboss eingesteckt. Schmiedezangen dienen zum Festhalten der warmen Werkstücke. Mit Schmiedehämmer wird die Umformkraft erzeugt.

Schmiedemaschinen

Maschinenhämmer formen durch Schläge, wobei grosse Werkstücke nicht bis in den Kern verdichtet werden. Schmiedepressen formen durch Druck und kneten den Werkstoff bis in den Kern durch.

Gesenkformen

Beim Gesenkformen wird ein schmiedewarmer Rohling in eine entsprechende Hohlform (Gesenk) geschlagen oder gepresst.

Beim Gesenkformen ist der Werkstoff ganz oder zu einem wesentlichen Teil von Gesenk umschlossen, während er beim Freiformen frei fliessen kann.

Gesenkschmieden

Gesenke bestehen meist aus zwei Hälften, dem Ober- und dem Untergesenk, deren Hohlräume der Form des fertigen Gesenkschmiedeteils entsprechen. Durch meist mehrmaliges Schlagen wird aus dem schmiedewarmen Rohling das Werkstück geformt.

Gesenkpressen

Das Umformen erfolgt durch die Druckkraft einer Schmiedepresse. Durch genaue Führung zwischen Ober-und Untergesenk erreicht man große Herstellungsgenauigkeit und besonders gute Formannäherung des Schmiedestückes an das Fertigteil.

Vorteile des Umformens gegenüber spanender Formgebung

– Höhere Festigkeit der Werkstücke.

– Werkstoffsparnis, da geringer Abfall. Gestaltungsoptimierung.

– Kurze Fertigungszeit. rationelle Fertigung.

– gute Masshaltigkeit, hohe Oberflächengüte.

Arbeitsregeln

– Wärmebehandlungsvorschriften der Werkstofflieferer beachten.

– Vorschlaghammer neben dem Körper führen. Rundschlag verboten!

WIEDERHOLUNGSFRAGEN

1. Was versteht man unter Schmieden?
2. Welche Vorteile hat das Gesenkformen gegenüber der spanenden Formgebung?

Neue Wörter

	ausreichen	足够用于		der	Spielsitz	滑配合
der	Formteil	成型件，砂型		der	Preßsitz	压配合
	im Mittelalter	在中时期			außerordentlich	特别的
	übertreffen	胜过，超过			nämlich	即
die	Wucht	动能，动力		der	Steuerstand	控制台，操纵台
die	Bedarfform	需要的形状			übersehen	忽视
	mehr und mehr	越来越多			im Mittel bis zu	平均达到
der	Industriezweig	工业部门			abgeben	排出
die	Walze	轧辊，辊子			entgraten	去飞翅，清除飞边
	serienmäßig	成批的，连续的		das	Schnittwerkzeug	刀具，切边模
	wertvoll	贵重的，有价值的		die	Richtarbeit	矫正工作
der	Abfall	倾斜，斜坡，下降		die	Biegearbeit	压弯
das	Freiformschmieden	自由锻造，手工锻造		der	Brückenhammer	桥式锻锤
das	Gesenkschmieden	模锻		die	Reinhydraulische Presse	水压机
die	Paßfläche	配合面，对准面				

Text 2 Forming 锻造技术（英文）

Forming under compressive conditions

Forming under compressive conditions is the forming of a workpiece by compressive forces.

Following are the different processes:

• **Rolling.** Sections, sheets, pipes and wires are produced between rotating rollers.

• **Extrusion.** In the case of extrusion moulding, heated materials are pressed through a die-plate and shaped into sections. In the case of impact extrusion, materials are pressed with a punch and die plate into solid or hollow bodies.

• **Free forming** (forging).

• **Die forming** (drop forging).

Forging (free forming and die forming)

Forging is the forming of hot metals under compressive conditions in a plastic state.

Forging involves forming workpieces without cutting, usually while red-hot, by means of beating or compression. Upsetting and stretching the material changes the structure, in the course of which the fibre orientation is not interrupted. A tight structure and favourable fibre orientation increases the strength and stability under load of the forgings.

Free forming

In the case of free forming, the materials can be freely displaced between an anvil and a hammer or press.

The following different processes are available:

- Upsetting. Height is reduced, cross-section size increases.
- Stepping. Forging a sharp-edged step.
- Extending (stretching). Extending by reducing cross-section.

Die forming

Die forming involves beating or pressing the hot blank into a hollow mould (die).

In the case of die forming, the material is completely or significantly enclosed in the die while, in the case of free forming, it can be freely displaced in all directions.

Drop forging. Dies are usually made up of two halves, the upper die and the lower die. The cavities correspond to the shape of the finished drop forging. The workpiece is formed for the most part by repeated beating from the blank hot from forging. The volume of the blank here is somewhat greater than the volume of the finished part. This ensures that the hollow mould is filled completely. The burr created acts as a buffer and prevents hard beating of the die parts. The deformation rate is high.

Pressure forging. The forming force is applied by a forging press. The accuracy of manufacture is high thanks to the exact guidance of the upper and lower parts. The deformation rate is dependent on the material. For example, the rate is lower for titanium than for steel.

Application: titanium connecting rods for use in motor racing.

Advantages of (re)forming over metal-cutting shaping:

- Increased strength of workpieces.
- Workpiece savings due to little waste.
- Efficient production with high production members.
- Good dimensional stability and high surface quality.

Internal high-pressure forming (IHPF)

Internal high-pressure forming involves pressing a sheet-metal section under high pressure from the inside against a hollow mould.

This process facilitates the manufacture of hollow sections, e.g. roof frame of a light-alloy body. During production, a sheet metal section is inserted in a two-part mould, sealed by cylinders and filled with a liquid. The liquid is then subjected to a pressure of approx. 1,700 bar. The forces generated cause the section to adapt to the shape of the tool.

Advantages over extruded components:

- Components with different cross-sections can be manufactured in one workstep.
- Lower weight of components.
- More efficient production of expensive components in one workstep.
- High accuracy.

REVIEW QUESTIONS:

1. What do you understand by forging?
2. What are the advantages of die forming over cut- ting-shaping?

New Words

rolling	压延，轧制	press	压头
section	型材	stepping	制阶
sheet	板材	blank	坯件、坯料
rotating roller	旋转辊	sharp-edged step	薄边台阶
extrusion	挤压	drop forging	锻模
impact extrusion	冲击挤压成型	deformation rate	变形率
punch	冲击	pressure forging	压力锻造
die plate	模板	forging press	锻压机
free forming	自由成形	connecting rod	连杆
die forming	模制成型	metal-cutting shaping	金属切削成形
upsetting	镦粗	internal high-pressure forming	内部高压成型
stretching	拔长	facilitate	使（行动、过程）更容易
fibre orientation	纤维走向	about-sledge	大铁锤
anvil	铁砧		

课文参考译文

锻造（自由锻和模锻）

锻造是加热的金属材料在塑性状态下受到压缩作用而进行成型的方法。

锻造是指借助于冲击力或压力对毛坯进行成型且多半情况下不需进行切削加工的一种成型方法。毛坯的镦粗和拔长会改变材料的组织，但纤维的走向并没有被切断。在锻造力的作用下，紧密的组织和有益的纤维走向提高了强度和稳定性。

1. 自由锻成形

在自由锻的情况下，将毛坯材料自由地放在铁砧与锻锤或压头之间。自由锻有下面几种不同的方法：

镦粗。高度变小，横断面变大。

制阶。锻造出一个薄边台阶。

延展（拔长）。通过减小横截面使毛坯件长度增加。

2. 模锻成型

模锻成型是在冲击力或压力的作用下，使加热的坯料被挤入锻模中的一种成型方法。

在模锻的情况下，坯料完全或基本完全被封闭在锻模内，而在自由锻的情况下，坯料在变形方向不受约束，自由流动。

1）锤上模锻。通常，锻模是由上、下模两部分组成。锻模的空腔的形状与成品锻件外形相同。大多数情况下，加热的坯料要经过反复锤击，才能成型为锻件。坯料的体积要略大于成品锻件的体积，以确保完全充满锻模空腔。锻造所形成的毛边形成了缓冲区，以防对锻模的过度冲击。

2）压力锻造。通过锻压机产生的成型力进行锻造。因为有上、下导向装置的精确导向，压力锻造具有制造精度高的特点。变形量取决于坯料材质。例如，钛的变形量小于钢的变形量。

3）应用举例：赛车发动机钛连杆。

与金属切削成形相比，锻制成型的优点是：

提高了工件的强度。

由于加工余量小，废料少，节省坯料。

在产量高的情况下，生产效率高。

锻件尺寸稳定性好，表面质量高。

3. 内部高压成型（IHPF）

内部高压成型是在高压力作用下，从内部向着凹陷的锻模冲压金属板型材的成型方法。

这种方法使中空的零件，如轻合金车身的车顶框架的制造变得容易。在制造期间，将一块钢板型材插入两半式锻模中，内部充有一种液体，两端与液压缸相连。然后，将这种液体加压，使压力达到大约170MPa所产生的张力使型材的外形与模具的形状相适应。

与挤压成型相比，这种方法的优点有：

用一个成型步骤能制造出不同横断面的零件。

零件重量轻。

用一个成型步骤实现昂贵零件的高效率生产。

成型件精度高。

Kapitel 2　Fertigungstechnik // Chapter 2　Production engineering

Teil 5　Trennen durch Spanen　切削加工
Part 5　Cutting and shaping with machine tools　切削加工

【知识目标】
1. 掌握与切削加工方面等相关的专业术语、单词和词汇。
2. 掌握切削加工的德文、英文表达方法。

【能力目标】
1. 能对切削加工内容进行中、德、英互译。
2. 能进行与切削加工相关的德文、英文资料的阅读和翻译。
3. 能在加工机床实物上标识出相应结构的德语、英语单词和词汇。

Text 1　Trennen durch Spanen切削加工（德文）

Spanen ist das mechanische Abtrennen von ungeformten Stoffteilchen. Der Zusammenhalt eines Stoffes wird örtlich aufgehoben.

Die Verfahren zur spanenden Formung werden nach Schnittbewegung und Schneidengeometrie unterschieden. Die Schnittbewegung kann durch das Werkzeug oder das Werkstück ausgeführt werden.

Die für die spanende Formung verwendeten Werkzeuge heben mit ihrer Schneide Späne vom Werkstoff ab. Dabei sind folgende vier Grundforderungen zu erfüllen:

– Die bearbeitete Fläche soll so glatt werden wie erforderlich.
– die Bearbeitungszeit soll möglichst kurz sein.
– der Kraftaufwand am Werkzeug soll möglichst klein sein.
– die Standzeit des Werkzeuges soll möglichst groß sein.

Grundlagen der spanenden Formung von Maschinen

Bei der spanenden Formung von Hand werden Werkstücke mittels einfacher Werkzeuge, wie z.B. Meißel, Säge, Feile bearbeitet.

Grundform der Werkzeugschneide aller Werkzeuge zur spanenden Formung ist der Keil (Schneidkeil).

Flächen und Winkel am Schneidkeil

Spanfläche ist die Fläche am Schneidkeil, an der Span abläuft. Freifläche ist die Fläche am Schneidkeil, die der entstehenden Werkstückoberfläche (Arbeitsfläche) gegenüberliegt.

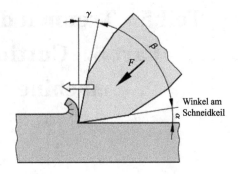

Bild : Winkel am Schneidkeil

Freiwinkel α ist der freie Winkel zwischen Schneidkeil und Werkstückoberfläche (Schnittfläche). Bei zu kleinem Freiwinkel reibt der Rücken des Schneidkeils auf der Werkstückoberfläche.

Keilwinkel β ist der Winkel des in das Werkstück eindringenden Schneidkeils, der von Freifläche und Spanfläche eingeschlossen wird.

Weiche Werkstoffe ermöglichen kleine Keilwinkel.

Harte Werkstoffe erfordern große Keilwinkel.

Spanwinkel γ ist der Winkel zwischen Spanfläche- an dieser gleitet der Span entlang- und einer gedachten Linie senkrecht zur Bearbeitungsrichtung. Der Spanwinkel kann positiv oder negativ sein. Bei negativem Spanwinkel wirkt das Werkzeug schabend, die Werkstoffabtragung ist dabei sehr gering.

Meißeln

Der Meißel dient zur Spanabnahme und zum Trennen.

Man unterscheidet am Meißel Schneide, Kopf und Schnittkraft. Die Meißelschaft ist an den Schmalseiten gerundet oder hat einen achtkantigen Querschnitt, damit er gut in der Hand liegt. Der Meißelkopf ist verjüngt und ballig.

Der Keilwinkel der Meißelschneide liegt zwischen 40° und 70°; zur Bearbeitung von mittelhartem Stahl wählt man etwa 60°.

Meißelarten

– Flachmeißel haben eine breite, gerade Schneide und dienen zur Spanabnahme und zum Trennen.

– Kreuzmeißel, mit schmaler und quer stehender Schneide zum Meißelschaft, dienen zum Ausmeißeln schmaler Nuten.

– Nutenmeißel mit breiter bogenförmiger Schneide werden zum Aushauen von Blechteilen verwendet.

– Hohlmeißel dienen zum Aushauen von Rundungen in Blechen.

– Trennstemmer haben vier gerade Schneiden und dienen zum Durchtrennen von Stegen zwischen Bohrungen.

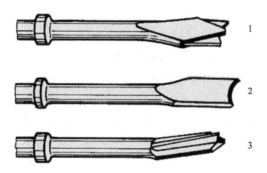

Bild : Meißeleinsätze

Zum Themen von Karosserieteilen, Lösen von Punktschweißungen, Schneiden und Trennen von Auspufftöpfen und Anschlüssen, Abscheren von Nieten können Meißeleinsätze in druckluftbetriebenen Meißelhämmern verwendet werden.

Meißelvorgang

Span-und Freiwinkel hängen von der Meißelhaltung ab. Eine flache Meißelhaltung ergibt einen kleinen Freiwinkel, der Meißel neigt dazu, aus dem Werkstück herauszutreten. Bei einem zu großen Freiwinkel dringt der Meißel zu tief in das Werkstück ein, der Span wird zu dick und die Schnittkraft zu groß.

Bei senkrechter Haltung des Meißels zur Werkstückoberfläche wirkt der Meißel trennend (zerteilend) und nicht spanend. Span- und Freiwinkel sind beim Trennen 0°.

Universaldrehmaschine

Bild: Universaldrehmaschine

Auf ihr können fast alle Vorkommenden Dreharbeiten ausgeführt werden. Da sie meist eine Leit- und Zugspindel besitzt, wird sie auch als Leit- und Zugspindeldrehmaschine (LZD) bezeichnet.

Hauptbaugruppen

- Gestell
- Drehmaschinenbett
- Spindelstock
- Werkzeugschlitten
- Leitspindel
- Zugspindel
- Reitstock.

Drehmaschinenbett. Es besteht aus den beiden, meist prismatischen Drehmaschinenwangen, mit gehärteten Führungsbahnen, auf denen Werkzeugschlitten und Reitstock geführt werden.

Spindelstock. In ihm ist die Arbeitsspindel gelagert und geführt. Die Arbeitsspindel dient zur Aufnahme der Spannmittel, z.B. Drehmaschinenfutter. Sie ist hoch, um Stangenmaterial hindurchführen zu können. Der Antrieb der Arbeitsspindel erfolgt über einen Elektromotor, dem ein Getriebe nachgeschaltet ist.

Werkzeugschlitten. Er dient zum Spannen und Bewegen der Drehwerkzeuge. Er besteht aus folgenden Hauptteilen

- Schlosskasten mit Schaltelementen für Zug- und Leitspindel.
- Bettschlitten.
- Querschlitten.
- Oberschlitten.

Schlosskasten. Er enthält die Schaltelemente zur Einleitung der Bewegungsvorgänge für Bett- und Querschlitten. Die Zugspindel besteht meist aus einer glatten Welle mit Längsnut. Sie überträgt die Kräfte für die Längs- und die Querbewegung der einzelnen Schlitten. Die Leitspindel besitzt ein genau gearbeitetes Trapezgewinde, das nur beim Gewindeschneiden zur Bewegung des Werkzeugschlittens verwendet werden darf. Der Bettschlitten dient zur Längsbewegung und der Querschlitten (Planschlitten) zur Querbewegung und des Drehwerkzeugs. Mit dem Oberschlitten kann das Drehwerkzeug in der Ebene der X- und der Z- Achse in beliebiger Richtung von Hand bewegt werden.

Reitstock. Er dient als Gegenlager beim Drehen zwischen den Spitzen, sowie zur Aufnahme von Werkzeugen, z.B. Bohr- und Senkwerkzeugen. Er wird auf den Drehmaschinenwangen geführt und kann an jeder beliebigen Stelle durch einen Spannhebel festgeklemmt werden.

Spannen der Werkstücke

Drehteile müssen entsprechend ihrer Form auf der Drehmaschine gespannt werden. Folgende Spannmittel werden dabei verwendet

- Spannfutter
- Zentrierspitzen
- Spannzange
- Planscheibe

Spannfutter. Es gibt Drei- und Vierbackenfutter. Zylindrische Werkstücke können in beiden

Spannfuttern gespannt werden. Mehrkantwerkstücke, deren Kantenzahl durch 3 teilbar ist, werden im Dreibackenfutter gespannt. Ist die Kantzahl durch 4 teilbar, so werden sie im Vierbackenfutter gespannt.

WIEDERHOLUNGSFRAGEN

1. Wie wirkt sich die Meißelhaltung auf Frei- und Spanwinkel aus?
2. Wovon ist der Keilwinkel der Meißelschneide abhängig?
3. Wodurch unterscheiden sich Spanen und Trennen?
4. Wie wird mit dem Trennstemmer gearbeitet?
5. Wie ist die Vorschubrichtung beim Längs- und beim Querdrehen?

Neue Wörter

die	Maschine	机床	die	Schmierung	润滑
die	Ebenfläche	平面	de	Querschnitt	横断面，横切口，截面
die	Zylinderfläche	柱面	das	Schruppen	粗加工
die	Längsbewegung	纵向运动	das	Schlichten	精整加工，修整，上涂料，上浆胶，精轧，光轧
die	Querbewegung	横向运动			
der	Span	木屑，铁屑	der	Freiwinkel	后角
die	Schnittkraft	切削力	die	Reibung	摩擦，摩擦力
das	Werkstück	工件		senkrecht	垂直的，立的
der	Spindelstock	主轴箱	die	Horizontale	水平线
die	Führungsbahn	导轨	die	Wende	转弯，回转，转弯处
das	Profil	外形，剖面图	die	Schneidplatte	刀片
das	Gewinde	螺纹		schneiden	切断，切割，切削，交会，(相)切
	rund	圆的			
der	Vorschub	走刀，送进，进给，送料	das	Futter	炉衬，衬里，衬垫，卡盘，饲料

Text 2 Cutting and shaping with machine tools 切削加工（英文）

Basics of cutting and shaping with machine tools

Machine tools for cutting and shaping can machine flat, cylindrical, tapered and curved surfaces.

To obtain a specific surface, it is necessary to move the workpiece and the tool towards each other accordingly.

Motions/movements on machine tools

There are three different types of cutting motion:

- Primary or cutting motion.

- Feed motion.
- Positioning motion.

Primary or cutting motion v_c. This is executed either by the tool or by the workpiece.

> The cutting speed v_c is the speed at which the chip is removed.

The cutting speed is generally given in m/min, but in the case of grinding is given in m/s.

Feed motion v_f. This can be executed manually (by hand) or automatically by the machine.

> The rate of feed v_f (mm/min) is the speed at which the workpiece and tool move towards each other during cutting.

Feed f is the travel of the tool, e.g. when drilling, grinding or milling. When turning, feed f is the travel of the tool during one rotation of the tool.

Positioning motion a_p, a_e. This is the motion between the workpiece and the tool which determines the thickness of the chip to be removed.

The cutting speed, rate of feed and positioning motion are dependent on:
- the operating process and the design of the machine.
- the material to be cut.
- the cutting material of the tool.
- the required surface quality.
- the cooling and lubrication of the tool's cutting edge.
- the required life of the tool.

Chip formation

> During each chipping operation, the material is upset, separated and removed in the form of a chip via the face by the penetrating cutting wedge of the tool cutting edge.

Types of chip

Tearing chips are produced from brittle materials, e.g. grey cast iron, at small cutting angles, low cutting speeds and a large cutting depth. In the process, the surface becomes rough and loses its dimensional and geometrical accuracy.

Shearing chips are produced from tough materials at medium cutting angles and low cutting speeds. These chips flake off, bond with each other partially and for the most part form short helical chips. They are not an impediment to the work sequence.

Flowing chips are produced from tough materials at large cutting angles, high cutting speeds and low to medium cutting depth. Smooth workpiece surfaces of high surface quality are obtained. These types of chips are therefore the desired end result. Long, continuous flowing chips can hinder the work sequence, for instance, where automatic lathes are used.

Built-up edge. This is formed during the cutting process on the face of the tool. A built-up edge may be formed at excessively slow cutting speeds or in the event of insufficient cooling lubrication or an excessively rough tool face. The deposit of material particles alters the angles at the cutting wedge unfavourably and causes a rough workspiece surface. A built-up edge is not formed on oxide-ceramic or diamond tools.

Cooling and lubrication during cutting

During cutting-shaping, heat is generated as a result of friction at the tool's cutting edge and in the edge zone of the workpiece. If there is inadequate cooling lubrication during cutting, temperatures in excess of 1,000 ℃ may arise at the tool and in the edge zone of the workpiece.

Possible consequences of inadequate cooling lubrication:
- Premature tool wear.
- Dimensional deviations.
- Reduced surface quality.
- Cracking in the workpiece edge zone.
- Reduced strength.

During metal-cutting manufacturing processes, the following are used, depending on the cutting speed: non-water-soluble cooling lubricants, e.g. cutting oils with additives, and water-soluble cooling lubricants, e.g. drilling oil with water (cooling lubricant emulsion).

Low cutting speed → small cooling effect required → non-water-soluble cooling lubricants, e.g. thread-cutting.

High cutting speed → large cooling effect required → water-mixable cooling lubricants, e.g. drilling, turning, milling.

Disposal. Used cooling lubricants must be handled as hazardous waste.

REVIEW QUESTIONS

1. What are the different movements/motions involved in cutting with machine tools?
2. What do you understand by cutting speed and rate of feed?
3. What are the potential consequences of inadequate cooling lubrication during cutting by machine?

New Words

machine tool	机床	feed motion	进给运动
flat surface	平面	positioning motion	吃刀运动
cylindrical surface	柱面	chip	碎片，碎屑
tapered surface	锥面	grind	磨碎，磨削
curved surface	曲面	drill	钻，钻削
cutting motion	切削运动	mill	铣，铣削
primary motion	主运动	rotation	旋转，转动

fate of feed	进给速度	built-up edge	切屑瘤，积屑瘤
lubrication	润滑	insufficient	不足的，不够的
penetrate	穿透，穿过，刺入	deposit	沉淀堆积
cutting wedge	切削楔	alter	改变，更改
tearing chip	粒状切屑	friction	摩擦
shearing chip	剪切切屑	inadequate	不充足的，不适当的
flowing chip	带状切屑	in excess of	多于，超出
brittle material	脆性材料	premature	过早的，提前的
grey cast iron	灰铸铁	tool wear	刀具磨损
cutting angle	切削角	deviation	偏离，偏差
dimensional accuracy	尺寸精确度	crack	破裂，开裂，断裂
geometrical accuracy	几何精确度	non-water-soluble	非水溶性的
tough material	韧性材料	water-soluble	水溶性的
flake off	剥落	thread-cutting	螺纹切削
bond with ...	与……相粘连，相黏结	turning	车削
helical chip	螺旋形切屑	disposal	废品处置
impediment	妨碍，障碍	hazardous	有危险的
lathe	车床		

课文参考译文

切削加工

机床切削成形基础

切削成形机床可以加工平面、柱面、锥面和曲面。为了获得特定的表面，必须使工件和工具发生相对运动。

1. 机床的运动

在机械加工时，机床有下面三种运动：

主运动即切削运动。

进给运动。

吃刀运动。

1）主运动（或叫切削运动）。主运动或由工具或由工件来执行。

切削速度v_c也是切屑退出的速度。切屑速度一般用m/min作单位，但在磨削的情况下用m/s作单位。

2）进给运动v_f。进给运动通过手动的方式来完成，或者通过机床自动完成。

制造技术篇

Kapitel 2　Fertigungstechnik // Chapter 2　Production engineering

进给运动的速度v_f（mm/min）是切削期间工件和工具相对运动的速度。

进给量f就是工具的运动量（例如，在钻削、磨削和铣削时），或者是在工具转一转期间工具的移动量（例如车削时）。

3）吃刀运动a_p、a_e。这是工件与工具之间的决定切屑厚度的运动。

切削速度、进给速度和吃刀量的大小取决于下列因素：
- 机床的操作过程和结构。
- 被切削的材料。
- 工具的切削刃材料。
- 要求的表面质量。
- 工具切削刃的冷却和润滑状况。
- 所要求的工具寿命。

2. 切削的类型

在每个切削成形工艺中，材料都要在工具切削刃的切削楔的作用下，先受到挤压和分离，然后以切削的形式经过工具的前刀面排出。

粒状切屑是由脆性材料（如灰铸铁）在切削角小、切削速度低、切削深度大的情况下所产生的切屑。在形成这种切屑的过程中，切削表面变粗糙，因而尺寸精度和几何精度下降。

剪切切屑是由韧性材料在切削角为中等大小、切削速度低、切削深度中等以下的情况下所产生的切屑。这些切屑剥落，部分相互粘结在一起，并且大多数形成短的螺旋形切屑。这种切屑对加工过程并无妨碍。

带状切屑是由韧性材料在切削角大、切削速度高、切削深度中等以下的情况下所产生的切屑。在这种情况下，会得到高质量的平滑的工件表面，因此，希望产生这种切屑。但是，在使用自动车床等情况下，长长的连续不断的切屑会妨碍加工过程。

切削刃沉积加厚是在切削期间在工具的前刀面上出现的一种现象。在切削速度极低，或在冷却和润滑不足，或在工具前刀面过于粗糙的情况下，刀具的切削刃就会出现沉积加厚的现象。材料颗粒的堆积改变了切削楔的角度，从而导致了工件表面变粗糙。在氧化物陶瓷刀具和金刚刀具上不会出现沉积加厚现象。

3.切削期间的冷却和润滑

在切削成形期间，由于刀具切削刃与工件之间的摩擦，会产生热量。如果在切削期间，冷却与润滑不足，刀具和工件切削区就会出现超过1000℃的温度。

冷却和润滑不足可能后果有：
- 刀具早期磨损。
- 尺寸偏差增大。
- 表面质量下降。
- 工件切削区开裂。
- 强度下降。

在金属切削的生产过程中，根据切削速度的不同，使用的切削液有：不溶于水的切削液（例如，带有添加剂的切削油）和水溶性切削液［例如，含有水的钻削油（冷却润滑乳液）］。

1）低切削速度。此时需要小的冷却强度，所以采用不溶于水的切削液，例如用于螺纹切削。

2）高切削速度。此时需要大的冷却强度，所以采用溶于水的切削液，例如用于钻削、车削和铣削。

切削液在报废时必须作为危险废物来处理。

制造技术篇

Kapitel 2　Fertigungstechnik // Chapter 2　Production engineering

Teil 6　Drehen　车削
Part 6　Turning　车削

学习目标

【知识目标】
1. 掌握与车削加工方面等相关的专业术语、单词和词汇。
2. 掌握车削加工的德文、英文表达方法。

【能力目标】
1. 能对车削加工内容进行中、德、英互译。
2. 能进行与车削加工相关的德语、英语资料的阅读和翻译。
3. 能在车床实物上标识出相应结构的德语、英语单词和词汇。

Text 1　Drehen 车削（德文）

Drehen ist ein maschinell spanendes Fertigungsverfahren mit geomdetrisch bestimmter Schneide. Mit einem einschneidigen Werkzeug werden dabei runde oder ebene Flächen herstellt.

Einteilung der Drehverfahren

Sie erfolgt nach der

— Lage der Bearbeitungsflächen in Außen- und Innendrehen.

— Vorschubrichtung in Längsdrehen (Runddrehen) und Querdrehen (Plandrehen).

— erzeugten Fläche in Runddrehen, Plandrehen, Profildrehen, Formdrehen, Gewindedrehen.

Vorschbbewegung. Sie erfolgt beim Längsdrehen in der Z-Achse (Werkstückachse), beim Querdrehen in X-Achse (quer zur Werkstückachse). Der Vorschub f wird in mm je Umdrehung angegeben. Er beeinflusst die Oberflächengüte der Drehfläche.

Bewegungsvorgänge beim Drehen

Schnittbewegung. Sie erfolgt durch das in der Drehmaschine eingespannte Werkstück, das die Drehbewegung aufführt. Aus dem Durchmesser und der Drehzahl ergibt sich die Schnittgeschwindigkeit, die in m/min angegeben wird. Die Schnittgeschwindigkeit ist von folgenden Faktoren abhängig:

- Werkstoff
- Kühlschmierung
- Schneidstoff
- Oberflächengüte

Zustellbewegung. Sie erfolgt beim Längsdrehen in der *X*-Achse, beim Querdrehen in der *Z*-Achse. Die Schnitttiefe *a* entspricht der Zustellung des Drehmeißels.

Spanbildung

Durch das Zusammenwirken von Schnittbewegung und Vorschubbewegung bei vorgegebener Zustellung entsteht ein Span mit dem Spanungsquerschnitt *A*.

Spanungsquerschnitt *A*. Er ist das Produkt aus dem Vorschub *f* und der Schnitttiefe *a*. Für eine möglichst kurze Fertigungszeit muss mit hoher Schnittgeschwindigkeit und großem Spanungsquerschnitt gedreht werden. Diese Forderungen werden begrenzt durch die Leistungsfähigkeit der Drehmaschine, die Standzeit des Drehwerkzeuges und die Oberflächengüte.

Daher muss bei großen Spanabnahmen in mehreren Stufen gedreht werden, z.B. erst Schruppen, dann Schlichten.

Schneidengeometrie am Drehmeßel

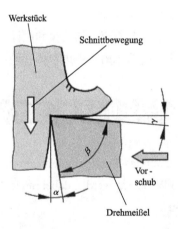

Bild: Winkel und Flächen am Drehmeißel

Winkel und Flächen. Der Drehmeißel entspricht in seiner Grundform einem Keil mit Freiwinkel α, Keilwinkel β, und Spanwinkel γ. Der Span wird an der Schnittfläche des Werkstücks durch den Drehmeißel abgenommen.

Haupt- und Nebenschneide. Die Hauptschneide weist zur Vorschubrichtung. Sie bewirkt das eigentliche Spanen. Haupt- und Nebenschneide bilden eine gerundete Schneidenecke. Sie wirkt sich auf die Tiefe der entstehenden Riefen aus.

Freiwinkel α. Er wird durch die Freifläche und die Senkrechte an die Schnittfläche begrenzt. Seine Größe bestimmt die Reibung bzw. die Flächenpressung zwischen Werkstück und Drehmeißel.

Keilwinkel β. Er wird von der Freifläche und der Spanfläche gebildet. Seine Größe richtet sich nach dem zu bearbeitenden Werkstoff und nach der Oberflächengüte.

制造技术篇

Kapitel 2　Fertigungstechnik // Chapter 2　Production engineering

Spanwinkel γ. Er wird von einer horizontalen Ebene durch die Drehachse und der Spanfläche gebildet.

Einstellwinkel χ. Er wird von der Hauptschneide und der Drehteilkontur gebildet. Zusammen mit der Zustellbewegung bestimmt er die beim Spanen wirksame Schneidenlänge.

Spannen der Drehmeißel

Der Drehmeißel muss möglichst kurz und fest gespannt werden. Die Schneidenecke wird dabei normalerweise auf Werkstückmitte (Höhe der Drehachse) eingestellt. In dieser Einstellung haben Frei- und Spanwinkel ihre richtige Größe.

Wendeschneidplatten. Sie besitzen mehrere Schneidkanten, die durch einfaches Drehen bzw. Wenden zum Einsatz gebracht werden können, wenn eine Schneide abgenützt ist. Dadurchentfällt das Nachschleifen des Drehmeißels. Wendeschneidplatten können durch unterschiedliche Klemmvorrichtungen im Klemmhalter befestigt werden.

Formen der Drehmeißel.

Man unterscheidet nach

– Schneidrichtung (R rechtsschneidend, L linksschneidend, N neutral)

– Lage der Eingriffsstelle (Außen-und Innendrehmeißel).

Neue Wörter

das	Drehwerkzeug (Drehstahl, Drehmeißel)	车刀			燕尾导轨，燕尾状导向装置
			die	Stirnfläche	端面，侧面
	widerstehen	抵抗，反对		aufspannen	夹紧
der	Langvorschub	纵走刀，纵向进给	die	Gradteilung	刻度，分度
der	Planvorschub	横走刀，横向进给		stillstehend	停顿的
	übernehmen	接受，承担	der	Neigungswinkel	倾斜角
der	Bettschlitten	纵滑板	der	Vorschubwinkel	进给角度
der	Planschlitten	横滑板		selbstständig	自动的
der	Oberschlitten	上滑板		ableiten	导出，引出
die	Drehscheibe	转盘，刻度盘	die	Schloßplatte	锁板
	ergeben	产生，引起	die	Drehmaschine	车床
das	Handrad	手轮		rund	圆的
	verschieben	移动，进给		spanabhebend	切削的
die	Mantelfläche	外表面，外壳面积		bearbeiten	加工
	abdrehen	车削，重车	das	Verfahren	方法
die	Deckfläche	盖板表面		außen	外部的
die	Schwalbenschwanzführung			innen	内部的

Text 2 Turning 车削（英文）

Turning is a machining manufacturing process with a geometrically defined cutting edge. Here, round or flat surfaces are produced with a single-edged tool.

Subdivision of turning processes

The processes are categorised in accordance with:

- the position of the machining surfaces into outside and inside turning.
- the feed direction into longitudinal turning (round turning) and lateral turning (facing).
- the created surface into round turning, facing, profiling, forming by turning and threading.

Motion processes when turning

Cutting motion. This is performed by the workpiece gripped in the lathe, which executes the rotary motion. The cutting speed is derived from the diameter and the rotational speed. It is important when selecting the cutting speed to take into account:

- Material
- Cutting material
- Cooling lubrication
- Surface quality

Feed motion. This is performed with longitudinal turning in the Z-axis (workpiece axis) and with lateral turning in the X-axis (transverse to the workpiece axis). The feed f is given in mm per revolution.

Positioning motion. This is performed with longitudinal turning in the X-axis and with lateral turning in the Z-axis. The cutting depth a corresponds to the positioning of the lathe tool.

The combination of cutting motion and feed motion with prespecified positioning results in a chip with the cutting cross-section A.

Cutting cross-section A. This is the product of the feed f and the cutting depth a. If large amounts of material are removed, it is essential to turn in several stages, e.g. first roughturn, then smooth.

Shapes of lathe tools. Lathe tools are distinguished according to:

- cutting direction (R right-hand cutting, L left-hand cutting, N neutral).
- position of contact — outside and inside lathe tools.

Cutting edge geometry on lathe tool

Angles and surfaces. In its basic shape, a lathe tool is a wedge with a clearance angle α, wedge angle β and cutting angle γ. The chip is removed at the tool's cutting surface by the lathe tool.

Major and minor cutting edges. The major cutting edge points to the feed direction and performs the actual cutting. The major and minor cutting edges together form a rounded nose, which affects the depth of the furrows created.

Clearance angle α. This is limited by the flank and the tangent to the cutting surface. Its size determines the friction or surface pressure between the workpiece and the lathe tool during the turning operation.

Wedge angle β. This is formed by the flank and the face. Its size depends on the material to be machined.

Cutting angle γ. This is formed by a horizontal plane through the rotational axis aid the face.

Indexable inserts. These have several cutting edges which can be brought into place simply by turning.

Gripping lathe tools

The lathe tool must be gripped as briefly and securely as possible. The nose is normally set to the centre of the workpiece (height of the rotational axis). The clearance and cutting angles are correctly sized in this setting.

Gripping workpieces

Parts to be turned must be gripped on the lathe on the basis of how they are shaped.

The following means of gripping are used:

- clamping chuck
- lathe centres
- collet chuck
- surface plate

Clamping chuck. There are three-and four-jaw chucks. Cylindrical workpieces can be gripped in both types of chuck. Multiple-edge workpieces whose number of edges is divisible by 3 are gripped in three-jaw chucks. If the number of edges is divisible by 4, then a four-jaw chuck is used.

REVIEW QUESTIONS：

1. What is the feed direction for longitudinal and for lateral turning?
2. Why should the lathe tool be set to the centre of the workpiece?
3. What working rules must be followed when turning?

New Words

single-edged	单刃的	right-hand cutting	右侧切削
subdivision	细分，分支	left-hand cutting	左侧切削
outside turning	外圆车削	outside lathe tool	外圆车刀
inside turning	内圆车削	inside lathe tool	内圆车刀
round turning	圆面车削	tangent to	正切
longitudinal	纵向的	indexable insert	可转位刀片，车刀镶块
lateral	横向的	clamping chuck	卡盘
profiling	仿形车削	lathe centre	车床顶尖
derive from	从……得到，推导出	surface plate	平板
take into account	考虑	divisible	可除尽的
revolution	旋转	shear force	剪力，剪切力
cross-section	横断面，横截面	chuck key	卡盘扳手，夹头钥匙

课文参考译文

车削

车削是使用规定几何形状的切削刃进行机械加工的一种方法。圆面或平面可用单切削刃工具进行加工。

（1）车削工艺的分类　车削按照下述方法进行分类

1）按照加工表面的位置可分为：外圆车削和内圆车削。

2）按照进给的方向可分为：纵向车削（圆面车削）和横向车削（端面车削）。

3）按照形成的表面的不同可分为：圆面车削、端面车削、仿形车削、车削成形和螺纹车削。

（2）车削时的运动

1）切削运动。夹紧在车床上的工件进行的旋转运动就是切削运动。切削速度可由直径和转速计算得出。选择切削速度时，必须考虑下列因素：材料、切削材料、切削料、表面质量。

2）进给运动。对于纵向车削，进给运动沿 Z 轴（工件轴线）方向；对于横向车削，进给运动则沿着 X 轴（与工件轴线垂直）的方向。进给量 f 的单位是mm/r。

3）吃刀运动。对于纵向车削，吃刀运动是沿 X 轴方向的运动；对于横向车削，吃刀运动是沿 Z 轴方向的运动；切削深度 a 等于车刀的吃刀量。

有了切削速度、进给速度和预定的吃刀量，就可以计算出切屑横断面积 A。

4）切削横断面积 A。切削横断面积 A 等于进给量 f 与切削深度 a 的乘积。如果需要去除大量的材料，必须分次车削。即先粗车，再精车。

5）车刀类型。车刀按照下列方式进行分类：

① 按照切削方向分 R（右侧切削）型、L（左侧切削）型和 N（两侧切削）型三种。

② 按照接触位置分外圆车刀和内圆车刀两种。

（3）车刀切削刃几何参数

1）车刀角度和表面。从基本形状来看，车刀就是一个带有前角 γ、楔角 β 和后角 α 的切削楔。切屑通过车刀的前刀面排出。

2）主切削刃和副切削刃。主切削刃朝向进给方向，完成实际切削工作。主、副切削刃一起形成圆滑的刀尖部分，这个部分将影响车削纹路的沟槽深度。

3）后角 α。后角的大小由主后刀面和主后刀面与切削面的切线所决定。后角的大小决定了工件与车刀之间的摩擦力或表面压力。

4）楔角 β。楔角是主后刀面与前刀面之间形成的夹角。其大小取决于待加工的材料。

5）前角 γ。前角是通过工件轴线的水平面与前刀面之间的夹角。

6）可转位车刀镶块。这些镶块具有若干个切削刃，只要转换位置就可更换切削刃。

（4）车刀的夹紧　车刀的夹紧必须尽可能简单和可靠。正常情况下，应将刀尖调到工件的中心高度，在这个高度，前角和后角的适当大小都能得到保证。

（5）工件的装夹　必须根据待车削的零件的成形方式，将其夹紧在车床上。可以采用下列夹紧方式：卡盘、套爪夹头、车床顶尖和平板。

卡盘：卡盘有三爪卡盘和四爪卡盘。圆柱形零件可以用这两种卡盘夹紧。多棱工件如果其棱数能被3除尽，也可用三爪卡盘夹紧。如果棱数能被4除尽，就用四爪卡盘夹紧。

Teil 7　Fräsen und Bohren　铣削和钻削
Part 7　Milling and Drilling　铣削和钻削

学习目标

【知识目标】
1. 掌握与铣削和钻削技术等相关的专业术语、单词和词汇。
2. 掌握铣削和钻削技术的德文表达方法。

【能力目标】
1. 能对铣削和钻削技术方面进行中、德、英互译。
2. 能进行与铣削和钻削技术相关的德文、英文资料的阅读和翻译。
3. 能在铣床和钻床实物上标识出相应结构的德语、英语单词和词汇。

Text 1　Fräsen und Bohren 铣削和钻削（德文）

Fräsen ist ein maschinell spanendes Fertigungsverfahren mit geometrisch bestimmten Schneiden. Dabei werden mit mehrschneidigen rotierenden Werkzeugen ebene und gekrümmte Flächen hergestellt.

Fräsvorgang

Das Fräswerkzeug führt eine kreisförmige Schnittbewegung (Hauptbewegung) aus. Vorschub- und Zustellbewegung erfolgen meistens durch das Werkstück. Nach der Lage der Fräserachse zum Werkstück unterscheidet man Umfangsfräsen und Stirnfräsen.

Umfangsfräsen. Hierbei liegt die Fräserachse parallel zur Fräsfläche. Beim Umfangsfräsen unterscheidet man Gegenlauffräsen und Gleichlauffräsen.

Gegenlauffräsen. Es erfolgt die Vorschubbewegung entgegengesetzt zur Schnittrichtung.

Gleichlauffräsen. Vorschub- und Schnittbewegung sind gleichgerichtet. Der Fräser hat eine längere Standzeit, Schnittleistung des Werkzeugs und Werkstückoberflächengüte nehmen im Vergleich zum Gegenlauffräsen zu. Gleichlauffräsen erfordert jedoch spezielle Werkzeugmaschinen.

Kapitel 2　Fertigungstechnik // Chapter 2　Production engineering

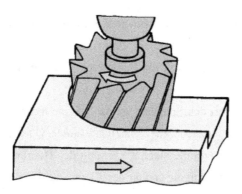

Bild: Stirnfräsen mit dem Walzenstirnfräser

Stirnfräsen. Bei diesem Verfahren steht die Fräserachse senkrecht zur Fräsfläche. Es schneiden mehrere Zähne gleichzeitig.

Bohren ist in der Metalltechnik ein maschinelles Spanen mit geometrisch bestimmten Schneiden und überwiegend mehrschneidigen Werkzeugen zur Herstellung von zylindrischen Löchern (Bohrungen).

Spiralbohrer. Er ist das meist verwendete Bohrwerkzeug. Seine Vorteile sind:

– günstige Winkel an den Schneiden.

– gute Einspanmöglichkeit.

– gleichbleibender Durchmesser beim Nachschleifen.

– selbsttätige Spanabfuhr.

– gute Zufuhr von Kühlschmierstoff.

Bohrvorgang. Die Haupt- bzw. Schnittbewegung ist immer eine Drehbewegung, die meist das Bohrwerkzeug ausführt. Gleichzeitig wird das Werkzeug in axialer Richtung gegen das Werkstück bewegt(Vorschub). Daraus ergibt sich eine kontinuierliche Spanbildung. Die Schnittgeschwindigkeit hängt im wesentlichen vom Werkstoff des Werkstücks und vom Schneidstoff des Bohrers ab. Der Vorschub ist vom Bohrerdurchmesser, vom zu bearbeitenden Werkstoff und vom Bohrverfahren abhängig.

Schneidengeometrie des Spiralbohrs

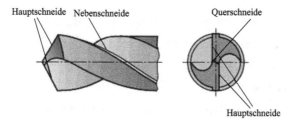

Bild: Spiralbohr

Hauptschneiden. Zwei schraubenförmige Spannuten bilden an der Bohrerspitze die Hauptschneiden. Sie übernehmen die eigentliche Zerspanungsarbeit.

Nebenschneiden. Sie werden durch die Spannuten an Schneidteil gebildet und glätten die Bohrung.

Querschneide. Sie erschwert den Spanungsvorgang, da sie nicht schneidet, sondern schabt. Bei großem Bohrerdurchmesser ist vorzubohren. Zusätzlich kann die Querschneide ausgespitzt werden.

Führungsfasen. Sie bewirken eine sichere Führung des Bohrers in der Bohrung. Außerdem vermindern sie die Reibung und somit die Gefahr des Klemmens des Bohrers in der Bohrung.

Spitzenwinkel. Er wird von den Hauptschneiden gebildet und ist abgestimmt auf den zu bearbeitenden Werkstoff. Für die Bearbeitung von Stahl, Stahlguss, Gusseisen, Temperguss, Kupfer-Zink- Legierungen beträgt er 118°.

Freiwinkel. Er ergibt sich durch Hinterschleifen der Hauptschneiden. Der Freiwinkel ermöglicht das Eindringen des Bohrers in den Werkstoff. Bei einem Spiralbohrer mit einem Spitzenwinkel von 118° ergibt sich bei richtigem Hinterschliff ein Querschneidenwinkel von 55°. Dies entspricht dem richtigen Freiwinkel für die Bearbeitung von Stahl.

Seitenspanwinkel γ. Es ist der Winkel der Spanflächen (Spannuten) mit der Achse des Bohrers. Er bestimmt den Spanwinkel. Seitenspanwinkel und Spanwinkel können durch Schleifen des Bohrers nicht geändert werden. Bei Spiralbohrern der Typen N,H und W hat der Seitenspanwinkel je nach Bohrerdurchmesser und zu bearbeitendem Werkstoff eine bestimmte Größe. Für die Bearbeitung von Stahl, Gusseisen und Temperguss eignet sich ein Seitenspanwinkel von 19°...40°.

Schleifen beim Spiralbohrer

Zum genauen Schleifen der Bohrerschneiden verwendet man Bohrer- Schleifvorrichtungen.

Fehler beim Schleifen von Hand sind

– Schneiden ungleich lang.

– Spitzenwinkel ungleich.

– Freiwinkel zu groß, zu klein.

Folgen dierser Fehler

– zu groß Bohrungsdurchmesser.

– verkürzte Bohrerstandzeit.

Um diese Fehler zu vermeiden muss der Anschrift des Bohrers mit der Schleiflehre geprüft werden. Bei zu großem Freiwinkel brechen die Schneidkanten des Bohrers aus, da der Werkzeugkeil geschwächt wird. Bei zu kleinem Freiwinkel ist die Reibung zwischen Bohrerfreifläche und Werkstück zu groß, der Bohrer glüht aus.

Bohrungen über 15 mm Durchmesser müssen vorgebohrt werden, da ansonsten der Bohrer verläuft. Außerdem wäre aufgrund der Querschneide eine zu große Vorschubkraft erforderlich. Aus diesem Grund werden häufig Bohrer ausgespitzt, d.h. die Querschneidenlänge wird auf rd. 1/10 des

制造技术篇

Kapitel 2　Fertigungstechnik // Chapter 2　Production engineering

Bohrerdurchmessers verkürzt.

Bohrmaschinen

Handbohrmaschinen eignen sich für Bohrungen, für die eine geringe Genauigkeit erforderlich ist. Sie sind meist mit einem Dreibackenbohrfutter ausgerüstet.

Elektrische Handbohrmaschinen durch nur in einwandfreiem Zustand benutzt werden. Beschädigt Kabel, Stecker oder Gchäuse sind tödliche Gefahren.

Tisch- und Säulenbohrmaschinen eignen sich für Bohrarbeiten mit hoher Genauigkeit und großer Zerspanungsleistung.

Spannen der Bohrer

Kleine Bohrer bis etwa 12 mm Durchmesser haben meist einen zylindrischen Schaft und werden in Dreibackenbohrfuttern, Spannzangen oder Klemmhülsen gespannt. Größere Bohrer haben in der Regel einen kegeligen Schaft.Sie werden mit dem Innenkegel der Bohrspindel durch axiales Einschieben kraftschlüssig verbunden. Ein Austreiber ist zum Lösen des Bohrers aus der Bohrspindel erforderlich.

Spannen der Werkstücke. Es ist sorgfältig durchzuführen. Dabei ist darauf zu achten, dass die Werkstücke, z.B. Bleche, vom Bohrwerkzeug nicht mitgerissen werden können. Beim Austritt des Bohrers aus der Bohrung hakt dieser leicht ein, dadurch können Unfälle entstehen. Kleinere Werkstücke spannt man in den Maschinenschraubstock.

WIEDERHOLUNGSFRAGEN:

1. Wie gross sind Spitzen-, Querschniden-, und Seitenspanwinkel für das Bohren von Stahl?
2. Wodurch werden zu grosse Bohrungsdurchmesser verursacht?
3. Geben Sie mögliche Ursachen für das Ausglühen von Bohrer an?
4. Worauf ist beim Spannen der Bohrwerkzeuge und Werkstücke zu achten?
5. Weshalb muss beim Bohren spröder Werkstoffe eine Schutzbrille getragen werden?

Neue Wörter

	mehrschneidig	多刃的		die Nebenschneide	副切削刃
das	Zahnrad	齿轮	die	Querschneide	横刃
der	Spiralbohrer	螺纹钻头，麻花钻头		schaben	剃齿，剃削
die	Einspanmöglichkeit	装夹能力，夹紧力	der	Spitzenwinkel	顶角
	gleichbleibend	一致的	der	Freiwinkel	后角
der	Durchmesser	直径	das	Gußeisen	铸铁
	axial	轴的，轴向的	die	Klemmhülse	套筒，套管
die	Spitze	顶端	der	kegelige Schaft	圆锥柄
die	Hauptschneide	主切削刃	die	Bohrspindel	钻床主轴

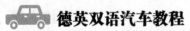

das	Einschieben	插入		im allgemein	一般，大概
der	Maschinenschraubstock	机用虎钳		ersparen	节约
die	Bohrmaschine	钻床	das	Umspannen	变压
die	Mehrzahl	多数		tief	深的
	aufweisen	显出		verlaufend	进行，经过
das	Durchgangsloch	通孔	die	Bohrspitze	钻头顶部
das	Grundloch	底孔	die	Mitte	中心
das	Fortleiten	传导		sich anpassen	配合
	nichtmetallisch	非金属的	das	Gütegrad	质量等级
	herausschneiden	切掉，割掉	die	Senkrechtbohrmaschine	立钻
	spanlos	无屑的	die	Auslegerbohrmaschine	悬臂钻床
das	Stanzen	冲孔，模压	das	Lehrenohrwerk	量规钻床
das	Lochen	钻孔	die	Mehrspindelbohrmaschine	多轴钻床
das	Aufdornen	冲孔	die	Handbohrmaschine	手持式钻床
das	Brennschneiden	火焰切割	die	ortfeste Bohrmaschine	固定式钻床
das	Eingießen	浇铸	die	waagerechte Bohrmaschine	卧式镗床
das	Reiben	研磨			

Text 2　Milling and Drilling 铣削和钻削（英文）

Milling is a machining manufacturing process with geometrically defined cutting edges. Here, flat and curved surfaces are produced with multiple-edged, rotating tools.

Applications. Such as in the manufacture of: gear wheels, end faces, solid faces (freeform milling) and helicoidal faces.

Drilling

Drilling in metal technology is the cutting by machine with geometrically defined cutting edges and predominantly multiple-edged tools for producing cylindrical holes (bores).

Twist drill bit. This is the most commonly used drilling tool. Its advantages are:
- Favourable angles at the cutting edges.
- Good chucking capability.
- Consistent diameter when regrinding.
- Automatic chip removal.
- Good supply of cooling lubricant.

Drilling process. The primary or cutting motion is a rotary motion which is mostly executed by the drilling tool. At the same time, the tool is moved in the axial direction against the workpiece (feed).

This results in continuous chip formation. The cutting speed is primarily dependent on the workpiece material and the drill-bit cutting material. The feed is dependent on the drill-bit diameter, on the material to be machined and on the drilling process.

Cutting edge geometry of twist drill bit

Major cutting edges. Two helicoidal flutes form the major cutting edges on the tip of the drill bit and perform the actual cutting.

Minor cutting edges. These are formed by the flutes on the cutting wedge and smooth the bore.

Chisel edge. This hinders the cutting process, since it scrapes as opposed to cuts.

Lands. These ensure that the drill bit is securely guided in the bore. They also reduce friction and thus the risk of the drill bit jamming in the bore.

Point angle. This is formed by the major cutting edges and is matched to the material to be machined. It is 118° for the machining of steel, cast steel, cast iron and malleable cast iron.

Clearance angle. This is produced by relief-grinding of the major cutting edges. The clearance angle enables the drill bit to penetrate into the material. A point angle of 118° produces a chisel-edge angle of 55° with correct relief-grinding. This corresponds to the correct clearance angle for the machining of steel.

Tool side rake γ. This is the angle of the faces (flutes) with the axis of the drill bit. The tool side rake cannot be altered by grinding the drill bit. In the case of twist drill bits of the N, H and W types, the tool side rake has a specific size, depending on the drill-bit diameter and the material to be machined. A tool side rake of 19° to 40° is suitable for machining, for example, steel or cast iron.

Grinding twist drill bit

Drill bit grinders are used to precision-grind the drill bit cutting edges.

Errors when grinding by hand

- Cutting edges unequal in length.
- Point angles unequal.
- Clearance angle too high, too low.

Consequences of these errors

- Bore diameter too large
- Reduced drill bit life

In order to avoid these errors, it is essential to check the grinding of the drill bit with a grinding gauge. If the clearance angle is too large, the cutting edges of the drill bit will break off because the tool wedge is weakened. If the clearance angle is too small, the friction between drill bit flank and workpiece will be too great and the drill bit will burn out. Bores over 15 mm in diameter can be predrilled if necessary because an excessive feed force is required on account of the chisel edge. For this reason, drill bits are often pointed out, i.e. the chisel-edge length is shortened to roughly 1/10 of the drill bit diameter.

Drills

Hand drills are suitable for bores for which low levels of precision are required. These are usually equipped with three-jaw drill chucks.

Electric hand drills must be in perfect condition when used. Damaged cables, plugs or housings could result in serious injury or death.

Bench and upright drills are suitable for drilling which requires high levels of precision and cutting performance.

Chucking drill bits

Small drill bits up to approx. 12 mm in diameter usually have parallel shanks and are chucked in three jaw drill chucks, collet chucks or clamping sleeves. Larger drill bits generally have tapered shanks. They are non-positively connected to the inner taper of the drilling spindle by means of axial insertion. An ejector is required to release the drill bit from the drilling spindle.

Clamping workpieces

Caution must be exercised. It is essential to ensure that the workpieces, e.g. metal sheets, cannot be carried along by the drilling tool. The drill bit can easily catch as it emerges from the bore, which can cause accidents. Smaller workpieces must be clamped in a machine vice.

New Words

multiple-edged	多刃的	cast steel	铸钢
gear wheel	齿轮	cast iron	铸铁
helicoidal face	螺旋面	malleable	可锻造的
twist drill bit	麻花钻头	relief-grind	铲磨
chucking capability	装夹能力，夹紧力	correspond to	符合，一致，相应
consistent	一致的	tool side rake	刀具侧前角，斜角
diameter	直径	precision-grind	精密磨削
axial	轴的，轴向的	grinding gauge	外圆磨床用钩形卡规
flute	（柱上的）凹槽，排屑槽	flank	侧面
tip	顶端	three-jaw drill chuck	三爪钻头卡盘
major cutting edge	主切削刃	housing	外罩，电动钻外壳
minor cutting edge	副切削刃	bench drill	台式钻床
chisel edge	横刃	upright drill	立式钻床
scrape	擦，刮，刮削	parallel shank	直柄
jamm	干扰	collet chuck	套爪卡盘
point angle	顶角	clamp	夹住，夹紧
clearance angle	后角	sleeve	套筒，套管

制造技术篇

Kapitel 2　Fertigungstechnik // Chapter 2　Production engineering

tapered shank	锥柄	locating taper	定位锥体
drilling spindle	钻床主轴	reducing sleeve	转接套，变径套
insertion	插入	align	使成一线，对正，排整齐
ejector	操纵杆，顶杆	centre punch	中心冲头
emerge from	从……摆脱	commencement	开始，开端
machine vice	机用台虎钳		

课文参考译文

铣削

　　铣削是指用几何形状确定的切削刃进行机械加工的一种制造工艺。在这种加工工艺中，用多刃旋转刀具来加工平面和曲面。

　　应用举例：加工齿轮、平面、连续平面（自由成形铣削）和螺旋面。

钻削

　　在金属加工工艺中，钻削是指使用具有一定几何形状的切削刃，主要是多切削刃刀具的机械来加工圆柱形孔的切削方法。

　　1）麻花钻头。这是一种最常用的钻削工具，其优点有：

　　① 切削刃上具有合适的刀具角度。

　　② 良好的装夹能力。

　　③ 重磨后直径不变。

　　④ 自动排屑。

　　⑤ 切削液供给充足。

　　2）钻削过程。主运动即切削运动是旋转移动，并且大多数情况下是由钻削工具来完成的。同时，钻削工具还要在轴线方向朝着工件的方向运动（进给运动），这就导致了切屑连续不停地形成。切削速度主要取决于工件材料和钻头的材料。进给量取决于钻头的直径、被加工的材料和钻削工艺规程。

　　3）麻花钻头的切削刃几何参数。

　　① 主切削刃。两个螺旋形的排屑槽在钻头尖上形成了主切削刃，主切削刃完成实际切削工作。

　　② 副切削刃。排屑槽使切削楔上形成了副切削刃。副切削刃使孔变得光滑。

　　③ 横刃。由于横刃产生刮削作用而不是切削，所以它对切削过程起了妨碍作用。

165

④ 副后刀面。副后刀面能确保钻头在孔中得到正确的引导，并且还能减小摩擦，防止钻头被卡住在孔内。

⑤ 顶角。顶角是两个主切削刃之间的夹角，其大小必须与待加工的材料相适应。在钢、铸钢、铸铁和可锻铸铁上钻孔，顶角为118°。

⑥ 后角。此角是由于主切削刃的铲磨所形成。后角能使钻头刺入材料。在正确铲磨的情况下，118°顶角会形成55°的横刃斜角。这样，就能获得加工钢的正确的后角。

⑦ 斜角γ。这是前刀面（排屑槽）与钻头轴线之间的夹角。磨削钻头不会改变倾斜角。对于N、H和W型钻头，根据钻头直径和待加工的材料的不同，倾斜角具有特定的大小。19°~40°的倾斜角适合于加工钢或铸铁等材料。

4）麻花钻头的磨削。钻头磨削机可对钻头切削刃进行精密磨削。

手工磨削时会出现的误差：

- 切削刃长度不等。
- 顶角不对称。
- 后角过大或过小。

产生这些误差的后果：

- 钻孔直径过大。
- 降低钻头寿命。

为了避免出现这些误差，要用外圆磨床用钩形卡规检查钻头的磨削情况。如果后角过大，就会因为钻头切削刃被削弱，而导致钻头切削刃的破坏。如果后角过小，钻头主后面与工件之间的摩擦就会过大，从而导致钻头烧坏。如果钻孔直径超过15mm，如果必要的话(因为横刃上需要有更大的进给力)，就需要预先钻孔。为此，常常有人提出钻头横刃长度应缩短为钻头直径的1/10左右。

5）钻床。手动钻适合于加工精度要求低的孔。这些钻通常装备有三爪钻头卡盘。电动钻只有在条件完善的情况下使用。电缆线、插头和电动钻外壳损坏都可能导致生命危险。台式即立式钻床适合于精度要求高、需要有良好切削性能的场合。

6）钻头的装夹。直径约为12mm以下的小型钻头通常带有直柄，并用三爪卡盘、套爪卡盘或夹套装夹。大型钻头一般带有锥柄，因此，这些钻头轴向插入钻床主轴的内锥孔，便能夹住钻头。为了从钻床主轴上拆下钻头，需要一个顶杆。

7）工件的装夹。必须执行预防措施，确保工件(例如金属件）不能被钻削工具带着一起转动。钻孔时钻头很容易带着工件转动，从而导致事故。小型工件必须用工作台装夹。

制造技术篇

Kapitel 2　Fertigungstechnik // Chapter 2　Production engineering

Teil 8　Schweiβen　焊接技术
Part 8　Welding　焊接技术

学习目标

【知识目标】
1. 掌握与焊接技术等相关的专业术语、单词和词汇。
2. 掌握焊接技术的德文、英文表达方法。

【能力目标】
1. 能对焊接技术方面进行中、德、英互译。
2. 能进行与焊接技术相关的德语、英语资料的阅读和翻译。
3. 能在焊接实物上标识出相应结构的德语、英语单词和词汇。

Text 1　Schweiβen焊接技术（德文）

Metalllichtbogenschweissen

Beim Metalllichtbogenschweissen wird die Wärme des elektrischen Lichtbogens zum Schmelzen der Werkstoffe an der Schweissteile ausgenützt. Der Lichtbogen entsteht nach einem kurzzeitigen Kurzschluss zwischen Elektrode und Werkstück und bildet eine elktrisch leitende Gasstrecke hoher Temperatur. Der von der Elektrode abschmelzende Werkstoff bildet mit dem aufgeschmolzenen Werkstoff des Werkstücks die Schweissraupe. Der Lichtbogen soll kurz sein (Lichtbogenlänge= Elektrodendurchmesser), um die Aufnahme von Sauerstoff und Stickstoff in das Schmelzbad gering zu halten.

Schweissstromquellen. Als Schweissstromquellen werden Schweisstransformatoren zum Schweissen mit Wechselstrom verwendet bzw. Schweissgleichrichter zum Schweissen mit Gleichstrom. In K_{fz}-Werkstätten wird häufig unter einem räumlichen Verhältnis oder zwischen elektrisch leitenden Teilen geschweisst. Die Leerlaufspanung darf dort beim Schweissen mit Wechselstrom 48V und beim Schweissen mit Gleichstrom 113V nicht überschreiten.Solche Schweistromquellen sind besonders gekennzeichnet（Tab.1）.

Tab.1:Kennzeichnung von Schweissgeräten unter erhöhter elektrischer Gefährdung

Schweissgerät	Max Leelaufspannung	Kennzeichen
Schweisstransformator	48V	S
Schweissgleichrichter	113V	S

Stabelektroden bestehen aus dem Kerndraht und der Umhüllung. Der abschmelzende Kerndraht bildet mit dem aufschmolzenen Werkstoff des Werkstücks die Schweissraupe. Die Umhüllung schmilzt mit dem Kerndraht ab und bildet auf der Schweissnaht die Schlacke. Durch die Schlacke wird das Abkühlen der Naht verlangsamt, dadurch werden Schrumpfspannungen vermindert. Ein Teil der Umhüllung vergast beim Abschmelzen und schirmt als Gasschlauch den Lichtbogen sowie die Schweissnaht in der Umgebung des Schmelzbades gegen die Umgebungsluft ab und vermindert dadurch den Abbrand von Legierungsbestandteilen. Der elektrisch leitende Gasschlauch ermöglicht auch einen gleichförmigen Lichtbogen; beim Schweissen mit Wechselstrom müsste der Lichtbogen sonst ständig neu gezündet werden, da die Stromrichtung dauernd wechselt.

Schweisswerkzeug. Im Elektrodenhalter sind zum Schutz vor elektrischer Spannung und vor Verbrennungen Griffstück und Spannvorrichtung, mit Ausnahme der Kontaktfläche für die Elektrode, isoliert.Pickhammer und Drahtbürste dienen zum Entfernen der Schlacke. Der Schweisserschutzschild ist mit dunklen Spezialgläsern (Schweissschutzfilter) versehen, denen meist Klargläser vorgesetzt sind.Stulpanhandschuhe und Schürze, meist aus Leder, schützen gegen Strahlen, Funkenflug und Verbrennungen.

Schutzgasschweissen

Das Schutzgasschweissen ist ein Lichtbogenschweissen, bei dem der Lichtbogen und das Schmelzbad in eine Schutzgasatmosphäre eingehüllt und dadurch gegen die Umgebungsluft abgeschirmt sind. Das Schutzgas wird der Schweissstelle durch den Schweissbrenner zugeführt.

Man unterscheidet das Wolfram-Inertgasschweissen mit einer nichtabschmelzenden Wolframelektrode und das Metall-Schutzgasschweissen mit einer abschmelzenden Drahtelektrode. Das jeweils verwendete Schutzgas richtet sich nach dem Schweissverfahren und dem zu schweissenden Werkstoff.

Der Schweissbrenner wird von Hand oder vollmechanisiert oder automatisch geführt. Schweissbrenner für die Schweissung dünner Bleche sind luftgekühlt. Für dicke Bleche und grosse Schweissstromstärken sind die Brenner wassergekühlt.

Die Vorteile des Schutzgasschweissens sind:

– keine Umgebungsluft im Schmelzbad.

– kein Verbrennen von Legierungsbestandteilen.

– keine Schlackenbildung.

– hohe Schweissgeschwindigkeit.

– schmale Erwärmungszone.

– geringe Verzug.

Punktschweissen

Punktschweissen ist ein Widerstandspressschweissen. Es entsteht eine unlösbare stoffschlüssige Verbindung dadurch, dass zwei aufeinander liegende Bleche in teigigem Zustand ohne Zusatzwerkstoffe an einzelnen Schweisspunkten durch Wärme und Druck mit einander verbunden werden.

Der benötigte Druck wird über die stiftförmigen Kupferelektroden ausgeübt. Über die Kupferelektroden und die zusammengepressten Bleche fliesst kurzzeitig ein grossee Strom. Die erforderliche Schweisswärme entsteht sehr schnell durch den großen elektrischen Widerstand an der Verbindungsstelle. Druck, Stromstärke und Schweisszeit müssen aufeinander abgestimmt sein.

Für die Kfz-Instandsetzung gibt es kleine tragbare Punktschweisszangen mit eingebautem Transformator. Die Elektroden werden bei Betätigen des Handhebels zusammengepresst. Elektrodenarme gibt es in verschiedenen Ausführungen, um auch an sonst unzugänglichen Stellen der Karosserie Schweisspunkte setzen zu können. Die Schweissstelle muss jedoch für die Schweisszange immer von beiden Seiten zugänglich sein.

Mit dem Stosspunkter kann gearbeitet werden ,wenn die Schweissstelle nur von einer Seite zugänglich ist.Zum Punktschweissen wird die Elektrode der Schweisspistore so gegen die Schweissstelle gepresst,dass sich beide Bleche berühren,und dann der Schweisspunkt gesetzt.

Der Stosspunkter ist vielseitig einsetzbar:

– Einseitiges Punktschweissen.

– Ausbeulen von Blechen (in Verbindung mit dem Ausziehhammer).

– Einziehen von Blechen.

– Ausschweissen von Gewindebolzen und Stiften.

WIEDERHOLUNGSFRAGEN:

1. Welche Schmelzschweissverfahren unterscheidet man?
2. Welche Aufgabe hat die Umhüllung einer Elektrode?
3. Welche schweissrichtungen werden beim Schutzgasschweissen angewendet?
4. Welche Vorteile hat das Schutzgasschweissen gegenüber anderen Schweissverfahren?

Neue Wörter

das	Metalllichtbogenschweissen	金属电弧焊接	der	Sauerstoff	氧
die	Elektrode	电极	der	Stickstoff	氮
	leitend	传导的，导电的	da	Schmelzbad	熔池
die	Schweissraupe	焊缝	die	Stromquelle	电源
die	Aufnahme	吸收	der	Transformator	变压器

der	Gleichstrom	直流电	die	Schrumpfspannung	收缩应力
die	Leerlaufspanung	开路电压		schützen	保护
	Überschreiten vi	超出，超过		in der Nähe	在……附近，邻近
das	Gerät	仪器，器械，设备	die	Umgebungsluft	环境空气，周围空气
die	Stabelektrode	棒式电极，焊条	das	Legierungsbestandteil	合金成分
das	Kerndraht	焊芯	das	Punktschweissen	点焊
die	Umhüllung	涂层	die	Punktschweisszangen	点焊钳
die	Schlacke	熔渣	das	Handhebel	手柄
die	Schweissnaht	焊缝	der	Ausziehhammer	鹤嘴锤

Text 2　Metal-arc welding 金属焊接（英文）

In the case of metal-arc welding, the heat of the electric arc is utilised to melt the materials at the weld.

Electrically conductive gas trace of high temperature. The material melting off the electrode forms the welding bead with the melted-on workpiece material. The arc should be as short as possible (arc length ≈ electrode diameter) in order to keep the absorption of oxygen and nitrogen into the melting bath at a low level.

Welding current sources. Welding transformers are used as the welding current sources for welding with alternating current while welding rectifiers are used for welding with direct current. In garages/repair shops welding is often performed in confined spaces or between electrically conducting parts. In such situations the open circuit voltage must not exceed 48 V when welding with alternating current，or 113 V when welding with direct current. Such welding current sources are specifically marked (Tab.1).

Tab.1: Marking of welding apparatus for welding under increased electrical hazard conditions

Welding apparatus	Max. open Circuit voltage	Marking
Welding transformer	48V	S
Welding rectifier	113V	S

Stick electrodes consist of core wire and a coating.

The melting-off core wire forms the welding bead with the melted-on workpiece material. The coating melts off with the core wire and forms the slag on the weld seam. The slag slows down the rate at which the seam cools. This reduces contraction strains.

Part of the coating reduces to gas as it melts off and forms a volatile covering to shield the arc and the weld seam in the vicinity of the melting bath against ambient air and thereby reduces the melting loss of alloying constituents. The electrically conductive volatile covering also facilitates a uniform arc. When welding with alternating current, the arc would otherwise have to be constantly reignited, since the current direction alternates constantly.

Welding tools. Except for the electrode contact surface in the electrode holder, the handle and clamping fixture are insulated to protection against voltage and burns. The pick hammer and wire brush are used to remove the slag. The welder's face shield is fitted with a special lens shade (protective filter), in front of which clear glass is usually fitted. Gauntlet gloves and aprons, usually made of leather, provide protection against jets, flying sparks and burns.

> Always wear personal protective clothing and equipment when welding !

Inert-gas-shielded welding

Inert-gas-shielded welding is a type of arc welding in which the arc and the melting bath are surrounded by an atmosphere of inert gas and thereby shield against the ambient air. The inert gas is delivered to the weld location by the welding torch.

Two different methods may be used: tungsten inert-gas-shielded welding with a non-melting-off tungsten electrode and gas-shielded metal-arc welding with a melting-off wire electrode.

> The inert gas used in each case is dependent on the welding process and the material to be welded.

The welding torch is guided by hand, by fully mechanised means or automatically. Welding torches for welding thinner metal sheets are air-cooled. The torches are water-cooled for thick sheets and high welding currents.

The advantages of inert-gas-shielded welding are:
- No ambient air in the melting bath.
- No burning of alloying constituents.
- No slag formation.
- High welding speed.
- Narrow heating zone.
- Low distortion.

Welding direction. Both "forehand" and "backhand" welding are used.

Tungsten inert-gas-shielded welding

The arc burns between a tungsten electrode, which does not burn off, and the workpiece. The welding rod is guided by hand from the side into the melting bath. Depending on the workpiece material, welding with direct current or with alternating current is used. The slow-to-react noble gas argon or a mixture of argon and helium is used as the inert gas.

TIG welding is suitable mainly for welding metal sheets, profile sections and pipes up to approx. 5 mm thick made of heat-resistant, acid-resistant or stainless steels, of copper or copper alloys and of aluminium or aluminium alloys.

Gas-shielded metal-arc welding

The arc burns between the melting-off wire electrode and the workpiece. The wire electrode is wound on a wire reel and delivered to the welding torch with the wire feed motor through a flexible hose in the hose pack.

Gas metal-arc welding makes use of direct current which is fed to the wire electrode in the welding torch at the current contact nozzle shortly before the arc. The positive terminal is usually connected to the wire electrode. The small electrode cross-section provides for a high current density, high melt-off, high welding speed and low penetration

Metal inert-gas-shielded welding

In this case, inert welding gases (e.g. argon), which undergo no chemical reactions during the welding process, are used.

MIG welding is suitable for welding thick sheets of high-alloy steels, of copper or Cu alloys or aluminium or Al alloys. When light-alloy bodies are manufactured, thin sheets of Al alloys are MIG-welded to each other and with pressure die castings and extruded sections made of Al alloys.

Metal active-gas-shielded welding

Here gas mixtures of argon, carbon dioxide and oxygen or pure carbon dioxide are used as the inert gas. MAG welding is a method of inert-gas-shielded welding for welding unalloyed and alloyed steels. With carbon dioxide and oxygen, the inert gases contain active constituents which react with the melting bath. The wire electrode therefore contains manganese and silicon as important alloying constituents for deoxidising the melting bath. Both materials combine with oxygen, which either is released when the carbon dioxide decomposes or is present as a constituent of the mixture gas.

Inert-gas-shielded welding is carried out in garages/repair shops usually with one wire-electrode diameter only; mainly a 0.8 mm wire electrode is used, but 1 mm may also be used.

Laser welding

> In the case of this welding process, the heat required for melting on the material and the filler metal is introduced by a high-energy laser beam.

In a laser (Light Amplification by Stimulated Emission of Radiation), a medium, e.g. a helium/neon gas mixture, is brought to a higher energy level by "collision" with electrons. The energy is then given off again in the shape of an electromagnetic wave (e.g. as red light) in a highly concentrated form.

Welding process: The contact roller ensures that the parts to be joined are fixed in place and that the filler material is delivered to the weld. The thin laser beam enables a high-precision weld seam to be produced. The melting mass is protected by an inert gas to prevent it reacting with the ambient air.

制造技术篇

Kapitel 2　Fertigungstechnik // Chapter 2　Production engineering

Laser welding is used in industrial car manufacturing for body shells. Steels, light alloys and plastics can be welded.

Features of laser welding:
- Clean seam.
- Minimal material distortion thanks to low heat application during welding.
- High productivity and rigidity.
- Weight saving due to low or no overlapping.
- High strength.

Spot welding

> Spot welding is a form of resistance pressure welding. A non-removable, material-based connection is created when two stacked metal sheets are joined in a paste-like state without filler metals at individual welding spots by means of heat and pressure.

The required pressure is exerted via the pin-shaped copper electrodes. A high current passes briefly through the copper electrodes and the metal sheets which are pressed together. The necessary welding heat is generated very quickly due to the high electrical resistance at the joint. Pressure, current intensity and welding time must be matched to each other.

Small, portable spot-welding tongs with an integrated transformer are used for motor-vehicle repairs. The electrodes are pressed together when the hand lever is actuated. Different types of electrode arms are available to enable welding spots to be applied even in otherwise inaccessible areas of the body. However, the weld must always be accessible to the welding tongs from both sides.

Joint spot-welder. This can be used when the weld is only accessible from one side. For spot welding, the electrode of the welding gun is pressed against the weld in such a way that the two metal sheets touch each other and then the welding spot is applied.

The joint spot-welder has many uses:
- Spot welding from one side.
- Removal of dents from metal sheets (in conjunction with a pulling hammer).
- Drawing-in of metal sheets.
- Welding-on of stud bolts and pins.

REVIEW QUESTIONS:

1. Why should oil and grease not be permitted anywhere near the locks/seals of oxygen bottles?
2. How can you recognise an acetylene bottle?
3. Which measured values are read off on the reducing regulator?
4. Why is the welding flame adjusted to neutral for the acetylene welding of steel?
5. What is flame cutting based on?

New Words

metal-arc	金属电弧	core wire	焊芯
welding	焊接，锻接	coating	涂层
circuit	电路，电流	slag	熔渣
electrode	电极	weld seam	焊缝
conductive	传导的，导电的	contraction	收缩
welding bead	焊缝	strain	应力
absorption	吸收	volatile	易变的，不稳定的
oxygen	氧	shield	保护
nitrogen	氮	in the vicinity of	在……附近，邻近
melting bath	熔池	ambient air	环境空气，周围空气
current source	电源	alloying constituent	合金成分
transformer	变压器	facilitate	促进，帮助，有助于
alternating current	交流电	reignite	重新点火，重新起弧
rectifier	整流器	alternate	交替，轮流
direct current	直流电	electrode holder	电焊钳，电极夹
open circuit voltage	开路电压	handle	手柄
exceed	超出，超过	clamping fixture	夹具
apparatus	仪器，器械，设备	pick hammer	鹤嘴锤
stick electrode	棒式电极，焊条		

课文参考译文

焊接技术

电弧焊

电弧焊是利用电弧的加热作用来熔化焊接材料的一种焊接方法。

电极与焊件之间短时间短路之后产生电弧，从而形成了高温导电气体轨迹。从电极上熔化下来材料与熔化的焊件材料一起形成了焊缝。为了使熔池少吸收氧和氮，电弧应该尽可能短（电弧长度约等于电极直径）。

1）焊接电源。焊接变压器用作交流焊接的电源，而焊接整流器用作直流焊接的电源。在车库或修理车间内，常常需要在空间受限制的场合下完成焊接操作，甚至在导电部件之间进行焊接。在这种情况下，用交流电焊接的开路电压不得超过48V，用直流电焊接的开路电压不得超过113V。这样的电源有专门的标识。

制造技术篇

Kapitel 2　Fertigungstechnik // Chapter 2　Production engineering

表1　焊接时具有较大危险性的焊接设备标识

焊接设备	最大开路电压	标识	焊接设备	最大开路电压	标识
焊接变压器	48V	S	焊接整流器	113V	S

2）棒式电极（焊条）。焊条是由焊芯和药皮组成的。熔化的焊芯与熔化的焊件材料一起形成焊缝。药皮从焊芯上熔化下来并在焊缝上形成熔渣。熔渣降低了焊缝冷却的速度，从而降低了收缩的应力。部分药皮在熔化时变为气体，因而在熔池的附近形成一个能隔离环境空气、保护电弧和焊缝的临时覆盖层，因此就降低了在熔化时合金成分的损失。这种导电的临时覆盖层也有利于电弧的稳定。当用交流电进行焊接时，如果没有这个覆盖层，由于电流方向不断改变，就必须不断地重新起弧。

3）焊接工具。为了防止触电和烫伤，除了焊条的接触表面之外，焊钳的手柄和夹具均要绝缘。鹤嘴锤和钢丝刷的用途是除去熔渣。焊接面具上装有特制的遮光玻璃(防护滤镜)，遮光玻璃前面通常装有透明玻璃。通常用皮革制成的长手套和围裙能防止火花飞溅和烧伤。

焊接时，一定要穿好防护服并使用保护装置。

惰性气体保护焊

惰性气体保护焊是电弧焊的一种。在这种电弧焊中，电弧和熔池的周围有惰性气体，因此电弧和熔池不会直接接触到大气。惰性气体通过焊炬被输送到熔池的附近。

惰性气体保护焊可以采用两种不同的方法：采用不熔钨电极的钨惰性气体保护焊和采用可熔焊丝电极的气体保护金属电弧焊。

每种情况下所用的惰性气体取决于焊接方法和待焊接材料。

焊炬的移动可以手动、全机械化或全自动操纵。焊接薄金属板的焊炬要使用空气冷却。焊接厚金属板和焊接电流大时，要对焊炬进行水冷。惰性气体保护焊的优点是：

- 环境空气不会进入熔池。
- 合金成分不会被烧掉。
- 不会形成熔渣。
- 焊接速度快。
- 受热范围小。
- 变形小。

焊接方法：可以采用"刺穿"焊接和"牵拖"焊接。

钨惰性气体保护焊

对于钨惰性气体保护焊（TIG焊)，电弧在不熔钨电极与焊件之间形成。焊条用手动的方式从一侧送入熔池。根据焊件材料的不同，确定采用直流焊接还是交流焊接。稳定的惰性气体氩气或氩气与氦气的混合气用作焊接用惰性气体。

TIG焊接主要适合于焊接金属板，型材和壁厚约为5mm，由耐热、耐酸的不锈钢，或用铜或铜合金，以及用铝或铝合金制成的管件。

气体保护金属电弧焊

对于气体保护金属电弧焊（MIG焊），电弧在熔化焊丝电极与焊件之间形成。焊丝缠绕在绕线盘上，并通过焊丝进给电动机，经过软管盘上的软管，被送给焊炬。

气体保护金属电弧焊采用直流电。就在电弧之前，在电流接触嘴处，直流电进入焊炬内的焊丝电极。通常，正极与焊丝电极相连。电极断面很小，从而产生了大的电流、高的熔化功率、高的焊接速度和低的熔深。

金属惰性气体保护焊

在这种情况下，采用焊接期间根本不会参与化学反应的惰性焊接气体（例如氩气）。

MIG焊适合于焊接高合金钢、铜或铜合金，以及铝或铝合金厚金属板。生产轻合金车身时，使用铝合金制造的压铸件和挤压型材，并采用MIG焊对薄铝合金板进行焊接。

金属活性气体保护焊

在金属活性气体保护焊（MAG焊）中，将氩气、二氧化碳和氧或纯二氧化碳用作惰性气体。

MAG焊是对非合金钢或合金钢进行惰性气体保护焊接的一种方法。在有二氧化碳和氧存在的情况下，惰性气体内便含有与熔池发生反应的活性成分。因此，焊丝内含有熔池脱氧的重要成分锰和硅。无论是二氧化碳分解时会释放出氧，或者将氧作为混合气体的一种构成成分，而锰和硅都会与这些氧结合。

在车库或修理车间进行惰性气体保护焊通常仅使用一个焊丝电极直径，主要采用 0.8mm 焊丝电极，但是也可以采用1mm直径的。

激光焊接

在激光焊接的情况下，熔化焊件材料和填充金属所需要的热量由高能激光束提供。

在激光器中，通过电子"碰撞"使一种介质（例如氦与氖的混合气）进入更高的能级。然后，再以高度密集的电磁波（如红外线）形式，将这些能量重新释放出来。

1）焊接过程。接触辊确保将焊件固定到合适的位置，并确保将填充材料输送到焊缝处。细激光束能够形成一个高精度焊缝。熔化的金属受到惰性气体的保护，以免与周围的空气发生反应。

在汽车制造业，激光焊接用于生产车身。钢、轻合金和塑料都可以采用激光焊接。

2）激光焊接的特点：

①焊缝干净整洁。

②由于焊接过程中需要热量少，使材料变形大大减小。

③生产率高，刚性大。

④由于焊件重叠小甚至无重叠，节省了材料。

⑤强度高。

点焊

点焊是一种电阻压焊。当借助于加热和加压的手段，将两块一上一下叠放的金属板在各个焊点处采用膏状连接，而不采用填料金属的时候，就会形成一种不可拆的材料连接。

点焊所需要的压力通过销状铜电极来产生。大电流短时通过铜电极和叠放在一起的两层金属板。连接点处的高电阻会迅速地产生必要的焊接热。压力、电流和焊接时间必须相互匹配。

1）焊钳。这种内装焊接变压器的手提式小型点焊机可用于汽车车身修理。当操作手柄时，便可将电极压在一起。可以使用不同类型的电极臂，从而即使在不易接近的车身区域，也能够进行点焊操作。不过，使用这种点焊机，必须使焊钳从两侧都能够到才行。

2）连接点焊机。当只能从一侧够着焊接部位时，就要使用这种焊机。进行点焊时，焊枪的电极要压向焊接点，从而使两个金属板相互接触，然后再加焊接电流。

连接点焊机具有多种用途：

- 从一侧进行点焊。
- 除去金属板的一侧凹痕（与拉锤配合）。
- 金属板的引入。
- 螺钉和销钉的焊接。

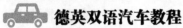

Teil 9　Fahrzeuglackierung　汽车涂装技术
Part 9　Vehicle paintwork　汽车涂装技术

学习目标

【知识目标】
1. 掌握与涂装技术等相关的专业术语、单词和词汇。
2. 掌握涂装技术的德文、英文表达方法。

【能力目标】
1. 能对汽车涂装方面进行中、德、英互译。
2. 能进行与汽车涂装相关的德语、英语资料的阅读和翻译。

Text 1　Fahrzeuglackierung汽车涂装（德文）

Fahrzeuglackierung haben die Aufgabe,die Karosserieoberfläche gegen äussere Einflüsse,z. B.aggressive Stoffe in Wasser und Luft gegen Steinschlag zu schützen.

Weiterhin soll die Fahrzeuglackierung

– einen dichten und zusammenhängenden Schutzfilm bilden.

– hart und gleichzeitig elastisch sein.

– lichtecht sein.

– Signalwirkung erzeugen.

– sich leicht reinigen und pflegen lassen.

Auftragsverfahren

Das Auftragen der Lacke kann durch Spritzen, Tauchen oder elektrische Spritzverfahren erfolgen.

Spritzen.Spritzpistore arbeiten meistens mit Druckluft.Dabei wird nach dem Injektorprinzip der Lack von der am Injektor vorbeiströmenden Luft angesaugt und zur Düse transpotiert. Beim Austritt aus der Düse entsteht ein Farbnebel, der sich auf der Oberfläche niederschlägt.

Man unterscheidet Kalt-und Heissspritzen.

Kaltspritzen. Der Lack wird durch Lösemittel so weit verdünnt (Änderung der Viskosität), bis er gut spritzbar wird. Nach dem Lackieren verdunstet das Lösemittel. Bei zu schneller Verdunstung des Lösemittels kann eine Schrumpfung der Lackoberfläche eintreten.

Heissspritzen. Der Lack wird mittels einer Heizvorrichtung im Farbbecher auf 50℃ bis 120℃ vorgeheizt. Dadurch verringert sich die Viskosität des Lackes, so dass er ohne Lösemittel spritzbar ist.

Spritzen mit elektrostatischer Aufladung. Das elektrostatische Spritzverfahren wird in der Serienfertigung angewendet.An der Karosserie wird der Pluspol, an die Farbspritzdüsen der Minuspol einer Gleichspannungsquelle angelegt. Die Spannung kann bis zu 200000V betragen. Die negativ aufgeladenen Farbnebel werden von der positiv aufgeladenen Karosserie angezogen. Der Farbverlust wird dadurch verringert.

Anstelle von Spritzpistolen kann der Lack durch Hochrotationsglocken im elektrostatischen Spritzverfahren aufgebracht werden.Mit Spritzrobotern werden die Bereiche der Karosserie lackiert, die durch den Farbnebel der Hochrotationsglocken nicht erreicht werden.

Airress-Spritzen (Hochdruckspritzen). Das Lackmaterial wird unter hohem hydrostatischem Druck (100 bar bis 200 bar) gesetzt. Es zerstäubt beim Entspannen am Austritt der Spritzdüse. Airless-Spritzen ermöglicht eine feinneblige Zerstäubung auch zäflüssiger Beschichtungsstoffe. Um mit einem geringeren hydrostatischen Druck (40 bar bis 60 bar) arbeiten zu können, ist es möglich ,die Zerstäubung des Lackmaterials mit Druckluft zu unterstützen. Diese Verfahren werden hauptsächlich zum Auftragen von Unterboden-und Korrosionsschutz eingesetzt.

Tauchen. In der Serienfertigung kann die Grundierung durch Tauchen der Karosserie in eine mit Grundierlack gefüllte Wanne hergestellt werden. Überschüssiger Lack an der Karosserie kann durch Hängelage und Ablaufbohrungen beseitigt werden.

Elektrophorese-Verfahren. Die in einem Elektrolyt schwebenden Lackteilchen z.B. einer Wasser-Kunstharz-Emulsion werden elektrisch aufgeladen und zur entgegengesetzt geladenen Karosserie bewegt, auf der sie eine gleichmässige Lackschicht bilden. Der Vorgang dauert so lange, bis die letzte blanke Stelle mit Lack bedeckt, d.h. isoliert ist. Diese Verfahren ist nur für den ersten Lackauftrag, die Grundierung, geeignet. Man unterscheidet Kataphorese und Anaphorese.

Kataphorese. Die Karosserie ist negativ, das Tauchbad positiv aufgeladen. Die bei der Wasserzerlegung durch Elektrolyse erzeugten positiven Wasserstoffionen wandern zur negativ geladenen Karosserie und verhindern dort während des Beschichtungsvorgangs eine Oxidbildung auf dem Blech.

Anaphorese. Die Karosserie ist positiv, das Tauchbad negetiv aufgeladen. Die bei der Wasserzerlegung durch Elektrolyse erzeugten negativen Sauerstoffionen wandern zur positiv geladenen Karosserie. Sie wird zum Grundieren von Rohkarosserie nicht mehr verwendet, da während des Beschichtungsvorgangs am Blech und in der Lackschicht nachteilige Oxidationsvorgänge entstehen.

Aubau einer Lackierung

Eine Kraftfahrzeuglachierung besteht aus folgenden Schichten:

– Phosphatschicht.

– Elektrotauchgrundierung.

– Steinschlagzwischengrund.

– Füller (Spritzgrund).

– Decklackierung (Uni-oder Metallic-Lackierung).

Bevor die erforderlichen Schichten für den Lackaufbau aufgetragen werden können, muss die Karosserievorgehandelt werden. Dazu muss sie gereinigt, entfetet und anschliessend mit einer Phosphatschicht versehen werden.

Phosphatschicht. Durch Phosphatieren wird eine poröse Eisenphosphatschicht auf der Blechoberfläche erzeugt. Sie ist die Voraussetzung für eine gute Haftung der nachfolgenden Schichten und ein sehr guter Korrosionsschutz.

Grundierung. Sie ergibt eine Haftschicht für den Steinschlagzwischengrund, den Füller und den Decklack. Der Auftrag der Grundierung erfolgt meist im Tauch-oder Elektrophoreseverfahren.

Steinschlagzwischengrund. Er kann an besonders steinschlaggefährdeten Aussenhautflächen der Karosserie z.B. die seitlichen Flächen der Karosserie bis zu den Unterkanten der Fensterausschnitte sowie der Motorhaube auftragen werden.

Füller (Spritzgrund). Er dient dazu, um kleinere Unebenheiten, Schleifrillen und Poren an der Oberfläche auszugleichen. Der Füller wird meist maschnell durch elektostatisches Spritzen aufgetragen.Er bildet den Untergrund für die Vor-und Decklackierung. Wird auf die Füllerschicht direkt der Decklack aufgetragen, übernimmt der Füller auch die Aufgabe des Vorlacks.

Uni-Lackierung

Vierschicht-Lackaufbau. Neben Grundierschicht und Füllerschicht werden zwei weitere Schichten durch elektrostatisches Spritzen aufgetragen.

– Aufspritzen des Vorlacks und Trocken bei ca.140℃.

– Aufspritzen des Decklacks und Trocken bei ca.130℃.

Dreischicht-Lackaufbau. Er besteht aus Grundierung Füller und Decklackierung. Dabei wird auf die Füllerschicht sofort der Decklack nass in nass aufgespritzt und anschliessend getrocknet.

Der Vorteil des Vierschicht-Lackaufbau gegenüber dem Dreischicht-Lackaufbau ist, dass die Gesamtdicke der Lackschicht über die gesamte Karosserieoberfläche sehr gleichmässig wird, da die Vorlackschicht und die Decklackschicht gleich dick sind.

Metallic-Lackierung

Im Gegensatz zur Uni-Lackierung werden bei der Metallic-Lackierung ein Metallic-Basislack als farb-und effektgebende Schicht und ein Klarlack als glanzgebende und schützende Schicht aufgetragen. Der Metallic-Basislack wird durch Luftzerstäubung, der Klarlack im elektrostatischen

Spritzverfahren aufgetragen. Die Verarbeitung erfolgt im „Nasse in Nasse Verfahren ", d.h. dass auf den Basislack ohne Zwischentrocknung der Klarlack aufgespritzt wird. Anschliessend werden beide Lackschichten bei ca.130 ℃ getrocknet.

Lacke

Sie bestehen aus nicht flüchtigen Bestandteilen (Tab.1).

Tab.1: Lackbestandteile

nicht flüchtige Bestandteile	
Bindemittel	Harze, Filmbildner
Farbstoffe	Farbpigmente, Füllstoffe
Zusatzstoffe	Katalysatoren, Filmbildungsverbesserer, Weichmacher, Glanzverbesserer
flüchtige Bestandteil	
Lösemittel	Verdünnungsmittel, Reaktionsprodukte

Lackarten

— Man unterscheidet.

— Nitrolacke.

— Kunstharzlacke.

— Effektlacke.

— Wasserlacke.

— High-Solid-Lacke.

— Pulverlacke.

WIEDERHOLUNGSFRAGEN:

1. Welche Aufgaben haben Lackierungen?
2. Welche Lackarten werden unterschieden?
3. Was sind Pulverlacke?
4. Welche Möglichkeiten des Lackauftrages werden am Kraftfahrzeug angewenden?

Neue Wörter

	spritzen	喷，喷射，喷雾		elektrostatisch	静电的，静电学的
	tauchen	沉浸，浸没		hydrostatisch	流体静力学的，静水力学的
der	Injektor	注射器；喷嘴		feinneblig	雾化
die	Düse	喷嘴，喷射管	die	Grundierung	底面涂层，底层漆
das	Lösemittel	溶剂		elektrochemisch	电化学的
die	Viskosität	黏性		manuell	手工的
	verdünnen	挥发；蒸发		entlegen	偏僻的
die	Schrumpfung	收缩，皱缩；缩水		optimal	最佳的

der	Winkel	角度		die	Kante	角，边
der	Rost	锈		das	Bördeln	弯边
	entfetten	脱脂		der	Fransch	凸缘
	hauchdünn	极薄的			installieren	安装
der	Ölfilm	油膜		der	Sprühautomat	自动喷漆装置
der	Span	铁屑			auftragen	涂上
	sonstig	其他的		das	Lösungsmittel	稀释剂
der	Rückstand	残渣			elektrostatisch	静电的
die	Unterwanderung	外力渗入引起的破坏			konstruieren	设计
	vertikal	垂直的			elastisch	有弹性的
die	Tauchgrundierung	电泳底漆			übernehmen	验收
die	Lackpartikel	油漆粒子		der	Fertigungsfluss	生产流程

Text 2 Vehicle paintwork 汽车涂装（英文）

The function of vehicle paintwork is to protect the body surface against external influences, e.g. aggressive substances in water and air, and against stone impacts.

Furthermore, the vehicle paintwork is intended to:

- form a tight and cohesive protective film.
- be hard and at the same time elastic.
- be colourfast.
- generate a signal effect.
- be easy to clean and maintain.

Application processes

Paints can be applied by spraying, immersing or using electric spraying processes.

Spraying. Spray guns operate for the most part with compressed air. Here, the paint is drawn in according to the injector principle by the air flowing past the injector and transported to the jet nozzle. As the paint emerges from the jet nozzle, a paint mist is created which settles on the surface.

There are two different methods of spraying: cold and hot spraying.

Cold spraying. The paint is thinned by a solvent (change in viscosity) until it can be easily sprayed. The solvent evaporates after painting. Excessively quick evaporation of the solvent may cause the painted surface to shrink.

Hot spraying. The paint is preheated by a heater in the paint canister to 50℃ to 120℃. In this way the viscosity of the paint is reduced to such an extent that it can be sprayed without a solvent.

Spraying with electrostatic charge. Electrostatic spraying is used in mass production. The positive pole and the negative pole of a direct voltage source are applied to the body and to the paint spraying nozzles respectively. The voltage can range up to 200,000 V. The negatively charged paint mist is attracted by the positively charged body. The loss of paint is thereby reduced.

In the electrostatic spraying process, the paint can be applied by high-rotation bells instead of by spray guns. Spraying robots are used to paint those areas of the body which cannot be reached by the paint mist from the high-rotation bells.

Airless spraying (high-pressure spraying). The paint material is subjected to high hydrostatic pressure (100 bar to 200 bar). It atomises as it relaxes at the outlet of the spray nozzle. Airless spraying facilitates fine mist atomisation even of viscous coating substances. To be able to work with a lower hydrostatic pressure (40 bar to 60 bar), it is possible to support the atomisation of the paint material with compressed air. These processes are primarily used to apply undercoating and corrosion inhibitors.

Immersing. In mass production the priming coat can be applied by immersing the body in a tank filled with priming paint. Excess paint on the body can be removed by suspension and through drain holes.

Electraphoresis process. The paint particles of a water/artificial-resin emulsion suspended in an electrolyte, for instance, are electrically charged and transpored to the opposite-charged body, on which they form a uniform coat of paint. The process continues until the last bare area is covered with paint, i.e. insulated. This process is only suitable for the first coat of paint: the priming coat. The positive hydrogen ions generated by electrolysis during the decomposition of water stray to the negatively charged body, where they prevent oxide formation on the panel/plate during the coating process.

Build-up of paint

The paintwork of a motor vehicle is made up of the following layers:
- Phosphate layers.
- Electro-dipcoat priming.
- Intermediate anti-chip foundation.
- Filler (spray foundation).
- Top coat (plain or metallic paint).

The body must be preheated before the necessary layers can be applied for the build-up of paint. For this purpose, it must be cleaned, degreased and then provided with a phosphate layer.

Phosphate layer. A porous iron-phosphate layer is created on the sheet-matal surface by phosphatising. This is essential to the sound adhesion of the subsequent layers and to very good corrosion protection.

Priming coat. This creates an adherent layer for the intermediate anti-chip foundation, the filler and the top coat. The priming coat is usually applied in immersion or electrophoresis processes.

Intermediate anti-chip foundation. This can be applied to outer skin areas of the body particularly exposed to the risks of stone impacts, for example the side surfaces of the body up to the lower edges of the window apertures and bonnet/hood.

Filler (spray foundation). This serves to correct smaller irregularities, grinding marks and pores on the surface. The filler is usually applied by an electrostatic spraying machine. It forms the background for the undercoat and the top coat. If the top coat is applied directly to the filler layer, the filler also assumes the function of the undercoat.

Top coat

A distinction is made between plain paintwork and metallic paintwork.

Plain paintwork

Four-layer paint structure. In addition to the priming and filler layers, two further layers are applied by electrostatic spraying.

- Spraying on of the undercoat and drying at approx. 140℃.
- Spraying on of the top coat and drying at approx. 130℃.

Three-layer paint structure. This consists of primer, filler and top coat. Here, the top coat is sprayed immediately onto the filler layer wet on wet and then dried. The advantage of the four-layer paint structure over its three-layer counterpart is that the overall thickness of the paint layer is very uniform over the entire body surface since the undercoat layer and the topcoat layer are of equal thickness.

Metallic paintwork

In contrast to plain paintwork, metallic paintwork involves the application of a metallic base paint as the colouring, effect-giving layer and a clear lacquer as the glossy, protective layer. The metallic base paint and the clear lacquer are applied by air atomisation and electrostatic spraying respectively. They are applied in a "wet-on-wet" process, i.e. the clear lacquer is sprayed onto the base paint without intermediate drying. The two paint layers are then dried at roughly 130℃.

Paints

These consist of non-volatile and volatile components（Tab.1）.

Tab.1 Paint components

Non-volatile components	
Binders	Resins, film-forming media
Pigments	Insoluble paint particles
Additives	Catalysts, antioxidant agents, extender, rust inhibitors
Volatile components	
Solvents	Thinners, reaction products

Binders. These form the paint film after the coating and drying processes. Here, the colouring pigments are combined with each other by the resins. Film-forming media speed up the layer formation process and improve the processability of the paint.

制造技术篇

Kapitel 2　Fertigungstechnik // Chapter 2　Production engineering

Pigments. These lend the coating the desired colour appearance. Pigments are paint particles which are present in insolubly solid form in the paint.

Additives. Catalysts speed up the curing and drying process. Antioxidant agents prevent the paint from forming a skin and thickening. The extenders improve the shine and film formation of the paint. The protective properties of the paint are improved by rust inhibitors.

Solvents. These dissolve the solid and viscous components of the paint and establish the viscosity required for processing. Solvents and reaction products evaporate during processing and during drying of the paint film. Reaction products are created during the stoving process and during the film-formation process, e.g. dehydration by polycondensation.

Types of paint

The following different types are available:

- Nitrocellulose paints.
- Synthetic paints.
- Effect paints.
- Water-based paints.
- High-solid paints.
- Powder-based paints.

Nitrocellulose paints. These are normally no longer used in painting vehicles today. Nitrocellulose paints harden rapidly due to the evaporation of the solvent. They are highly inflammable, non-resistant to fuels and require regular upkeep in order to maintain the high-gloss surface. Nitrocellulose paints are mainly used today in painting classic cars.

Synthetic paints. These use, for example, duroplastics (alkyd resins, melamine resins) as binders. These paints cure under the influence of atmospheric oxygen. This is known as oxidative curing. Application: top coat.

Acrylic resin paints. These use acrylic resins (thermoplastics) as binders. They cure through physical drying, i.e. through evaporation of the solvents. These paints can be dissolved again with the aid of solvents; they are reversible. Silicone resins are used as binders for heat-resistant paints. Application: they are used both as priming coats and as top coats on vehicles. Acrylic resin paints are subdivided into

- one-component paints (1C paints).
- two-component paints (2C paints).

One-component paints (1C paints). These usually cure under the influence of atmospheric oxygen through cross-linking of the molecules (polymerisation). Solvents and reaction products evaporate in the process. A high-gloss paint layer is created. The ultimate hardness of the paint layer is usually only established after a period of several weeks. The curing process can be sped up by stoving at temperatures between 100℃ and 140℃.

Two-component paints (2C paints). These consist of extenders and hardeners. In mass-production painting these paints are usually mixed in the correct proportions in a spray gun. Between the two components a chemical reaction (polyaddition) takes place which gradually cures the applied paint film without reaction products even at room temperature.

The curing process can be sped up at temperatures up to roughly 130 ℃. Acrylic resin paints are chemical, scratch and weather resistant.

Effect paints (metallic paints). In addition to the colour pigments, these contain mica or flakes of aluminium in the base paint. Because these additives reflect the incident light, a metallic effect is created on the surface. Once the base paint has been applied, a second layer of clear paint is applied wet on wet to protect the base paint.

Water-based paints. Plastic-based resins serve as binders. In the case of fillers and base paints the organic solvent components are almost completely replaced by water. Only in the case of clear paint is the proportion of organic solvents approximately 10% and the water content as solvent is up to 80%.

The following different types exist:

True water-based paints. The resin molecules are dissolved in water.

Water-thinnable paints (dispersion). The resin particles are finely distributed in the water.

After application, the water and solvent in the paint layer are evaporated in drying systems. A tight, water-proof and chemical-resistant paint layer is formed. However, the drying process takes longer due to the low solvent content, although damage to the environment by solvent emissions is lower.

High-solid paints (HS paints) and medium-solid paints (MS paints). These are paints which contain a high proportion of non-volatile components (solid content up to 70%). The solvent content on the other hand is greatly reduced (20% to 30%) for reasons of environmental protection. These paints are primarily used in repair applications. They are characterised by very good coverage, rapid thorough drying and a high-gloss finish. Furthermore, the large layer thickness possible in each work operation greatly reduces the labour expenditure.

Powder-based paints. A plastic which is processed into powder with a grain size of 20μm to 60μm is used as the binder. The powder is then sprayed with special spray guns onto cold or warm workpiece to be coated. The paint powder sticks to cold materials electrostatically and to warm workpieces by melting on. The paint film must then be established on the coated parts. By baking for example with infrared radiators at approx. 120℃ or in a stove furnace at temperatures above 130℃, the powder melts and the macromolecules of the binder cross-link (polyaddition). During cooling, a tight, shockproof, chemical-resistant paint layer with a thickness of up to 120μm is created. The advantage of this process lies in the fact that there is no emission of solvents. Furthermore, there are no spraying losses, since the powder-based paint that does not stick (overspray) can be returned to the production process.

REVIEW QUESTIONS:

1. What are the functions of paintwork?

2. What different types of paint are there?
3. What are powder-based paints?
4. What different ways of applying paint are used on a motor vehicle?

New Words

spray	喷，喷射，喷雾	porous	有毛孔或气孔的
immerse	沉浸，浸没	adhesion	黏连，黏合；黏附力
injector	注射器；喷嘴	subsequent	随后的
jet nozzle	喷嘴，喷射管	adherent	粘着的
solvent	溶剂	hood	发动机舱盖
viscosity	黏性	irregularity	不整齐；不规则
evaporate	挥发；蒸发	pore	细孔；气孔；毛孔
shrink	收缩，皱缩；缩水	lacquer	漆，天然漆
electrostatic	静电的，静电学的	glossy	有光泽的
be subjected to	遭受	binder	黏合剂，黏结剂
hydrostatic	流体静力学的，静水力学的	pigment	颜料；色料；色素
atomise	将……喷成雾状	additive	添加剂
atomisation	雾化	catalyst	催化剂
viscous	黏的，黏性的	antioxidant agent	抗氧化剂
corrosion inhibitor	腐蚀抑制剂，防腐剂	extender	添加物，填充剂
priming coat	底面涂层，底层漆	rust	铁锈，锈
priming paint	底漆	rust inhibitor	防锈剂
suspension	悬浮，悬架	stove	用火炉烤，使干燥
drain hole	排出孔；排水孔	dehydration	脱水；干燥
electraphoresis	电泳，电泳疗法	polycondensation	缩聚作用
artificial-resin	人造树脂，合成树脂	nitrocellulose	硝化纤维
emulsion	乳状液；乳胶漆	nitrocellulose paint	硝基漆
electrolyte	电解液；电解质	effect paint	外观漆
hydrogen	氢	inflammable	易燃的
ion	离子	duroplastic	硬质塑料
phosphate	磷酸，磷酸盐	alkyd	醇酸
dipcoat	浸渍涂层	melamine	三聚氰胺
undercoat	底漆层	oxidative curing	氧化固化
top coat	表面层	acrylic	丙烯酸
degrease	脱脂	thermoplastic	热塑塑料

cross-linking	交联；交叉连接	radiator	辐射器
polymerisation	聚合，聚合作用	furnace	熔炉
ultimate	最大的，极限的	shockproof	防振的，抗冲击的
hardener	硬化剂，固化剂	grease	油脂
polyaddition	加（成）聚（合）作用	residue	残余，残渣
scratch	擦，刮，划	knifing filler	细填料
mica	云母	polyester	聚脂
incident light	入射光	putty	油灰；腻子
true water-based paint	纯水漆	pulling paste	张力膏
water-thinnable paint	水稀释漆	galvanised	镀锌的
labour expenditure	工时费	flash point	闪点
paint film	漆膜	extinguisher	灭火器，消火器
infrared	红外线的		

课文参考译文

汽车喷漆

汽车喷漆的作用是保护车身表面，以防止外部物质的影响，如水和空气中的腐蚀性和磨损性物质，或防止石子的冲击。

汽车喷漆还有以下作用：

① 形成致密而牢固的保护膜。

② 形成坚硬且有一定弹性的表面。

③ 色彩持久而美观。

④ 产生标识的效果。

⑤ 易于清洁和维护。

1. 喷漆方法

汽车漆面可以通过气压喷漆、沉浸或电喷漆的方法获得。

（1）气压喷漆 对大部分部件都是利用压缩空气通过喷枪进行喷漆。

采用这种方法时，根据喷枪的工作原理，漆被气流吸入喷枪并输送到喷嘴。当漆射出喷嘴时，形成漆雾并沉落在车身表面上。

通常，采用两种不同的气压喷漆方法，即冷态喷漆和热态喷漆。

1）冷态喷漆。首先用溶剂将漆稀释（改变其黏度），直到漆能容易地喷雾。溶剂在喷漆后会自行挥发。溶剂过度迅速地挥发可能会引起漆面的收缩。

2）热态喷漆。喷漆时，通过漆罐中的加热器对漆进行预加热至50~120℃。这样，漆的黏度减小，因而可以在不需溶剂的情况下进行喷涂。

（2）静电喷漆　静电喷漆用于大批量生产。直流电源的正极和负极分别连接到车身上和漆的喷嘴上。电压高达200000V。带有负电荷的漆雾被带有正电荷的车身吸引。因而，减少了漆的损失。

在静电喷漆过程中，漆是通过高速转动的喇叭口喷出的，而不是通过喷枪。对那些高速转动喇叭口的漆雾不能到达的区域，需要使用喷涂机械手进行喷漆。

（3）无空气喷漆（高压力喷漆）　在这种喷漆中，液态漆受到高的液压力（10~20MPa），当漆从喷嘴出口释放出来时即被雾化。即使比较黏稠的漆采用无空气喷漆也容易获得精细的漆雾。为了使用较低的喷漆工作压力（4~6MPa），也可以利用压缩空气来帮助漆的雾化。这种方法主要用于喷涂漆面底层和防腐剂。

（4）浸漆　在大批量生产中，第一道底漆可以通过将车身板沉浸在盛有底漆的漆池里得以完成。车身板上过多的漆可以采用悬挂方法并通过排泄孔去掉。

（5）电泳涂漆　漆的颗粒，如悬浮在电解液中的水与人造树脂乳液被充以电荷，并被传送到带有相反电荷的车身板上，在车身板上，它们形成均匀的涂层。这个过程一直持续到车身板最后裸露的区域被漆覆盖，即被隔绝。电泳程序只适合于第一层底漆。由水的电解产生的正的氢离子游向带负电荷的车身板，在这里它们防止了电泳过程中车身板上氧化层的形成。

2. 漆层的组成

汽车漆层是由以下几层组成的：

1）磷酸层。

2）电泳浸涂底层。

3）中间防裂基层。

4）填充层（喷涂层）。

5）表面层（普通漆或金属漆）。

为使车身形成漆层，在施加必要的底层之前必须先对车身进行预热。为达到这一要求，应对车身进行清洗、脱脂，然后施加磷化层。

（1）磷化层　通过磷化的方法在薄金属板表面形成一层多孔磷酸铁层。这对于接下来施加良好黏附的涂层，以及形成很好的腐蚀防护都是十分必要的。

（2）电泳浸涂底层　该底层成为中间防裂基层、填充层和表面层的粘附层。这一底层通常通过沉浸或电泳的方法形成。

（3）中间防裂基层　汽车车身，特别是暴露而易于受到石子冲击的外表皮区域，如车身侧面车窗口下缘以下部分和发动机舱盖，应当施加中间防裂基层。

（4）填充层（喷涂层）　填充层的作用是修正表面上较小的不平整、磨痕和细孔等。填充层通常使用静电喷涂设备进行施加。它形成了底漆层和表面层的基础。如果表面层直接施加在填充层上，则填充层也承担着底漆层的作用。

（5）表面层　表面层分为普通漆面和金属漆面。

1）普通漆面。普通漆面通常是以四层漆结构或三层漆结构形成的。

① 四层漆结构。除了电泳浸涂底层和填充层外，还有两层漆通过静电喷涂的方法被施加。

a) 喷涂在底漆层上，并以约140℃的温度进行干燥。

b) 喷涂在表面层上，并以约130℃的温度进行干燥。

② 三层漆结构。三层漆结构由电泳浸涂底层、填充层和表面层组成。这种情况下，表面层被湿对湿地直接喷涂在填充层上，然后进行干燥。

四层漆结构与三层漆结构相比的优点是它在整个车身表面上的漆层厚度非常均匀，因为底漆层和表面层具有相同的厚度。

2）金属漆面。与普通漆面相比，金属漆面需要使用金属底漆作为色彩和外观表现层，而透明的清漆作为光亮和保护层。金属底漆和透明清漆分别通过空气雾化和静电喷涂的方法进行施加。它们以"湿对湿"的方法，即清漆被喷涂在没有立即干燥的底漆上。喷涂后使两种漆层以大约130℃的温度进行干燥。

3. 汽车漆

汽车漆由非蒸发成分和蒸发成分组成（表1）。

表1 汽车漆的成分

成分类型	成分名称	
非蒸发性成分	粘结剂	树脂、成膜介质
	颜料	非溶解颗粒
	添加剂	催化剂、抗氧化剂、填充剂、防锈剂
蒸发性成分	溶剂	稀释剂、反应生成物

（1）粘结剂　粘结剂在喷涂和干燥程序后形成漆膜。这样，颜料通过树脂相互结合。成膜介质加速漆层形成过程，并改善漆的成形性能。

（2）颜料　颜料给漆层增加了色彩效果。颜料是漆的颗粒，它们以非溶解固体形式存在于漆中。

（3）添加剂　包括：催化剂，加速固化和干燥过程；抗氧化剂，防止漆形成结皮和变稠；填充剂，改善光泽和漆膜的形成；防锈剂，能改善漆的保护性能。

（4）溶剂　溶剂能溶解漆中的固体和黏稠成分，使其达到喷涂漆所需要的黏度。溶剂和反应生成物在喷涂漆过程中和漆膜的干燥（如通过缩聚作用进行干燥）过程中蒸发。

4. 汽车漆的类型

汽车漆有以下几种类型：

1）硝基漆。

2）外观漆。

3）高固体含量漆。

4）合成漆。

5）水溶性漆。

6）粉末基漆。

（1）硝基漆　这种漆现在一般不再用来喷涂汽车。硝基漆面由于溶剂的蒸发会迅速固化。它们具有高的易燃性，易受燃油的侵蚀，需要定期保养以保持良好的光泽。硝基漆现在主要用于古典老爷车的喷漆。

（2）合成漆　合成漆使用硬质塑料（醇酸树脂、三聚氰胺树脂）作为粘结剂。这种漆在大气中氧的影响下固化，这叫做氧化固化。它主要用作汽车表面漆。

（3）丙烯酸树脂漆　这种漆采用丙烯酸树脂（热塑性塑料）作为粘结剂。它们通过物理干燥，即通过溶剂的蒸发而干燥。丙烯酸树脂漆能够借助于溶剂而溶解，而且它们是可逆的硅树脂，被用作耐热漆的粘结剂。这种漆既被用作电泳浸涂底层漆，也被用作汽车表面漆。丙烯酸树脂漆又被分为：

① 单成分漆（1C漆）。

② 双成分漆（2C漆）。

1）单成分漆（1C漆）。这种漆通常在大气中氧的影响下通过分子的交联键（聚合作用）而固化。溶剂和反应生成物在这个过程中蒸发，形成高光泽度的漆层。漆层的最大硬度通常几周以后才能形成。使用干燥室以100~140℃的温度加热，可以加快固化过程。

2）双成分漆（2C漆）。这种漆由填充剂和固化剂组成。在大量生产过程中，这种漆通常以正确的比例在喷枪中进行混合。在这两种成分之间，发生化学反应（加成聚合作用），从而逐步固化喷涂的漆膜，即使在室温下也没有反应生成物。

丙烯酸树脂漆在温度达到130℃时，能加速固化过程。这种漆具有耐化学剂、抗划伤、耐风雨侵蚀的能力。

（4）外观漆（金属漆）　这种漆除含有色彩颜料外，底漆中还含有云母或铝的小薄片。由于这些添加物能反射入射光，因而在汽车表面上形成了金属感的外观效果。这种底漆被喷涂后，接着"湿对湿"地喷涂第二层清漆，以便对底漆形成保护。

（5）水溶性漆　塑料基树脂起着粘结剂的作用。在作为填充层和底层时，漆中的有机溶剂成分几乎完全被水代替。只有在透明涂料中，才含有大约10%质量分数的有机溶剂，而水的质量分数高达80%。

水溶漆有以下不同种类：

1）纯水漆。纯水涂料的树脂分子溶解在水中。

2）水稀释漆（悬浮液）。树脂颗粒细微地分布在水中。

这种漆被使用后，漆层中的水和溶剂在干燥设备中蒸发，形成致密的防水、耐化学剂的漆层。然而，因为溶剂含量低，所以干燥过程耗费时间较长。但因溶剂蒸发而导致的对环境的损害也较低。

（6）高固体含量漆（HS漆）和中等固体含量漆（MS漆）　这种漆含有高比例的非蒸发成分（固体成分质量分数达70%）。另一方面，因为保护环境的缘故，漆中的溶剂质量分数有较大幅度地减小（约为20%~30%）。这种漆主要在汽车漆面修理时使用。它们具有非常好的覆盖能力、迅速的干燥能力和高的表面光泽度。另外，每一次喷涂操作可以施加较大厚度的漆层，因而大大减少了工时费。

（7）粉末基漆　这种漆是以20~60μm的粒度加工成粉末的塑料作为粘结剂。然后，用专门的喷枪将这些粉末喷涂在需要涂层的冷或热的工件上。漆的粉末以静电的方法粘附在冷的材料上，或以熔化的方法粘附在热的工件上。然后，在喷涂的部分上必须施加漆膜。使用红外辐射器烘烤至大约120℃，或在干燥炉中烘烤至130℃以上，使粉末熔化，并且使粘结剂中的大分子交联（加成聚合作用）在一起。冷却的过程中，形成了厚度达120μm的致密的、抗冲击的、耐化学剂的漆层。这种方法的优点在于整个过程没有溶剂的蒸发排放。此外，由于没有粘附到被涂表面的粉末基漆（过度喷涂）能够返回再用，因而不存在喷涂损失。

Teil 10　Arbeitssicherheit　劳动安全
Part 10　Working-Safety　劳动安全

学习目标

【知识目标】
1.掌握与劳动安全技术原理等相关的专业术语、单词和词汇。
2.掌握劳动安全技术主要知识的德文、英文表达方法。

【能力目标】
1.能对劳动安全技术进行中、德、英互译。
2.能进行与劳动安全技术相关的德语、英语资料的阅读和翻译。
3.能在劳动安全实物上标识出相应结构的德语、英语单词和词汇。

Text 1　Arbeitssicherheit und Unfallverhütung 劳动安全与事故防护（德文）

Bild：Zeichen der gewerblichen Berufsgenossenschaften

　　Der Betrieb von Maschinen und der Umgang mit technischen Systemen sowie mit Werk- und Hilfsstoffen birgt stets Gefahren in sich. Durch unfallverhütende Maßnahmen im Arbeitsbereich sollen sowohl der Mensch als auch Einrichtungen, Gebäude und die Umwelt vor Schaden bewahrt werden. Zur Förderung der Arbeitssicherheit und damit zur Verminderung des Unfallrisikos gibt es für jeden Berufszweig verbindliche Unfallverhütungsvorschriften (UVV). Sie werden von den jeweils zuständigen Berufsgenossenschaften erlassen. Die Berufsgenossenschaft Metall ist z.B. für Kfz- Reparaturbetriebe verantwortlich. Die Unfallverhütungsvorschriften müssen in jedem Betrieb gut erkennbar und leicht zugänglich und ausgelegt sein. Jeder Betriebsangehörige ist verpflichtet, dass er diese Vorschriften genau einhält. Durch sicherheitswidriges Verhalten können schwere oder gar tödliche Verletzungen entstehen, Krankheiten ausgelöst, sowie hohe Sach- und Umweltschäden verursacht werden.

Sicherhheitswidrig verhält sich jeder, der Sicherheitsvorschriften und Sicherheitszeichen nicht beachtet oder missachtet und somit seine Mitmenschen, die Einrichtungen und Anlagen des Betriebes und die Umwelt gefährdet.

Sicherheitszeichen

Sie sollen die Sicherheit am Arbeitsplatz erhöhen. Es wurden dazu Gebots-, Verbots-, Warn- und Rettungszeichen genormt.

Bild: Gebotszeichen

Gebotszeichen sind runde Scheiben in den Farben blau und weiß. Skizzen zeigen die gebotene Schutzmaßnahme als zwingende Verhaltensweise an. So muss z.B. bei Arbeiten unter hohen Lärm (ab 90 dB(A)) ein Gehörschutz verwendet werden.

Verbotszeichen sind weißgrundige, runde Scheinen, die die verbotene Handlung als schwarze Skizze zeigen. Ein roter Querbalken und rote Umrandung heben die Verbotszeichen hervor.

Bild: Verbotszeichen

Brennbare Flüssigkeiten, die bei Raumtemperatur verdunsten (z.B. Benzin) oder brennbare Gase (z.B. Wasserstoff) oder auch Feinstäube(z.B. Mehl) können in einem geschlossenen Raum mit der Luft ein hochexplosives Gemisch bilden. In diesen Räumen muss das Zeichen, das Feuer, offenes Licht und Rauchen untersagt, gut sichtbar angebracht sein.

Bild: Warnzeichen

Warnzeichen sind gelbgrundige Schilder in der Form eines gleichseitigen Dreiecks, dessen Spitze nach oben zeigt. Warnbild und Umrandung sind schwarz. Mit dem Warnzeichen, das gut sichtbar angebracht sein muss, wird ein Umfeld gekennzeichnet, in dem vor einer bestimmten Gefahr gewarnt wird. Lagerräume, in denen z.B. ätzende Schwefelsäure für Starterbatterien gelagert wird, müssen mit dem entsprechenden Warnzeichen versehen sein.

Rettungszeichhen sind grüngrundige Schilder in Rechteckform. Sie weisen durch weiße Piktogramme (Symbolbilder) und ggf. Pfeile auf Stellen hin, an denen sich Rettungsmittel (z.B. Tragen) befinden. Sic kennzeichnen auch die Fluchtwege und die Fluchtrichtungen, über die Gefahrenbereiche schnell und sicher verlassen werden können. Diese Fluchtwege müssen stets frei sein, sie dürfen nie durch Gegenstände blockiert oder durch abgeschlossene oder gegen die Fluchtrichtung öffnende Türen gehemmt sein.

Unfallursachen

Trotz größter Sorgfalt und umfangreichster Sicherheitsvorkehrungen werden sich Unfälle nie ganz vermeiden lassen. Ihre Zahl kann aber sehr wohl durch Untersuchung und Auswertung der Unfallursachen mit den sich daraus ergebenden Unfallverhütungsvorschriften eingedämmt werden. Bei den Unfallursachen ist zu unterscheiden

– meschanisches Versagen durch Unkenntnis der Gefahr, Gedankenlosigkeit, Leichtsinn und Bequemlichkeit. Diese Unfallursache kann durch gründliche Schulung, Erziehung zu sicherheitseinrichtungen, z.B. Schutzgitter, Sicherheitsschhalter, entschärft werden.

– technisches Versagen, z.B. durch Werkstoffermüdung oder umvorhersehbare Überlastung. Hier können Unfälle durch technische Sicherheitsvorkehrungen, z.B. Verstärkung des Bauteils, das durch Bruch zu einem Unfall geführt hat, verhindert werden.

– höhere Gewalt durch nicht vorhhersehbare Fremdeinwirkung, z.B. abnormaler Witterungseinfluss.

Sicherheitsmaßnahmen

Viele Unfälle können durch vorbeugende Sicherheitsmaßnahmen vermieden oder zumindest in ihren Folgen vermindert werden.

Gefährdung muss verhindert werden.

– Elektrische Geräte, z.B. Handbohrmaschinen mit beschädigten Anschlussleitungen dürfen nicht benutzt werden.

– Gefahren für Augen und Gesicht, z.B. beim Schweißen oder durch Metallsplitter beim Schleifen, sind durch Schutzbrillen, Schutzschirme und Schutzschilder abzuwenden.

Bild : Warnzeichen und Rettungszeichen

Gefahrenstellen sind abzuschirmen und auffallend zu kennzeichnen.

— Rädertriebe, Spindeln, Wellen und bewegte ineinander greifende Teile müssen abgestimmt sein, z.B. durch Schutzgitter.

— Behälter mit Gefahrstoffen (z.B. Benzin, Säuren, Brenngase) müssen vorschriftsmäßig, z.B. mit den entsprechenden Warnzeichen, gekennzeichnet und sicher aufgestellt sein.

Gefahren müssen beseitigt werden.

— Maschinen und Werkzeuge mit Sicherheitsmängeln müssen sofort von der Verwendung ausgeschlossen werden. Sie sind umgehend der Instandsetzung oder der Ausmusterung zuzuleiten.

— Scharfe, spitze Werkzeuge dürfen nicht offen (z.B. ohne Schutztasche) in der Arbeitskleidung getragen werden.

— Ringe, Uhren, Schmuckstücke sind ggf. vor der Arbeit abzulegen, so dass sie von rotierenden Teilen nicht erfasst werden.

— Verkehrs- und Fluchtwege müssen stets frei von Hindernissen sein.

WIEDERHOLUNGSFRAGEN:

1. Nennen Sie 3 Beispiele für sicherheitswidriges Verfahren im Kfz- Reparaturbetrieb.
2. Welche Berufsgenossenschaft ist für Kfz-Reparaturbetriebe zuständig?
3. Welche Gruppen der Sicherheitszeichen werden unterschieden?
4. Nach welchen Gesichtspunkten können Unfallursachen eingeteilt werden?

Neue Wörter

die	Arbeitssicherheit	劳动安全	das	Rettungszeichen	救援标识
die	Unfallverhütung	事故防护	das	Gehörschutz	听力保护装置
das	Zeichen	标识		weißgrundig	底色为白色的
die	Einrichtung	设备	die	brennbare Flüssigkeit	可燃液体
das	Gebäude	建筑物	das	brennbare Gas	可燃气体
die	Umwelt	环境		hochexplosiver	爆炸性危险较高的
das	Unfallrisiko	事故风险	das	Feuer	火焰
die	Berufsgenossenschaft	工会		sichtbar	明显可见的
der	Kfz- Reparaturbetrieb	汽车维修企业		gelbgrundig	黄色底色
die	Krankheit	疾病	die	Gefahr	危险
die	Verletzung	受伤	die	Schwefelsäure	硫酸
das	Sicherheitszeichen	安全标识		versehen	张贴
der	Arbeitsplatz	工位		grüngrundig	绿色底色
das	Gebotszeichen	指示标识	das	Rettungsmittel	救生设备
das	Verbotszeichen	禁止标识	die	Tragen	支座，托架
das	Warnzeichen	警示标识			

Text 2　Working-Safety 劳动安全（英文）

Safety signs

These are intended to enhance safety in the workplace. Signs that are used include mandatory instructions, prohibitions, warnings, first-aid and hazardous substance information.

Mandatory information signs are round, and coloured in blue and white. Symbols indicate that the required safety measures are mandatory procedures. One example is the use of eye and ear protection required for employees performing cutting operations with grinders.

Prohibition signs are round signs with a white background in which the prohibited action is represented in black. A diagonal red bar and red periphery are the distinctive features of the prohibition sign. Fire, open flames and smoking are prohibited in areas where explosive gases may form.

Warning signs are triangular notices featuring black symbols and a black periphery against a yellow background. Warning signs warn against specific hazards that may be encountered within an individual area. The relevant warning signs are required in areas such as warehouses in which caustic sulphuric acid for use in starter batteries is being stored.

First-aid and emergency exit signs are rectangular signs bearing white symbols on a green background. Arrows indicate the directions to the location where first-aid and lifesaving equipment such as stretchers or first-aid kits are stored. They also identify exits and directions for the fast evacuation of hazardous areas.

Safety measures

Safety measures may be of a technical, organisational or personnel-related nature. Technical measures should always be implemented first. Personnel-related measures should only be implemented in exceptional cases.

- Examples of technical measures:
  ➢ Avoiding the hazard by routing supply lines from the ceiling instead of the floor.
  ➢ Separating personnel from the hazard by providing an enclosure for a dangerous machine.
  ➢ Replacing a hazardous substance with a non-hazardous substance.
- Examples of organizational measures:
  ➢ Posting relevant warning signs.
  ➢ Controlling access to hazardous areas.
- Examples of personnel-related measures:
  ➢ Supplying personnel with personal protective equipment.
  ➢ Instruction and training courses.

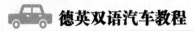

Deutsch – English Kraftfahrzeugtechnik // German – English Automotive Engineering

New Words

enclosure	围栏，围墙	evacuation	撤离，疏散
mandatory	强制性	pictogram	象形图
grinder	研磨机，磨床	preparation	配制品
diagonal	斜线的，斜的	hazard	危险，风险
encounter	遇到（困难或不利的事），碰到，面临	working-safety	劳动安全
		safety signs	安全标识
caustic	腐蚀性的，苛性的	instructions signs	指示标识
sulphuric acid	硫酸	prohibitions signs	禁止标识
rectangular	长方形的，矩形的	warnings signs	警示标识
stretcher	担架	first-aid signs	救援标识

课文参考译文

安全标志

安全标志的作用是提高工作场所的安全性。标准化的标志形式明确传达了指令、禁止、警告、急救和危险物质等信息。

指令标志为圆形，颜色为蓝色和白色。这种标志符号表明了规定的安全措施是严格要求和强制执行的。例如，利用磨床或砂轮机进行切割操作的人员必须佩戴护目镜和护耳器。

禁止标志也是圆形标志，其底色为白色，禁止的行为以黑色标出。斜红杠和红色圆周是禁止标志的显著特点。在爆炸性危险较高的区域，如汽油和可燃气体存在的地方，火、明火焰和吸烟是被禁止的。相应的禁止标志必须悬桂或张贴在室内明显的位置。

警告标志为三角形告示，其特点是黑色符号和黑色边框，具有对比明显的黄色底色。警告标志应当总是悬挂在较高的可见位置。这种标志警告人们在个别区域防止可能遇到的特有危险。在仓库等区域，如果存储具有腐蚀性的蓄电池硫酸，则需要张贴相应的警告标志。

急救和安全出口标志为长方形边框，其中有白色符号和绿色底色。符号表示急救和救生设备，如担架的位置。还有为脱离危险区域而迅速和安全逃生的明确标注的出口和方向指示。

安全措施

安全措施具有与技术、组织或人员相关的性质。应始终首先实施技术措施。只应在特殊情况下实施与人员相关的措施。
- 与技术相关的措施举例：
  - ➢ 在天花板，而不是地板上铺设供电线路以避免危险。
  - ➢ 通过为危险机器提供围栏，将人员与危险物分离。
  - ➢ 用非危险物质替换危险物质。
- 与组织相关的措施举例：
  - ➢ 张贴相关警告标志。
  - ➢ 限制进入危险区域。
- 与人员相关的措施举例：
  - ➢ 为人员提供个人防护装备。
  - ➢ 指导和培训课程。

Kapitel 3
Neue Technologie

新技术篇

Chapter 3
New Technology

新技术篇

Teil 1　Benzineinspritzung　汽油直喷
Part 1　LH-Motronic　汽油直喷

【知识目标】
1. 掌握与系统结构、分类、运行原理等相关的专业术语、单词和词汇。
2. 掌握系统主要结构的德文、英文表达方法。

【能力目标】
1. 能对系统总体结构的各部分细节进行中、德、英互译。
2. 能进行与系统大体构造相关的德语、英语资料阅读和翻译。
3. 能在系统实物上标识出相应结构的德语、英语单词和词汇。

Text 1　Benzineinspritzung汽油直喷（德文）

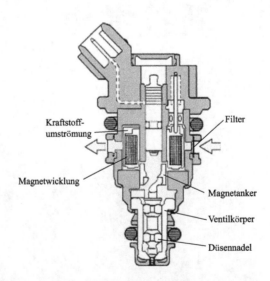

Bild: Einspritzventil

Einspritzventil. Jedem Zylinder des Motors ist ein elektromagnetisch betätigtes Einspritzventil

新技术篇

Kapitel 3　Neue Technologie // Chapter 3　New Technology

(Aktor) zugeordnet.

Luftumspülte Einspritzventile. Sie verhindern durch die Luftumspülung des Einspritzstrahls eine Tröpfchenbildung. Dabei werden kleinste Kraftstoffmengen fein zerstäubt und mit Luft vorgemischt. Dies ist besonders günstig für das Leerlaufverhalten und die Abgaszusammensetzung. Gleichzeitig wird der Anteil schädlicher Abgasanteile verringert.

Simultaneinspritzung. Alle Einspritzventile sind elektrisch parallel geschaltet und spritzen je Kurbelwellenumdrehung jeweils die Hälfte der für die Verbrennung notwendigen Kraftstoffmenge ein. Dadurch ist eine genaue Zuordnung zwischen Kurbelwinkel und Einspritzzeitpunkt nicht notwendig. Die Steuerung des Auslösezeitpunktes erfolgt drehzahlabhängig vom Steuergerät.

Einspritzdauer. Sie hängt im wesentlichen von der Stauklappenstellung im Luftmengenmesser ab. Stauklappenstellung und Motordrehzahl sind die Hauptinformation für das Steuergerät.

Außerdem erhält das Steuergerät folgende Korrekturgrößen von den Sensoren:

– Luft- und Motortemperatur über Temperaturfühler (NTC- Widerständer).

– Schubabschaltung und Vollastanreicherung über den Drosselklappenschalter.

– Gemischzusammensetzung über die Lambda-Sonde.

Alle diese Informationen werden im Steuergerät verarbeitet. Daraus werden die Einspritzzeitpunkte sowie die Öffnungszeit der Einspritzventile d.h. die Einspritzmenge bestimmt.

Luftmengemesser. In ihm befindet sich die Stauklappe, die unter der Federspannung einer Spiralfeder steht. Die Stauklappe wird entsprechend der Luftströmung beim Ansaugen gegen die Federkraft in eine bestimmte Winkelstellung gebracht. Sie ist das Maß für die angesaugte Luftmenge. Diese Winkelstellung wird auf ein Potentiometer übertragen und als eine Hauptinformation an das Steuergerät gegeben. Die mit der Stauklappe fest verbundene Kompensationsklappe gleicht im Zusammenwirken mit dem Luftpolster der Dämpfungskammer von außen einwirkende mechanische Schwingungen(Erschütterungen, Motorvibrationen) und vom Luftstrom kommende Rückschwingungen aus. Die Zusammensetzung des Mischungsverhältnisses von Kraftstoff zu Luft im Leerlauf kann über einen einstellbaren Bypass beeinflusst werden. Dabei kann eine geringe Luftmenge die Stauklappe umgehen.

Startanreicherung

Beim Kaltstart entstehen Kondensationsverluste der Kraftstoffanteile im Kraftstoff-Luft-Gemisch z.B. als Wandfilmbenetzungen an den kalten Wänden des Ansaugsystems. Zum Ausgleich und zum Starten muss in Abhängigkeit von der Motortemperatur zusätzlich Kraftstoff eingespritzt werden (fettes Gemisch $\lambda < 1,0$).

Die Startanreicherung kann durch eine Startsteuerung oder durch ein Kaltstartventil erfolgen.

Startsteuerung. Sie erfolgt durch die Signalauswertung vom Startschalter und Motortemperaturfühler. Durch Verlängerung der Öffnungszeit der Einspritzventile (Aktor) erfolgen. Es wird beim Kaltstart abhängig von Luft- und Motortemperatur über das Steuergerät angesteuert und liefert dann den zuszätzlich benötigten Kraftstoff.

Warmlaufphase. Sie folgt nach dem Kaltstart des Motors. Da hierbei noch ein Teil des Kraftstoffes kondensiert, muss das Einspritzsystem das Kraftstoff- Luft- Gemisch anfetten. In der Warmlaufphase erfolgt eine zusätzliche Gemischanreicherung, entweder über eine Verlängerung der Einspritzzeit oder über das Kaltstartventil.

Zur Überwindung der erhöhten Reibungswiderstände des kalten Morors muss im Leerlauf eine größere innere Leistung (Innenleistung) des Motors aufgebracht werden. Um diesen Leistungsbedarf auszugleichen, benötigt der Motor in der Warmlaufphase mehr Kraftstoff- Luft-Gemisch.

Durch einen veränderlichen Bypass, der die Drosselklappe umgeht, und eine Einspritzverlängerung wird dies erreicht.

Mit steigender Motortemperatur wird die Warmlaufanreicherung verringert und bei Erreichen der Betriebstemperatur eingestellt.

Leerlaufdrehzahl-Regelung mittels Leerlaufsteller. Er bewirkt bei allen Betriebsbedingungen des Motors eine stabile Abgaswerte und berücksichtigt teilweise auch alterungsbedingte Veränderungen des Motors. Das Steuergerät liefert ein Signal, abhängig von Motordrehzahl und Motortemperatur an den Leerlaufsteller. Danach verstellt der Drehmagnetantrieb den Drehschieber und verändert den Querschnitt im Bypasskanal. Die geforderte Leerlaufdrehzahl stellt sich so unabhängig von der Belastung des Motors ein.

Drosselklappenschalter. Er wird durch die Drosselklappe betätigt. Im Drosselklappenschalter befinden sich Kontakte für Leerlauf- und Volllastbetrieb. Beim Schließen der entsprechenden Kontakte erhält das Steuergerät Informationen über Leerlauf- oder Volllaststellung und verarbeitet diese bei der Festlegung der Einspritzdauer.

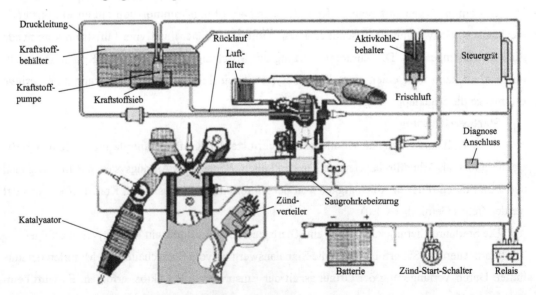

Bild: Benzineinspritzung mit Luftmassenmessung

Lambda-Sonde. Sie gibt Informationen an das Steuergerät zur exakten Kraftstoffzuteilung für das geforderte Mischungsverhältnis.

Benzineinspritzung mit Luftmassenmessung (LMM)

Bei diesem System wird die Luftmasse dadurch erfasst, dass ein „thermischer Lastsensor" (Hitzdraht oder Heißfilm) von der vorbeiströmenden Luft abgekühlt wird. Dadurch ändert sich der Sensorwiderstand.

Eine Elektronik regelt den Heizstrom so, dass die Temperatur des Sensors bzw. der Sensoroberfläche konstant bleibt. Das daraus abgeleitete variable Spannungssignal ergibt das Messsignal für das elektronische Steuergerät.

Luftmassenmesser messen direkt die dem Motor zugeführte Luftmasse, d.h. die Messung ist unabhängig von der Luftdichte, die von Luftdruck (Höhenlage) und Lufttemperatur abhängig.

Da das Kraftstoff-Luft-Gemisch als Masseverhältnis angegeben wird, z.B. 1 kg Kraftstoff zu 14,8 kg Luft, ist die Luftmassenmessung das genaueste Messverfahren für die Gemischbildung.

Luftmassenmessung mit Hitzdraht, LH-Motronic

Die LH-Motronic ist eine Weiterentwicklung der L-Jetronic. Einspritzsystem und Zündsystem werden von einem gemeinsamen Steuergerät versorgt.

Bei diesem Benzineinspritzsystem ist im Ansaugkanal ein Hitzdraht aufgespannt. Der Hitzdraht wird durch elektrischen Strom auf einer konstanten Temperatur von 100℃ über der Ansaugtemperatur gehalten. Wird durch wechselnde Fahrzustände vom Motor mehr oder weniger Luft angesaugt, verändert sich die Temperatur im Hitzdraht. Der Wärmeentzug muss durch den Heitz strom ausgeglichen werden. Die Größe des benötigten Heizstromes ist damit ein Maß für die angesaugte Luftmasse. Die Luftmassenmessung erfolgt etwa 1000-mal je Sekunde. Bei Bruch des Hitzdrahtes schaltet das Steuergerät auf Notlauf. Das Fahrzeug bleibt eingeschränkt fahrbereit.

Da der Hitzdraht im Ansaugkanal sitzt, können sich Ablagerungen bilden, die das Messergebnis beeinflussen. Nach jedemAbstellen des Motors wird durch ein Signal vom Steuergerät deshalb der Hitzdraht kurzzeitig auf etwa 1000℃ erwärmt. Drahtgitter schützen den Platin-Hitzdraht (Durchmesser 0,07 mm) vor mechanischen Einflüssen.

Das Hitzdrahtelement kann auch in einem Bypasskanal zum Innenrohr angebracht sein. Durch das Luftleitgitter werden Lufturbulenzen an der Messstelle verhindert. Im Innenrohr befinden sich keine beweglichen Bauteile, die als Strömungswiderstand wirken. Eine Verschmutzung des Hitzdrahtelementes wird durch seine Glasbeschichtung und die hohe Luftgeschwindigkeit im Bypasskanal vermieden. Das Freibrennen ist bei dieser Anlage nicht mehr nötig.

Luftmassenmessung mit Heißfilm (HFM)

In einem zusätzlichen Messkanal zum Innenrohr ist ein Heißfilm- Luftmassensensor eingebaut. Der Heißfilm ist weitgehend unempfindlich gegen Verschmutzungen. Ein Freibrennen – wie bei der Hitzdraht-Luftmassenmessung im zylindrischen Messkanal – ist nicht notwendig.

Wirkungsweise. Die vom Motor angesaugte Luftmasse durchströmt den Luftmassenmesser und beeinflusst so die Temperatur am Heißfilmsensor. Der Heißfilmsensor besteht aus drei elektrischen Widerständen:

- Heizwiderstand R_H (Platinfilmwiderstand).
- Sensorwiderstand R_S.
- Temperaturwiderstand R_L (Ansauglufttemperatur).

Die elektrische Brückenschaltung besteht aus dünnen Filmwiderständen, die auf einer Keramikschicht aufgebracht sind.

Die Elektronik im Heißfilm-Luftmassenmesser regelt über eine veränderliche Spannung die Temperatur des Heizwiderstandes R_H, so dass sie 160℃ über der Ansauglufttemperatur liegt. Die Ansauglufttemperatur wird vom temperaturabhängigen Ansauglufttemperaturwiderstand R_L erfasst. Die Temperatur des Heizwiderstandes wird durch den Sensorwiderstand R_S ermittelt. Bei erhöhtem oder verringertem Luftmassendurchsatz wird der Heizwiderstand mehr oder weniger abgekühlt. Die Elektronik regelt über den Sensorwiderstand die Spannung am Heizwiderstand nach, um die Temperaturdifferenz von 160℃ wieder zu erreichen. Aus dieser Regelspannung erzeugt die Elektronik für das Steuergerät ein Signal für die angesaugte Luftmasse (Durchsatz).

Bei Ausfall des Luftmassenmessers kann das elektronische Steuergerät einen Ersatzwert für die Öffnungszeit der Einspritzventile bilden (Notlaufbetrieb). Der Ersatzwert wird gebildet aus Drosselklappenwinkel und Drehzahlsignal.

Vorteile der Luftmassenmessung:

- Exaktes Erfassen der Luftmasse.
- schnelles Ansprechen des Luftmassenmessers.
- keine Messfehler durch Luftdruckunterschiede.
- keine Messfeher durch Temperaturunterschiede der Ansaugluft.
- einfacher Aufbau und keine bewegten Teile im Luftmassenmesser.
- sehr geringer Strömungswiderstand im Ansaugkanal.

WIEDERHOLUNGSFRAGEN

1. Welche Verfahren gibt es zur Luftmassenmessung bei Benzineinspritzanlagen?
2. Wie erfolgt die Luftmassenmessung mittels Hitzdraht?
3. Was versteht man unter „Freibrennen"?
4. Wie erfolgt die Luftmassenmessung mittels Heißfilmsensor?
5. Welcher Unterschied besteht in der Lufrmassenmessung mittels Hitzdraht oder Heißfilm?

新技术篇

Kapitel 3　Neue Technologie // Chapter 3　New Technology

Neue Wörter

die	Benzineinspritzung	汽油直喷		die	Lambda-Sonde	氧传感器
das	Einspritzventil	喷油器		die	Spiralfeder	螺旋弹簧
der	Düsennadel	喷嘴		das	Steuergerät	电控单元
die	Magnetwicklung	电磁线圈		die	Motorvibration	发动机抖动
der	Magnetanker	衔铁		das	Bypass	旁通
der	Filter	过滤器		der	Kaltstart	冷起动
der	Ventilkörper	阀体		das	Ansaugsystem	进气系统
der	Aktor	致动器，执行器		das	Kraftstoff-Luft-Gemisch	油气混和气
die	Luftumspülung	扫气		das	Ausgleich	平衡，补偿
der	Einspritzstrahl	喷射束		der	Startschalter	起动开关
das	Leerlaufverhalten	怠速特性		die	Warmlaufphase	热运行阶段
die	Kraftstoffmenge	燃油量		die	Verlängerung	延长
die	Abgaszusammensetzung	废气成分		die	Leistung	功率
der	Kurbelwinkel	曲轴转角		die	Reibungswiderstände	摩擦阻力
der	Einspritzzeitpunkt	喷射正时		die	Leerlaufdrehzahl-Regelung	怠速调节器
der	Einspritzdauer	喷射持续时间		die	Betriebsbedingung	工况条件
der	Temperaturfühler	温度传感器		die	Luftmassenmessung	空气质量测量
der	Drosselklappenschalter	节气门开关				

Text 2　LH-Motronic 汽油喷射（英文）

LH-Motronic is a further developed variant of L-Jetronic. The electromagnetic fuel injectors are sequentially actuated by the ECU. The fuel is injected into the intake manifold shortly before the engine inlet valves, which are still closed at the start of injection. Engine speed and inducted air mass are used as the main controlled variables (m/n-system). The latter is determined by a hot wire or hot film air mass sensor, which is also the external feature of LH-Motronic.

LH-Jetronic subsystems

Air intake system. The air filtered by the air filter and inducted by the engine flows into the intake manifold. There the air mass is recorded by the mass airflow sensor and transmitted to the ECU in the form of a voltage signal. An NTC resistor, which can also be integrated in the mass airflow sensor, is used as the air temperature sensor. The voltage drop at the thermistor is the measure of the intake air temperature.

Fuel system. Two-line systems are usually used in LH-Jetronic. An electric fuel pump, which is located either in the fuel tank (in-tank pump) or on the vehicle underbody (inline pump), delivers the fuel from the fuel tank via a fuel filter to the fuel rail. All the fuel injectors are supplied with fuel from the fuel rail. At the end of the fuel rail is a pressure regulator, which keeps the differential pressure constant at approx. 3.5 bar. The excess fuel returns from the pressure regulator to the fuel tank.

Regenerating system. The hydrocarbons temporarily stored in the carbon canister must be supplied for combustion in an appropriate operating state, e.g. part load. For this purpose, the regenerating valve (tank vent valve) is clocked by the engine ECU so that air and hydrocarbons can be drawn in by the vacuum pressure acting in the intake manifold.

Exhaust gas recirculation. An exhaust gas recirculation system can be used to improve the exhaust gas values.

The internal resistance levels of the engine when the engine is cold are greater than when it is hot on account of the viscous engine oil and increased friction. In order to overcome this resistance and facilitate stable idle speeds, the engine must generate more power. This is achieved by an increased amount of mixture. Furthermore, idle speed fluctuations must be compensated by a loaded vehicle electrical system or by a cut-in A/C compressor.

The ECU requires the signals from the following sensorsfor idle speed control:

- Engine speed sensor (actual speed).
- Engine temperature sensor (determination of the setpoint speed).

One of the following actuators is used for speed control.

Idle speed actuator. This permits additional airdepending on the requirement to flow in a bypass around the closed throttle valve. For this purpose, it is actuated by the ECU by means of pulse-width- modulated signals, a process which opens the air ductto a lesser or greater extent.

Throttle valve actuator. This subassembly consists of an electric motor, a gearing and the throttle valve. At idle the electric motor is actuated by the engine ECU in such a way that it opens or closes the throttle valve depending on the actual speed so that a prespecifiedsetpoint speed is maintained.

When the engine is running with increased revs and with the throttle valve closed (overrunning, e.g. in downhill-driving situations), overrun fuel cut-off prevents fuel from being injected. Fuel injection resumes when the throttle valve opens or when the engine speed drops below a stored threshold, e.g. 1,200 rpm.

The ECU requires the following information for overrun fuel cut-off:

- Throttle valve position from the throttle valve switch or throttle valve potentiometer.
- Engine speed from the engine speed sensor.

Engines with three-way catalysts are operated as far as possible in the $\lambda = 1$ range on account of exhaust gas regulations. To be able to output the maximum engine power, the inducted mixture is enriched, depending on the engine, to lambda 0.85 to 0.95. Lambda closed-loop control must be cut out for this purpose. Enrichment begins when the throttle valve potentiometer signals full load to the ECU or the voltage change per unit of time at the potentiometer exceeds a specific stored value. Extremely powerful engines do not necessarily require full-load enrichment.

Altitude adaptation

There is no need for special altitude adaptation in non-supercharged engines because the mass airflow sensor takes into account a reduced air density, for instance at greater altitudes.

Engine speed limitation is activated when the ECU receives from the engine speed sensor a signal from which it detects that the stored maximum speed has been reached. The moment of ignition is moved in the retard direction to limit the power and with it the maximum speed as well as the top road speed. Fuel injection is cut out in exceptional cases only.

LH-Jetronic as Motronic

All LH-Jetronic systems (fuel injection systems) are essentially designed as Motronic systems, i.e. both mixture formation and ignition of the fuel-air mixture is controlled by a common engine ECU. Here, depending on the manufacturer's requirements and year of manufacture, different ignition systems can be combined with LH-Jetronic. By using Motronic systems, it is possible to reduce design complexity, increase operational reliability and improve the efficiency of the systems.

LH-Motronic fuel injectors

Function. When the valve field winding is supplied with power by the ECU, a magnetic field is generated in it which attracts the solenoid armature. This raises the nozzle needle off its seat and fuel is injected. The needle stroke, depending on the valve design, is 0.05 mm to 0.1 mm. When the ECU stops supplying power as a function of the operating state (after 1.5 ms to 18 ms), the magnetic field collapses and the closing spring forces the nozzle needle into its seat. Fuel injection is terminated. The mass of the injected fuel is dependent on:

- the valve opening time.
- the injected fuel quantity per unit of time (valve constant).
- the fuel density.
- the fuel pressure.

Powering of valves. The fuel injectors are switched to negative by the ECU. In this way, the ECU can be protected against being destroyed by the short-circuit current in the event of a short circuit to earth/ground. The positive supply is provided via a relay switched by the ECU from terminal 15. The valve opening time can be determined by displaying the injection operation on an oscilloscope. The voltage peak during the closing operation is created by the switch-off induction of the field winding.

Types. With LH-Motronic different fuel injectors are used for engines with two- or multiple-valve technology. They differ in the shape of the fuel jet or spray and in the angle at which the fuel is injected by the nozzle.

Air-shrouded fuel injectors are used for finer atomisation of the fuel and for better mixing with air. For this purpose, air is diverted before the throttle valve and routed via a line into the injector. In the narrow injector air gap the air is greatly accelerated by the pressure differential acting in the intake manifold at part load. The air emerging at high speed is mixed with the injected fuel and this process finely atomises the fuel.

When the fuel injectors are supplied with fuel from the fuel rail, this fuel is fed from the top (top-feed). The top end of the injector, sealed by an O-ring, is integrated in the fuel rail while the bottom end, also sealed by an O-ring, is integrated in the intake manifold. In the interests of saving space, the fuel injectors are often integrated in fuel-rail modules. In this case, so-called bottom-feed fuel injectors are used. The fuel is supplied from the side with these injectors. These injectors have good fuel-cooling properties and thus exhibit a good hot-start response.

Hot film air mass sensor B3. This determines the inducted air mass and transmits it in the form of a voltage signal to the ECU, which calculates the basic injection quantity (quantity) from it together with the engine speed. If the sensor falls, the system can generate a substitute signal from the throttle valve position. The vehicle can continue to be driven under restricted conditions (limp-home operation). The mass airflow sensor is supplied with power from pin 10 and receives earth/ground from terminal 31. The voltage signal transmitted to the ECU can be taken at pins 10 and 12.

Engine speed sensor B1. The signal from this sensor serves first and foremost, together with the signal from the mass airflow sensor, to calculate the basic injection quantity. The system uses inductive speed sensors which are accommodated in the area of the crankshaft and scan a specific pulse generator wheel. These sensors more often than not also supply the reference mark which is needed to determine the exact TDC of cylinder No. 1. The engine cannot be operated should this sensor fail. The signal is also needed for idle speed control, overrun fuel cut-off and engine speed limitation. Oscilloscope readings can also be taken at pin 6 and pin 7.

Throttle valve potentiometer B4. This is located on the throttle valve and serves to record both the throttle valve position and the opening speed. The integrated idle switch signals to the ECU when the throttle valve is closed. If the sensor fails, a default value stored in the ECU is taken as the basis for the minimum speed. This is usually expressed in an increased idle speed. Idle speed control, overrun fuel cut-off and full-load and acceleration enrichment are no longer possible. The potentiometer signal readings can be taken at pins 13 and 14 or pin 12. The throttle valve switch is checked at pin 15 to terminal 31.

Some systems, especially when a throttle valve actuator is utilised, use a double potentiometer for reasons of safety and accuracy.

Intake air temperature sensor B7. This is an NTC resistor, the function of which is to record the temperature of the intake air. It is located in the intake manifold. The ECU needs this signal to adapt the fuel quantity. The injection time can be extended by up to 20% when the air is very cold. If the signal fails, it is possible to switch to a stored default value. The resistance of the sensor can be checked at pin 18 and pin 19.

Engine temperature sensor B5. This NTC resistor records the engine temperature. Depending on the voltage drop at the resistor, the engine ECU adapts the injected fuel quantity to the operating state as a function of temperature. Thus the injection time is extended by up to 70% when the engine is cold. In addition, the moment of ignition, idle speed, exhaust gas recirculation and knock control are modified when the engine is cold. The ECU can switch to a stored default value in the event of a signal interruption or a short circuit. An increased resistance, for example at a plug connection, is not detected however. This fault results in an enrichment of the mixture and thus among other things in increased CO emission. The resistance of the NTC resistor can be checked at the ECU plug at pin 12 and pin 16.

Reference mark sensor B2. The signal from the inductive reference mark sensor on the crankshaft and the signal from the Hall-effect sensor mounted on the camshaft are needed for the purpose of clearly identifying firing TDC. From both signals together with the engine speed the ECU calculates the correct moment for injection into the respective cylinder and the corresponding ignition angle. Oscilloscope readings of the sensor signal can be taken at pin 8 and pin 5. Terminals on the sensor: 7(1)=signal positive; 31d (31)=earth/ground supply. Power is supplied via pin 9 = terminal 8h (2).

Oxygen sensor (voltage-jump sensor) B6. This registers the residual oxygen in the exhaust gas and, by means of feedback in the form of a voltage signal to the ECU, enables the injected fuel quantity to regulated to $\lambda=1$. Since the sensor is only operated at approx. 250℃ to 300℃, it is electrically heated in order to achieve the quickest possible response. If the sensor fails, λ regulation is no longer possible. The failure is detected by the ECU. The mixture formation system then operates as an open-loop control system. Oscilloscope readings of the sensor signal can be taken at pin 17 and terminal 31. The sensor heater receives positive from terminal 87 of K2 and negative from terminal 31.

Main relay K1. When the ignition is switched on, the main relay receives positive to terminal 85 from terminal 15 and negative to terminal 86 from ECU pin 3. In this way, the relay operating circuit closes and the ECU is supplied with power to pin 4. Likewise, solenoid valves Y1 to Y7 and the control circuit are supplied with power by K2 to terminal 85.

Fuel pump relay K2. This relay closes when main relay K1 terminal 85 is supplied with positive and ECU terminal 86 is supplied with earth/ground. In order to establish the earth/ground connection, pin 30 must be connected to earth/ground. The operating circuit supplies fuel pump M and the oxygen sensor heater with power. The power supply is interrupted if the speed signal from the engine speed sensor fails.

Fuel injectors Y1 to Y4. Like fuel pump relay K2, these receive power from main relay K1. If the fuel injectors are top open, the ECU must connect in each case pins 26,27,28,29 to earth/ground.

Idle speed actuator Y5. The ECU uses this actuator to regulate the idle speed as a function of engine temperature. It is supplied with positive by K1 terminal 87. To facilitate stepless opening and closing of the bypass cross-section, the actuator is clocked by the ECU by means of pulse-width-modulated signals with negative.

Tank vent valve Y6. This solenoid valve opens and closes the connecting line between the intake manifold and the carbon canister. It is opened by pulse- width-modulated signals, during which the positive supply is provided by terminal 87 K1 and the negative supply by the ECU via pin 24. The valve remains closed if the signal fails.

Exhaust gas recirculation valve Y7. This solenoid valve for exhaust gas recirculation opens and closes the connecting line between the exhaust manifold and the intake manifold. It is opened by a pulse-width-modulated signal, during which it receives positive from terminal 87 K1 and negative from ECU pin 23. The valve closes if the signal fails.

REVIEW QUESTIONS

1. From which signals is the basic injection quantity calculated in LH-Motronic?

2. Which subsystems are featured in LH-Motronic?

3. Describe the various idle speed control possibilities.

4. Which sensors does the ECU require for overrun fuel cut-off?

5. Explain the term "Motronic".

New Words

air mass sensor	空气流量传感器	rev	(发动机的)旋转
induct	感应	threshold	临界值
manifold	集合管	rpm	每分钟转数
resistor	电阻	three-way catalyst	三效催化转化器
thermistor	热敏电阻	potentiometer	电位计
pressure regulator	压力调节器	density	浓度，密度
hydrocarbon	碳氢化合物，烃	solenoid	螺线管
carbon canister	炭罐	armature	转子，电枢
viscous	黏性的	bypass	旁通
friction	摩擦，阻力	nozzle needle	喷嘴针阀
speed fluctuation	速度波动	oscilloscope	示波器
actuator	执行器	atomise	将……喷成雾状
throttle	节流阀	resistor	电阻（器）
pulse-width- modulated	脉宽调节	tank vent valve	油箱通风阀
subassembly	组件，部件	circuit	电路，回路

新技术篇

Kapitel 3　Neue Technologie // Chapter 3　New Technology

课文参考译文

汽油喷射

汽油喷射系统的功用：

汽油喷射系统的功用是将细雾状的燃油喷入进气中，在喷射过程中，混合气的数量及其空燃比必须与工况相适应。

在燃油喷射系统中，借助于喷油器以及燃油泵所产生的压力，将燃油以细雾状喷入空气中。这样，燃油表面积增加，汽化速度加快，混合更充分，燃烧更完全，排气更洁净。

在间接喷射（混合气缸外形成）的情况下，通过喷油器的布置，能将燃油喷射到进气管内或节气门体内。而对于直接喷射（混合气缸内形成）来说，也是通过喷油器的布置，能将燃油喷射到燃烧室内。

通过对燃油喷射系统实现电子控制，能将混合气的空燃比（质调节）或将混合气的数量（量调节）与发动机工况相适应。

采用燃油喷射，会实现下列目标：

- 提高发动机转矩。
- 提高发动机功率。
- 改善发动机性能曲线。
- 降低油耗。
- 降低废气排放。

燃油喷射的类型：

间接喷射：采用这种方式，燃油与空气在气缸外面开始混合。在进气和压缩行程期间，在整个燃烧室内会形成均匀分布的均质混合气。间接喷射又分为单点喷射和多点喷射两种。

单点喷射。单点喷射是从中心部位将燃油喷入节气门体内的节气门前面（也叫中央喷射）。在节气门附近的空间中雾化。热的进气歧管内壁和外加的加热元件上的燃油蒸发，都将有助于混合气的形成。进气管或进气歧管长度不等，对各缸的燃油均匀分配不利。周边涡流和低温发动机上特别容易出现的壁面油膜现象，都会导致混合气成分不均匀。这些对混合气的形成都会产生不利影响。单点喷射系统的结构比多点喷射系统简单。

多点喷射。每个气缸设有一个喷油器。这些喷油器位于进气歧管上，通常就在进气门前面的位置。因此，混合气的进气路径长度相等，各缸混合气分配均匀。喷油器靠近进气门布置，使发动机低温时的壁面油膜减少，因而减少了有害废气排放物。

直接喷射。采用直接喷射的燃油喷射系统也属于多点喷射系统。电子控制喷油器将高压（可高达12MPa)燃油直接喷入燃烧室（混合气缸内形成）。这样，根据发动机的设计和工况的不同，就会形成均质或非均质混合气。

直接喷射消除了像壁面油膜和燃油分配不均这样的一些问题产生的不利影响。当然这种喷射方式对燃油系统的电子控制提出了极高的要求。

喷油器的控制

喷油器在燃油压力的作用下开启，或在电磁力的作用下开启。

连续喷射。喷油器在燃油压力的作用下开启，并在整个发动机工作期间一直保持开启状态。喷油器连续不断地喷油。通过改变系统压力来改变喷油量。

间歇喷射。在电磁力的作用下，喷油器开启很短的时间。一旦喷完计算的喷油量，油器就关闭。通过改变喷油器开启时间来改变喷油量。

根据ECU控制喷油器的方式不同，间歇喷射有四种类型：

同时喷射。

分组喷射。

顺序喷射。

特定气缸喷射。

同时喷射。发动机的所有喷油器都同时动作。对各个气缸来说，燃料蒸发所用的时间有很大的不同。因此，为了获得尽可能成分均匀的混合气和实现充分燃烧，在曲轴的每一圈中，喷射燃烧所需要的喷油量的一半。

分组喷射。对于4缸发动机每个做功循环，1、3缸燃油器或2、4缸燃油器各喷油一次。在每种情况下，整个喷油量都被喷在关闭的进气门之前。这些燃油的蒸发时间不同。

顺序喷射。就在进气行程开始之前，各缸喷油器按照点火顺序一个接一个地将相同数量的总喷油量喷入进气歧管。这就促进了最佳混合气的形成，并改善了机内冷却效果。

特定气缸喷射。这种喷射也是一种顺序喷射。由于传感器技术的进步，控制复杂程度的提升，ECU能够给每一个单个气缸分配特殊的喷油量。

电子控制汽油喷射系统的组成和功用

电子控制汽油喷射系统的组成至少包括三个子系统：

空气供给系统。组成包括：空气滤清器、进气歧管、节气门和各个进气管。

燃油供给系统。组成包括：燃油箱、燃油泵、燃油滤清器、压力调节器和喷油器。开、闭环电子控制系统。组成包括：传感器（温度传感器）、ECU和执行器（燃油泵继电器）。

开、闭环电子控制系统根据IPO理论来工作。IPO理论的意义如下：

输入（I）。传感器以电压信号的形式记录和传送信息给ECU。

处理（P）。ECU对这些饱含在电压信号里的信息进行处理，并对实测值与通常存储在程序脉谱图中的预定值进行比较，计算出相应执行器的操作值。

输出（O）。ECU给相关执行器（喷油器）通电。实现所希望的系统工作状态。

电子控制燃油喷射系统按照下面的程序工作：

对于形成均质混合气的系统来说，发动机将大量的经过空气滤清器过滤并经过节气门控制的空气吸入气缸。这些空气的流量经过一只记录器记录下来。

ECU根据发动机转速和空气量（主控参数），利用存储的程序脉谱图计算基本喷油量。

如果需要混合气的成分与特定工况相匹配，那么，就必须通过另外的传感器将这些工况以电信号的形式记录下来，并将这些信号传送给ECU。ECU将喷油器的喷油持续时间按照变化的工况进行调整，并给喷油器按照计算的通电时间进行通电。

这样，电磁式喷油器开启，喷出燃料。喷油压力由压力调节器控制。当ECU停止通电时，在弹簧的作用下，喷油器关闭，喷油过程结束。

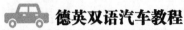

Teil 2　Elektronische Dieselregelung (EDC)
柴油机电子调节系统
Part 2　Injection systems for diesel engines
柴油机喷射系统

【知识目标】
1. 掌握与柴油机电子调节系统结构、分类、运行原理等相关的专业术语、单词和词汇。
2. 掌握柴油机电子调节系统主要结构的德文、英文表达方法。

【能力目标】
1. 能对柴油机电子调节系统总体结构的各部分细节进行中、德、英互译。
2. 能进行与柴油机电子调节系统大体构造相关的德语、英语资料阅读和翻译。
3. 能在柴油机电子调节系统实物上标识出相应结构的德语、英语单词和词汇。

Text 1　Elektronische Dieselregelung (EDC) 柴油机电子调节系统（德文）

　　Der Einsatz elektronisch geregelter Einspritzsysteme ermöglicht eine exakte Regelung des Einspritzbeginns, verbunden mit einer äußerst genauen Kraftstoffmengenzumessung.

　　Zusätzlich wird eine Leerlaufregelung, Vollastmengenbegrenzung, abhängig von Ladedruck, Lufttemperatur und Kraftstofftemperatur, eine Begrenzung der Enddrehzahl und eine Startmengenbegrenzung durchgeführt.

　　Weiterhin werden die Regelung der Abgasrückführung zur Schadstoffminderung und die Ladedruckregelung bei aufgeladenen Motoren von der Elektronikausrüstung übernommen.

　　Somit ergeben wesentliche Verbesserungen:

　　– Einhaltung verschärfter Abgasgrenzwerte.

　　– Verminderung des Kraftstoffverbrauchs.

　　– Optimierung von Drehmoment und Leistung.

　　– Verbesserung des Ansprechverhaltens.

- Verminderung des Motorgeräusches.
- Optimierung der Laufruhe.
- Problemlose Ausrüstung des Fahrzeugs mit einer Geschwindigkeitsregelung.
- Vereinfache Anpassung eines Motortyps an unterschiedliche Fahrzeuge.

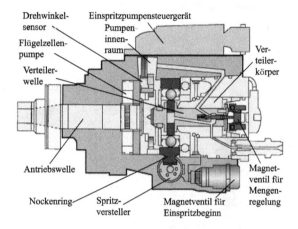

Bild :Die elektronisch geregelten Dieseleinspritzsysteme

Aufbau

Die elektronisch geregelten Dieseleinspritzsysteme (Bild) bestehen stets aus:

– Sensorausrüstung. Sie erfasst die Betriebsdaten, z.B. Last, Drehzahl, Motortemperatur und die Umgebungsbedingungen, z.B. Ansauglufttemperatur und Luftdruck.

– Elektronischem Steuergerät. Es ist ein Mikrocomputer, der aus den Betriebsdaten, den Umgebungsinformationen und unter Berücksichtigung der in Kennfeldern gespeicherten Sollwerter die Einspritzmenge, den Einspritzbeginn festlegt und ggf. die Abgasrückführmenge und den Ladedruck regelt.

– Aktorausrüstung (Steller). Sie ermöglichen den elektrischen Eingriff in die Hochdruck-Einspritzausrüstung, ggf. in das Abgasrückführsystem und das Aufladesystem.

Abgas-Rückführungsregelung (ARF). Um den Stickoxidanteil im Abgas zu reduzieren, wird eine Abgasrückführungsanlage eingebaut. Diese ist um so wirkungsvoller, je genauer die Abgasrückführungsrate ist. Die Luftmenge, die der Motor ansaugt, kann mit einem Luftmengenmesser gemessen werden. Das Steuergerät ermittelt über die eingespeicherten Daten die Abgasrückführungssteller. Dieser führt über ein Ventil dem Motor mehr oder weniger Abgas zu. Dadurch werden die Emissionswerte verringert.

Notfahrfunktion. Elektronische Diesel-Control-Systeme (EDC) überwachen sich selbst. Es werden sowohl die Funktion des Steuergerätes als auch die Funktionen der elektrischen Bauteile überwacht. Bei Fehlern wird über eine Anzeige dem Fahrer ein Defekt mitgeteilt und die Anlage wird mit einem entsprechenden Notfahrprogramm oder Ersatzfahrprogramm betrieben. Es wird z.B. bei einem defekten Fußfahrgeber die Leerlaufdrehzahl erhöht, damit das Fahrzeug mit geringer Motordrehzahl gefahren werden kann. Als Hochdruck- Einspritzausrüstungen für elektronisch geregelte Systeme werden verwendet:

- Hubkolben – Verteilereinspritzpumpe.
- Radialkolben- Venteilereinspritzpumpe.
- Pumpe-Düse-Element.
- Commen- Rail.

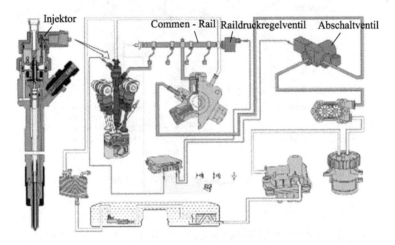

Bild: Einspritzausrüstung

Aufbau

Die Einspritzausrüstung (Bild) besteht aus:

– Niederdruckkreis. Er gliedert sich in den Saugdruckbereich, den Vorförderdruckbereich und den Kraftstoffrücklauf. Enthalten sind Kraftstoffbehälter, Kraftstoffvorwärmung, Kraftstofffilter, Kraftstoffförderpumpe, elektrisches Abschaltventil und Kraftstoffkühler.

– Hochdruckbereich. Er besteht aus der Hochdruckpumpe, den Hochdruckleitungen, dem Rail und einem Injektor je Zylinder.

– Elektronischer Steueung. Sie umfasst das elektronische Steuergerät, die Sensor-ausrüstung, das Raildruckregelventil, die Magnetventile der Injektoren und das Abschaltventil.

Wirkungsweise

Kraftstoffförderpumpe. Sie versorgt die Hochdruck-Kolbenpumpe mit Kraftstoff: Diese Pumpe ist häufig eine von der Motornockenwelle angetriebene Zahnradpumpe oder eine elektrisch angetriebene Rollenzellenpumpe. Sie fördert drehzahlabhängig zwischen etwa 40 L/h und etwa 120 L/h Kraftstoff. Das ist mehr als zum Einspritzen benötigt wird. Der überschüssige Kraftstoff durchströmt im Rücklauf den Kraftstoffkühler. Dies ist notwendig da sich der Kraftstoff im Hochdruckbereich stark erhitzt. Die Abwärme kann somit auch zur Verbesserung der

新技术篇

Kapitel 3　Neue Technologie // Chapter 3　New Technology

Fahrzeuginnenraumheizung genutzt werden.

Um kleine Kraftstoffmengen einzuspritzen, z.B. Voreinspritzung, wird das Magnetventil nur kurz bestromt. Die Düsennadel wird leicht angehoben. Das Einspritzventiel öffnet kurzzeitig und gibt dabei nicht den gesamten Öffnungsquerschnitt frei. Durch die Voreinspritzung wird im Verbrennungsraum eine Vorverbrennung ausgelöst. In diese Verbrennung wird die Haupteinspritzmenge eingespritzt. Dadurch ergeben sich folgende Vorteile gegenüber den herkommlichen Einspritzsystemen:

– Verkürzung des Zündverzugs für die Haupteinspritzmenge.

– weichere Verbrennung.

– Verminderung der Schadstoffe im Abgas.

– Verbrauchsminderung.

– geringere Verbrennungsgeräusche.

WIEDERHOLUNGSFRAGEN

1. Was kann der Einsatz elektronisch geregelter Einspritzsysteme ermöglichen?
2. Welche wesentliche Verbesserungen damit ergeben?
3. Woraus bestehen die elektronisch geregelten Dieseleinspritzsysteme？
4. Was ist ARF?
5. Was werden als Hochdruck- Einspritzausrüstungen für elektronisch geregelte Systeme verwendet?

Neue Wörter

die	elektronische Dieselregelung (EDC)	柴油机电子调节系统
das	Einspritzsystem	喷射系统
die	Leerlaufregelung	怠速调节
die	Abgasrückführung	废气再循环
die	Ladedruckregelung	增压压力调节
die	Abgasgrenzwerte	废气排放限值
der	Kraftstoffverbrauch	燃油消耗
das	Drehmoment	转矩
das	Ansprechverhalten	响应性
das	Motorgeräusch	发动机噪声
die	Laufruhe	运转平稳
die	Geschwindigkeitsregelung	车速控制器
die	Sensorausrüstung	传感器装置
die	Betriebsdaten	运行数据
das	elektronische Steuergerät（ECU）	电子控制单元
die	Umgebungsinformation	环境信息
die	Kennfelder	特征曲线，脉谱图
die	Aktorausrüstung	执行器
der	Eingriff	嵌接，干预
die	Abgas-Rückführungsregelung (ARF)	废气再循环系统
die	Notfahrfunktion	紧急情况行驶功能

Text 2　Injection systems for diesel engines 柴油机喷射系统（英文）

In order to comply with the stricter emission limits for diesel engines, modern electronically controlled injection systems inject fuel at increasingly higher pressures and with increasingly greater precision. Mechanically controlled in-line and distributor fuel injection pumps cannot meet the demands set. They have therefore virtually disappeared from the market altogether.

In addition to the common-rail system, the following different systems are found in passenger car:

- Unit injector systems.
- Axial-piston distributor fuel injection pump.
- Radial-piston distributor fuel injection pump.

Advantages of a map-controlled diesel injection system:

- Compliance with stricter emission limits.
- Reduced fuel consumption.
- Optimised torque and power.
- Improved response.
- Reduced engine noise.
- Optimised quiet running.
- Problem-free addition of cruise control system in vehicles.
- Simplified adaptation of an engine type to different vehicles.

Design. EDC consists of:

• Sensors. These record the operating data, such as load, engine speed, engine temperature, boost pressure, and environmental conditions, e.g. intake air temperature and air pressure.

• Electronic control unit. This is a microcomputer which, from the operating data and environmental information and while taking into account the set-point values stored in program maps, determines the injected fuel quantity and the start of injection, and if necessary controls the exhaust gas recirculation quantity and the boost pressure.

• Actuators. These allow interventions to be made in the fuel injection system, the exhaust gas recirculation system and supercharging system.

Function of map-based control

Main controlled variable. A basic start of injection and a basic injection quantity are determined in the ECU using program maps from the two main controlled variables, i.e. load and engine speed. The load signal is recorded by an accelerator pedal travel sensor while the engine speed is recorded by the crankshaft speed sensor.

Correction-controlled variables. These adapt the basic injection times optimally to the respective driving situation and ambient conditions. Additional program maps are stored in the ECU for each correction-controlled variable. Examples:

- Engine temperature.
- Fuel temperature.
- Boost pressure.
- Intake air temperature .

Setpoint/actual-value adjustment. Sensors inform the ECU whether the control intervention was sufficient. If necessary, the ECU effects a readjustment of the relevant actuators.

Particular features. The following additional functions can also be adapted (=applied) via EDC to the respective vehicle:

- Idle speed control. For emission and consumption reasons the idle speed is kept as low as possible, regardless of torque requirements, e.g. by the A/C compressor and alternator.
- Overrun fuel cut-off. In overrunning situations, e.g. downhill driving, the injected fuel quantity is reduced to zero.
- Smooth running control. Not all the cylinders of an engine generate the same torque with the same injected fuel quantity.

Wear and manufacturing tolerances of the components are possible causes. Thus each cylinder has a different actual speed during the power stroke. This results in irregular engine operation and increased emissions. Smooth running control detects this from the crankshaft acceleration with the aid of the speed sensor and compensates for it by specifically adapting the injected fuel quantity of the relevant cylinder.

- Active surge damping.In the event of sudden load changes, such as when pulling away, the torque change of the engine induces bucking oscillations in the vehicle drivetrain. These oscillations/vibrations are detected from the engine speed signal and damped by means of active control. The injected fuel quantity is reduced as speed increases and is increased as speed decreases in order to counteract the speed oscillations/vibrations.
- External torque intervention. The injection time is influenced by other ECUs, e.g. transmission control, TCS/ASR, ESP. Independently of the driver command they inform the engine ECU via data bus whether and by how much the engine torque is to be altered when they are engaged.
- Electronic immobiliser. To prevent the vehicle from being driven without authorisation, the engine can only be started when the engine ECU provides clearance.
- Cruise control. This adjusts the vehicle speed to the desired value. The injected fuel quantity is increased or reduced until the measured actual speed corresponds to the established setpoint speed.
- Altitude compensation system. As altitude increases, atmospheric pressure drops.The amount of combustion air available for cylinder charging also drops. Increasing the boost pressure

or reducing the injected fuel quantity compensates for the resulting heavy smoke emissions. The atmospheric pressure is detected by the barometric pressure sensor in the ECU. The atmospheric pressure also affects the torque limitation.

– Speed limiter (governor). Speed limiters, or governors, protect the engine from excessive rotational speeds. They reduce the injected fuel quantity, weakening the combustion process to prevent abrupt engine cut-off during acceleration.

– Diagnostic capability. Input and output signals are checked. Detected faults are stored in the ECU and are indicated to the driver when necessary.

– orque limiter. The maximum torque can be restricted to protect drive components. Engine torque curves do not show the peaks, but rather a constant torque over a greater speed range.

Limp-home function. The ECU activates an appropriate limp-home program to match the existing fault.

New Words

Electronic Diesel Control (EDC)	柴油机电子调节系统	boost pressure	增压压力
		electronic control unit（ECU）	电子控制单元
injection system	喷射系统	actuator	执行器
injection pump	喷射泵	compressor	压缩机
axial	轴，轴承	alternator	交流发电机
piston	活塞	cylinder	气缸
radial	径向的	crankshaft	曲轴
axial-piston	轴向活塞	compensate	补偿
radial-piston	径向活塞	oscillations	振动，振幅
distributor	分油器	vibrations	振动
emission limits	排放限值	immobiliser	防盗
fuel consumption	耗油率	cruise control	巡航控制
torque	转矩	speed limiter	限速器
map-controlled	图像控制	torque limiter	转矩限制器
sensor	传感器	limp-home	跛行

222

Kapitel 3　Neue Technologie // Chapter 3　New Technology

课文参考译文

柴油机电子控制系统 (EDC)

柴油机电子控制系统 (EDC) 是一种用脉谱图控制的电子燃油喷射系统。使用该系统，能对喷油始点实现准确控制，燃油计量具有极高的精度。

采用EDC的柴油机燃油喷射系统的优点：

1）满足了更加严格的排放法规。
2）降低了燃油消耗。
3）优化了转矩和功率。
4）改善了响应性。
5）降低了发动机噪声。
6）优化运转平稳性。
7）装备在采用车速控制器的车辆上，没有出任何问题。
8）能使发动机的型号与不同车辆的匹配得到简化。

结构。

EDC由以下三部分组成：

1）传感器。传感器检测各种运行数据，如发动机负荷、发动机转速、发动机温度、增压压力，以及进气温度和大气压力等环境条件。

2）电子控制单元（ECU）。ECU是一个微型计算机，它能够根据运行数据和环境信息，并考虑程序脉谱图中存储的预定值，来确定供油量和喷油始点。必要的话，ECU还要控制废气再循环流量和增压压力。

3）执行器。执行器能够对喷油系统进行干预，必要时对废气再循环系统和增压系统进行干预。

基于脉谱图控制的EDC系统的控制功能

主控参数。ECU利用程序脉谱图确定基本喷油始点和基本供油量所用的两个主控参数是负荷和发动机转速。负荷由加速踏板行程传感器检测。

修正参数。这些参数能使基本喷油正时更好地与各种不同的行驶条件和环境条件相适应。另外，对于每个修正参数，ECU中都存储了一个程序脉谱图。这些修正参数有：

发动机温度。

燃油温度。

进气温度。

增压压力。

预定值/实测值调整。传感器告诉ECU控制干预是否足够。必要时，ECU将对相关执行器发送再调节的信号。

特殊功能。除了上述功能外，通过采用EDC，还能使下列功能应用于不同的车辆上。

怠速控制。为了降低排放和油耗，根据转矩需求（如A/C压缩机和发电机）的变化，将怠速转速保持在尽可能低的数值上。

平稳运行控制。在喷油量相同的情况下，并非各个气缸会产生相同的转矩。这可能是零件磨损不同、制造误差不同的缘故。这会引起发动机运转不稳定，排放增加。平稳运行控制就是借助于转速传感器来检测曲轴的加速度，从而确定运转不平稳的情况，然后再通过调节相应气缸的喷油量，对转速进行补偿调整。

超速断油。在超速运行的情况下，如下坡，将喷油量减小为零。

转速主动控制。在负荷突然变化的情况下，发动机转矩的变化会激发车辆传动系统的振动。这些振动反过来传给曲轴，通过发动机转速传感器信号可以将这种振动激发的转速波动检测出来，并且借助于主动控制来衰减这种振动。为了消除这种振动，在转速增加时，减小喷油量；转速减小时，增加喷油量。

外部转矩干预。喷油正时还要受到其他ECU（如变速器控制、TCS/ASR、ESP系统的ECU）的控制。不管驾驶人有怎样的要求，这些ECU会通过数据总线，不受驾驶人影响地通过发动机ECU是否调整发动机转矩和调整多少。

电子控制防盗。为了防止车辆被非法开走，只有在发动机ECU获得准许之后，才可能起动发动机。

车速控制器。该装置（即巡航控制）能将车速调整到所希望的数值上。该装置增加或减小喷油量，直至实际车速测量值达到设定的车速为止。

诊断功能。对输入和输出信号进行检查，并将发现的故障存储在ECU中。必要时，提醒驾驶人注意。

应急功能。为了适应故障，ECU启动一个相应的应急运行程序，从而实现以下不同的功能：

功率降低30%。

提高怠速转速。

应急关机。

新技术篇

Kapitel 3　Neue Technologie // Chapter 3　New Technology

Teil 3　Katalysator　废气催化净化技术
Part3　　Catalyst　　废气催化净化技术

学习目标

【知识目标】
1. 掌握与废气净化技术结构、分类、运行原理等相关的专业术语、单词和词汇。
2. 掌握废气净化技术主要结构的德文、英文表达方法。

【能力目标】
1. 能对废气净化技术总体结构的各大总成进行中、德、英互译。
2. 能进行与废气净化技术大体构造相关的德语、英语资料的阅读和翻译。
3. 能在废气净化装置实物上标识出相应结构的德语、英语单词和词汇。

Text 1　Katalysator催化器（德文）

Katalysator-Funktionen

Der Katalysator ist das zur Zeit wirkungsvollste System zur Abgasreinigung. Er ist kein Filter im üblichen Sinn, sondern bewirkt in einem thermochemischen Prozeß die Umwandlung der Schadstoffe Kohlenmonoxid (CO), Kohlenwasserstoff (HC) und Stickoxid (NO_x) in unschädliche Abgasbestandteile wie Wasser, Kohlendioxid und Stickstoff. Mit dem geregelten Katalysator werden rund 90 Prozent der Schadstoffe im Abgas in unschädliche Bestandteile umgewandelt.

Der Katalysator selbst besteht aus einem Edelstahlgehäuse, in dem sich ein Keramikkörper als Katalysatorträger befindet. Um eine möglichst große Oberfläche auf kleinstem Raum zu erhalten, ist der Keramikkörper von mehr als 6000 Kanälen durchgezogen. Durch ein besonderes Verfahren wird die Oberfläche der vielen Kanäle sehr porös und dadurch um das ca. 7000 fache vergrößert. Das ergibt eine sehr große aktive Oberfläche. Darauf werden ein bis zwei Gramm der eigentlichen Katalysator mittel Platin und Rhodium aufgebracht. Je größer die Oberfläche, um so sicherer ist es, dass jedes Schadstoffmolekül mit dem Katalysator in Berührung kommt.

Der ungeregelte Katalysator ist im Aufbau und in der Funktion mit dem geregelten Katalysator identisch. Ein zusatzliches System zur Regelung des Kraftstoff-Luftgemisches, wie zum Beispiel die Lamda-Sonde und ein elektronisches Steuergerät, ist bei dieser kostengünstigen Abgasreinigung nicht vorhanden. Die Umwandlung der Abgas-Komponenten in unschädliche Bestandteile ist etwas weniger effektiv als beim geregelten Katalysator. Die Katalysatoren werden an Stelle des Vorschalldämpfers in das Abgassystem eingebaut. Alle abgasführenden Teile sind aus Edelstahl. Dadurch erreichen die Abgasanlagen etwa die doppelte Lebensdauer herkömmlicher Anlagen.

Die Lambda Sonde

Der geregelte Katalysator erreicht seinen hervorragenden Wirkungsgrad von ca. 90 Prozent bei der Abgasreinigung, weil ihm die Abgasbestandtile in optimaler Zusammensetzung zur Nachbehandlung zugeführt werden. Ein wichtiges Bauteil in diesem system ist die Lambda Sonde. Sie prüft die Abgasqualität und meldet sofort dem Steuergerät, wenn die Gemischzusetzung vom optimalen Wert abweicht. Dann entscheidet das Steuergerät in kürzester Zeit, wie die ein einzuspritzende Kraftstoffmenge zu verändern ist, damit das Abgas wieder in optimaler Zusammensetzung zum Katalysator gelangt. Dieses Gemischverhältnis wird auch mit Lambda = 1 bezeichnet und kennzeichnet das sogenannte " stöchiometrische Gemisch. "

Die Lambda-Sonde „ lebt " vom Restsauerstoff im Abgas wegen der kurzen Zeit, die zur Verbrennung des Kraftstoff Luftgemisches zur Verfügung steht, findet nicht jedes Sauerstoffmolekül ein Kraftstoffmolekül. Es wird dann, ohne an der Verbrennung teilzunehmen, aus dem Brennraum an der Lambda-Sonde vorbei durch den Auspuff befördert. Bei einem mageren Gemisch sind zu viele, bei einem fetten Gemisch sind zu wenig freie Sauerstoffmoleküle im Abgas enthalten. Der wirkungsgrad des Katalysators wird ganz wesentlich vom Abgassauertstoffanteil bestimmt. Er beeinflusst die elektrische Spannung, die die Lambda- Sonde an das Steuergerät abgibt.

Für den ungeregelten wie für den geregelten Katalysator darf nur unverbleiter Kraftstoff verwendet werden. Sonst würde die feinporige Katalysatorfläche durch Ablagerung von Bleibstandteilen im Abgas zugedeckt und entsprechend die Schadstoffreinigung vermindert.

Neue Wörter

die	Sonde	探测器，探针，传感器		befördern	输送
	abweichen	偏离，与……有偏差	der	Katalysator	催化剂，催化器
die	Qualität	质量		erreichen	取得，达到
	einspritzen	注射，喷射		hervorragend	突出的，优秀的
der	reste Sauerstoft	残余的氧气	das	Prozent	百分率，百分数
	stöchiometrisch	化学数量的，化学计算的		Circa = zirka (缩写 ca.)	大约，大概
das	Kraftstoffmolekül	燃料分子	der	Wirkungsgrad	效率
das	magere Gemisch	稀混合气	der	Abgasbestandteil	废气成分
das	fette Gemisch	浓混合气		optimal	最佳的，最理想的

Kapitel 3 Neue Technologie // Chapter 3 New Technology

die	Zusammensetzung	成分，构成		die	Abgasreinigung	废气净化
die	Nachbehandlung	后处理，进一步加工		der	Filter	过滤器
	wichtig	重要的		der	Schadstoff	有害物质
der	Bauteil	构件，组成部分		das	Stickoxid	氮氧化物
	prüfen	检查，试验，证明		der	Keramikkörper	陶瓷物体
	melden	报告、申报		der	Kanal	管道
	kennzeichnen	标明，标出，表明		die	Umwandlung	转变
das	Gesmisch	混合物			bewirken	促使，导致
	kurz	短的		das	Kohlenmenoxyd	一氧化碳
die	Verbrennung	烧毁，点燃		der	Kohlenwasserstoff	碳氢化合物
der	Brennraum	燃烧室			bestehen	由……组成
der	Auspuff	排气（管）			vergrößern	扩大
die	Spannung	拉紧，电压			eigentlich	真正的
	beeinflussen	影响，对……有影响		die	Berührung	触点，联系
	zuführen	输入，供给			identisch	相同的
das	Steuergerät	控制器		die	Regelung	调整
die	Katalysatorfläche	催化剂表面			vorhanden	现存的
die	Ablagerung	沉积，储藏			effektiv	实际的
	zudecken	盖上		die	Komponente	成分
	vermindern	减少		der	Edelstahl	不锈钢
der	Bleibestandteil	铅成分				

Text 2 Catalyst 催化器（英文）

Aftertreatment of exhaust gases in catalyst

At present the most effective method is exhaust gas aftertreatment in a catalytic converter or catalyst. The catalyst chemically converts the pollutants into non-toxic substances without their being consumed in the process.

Catalyst design. The main components of a catalyst are:
- Ceramic substrate (aluminium magnesium silicate) or metal substrate.
- Intermediate layer (wash-coat).
- Catalytically active layer.

The substrate consists of several thousand fine channels, through which the exhaust gas flows. The channels of the ceramic or metal substrate are provided with a highly porous intermediate layer. This increases the effective surface of the catalyst by a factor of roughly 7,000. The catalytically active layer is attached to this intermediate layer. The catalytically active layer is dependent on the pollutant constituents which are formed depending on the engine concept and the associated mixture composition ($\lambda \approx 1; \lambda > 1$).

Advantages and disadvantages of ceramic substrate compared with substrate

Advantages: It has a more constant operating temperature. Also the noble-metal coating can be recovered more easily than from a metal substrate.

Disadvantages: The ceramic substrate is sensitive to jolts and vibrations. It must therefore be embedded in a heat-resistant wire mesh which is enclosed in a sheet-steel housing. Furthermore, the heating-up time is longer and the backpressure in the exhaust system is greater in the case of standard catalysts [cell density: 400 cpsi (cells per square inch)]. This results in reduced exhaust gas conversion and reduced engine power shortly after engine starting. Ultrathin-wall substrates with a cell density of 600 cpsi to 1,200 cpsi eliminate these disadvantages.

Operating principle of single-bed three-way catalyst

The single-bed three-way catalyst has a catalytically active layer of platinum (Pt), rhodium (Rd) and palladium (Pd). The term single-bed three-way catalyst indicates that three chemical conversions take place simultaneously in one housing. Depending on its operating temperature, the catalyst converts NO_X, CO and HC in the range $\lambda \approx 0.995$ to 1.005 (lambda window) up to 98% into CO_2, H_2O and N_2.

Only an air ratio of $\lambda \approx 1$ delivers an exhaust gas composition in which the oxygen released during the reduction of the nitrogen oxides is sufficient to oxidise the HC and CO content in the exhaust gas almost completely into CO_2 and H_2O. A richer mixture ($\lambda < 0.995$) results in an increase in the CO and HC content in the exhaust gas. A leaner mixture ($\lambda > 1.005$) results in an increase in nitrogen oxides. Engines which operate in specific operating ranges at $\lambda > 1$, e.g. direct-injection engines, therefore require catalysts which are able to store NO_X intermediately.

Operating conditions for single-bed three-way catalyst

Only from temperatures in excess of 300℃ does the catalyst have a conversion rate of more than 50% ("light off" temperatures). The attainment of this temperature after cold starting can be significantly shortened by the following measures: upstream installation, catalyst heating, air-gap-insulated exhaust manifolds, marked reversal of the ignition point (up to 15°) and secondary air injection. The catalytically active layer is subject to thermal ageing at temperatures above approx. 800℃. If temperatures of more than 1,000℃ are reached in the catalyst, the catalyst will be thermally destroyed. This can occur for example as a consequence of misfiring. Here unburned hydrocarbons enter the catalyst where they burn with the accumulated residual oxygen.

To ensure that the catalytically active layer is not rendered ineffective ("poisoned") by deposits, only unleaded petrol may used. Even combustion residues of engine oil, e.g. in the event of defective piston rings or cylinder wear, are deposited on the catalytically active layer and thereby reduce the effectiveness of the catalyst.

Catalyst with closed-loop mixture formation system (closed-loop catalyst)

Here an oxygen sensor utilises the residual oxygen contained in the exhaust gas to monitor the mixture composition within narrow tolerances $\lambda=1 \pm 0.005$ (λ window).

While conversion rates of 94% to 98% are achieved in the catalyst by closed-loop-controlled mixture formation systems, on average a conversion rate of 60% is possible in older vehicles with non-closed-loop-controlled mixture formation systems.

Lambda (λ) control loop. The λ or oxygen sensor (signalling device) is installed before the catalyst. Depending on the residual oxygen content in the exhaust gas, the oxygen sensor issues a corresponding voltage signal to the controller in the ECU. The ECU shortens the injection time if the amount of residual oxygen in the exhaust gas is low (rich mixture). The injection time is increased accordingly the amount of residual oxygen in the exhaust gas is high (lean mixture). The control operation is repeated at a prespecified frequency so that smooth engine operation is not affected.

A second oxygen sensor (monitor sensor) installed after the catalyst serves to monitor the catalyst function.

Adaptive lambda closed-loop control. If, for example, the residual oxygen value is constantly too low in a specific load range, the mixture is too rich, the basic injection quantity is reduced for this load range and stored as a pilot-control value in the ECU. In this way, disturbance values, such as incorrect fuel-system pressure, incorrect temperature values, engine ageing or unmetered air, can be corrected within a specific control range. At the same time the response time of λ closed-loop control is shortened and the exhaust gas quality improved.

New Words

aftertreatment	再处理	cell density	细胞密度
catalyst	催化器	ultrathin-wall	超薄壁
converter	换流器，变压器	platinum	铂，白金
pollutant	污染物	rhodium	铑
ceramic substrate	陶瓷基片	palladium	钯
noble-metal	贵金属	ratio	比率，比值
coating	涂层	nitrogen oxide	氮氧化物，氧化亚氮
jolt	颠簸	oxidise	（使某物）氧化，（使某物）生锈
heat-resistant	耐热的，抗热的	thermal ageing	热力老化

课文参考译文

催化器

催化器功能

催化器是目前用于废气净化最有效的系统。该系统没有通常意义的过滤器，而是依靠加热过程使有害物质，一氧化碳（CO）、碳氢化合物（HC）及氮氧化物（NO_x）转变为如水、二氧化碳、氮气等的无毒物质。使用可调节式催化器可以将废气中的90%的有害物质转换为无害物质。

催化器本身由优质钢外壳构成，其中装有作为催化载体的陶瓷体。为了在最小的空间获得最大的表面，可以使陶瓷体中间穿过6000个通道。通过特殊的方法使许多通道的表面都是透气的，并由此可放大约7000倍。这样就获得非常大的有效表面。表面上可以覆着1~2g实际的催化材料——铂及铑。表面越大越能保证有害分子与催化剂的接触。不可调催化器在结构及功能上与可调式催化器一样。用于油气混合气调节的附加系统，例如氧传感器以及电控器在这一低价的排气净化装置中不使用。废气成分转换为无害成分比与可调式催化器相比效果不大。催化器安装在排气系统中的预消声器的位置。所有通过废气的部分都使用优质钢制成。由此排气装置可达到传统装置的两倍的寿命。

氧传感器

- 可调式催化器在净化时可达到90%突出的效率，因为废气成分经后处理变成有用的组合。这一系统中重要的部分是氧传感器。它检测废气质量，如果混合气成分与最佳值有偏差的话，立刻通知控制器。然后控制器在短时间内决定，如何改变喷射的燃油量，以便使废气以最佳的组合进入到催化器中。这一混合比用$\lambda = 1$表示并被称为"定量混合"。

- 氧传感器"生存"在废气中残余氧气中，由于短时间内供给油气混合气进行燃烧，并不是每个氧分子都参与燃烧。不用参与燃烧的由经过氧传感器通往排气管。在废气中包括对于稀混合气燃烧后过多的及对于浓混合气燃烧后过少的自由的氧分子。催化器的效率完全由废气含氧量决定。它影响到在控制器上供给氧传感器的电压。

- 不可调及可调催化器都仅可使用无铅汽油。否则的话微孔的催化器表面会被废气中的铅成分覆盖并降低净化的效率。

Teil 4　Hybridantriebe　混合动力驱动技术
Part 4　Hybrid drive systems　混合动力驱动系统

学习目标

【知识目标】

1. 掌握与混合动力结构、分类、运行原理等相关的专业术语、单词和词汇。
2. 掌握混合动力主要结构的德文、英文表达方法。

【能力目标】

1. 能对混合动力总体结构的各大总成进行中、德、英互译。
2. 能进行与混合动力大体构造相关的德语、英语资料的阅读和翻译。
3. 能在混合动力实物上标识出相应结构的德语、英语单词和词汇。

Text 1　Hybridantriebe混合动力驱动(德文)

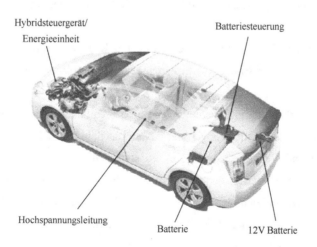

Die Entwicklung von alternativen Antriebskonzepten und alternativen Energieträgern soll dazu beitragen, dass die Luftschadstoffe (NO_X, HC, CO), Kohlendioxid (CO_2), der Kraftstoffverbrauch und die Geräuschemissionen vermindert werden.

Dadurch sollen die natürlichen Lebensgrundlagen erhalten bleiben und die Lebensqualität verbessert werden.

Als Energieträger stehen, außer Diesel und Benzin, einige alternative Kraftstoffe zur Verfügung. Zur Zeit laufen in Kleinserien bzw. in der Erprobungsphase Motoren mit

- Erdgas.
- Bio-Diesel, Bio-Gas.
- Ethanol, Methanol.
- Wasserstoff.
- elektrischer Energie.

Als alternative Antriebskonzepte bilden zur Zeit der Hybridantrieb und der Elektroantrieb mit Brennstoffzelle einen Entwicklungs- und Forschungsschwerpunkt.

Unter Hybridantrieben versteht man Fahrzeugantriebe, die mehr als eine Antriebsquelle besitzen, z.B. Elektromotor und Verbrennungsmotor.

Ziel von Hybridantrieben ist es, die Vorteile des jeweiligen Antriebskonzepts bei unterschiedlichen Betriebszuständen des Fahrzeugs zu nutzen. Folgende Hybridantriebsarten werden unter anderem erprobt:

- Verbrennungsmotor + Elektromotor (Series Hybrid).
- Verbrennungsmotor + Elektromotor + Batterie(Parallel Hybrid).
- Verbrennungsmotor + Elektromotor + externe Zufuhr von elektrischer Energie (Plug-in Hybrid).
- Gasturbine + Generator + Batterie + Elektromotor(Power-split Hybrid).

Eine vielfach erprobte Hybridantriebstechnik ist die Kombination von Verbrennungsmotor mit Elektromotor und Baterie (s.Bild).

Wirkungsweise. Im Kurzstreckenverkehr und bei Konstantfahrt versorgen Baterien den Elekrtomotor mit elektrischer Energie zum Antrieb. Dieser erfolgt über die Kupplung K2 zum Schaltgetriebe.

Im Langstreckenverkehr, beim Beschleunigen und bei Volllast sorgt der Verbrennungsmotor für den Antrieb. Hierbei wird die Kraft über K1 und K2 auf das Schaltgetriebe übertragen. Die zwischen Verbrennungsmotor und Getriebe liegende elektrische Baugruppe arbeitet jetzt als Generator und kann zum Laden der Batterien genutzt werden. Beim Bremsen öffnet die Kupplung K1, der Verbrennungsmotor wird zugleich abgeschaltet und der Elektromotor geht in den Generatorbetrieb. Über Kupplung K2 wird dabei der Rotor angetrieben. Damit nutzt man die Schwungenergie des Fahrzeugs zum Laden der Batterien.

Kapitel 3 Neue Technologie // Chapter 3 New Technology

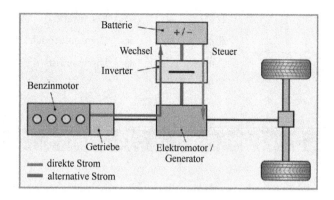

Bild: Hybridantriebskonzept

Verbrennungsmotor + Elektromotor

Vorteile dieses Antriebskonzeptes sind bei .

Antrieb durch Elektromotor .

— Geringe Geräuschemmission .

— keine Abgas .

— hoher Wirkungsgrad des Elektromotors (ca.90%).

Antrieb durch Verbrennungsmotor

— Große Reichweite des Fahrzeugs .

— im mittleren bis oberen Drehzahlbereich hohes Drehmoment .

— hohe Fahrzeuggeschwindigkeit möglich.

Merkmale

Da der Verbrennungsmotor bei dieser Antriebskombination häufiger im Lastbereich mit dem günstigsten Wirkungsgrad betrieben werden kann, wird der Gesamtwirkungsgrad positiv beeinflusst und der Energieverbrauch nimmt ab. Nachteilig sind die höheren Kosten für den Antrieb und das Gewicht der Batterien.

Neue Wörter

der	Antrieb	驱动装置	der	Hybridantrieb	混合动力驱动
der	Energieträger	能源载体	die	Brennstoffzelle	燃料电池
der	Kraftstoff	燃料	der	Elektromotor	电动机
die	Emission	排放	de	Verbrennungsmotor	内燃机
die	Kleinserie	小批量生产	die	Zufuhr	供给
das	Ethanol	乙醇	das	Schwungrad	飞轮
das	Methanol	甲醇	die	Gasturbine	燃气涡轮机
der	Wasserstoff	氢	der	Generator	发电机

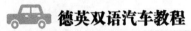

die	Kupplung	离合器	die	Reichweite	续驶里程
das	Schaltgetriebe	变速器	der	Drehzahlbereich	转速范围
die	Volllast	全负荷	das	Drehmoment	转矩
der	Rotor	转子			

Text 2 Hybrid drive systems 混合动力驱动系统（英文）

Design

In the case of hybrid drives, a distinction is made between series and parallel hybrid systems. It is possible to combine these two systems.

The electrical energy is stored in batteries via an inverter and can be called on as required, such as when driving exclusively with the electric drive system. An inverter converts the electrical energy generated in the generator as alternating current into direct current so that it can be stored in the battery. The inverter converts the direct current into alternating current to operate the electric motor.

Series hybrid systems also include electric vehicles that have an additional internal combustion engine.

Range extender. The electronics switch on the internal combustion engine as necessary in order to extend the range of the vehicle. The combustion engine in this case is used exclusively to supply electricity to the electric drive (on-board power generation). The electronics also include navigation data, e.g. the destination and route profile with uphill and downhill stretches.

Spark-ignition, diesel or wankel engines may be used as the internal combustion engine. For instance, diesel engines are used for buses. The advantage of the wankel engine is that it runs practically free of vibration, is more compact and weighs less. A passenger car fuel tank can hold 10 to 30 litres of fuel.

Vehicles with the range extender feature basically have a battery that is charged via an electrical connection, such as a domestic power outlet.

Charging the battery. The electric motor can also function as a generator and is therefore referred to as a motor generator. The battery is charged by switching over to the internal combustion engine or when braking while driving (recuperation).

Drive system. The connection between the combustion engine and electric motor is rigid in this system, e.g. due to flanged connections between the crankshaft and electric motor, which can be used simultaneously as the starter motor due to this connection. Its placement between the engine and gearbox is possible due to the flat layout. The electric motor (permanently exited three-phase synchronous motor) acts as a balancer shaft at the same time. A CVT (Continuously Variable Transmission) is usually used for the transmission.

The control unit consists of battery and the power unit (battery control unit, voltage converter, fan motor). A high-voltage cable supplies electric power to the drive unit in the front section of the vehicle.

Power-split hybrid system

The power-split hybrid system is a combination of the parallel and series hybrid systems. A power-split device, such as a planetary gear, is used to mechanically connect the internal combustion engine and one or two electric motors (MG1 and MG2) to each other.

The motive force of the internal combustion engine is distributed across the planetary gear unit. Part the motive force is transferred to the driving wheels, while another part is transferred to MG1 and is used to generate power. Since the drive wheels are connected to MG2, MG2 must be actuated, since it would otherwise cause a braking effect.

MG2 and the differential for the drive wheels are combined by way of a drive chain and gearwheels.

Drive unit design. This consists of the motor generators MG1 and MG2, the planetary gear unit and the differential. It also includes a connection to the inverter or battery.

The battery supplies the drive unit with 200 to 300 volts of power. The inverter converts the alternating current into direct current. A high-voltage cable connects the electric motors with the inverter. The high-voltage battery is located in the rear of the vehicle.

Operating principle

The internal combustion engine and the two motor generators MG1 and MG2 are linked via a planetary gear.

Connections between the drive and planetary gear:
- MG1 → Sun gear.
- MG2 → Internal gear with drive chain.
- Internal combustion engine → Planetary gear.

The ECU detects the driver's drive command via the accelerator pedal sensor. It also receives information on the driving speed and the gearshift position. Using this information, it controls the flow of energy and motive forces.

Pulling away. Propulsion is provided exclusively by MG2 when the vehicle pulls away. The engine remains switched off and MG1 rotates in the opposite direction without generating electrical energy.

Engine starting. If a higher torque is required for driving, MG1 starts the internal combustion engine as an auxiliary drive system. The engine is also started when the battery management system defects a low battery charge state or the battery temperature deviates grom the prescribed level.

MG1 operates as a generator once the engine has started. MG1 charges the high-voltage battery via the inverter.

Driving at low load. The planetary gear apportions the engine's motive force. Part of this force is applied to the drive wheels and the remainder is used to generate electrical energy with the aid of MG1. MG2 can provide the drive system with additional support.

Acceleration at full throttle. When the vehicle requires high propulsive power, the system increases the motive force from MG2 by drawing additional electrical energy from the HV battery.

Deceleration. The engine is switched off when the vehicle is braked or is in overrun mode. The drive wheels now drive MG2, which functions as a generator and charges the HV battery.

When the vehicle is decelerated from a higher driving speed, the engine maintains a predetermined engine speed. This prevents excessive speed discrepancies between the drives and protects the planetary gear from being destroyed.

Reversing. Propulsion is provided exclusively by MG2 when the vehicle is driven in reverse.

Energy accumulation

Battery system

Currently nickel metal hydride or lithium ion accumulators are used as batteries for hybrid and electric vehicle drive systems.

In addition to a high-voltage battery, a hybrid vehicle also has a conventional 12 volt battery to supply power to the vehicle electrical system.

Nickel metalhydridebatteries (NiMH)

The cells of a nickel metal hydride battery consist of multiple cells each of which is composed of a positive and a negative plate as well as electrolyte (potassium hydroxide solution).

Design. The positive plate (MH) consists of a metal alloy of a metal composition with a high percentage of rare earth elements (also known as rare earth metals) such as lanthanum, cerium and neodymium. The positive plate can store hydrogen. The hydrogen is deposited in the crystal lattice, thus forming a metal hydride.

Expensive procedures are required to mine rare earth elements. Since some are toxic, mining them is associated with high environmental risks.

New Words

hybrid	混合的	downhill	下坡
inverter	换流器，倒相器	wankel engine	转子发动机
range extender	范围扩充，域扩充	recuperation	同流节热
on-board	车载	gearbox	变速器
power generation	发电	synchronous	同步的
navigation	导航	balancer shaft	平衡器轴
uphill	上坡	（CVT）Continuously Variable Transmission	

新技术篇

Kapitel 3　Neue Technologie // Chapter 3　New Technology

	无级变速器	predetermine	预定，先定
power-split	功率分流，动力分配	reversing	换向
planetary gear	行星齿轮	accumulation	积累
accelerator pedal sensor	加速踏板传感器	lithium	锂
acceleration	加速度	electrolyte	电解质，电离质
propulsive	有推进力的	alloy	合金
propulsion	推进，推进力	lanthanum	镧
deceleration	减速	cerium	铈
generator	发电机	neodymium	钕

课文参考译文

混合动力装置

替代动力方案及替代能源载体的开发应致力于：降低有害废气（NO_X, HC, CO)、二氧化碳(CO_2)、燃料消耗和噪声排放。

由此可保持自然生存基础条件并改进生存质量。

除了汽油，柴油以外，作为能源载体还有其他一些替代燃料，目前小批量生产及正在试制阶段的发动机使用有：

1）天然气。

2）生物柴油，生物燃气。

3）甲醇，乙醇。

4）氢。

5）电能。

目前，作为替代驱动概念混合动力和利用燃料电池的电动驱动也已成为开发研究的重点。

混合动力装置是指具有不止一种动力源的汽车驱动装置，例如电动机和内燃机。

混合动力系统的目的是，在汽车不同的工况时充分利用该驱动方案的优点。

当前主要有以下几种混合动力类型正在试验中：

— 内燃机+电动机（串联式混合动力系统）。

— 内燃机+电动机+蓄电池（并联式混合动力系统）。

— 内燃机+电动机+外部电能的输入（Plug-in）（插电式混合动力系统）。

— 汽轮机+发电机+蓄电池+电动机（组合式混合动力系统）。

久经考验的混合动力技术方案是由内燃机和电动机以及蓄电池的组合。

工作原理　当短途行驶及在持续行驶时，蓄电池向电动机提供电能用于驱动汽车。此时，通过离合器K2与变速器连接进行工作。

当长途行驶时，在汽车加速及全负荷工况时内燃机用于驱动。此时，动力通过K1和K2传递到变速器上。位于内燃机和变速器之间的电气总成作为发电机进行工作，并为蓄电池充电。当汽车制动时，离合器K1打开，同时切断内燃机，电动机开始进行发电工作。通过离合器K2转子开始驱动。由此，可以利用飞轮能量为汽车蓄电池充电。

内燃机+电动机的混合动力方案

此方案的优点：

通过电动机驱动汽车

　－较低的噪声排放。

　－无废气排放。

　－充分利用电动机的高效率（约90%）。

通过内燃机驱动

　－汽车较长的续驶里程。

　－在中速及高速转速范围具有很高的转矩。

　－可以实现很高的行驶速度。

特征：因为内燃机在这一驱动组合方案中通常是在具有最有利的效率的负荷范围工作，可以对总效率造成积极的影响，并大大降低燃料消耗。缺点是此驱动系统的成本高以及蓄电池的重量问题。

新技术篇

Kapitel 3　Neue Technologie // Chapter 3　New Technology

Teil 5　Erdgasantrieb　天然气驱动技术
Part 5　Natural gas drives　天然气驱动技术

学习目标

【知识目标】
1. 掌握与天燃气驱动系统结构、分类、运行原理等相关的专业术语、单词和词汇。
2. 掌握天然气驱动系统主要结构的德文、英文表达方法。

【能力目标】
1. 能对天然气驱动系统总体结构的各部分细节进行中、德、英互译。
2. 能进行与天然气驱动系统大体构造相关的德语、英语资料阅读和翻译。
3. 能在天然气驱动系统实物上标识出相应结构的德语、英语单词和词汇。

Text 1　Erdgasantrieb天然气驱动技术（德文）

Als alternativer Kraftstoff hat Erdgas, das im wesentlichen aus Methan (CH_4) besteht beim Einsatz in Verbrennungsmotoren gegenüber Kraftstoffen (Benzin und Diesel) folgende Vorteile:

– Verbrennt nahezu Ruß- und Partikelfrei.

– weniger CO, im Durchschnitt 40%...50%.

– geringere NO_X-Emissionen.

– geringere Anteile an ozonbildenen Kohlenwasserstoffen.

– geringere Geräuschemissionen als bei Dieselmotoren.

– hohe Klopffestigkeit (135ROZ).

– direkt gewinnbares Naturprodukt; es bedarf keines aufwendigen Raffinerieprozesses. Daher weniger CO_2-Ausstoß und damit Verringerung von Treibhausgasen.

– lange Verfügbarkeit. Sie wird von Gaslieferanten auf bis zu 170 Jahre geschätzt.

Nachteile von erdgasbetriebenen Fahrzeugen:

– Geringere Leistung, da der Gemischheizwert von Erdgas kleiner als der von Benzin ist. Bei bivalenten Antrieben (Benzin oder Erdgas) beträgt der Leistungsverlust bis zu 15%; bei reinen Erdgasantrieben bis zu 12%.

- geringere Reichweiten.
- erhöhter Bedarf an Stauraum für Gasbehälter.
- verringerte Nutzlast durch Gasbehälter.
- schlechte Tankstelleninfrastruktur.
- höhere Kosten, wegen Kleinserienstandard.

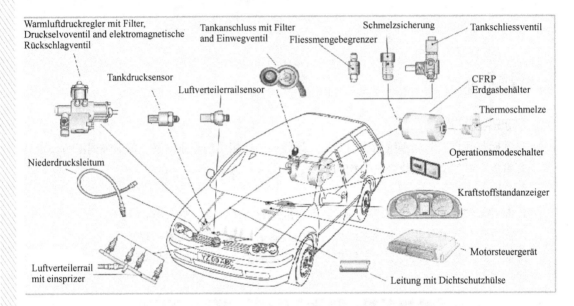

Eigenschaften. Erdgas ist in seinen Kenngrößen ähnlich dem Ottokraftstoff. Es muss aufgrund seiner Klopffestigkeit fremdgezündet werden. Benzinmotoren können deshalb ohne größeren bauliche Veränderungen auf NTG (Natural Gas Technology) umgerüstet werden. Bei Dieselmotoren ist ein erheblicher Umbauaufwand erforderlich. Das Verdichtungsverhältnis muss reduziert werden und der Klopffestigkeit des Erdgases angepasst werden. Es entfällt die Dieseleinspritzanlage, stattdessen ist eine Zündanlage mit entsprechender Steuerung erforderlich.

Prinzipielle Funktionsweise. Vom Gasbehälter gelangt das komprimierte Gas über einen Druckregler, der den Gasdruck reduziert, zu einem Verteiler mit Stellmotor für die Gasregelung weiter zu Einblaseventilen im Ansaugrohr. Der Stellmotor wird von einem elektronischen Steuergerät abhängig von Last, Drehzahl, Temperatur und λ-Signal gesteuert. Bei bivalenten Antrieben kann entweder per Knopfdruck auf Benzinbetrieb umgestellt werden oder bei leerem Gasbehälter schaltet die Anlage selbst um. Beim Ausschalten der Zündung sperrt ein Absperrventil die Gaszufuhr.

Neue Wörter

das	Methan	甲烷	die	Partikel	颗粒
der	Ruß	炭黑	die	Emission	排放

新技术篇

Kapitel 3 Neue Technologie // Chapter 3 New Technology

der	Kohlenwasserstoff	碳氢化合物		das	Ottokraftstoff	汽油
die	Klopffestigkeit	抗爆性		das	Verdichtungsverhältnis	压缩比
der	Raffinerieprozess	精炼工艺		die	Dieseleinspritzanlage	燃油喷射装置
das	Treibhausgas	引起温室效应的气体		der	Druckregler	调压器
der	Gemischheizwert	混合气热值		der	Stellmotor	伺服电动机
der	Gasbehälter	储气燃料箱		das	Einblaseventil	扫气阀
das	Kleinserienstandard	小批量标准		das	Ansaugrohr	进气管
die	Tankstelleninfrastruktur	加油（供气）基础设施		das	Absperrventil	止回阀
				die	Drehzahl	转速
die	Kenngröße	参数		die	Gaszufuhr	供气

Text 2 Natural gas drives 天然气驱动技术（英文）

Natural gas is a fossil fuel composed primarily of methane (CH_4). The percentage of actual methane contained in natural gas is 80% to 99%, depending on the region where the gas is extracted. The remaining sources comprise carbon dioxide, nitrogen and low-grade hydrocarbons.

Natural gas can be stored in a vehicle either in liquid form at -162℃ as LNG (Liquefied Natural Gas) or in compressed form at pressures of up to 200 bar as CNG (Compressed Natural Gas.). Natural gas is generally used in its compressed form because of the high cost of liquid storage.

The high knock resistance of natural gas (approx. 140 RON) allows a compression of roughly 13:1. However, this advantage cannot be exploited in bivalent drives, i.e. in a combination of petrol and natural gas drives, because the compression ratio must be tuned to petrol operation.

Advantages of natural gas drives over petrol and diesel:

• Very good combustion properties and low emissions of CO_2, NO_X, CO and virtually no soot and sulphur emissions.

• Less carbon fouling of spark plugs and reduced contamination of engine oil. Disadvantages of a natural gas drive over petrol and diesel:

• Stoichiometric ratio of 17.2:1 results in a lower fuel mass and thus lower engine power.

• Expensive storage of natural gas necessary.

• Shorter cruising range with the same tank volume.

• Extensive safety regulations with regard to operating, servicing and repairing natural gas vehicles.

Design. Natural gas drives are generally used in combination with petrol operation in spark-ignition engines (so-called bivalent drives). Various additional components must be installed in the vehicle for this purpose.

Operating principle. The natural gas stored at approx. 200 bar in the natural gas tank flows to the gas pressure regulator. This regulates the gas pressure in several reducing stages at approx. 9 bar. The gas injectors in the intake manifold are energised by the ECU as required and are thereby opened. The gas mixes with the inducted air and then flows as a gas-air mixture into the combustion chamber.

Safety features. Natural gas drives pose certain risks to the environment, e.g. as a result of unchecked discharge of gas or the danger of explosion caused by a rise in pressure. These systems are equipped with various safety features as a result.

• One-way check valves. These are located in the re-fuelling connection and on the tank shutoff valves and prevent the gas from flowing back via the re-fuelling valve.

• Gastight sheathing. This is wrapped around the lines and components routed inside the vehicle.

• Threaded joints. These are designed as double-clamping-ring threaded connections.

• Natural gas tanks. These are made of steel or CFRP. Each tank is connected to the vehicle by two retainers. The burst pressures are approx. 400 bar (steel) or approx. 500 bar (CFRP).

• Solder fuse and thermal cut-out on the natural gas tank. These prevent an excessive pressure increase, thus preventing the tank from exploding in the event of a fire.

• Flow-rate limiter. This prevents the natural gas tank from draining suddenly in the event of a pipe breakage.

• Electromagnetic shutoff valves. This valve, which is mounted on the natural gas tank, closes on changeover to petrol mode, in the event of a power failure, when the engine is stopped, or in the event of an accident. Another valve is located on the pressure regulator.

• Flexible gas lines. These prevent breaks caused by fatigue failure on the low-pressure side, i.e. between the pressure regulator and the gas injectors.

• Overpressure regulator. This is mounted on the pressure regulator and protects the low-pressure side against excessive pressures.

This calculates the appropriate values for actuation of the gas nozzles based on injection points and timing specified by the ECU. The control unit for the gas system includes diagnostic capabilities.

New Words

fossil	化石	bivalent drives	双驱动
methane	甲烷，沼气	one-way check	单项检查
Liquefied Natural Gas	液化天然气	sheathing	覆盖物，罩子
Compressed Natural Gas	压缩天然气	threaded joint	螺纹接头
soot	油烟，煤烟	fuse	熔化，熔合
sulphur	硫	regulator	调整器、校准器
stoichiometric	化学计量		

新技术篇

Kapitel 3　Neue Technologie // Chapter 3　New Technology

课文参考译文

天然气驱动系统

作为代用燃料的天然气实际上是一种以甲烷(CH_4)为主要成分的矿物燃料，与用汽油和柴油驱动的内燃机相比具有以下优点：

- 废气中几乎不含炭黑和颗粒排放物。
- 很低的CO排放，平均为40%~50%。
- 很低的NO_x排放。
- 碳氢化合物含量很低。
- 与柴油发动机相比具有很低的噪声排放。
- 极好的抗爆性（135RON）。
- 可直接获取的自然产物，不需要昂贵的再生工艺。因此，CO_2排放很低并由此减少温室气体的排放。
- 长期可供性。天然气供应商预计可提供170年的气体。

天然气驱动的汽车具有以下缺点：

- 较低的功率，因为天然气的混合气热值低于汽油。当双燃料（汽油或天然气）驱动时功率损失达15%，纯天然气驱动时达12%。
- 较短的续驶里程。
- 对储气罐安装空间很高的需求。
- 储气罐很低的有效负荷。
- 加气站设施很差。
- 由于小批量生产标准使其成本很高。
- 天然气存储费用高。

天然气动力系统的特性　天然气的特性值与汽油燃料近似。但是，由于其很高的抗爆性必须由外部点燃。因此，汽油发动机不用在部件上进行很大的改动就可以改造成NTG（天然气）发动机。柴油发动机改造则需要很大的花销。压缩比必须降低以便适应天然气的抗爆特性。不必使用柴油喷射装置，取而代之需要具有相应控制装置的点火系统。

天然气动力系统工作原理　天然气储气瓶内的气态天然气经过管路，到达调压器。ECU根据需要给进气歧管上的气体喷射器通电，从而使其开启。喷出的气体与进入的空气进行混合，然后进入燃烧室。点火切断后闭锁阀将进气道封闭。

Teil 6　Brennstoffzelle　燃料电池技术
Part 6　Drives with fuel cells　燃料电池驱动

【知识目标】

1.掌握与氢燃料电池驱动装置结构、分类、运行原理等相关的专业术语、单词和词汇。

2.掌握氢燃料电池驱动装置主要结构的德文、英文表达方法。

【能力目标】

1.能对氢燃料电池驱动装置总体结构的各部分细节进行中、德、英互译。

2.能进行与氢燃料电池驱动装置大体构造相关的德语、英语资料阅读和翻译。

3.能在氢燃料电池驱动装置实物上标识出相应结构的德语、英语单词和词汇。

Text 1　Wasserstoffantrieb – Brennstoffzelle氢燃料电池驱动装置（德文）

Wasserstoff (H_2) gilt als ein zukünftiger Energieträger. Verbindet sich Wasserstoff mit Sauerstoff, so entsteht Wasser unter Abgabe von Energie.

$2H_2+O_2 \rightarrow 2H_2O+Energie$

Bei der Wasserstoffantriebstechnik unterscheidet man zwischen der heißen Verbrennung und der kalten Verbrennung.

Heiße Verbrennung. Dabei reagiert reiner Wasserstoff mit Luftsauerstoff in einem Verbrennungsmotor und zeugt Wärmeenergie, die durch Kurbeltrieb in mechanische Energie umgewandelt wird.

Kalte Verbrennung. Dabei sorgt eine Brennstoffzelle für eine kontrollierte Reaktion bei der Verbindung von Wasserstoff und Sauerstoff, wobei elektrische Energie freigesetzt wird. Bei dieser Reaktion entstehen Temperaturen von etwa 80℃. Die erzeugte elektrische Energie wird zum Antrieb von Elektromotoren verwendet.

Kapitel 3 Neue Technologie // Chapter 3 New Technology

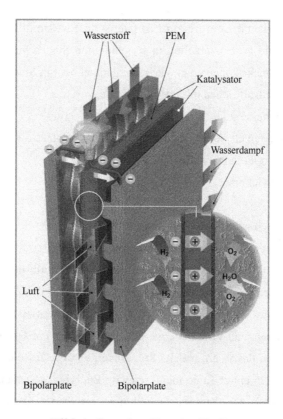

Bild: Aufbau einer Brennstoffzelle

Die Brennstoffzelle besteht im Kern aus einem festen protonenleitenden Elektrolyten aus Kunststofffolie (PEM: proton exchange membrane). Diese Folie ist beidseitig mit einem Platinkatalysator und Elektroden aus Graphitpapier beschichtet (Bipolarplatten). In die Bipolarplatten sind feine Gaskanäle eingefräst, durch die auf der einen Seite Wasserstoff und auf der anderen Seite Luft zugeführt wird.

Wirkungsweise der Brennstoffzelle

Die Wasserstoffmoleküle werden durch den Katalysator in positive Wasserstoffionen (Protonen) und negative Elektronen zerlegt. Danach wandern die Protonen durch den Elektrolyten zur Luftsauerstoffseite. Auf der Wasserstoffseite entsteht ein Elektronenüberschuss.

Der Katalysator auf der Luftseite bewirkt, dass die in der Luft enthaltenen Sauerstoffmoleküle zur Elektronenaufnahme angeregt werden. Verbindet man nun die beiden Bipolarplatten durch einen äußeren Stromkreis, so wandern die Elektronen unter Abgabe von elektrischer Energie von der Wasserstoffseite zur Sauerstoffseite und laden den Sauerstoff negativ auf. Die negativ geladenen Sauerstoffionen verbinden sich an der Grenzschicht mit den positiv geladenen Wasserstoffionen zu schadstofffreiem Wasserdampf (H_2O).

Die derzeitige Generation der Brennstoffzellen hat je Zelle eine Spannung von 0,6 Volt.

Um ausreichende elektrische Energie zum Antrieb von Elektromotoren zu erzeugen, wird eine entsprechende Anzahl an Einzelzellen in so genannten Stacks hintereinandergeschaltet (= Reihenschaltung). Diese Stacks können nun wiederum parallel oder in Reihe geschaltet werden.

Merkmale von Fahrzeugantrieben mit Brennstoffzelle:

– geringe Geräuschemission.

– besserer Wirkungsgrad als herkömmlicher verbrennungsmotorischer Fahrzeugantrieb.

– „keine" (sehr geringe) Schadstoffemission vor Ort.

– geringe Wärmeentwicklung.

– hoher Preis.

– erfordert derzeit noch zusätzlichen Stauraum.

Herstellung von reinem Wasserstoff für Fahrzeugantriebe

Die Wasserstoffherstellung kann durch Elektrolyse außerhalb des Fahrzeugs oder durch chemische Prozesse an Bord des Fahrzeugs erfolgen.

Elektrolyse. Dabei wird Wasser mit Hilfe von Gleichstrom in Wasserstoff und Sauerstoff zerlegt. Dazu sind erhebliche Mengen an Primärenergie erforderlich. Der Preis von Wasserstoff und seine ökologische Bilanz hängen davon ab, welche Primärenergieträger zu seiner Erzeugung eingesetzt werden. Zur Zeit werden in erster Linie nicht genutzte Energien, sogenannte „Abfallenergien", in der chemischen Industrie zur Wasserstofferzeugung verwendet. Ökologisch günstig wäre es regenerative (erneuerbare) Energieträger zu verwenden, z.B. Sonnenenergie, Wasserenergie, Windenergie, Biomasse.

Reiner Wasserstoff muss in speziellen Behältern mitgeführt werden, welche erheblichen Stauraum verbrauchen und die Nutzlast reduzieren.

Wasserstofferzeugung durch chemische Prozesse an Bord des Fahrzeugs

Dazu muss das Kraftfahrzeug mit flüssigem Methanol (CH_3OH) betankt werden. Das Methanol wird mit salzfreiem Wassser vermischt, bei 250℃ verdampft und in einem Reformer mit katalytischem Brenner in Wasserstoff und CO_2 umgewandelt. Das gereinigte Wasserstoffgas wird dann der Brennstoffzelle zugeführt. Bei diesem Prozess entstehen nur sehr geringe Mengen CO_2.

Neue Wörter

der	Antrieb	传动（装置），驱动装置	die	heiße Verbrennung	热燃烧
			der	Verbrennungsmotor	内燃机
die	Brennstoffzelle	燃料电池	die	Wärmeenergie	热能
der	Wasserstoff	氢，氢气	der	Kurbeltrieb	曲轴传动
der	Energieträger	能量载体	die	mechanische Energie	机械能
der	Sauerstoff	氧，氧气	die	kalte Verbrennung	冷燃烧

die	elektrische Energie	电能		das	Proton	质子
der	Elektromotor	电动机		der	Stromkreis	电路，回路
protonenleitend		质子传导的		die	Spannung	电压
der	Elektrolyt	电解质，电解液		die	Reihenschaltung	串联，串联电路
die	Kunststofffolie	塑料薄膜		der	Stauraum	储物空间
	PEM (proton exchange membranc) 质子交换膜			die	Elektrolyse	电解
der	Platinkatalysator	铂催化剂		der	Gleichstrom	直流（电流）
die	Elektrode	电极		die	Primärenergie	天然能
das	Graphitpapier	石墨纸		regenerativ		再生的
die	Bipolarplatte	双极板		der	Behälter	容器
das	Molekül	分子		das	Methanol	甲醇
die	Wasserstoffion	氢离子		der	Reformer	重整炉

Text 2　Drives with fuel cells 燃料电池驱动（英文）

Design. The core of the fuel cell consists of a proton-conducting plastic membrane (PEM: proton exchange membrane). This is coated on both sides with a platinum catalyst and graphite-paper electrodes (bipolar plates).

Fine gas ports are milled into the bipolar plates; through these ports hydrogen is supplied on the one side and air or oxygen is supplied on the other.

Operating principle. On one side of the fuel cell (cathode) hydrogen (H_2) is broken down by a catalyst into protons and electrons.

Only protons can pass through the plastic membrane (PEM: proton exchange membrane) to the other side of the cell (anode). Electrons cannot pass through the membrane. When the cathode and the anode are connected, the negatively charged electrons move to the positively charged side. This results in a flow of current which can drive a load/consumer, e.g. an electric motor. Protons, electrons and oxygen combine on the anode to form water.

Hydrogen formation. Hydrogen can be produced by electrolysis outside the vehicle or by chemical processes on board the vehicle.

Electrolysis. This occurs when water is broken down into hydrogen and oxygen using direct current. Pure hydrogen must be carried in special containers on board the vehicle, since the hydrogen is stored under high pressure.

Vehicle components in a fuel cell drive

High-pressure hydrogen storage tank. This tank has a fill port connection and is located in the rear of the vehicle. The storage tank capacity is approx. 170 litres and it is filled with roughly 350 bar of pressure. This gives the vehicle a range of approx. 460 kilometres.

Lithium-ion battery. The battery voltage is approx. 290 V. It is located in the floor assembly of the vehicle.

Fuel cell stack. The stack output is approx. 100 kW. It is also located in the floor assembly of the vehicle.

12 V on-board battery. The battery supplies the voltage to accessories as well as electrical auxiliary and equipment systems.

Drive unit. This unit comprises a permanently excited three-phase synchronous motor and the inverter.

Inverter. The inverter converts the electric DC voltage produced in the fuel cell to the AC voltage required by the drive motor. At the same time, the inverter supplies the HV battery and 12 V on-board battery with electric power.

Drive motor. The drive motor is designed as a motor generator set. This allows the vehicle to recover braking energy and store it in the battery.

On-board hydrogen formation. An alternative to storing hydrogen in the high-pressure tank is to produce hydrogen on board the vehicle.

The vehicle must be filled with liquid methanol (CH_3OH) for this purpose. The methanol is mixed with salt-free water, evaporated at 250 ℃ and converted in a reformer with a catalytic burner into hydrogen and CO_2. The purified hydrogen gas is then supplied to the fuel cell.

Small quantities of CO_2 are produced during the gas-purification process and are emitted into the environment.

New Words

proton-conducting	质子导电	electrolysis	点解
membrane	薄膜	lithium-ion battery	锂离子电池
graphite-paper	石墨纸	three-phase synchronous motor	三相同步电机
electrode	电极	inverter	变流器，逆变器
bipolar plate	双极板	methanol	甲醇
cathode	阴极	evaporate	使蒸发
anode	阳极	purification	净化

新技术篇

Kapitel 3　Neue Technologie // Chapter 3　New Technology

课文参考译文

燃料电池驱动系统

氢（H_2）将成为未来的能源载体。氢与氧反应产生水同时会产生能量：

$2H_2+O_2 \rightarrow 2H_2O+$能量

在氢燃料驱动技术中分为热燃烧和冷燃烧方法。

热燃烧即纯氢与含氧的空气在内燃机中发生反应并产生热能，并通过曲轴转动转换为机械能。

冷燃烧是在燃料电池中，氢与氧有控制地进行反应，化学能在燃烧空间内被转变成电能。在这一反应中产生约80℃的温度。所产生的电能用于驱动电动机。

燃料电池的结构。燃料电池的核心部件是质子传导塑料膜（PEM——质子交换膜）。PEM的两侧涂有铂催化剂和石墨纸电极（双极板）。在双极板中压制有细小的气孔，通过这些孔，从一侧供应氢，从另一侧供应空气或氧。

燃料电池的工作原理。在燃料电池的一侧（阴极），在催化剂的作用下，氢（H_2）分解成带正电的氢离子（质子）和电子。仅有质子才能通过这个塑料膜（PEM），到达电池的另一侧（阳极）。电子不能穿过PEM。当将阳极和阴极连接时，带负电的电子就会移向带正电的一侧。这就形成了驱动负载/用电设备（如电动机）工作的电流。氧、氢离子和电子在阳极上结合。

在当今的燃料电池中每个电池具有0.6V的电压。为了产生足够的电能用于驱动电动机，应将足够数量的单个电池串联成所谓的电池组（串联）。这一电池组又可以并联或串联接通。

使用燃料电池的汽车驱动装置的特征：

- 很低的噪声排放。
- 比传统内燃机汽车驱动装置具有更好的效率。
- "没有"（很低）有害物质排放。
- 较低的热排放。
- 价格偏高。
- 还需要额外的安装空间。

汽车驱动用纯氢的制备

可以在车外用电解制氢法，或在车上用化学制氢法来生产氢。

电解将水借助于直流电分解为氢和氧。为此需要大量的一次能源。氢的价格及其生态平衡取决于使用哪种一次能源用于其制备。目前，首先未使用的能源有所谓的"垃圾能源"，在化学工业中用于生产氢。对于生态有利的是使用再生（可更新）能源载体，例如，太阳能、水能、风能及生物燃料。

纯氢必须在特殊的容器中存放，需要很大的储藏空间，并且减少有效载荷。

利用化学反应在车上直接制氢

为此，车上必须加有液态甲醇（CH_3OH）。将甲醇与软化水混合，在250℃的条件下蒸发，并在带有催化燃烧器的重整炉中转化为氢和二氧化碳。然后，将这些提纯的氢送到燃料电池。在这个气体提纯过程中，会产生少量的二氧化碳。

Teil 7　Elektrische Fensterheber　电动车窗
Part 7　Comfort and convenience systems
舒适与便捷系统

【知识目标】

1. 掌握与电动车窗升降系统结构、分类、运行原理等相关的专业术语、单词和词汇。
2. 掌握电动车窗升降系统主要结构的德文、英文表达方法。

【能力目标】

1. 能对电动车窗升降系统总体结构的各部分细节进行中、德、英互译。
2. 能进行与电动车窗升降系统大体构造相关的德语、英语资料阅读和翻译。
3. 能在电动车窗升降系统实物上标识出相应结构的德语、英语单词和词汇。

Text 1　Elektrische Fensterheber 电动车窗（德文）

Sie ermöglichen ein elektrisches Öffnen und Schließen der Fenster und gegebenenfalls des Schiebedachs über einen Wippschalter (Tastschalter).

Als Fensterantrieb dient hauptsächlich ein Seilzugantrieb (Bild). Der Antriebsmotor betätigt über ein Schneckengetriebe einen Seilzug, der je nach Drehrichtung des Motors das Fenster öffnet oder schließt. Die selbsthemmende Wirkung des Schneckengetriebes verhindert ein gewaltsames Öffnen der Fenster.

Elektrische Betätigung der Fenster. Sie kann erfolgen durch

— Wippschalter (manuelle Betätigung).

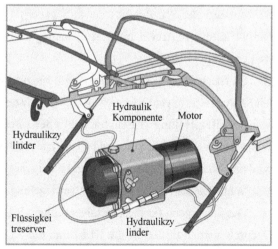

Bild. Seilzugantrieb

– Steuerelektronik kombiniert mit Wippschalter.

Betätigung mit Wippschalter. Über den jeweiligen Wippschalter, der dem Fensterhebermotor zugeordnet ist, kann das Fenster geschlossen oder geöffnet werden. Bei Zentralverriegelung können auch alle Fenster gleichzeitig schließen (Bild).

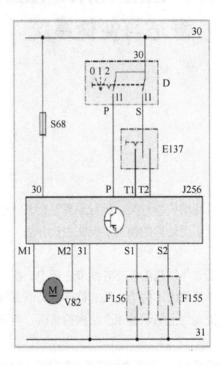

Bild: Schaltplan für die Betätigung mit Wippschalter

Wirkungsweise (Bild). Bei eingeschaltetem Fahrschalter wird über Klemme 15 das Hauptrelais angesteuert. Es zieht an, verbindet Kl.30 mit Kl.87 und legt Spannung an Kl.d von Schalter S1 und S2. Mit Hilfe des Schalters S5, der in Schalter S1 des Fahrers integrier ist, können die Schalter S3 und S4 für die hinteren Türen mit Spannung versorgt bzw. die Spannungsversorgung abgeschaltet werden.

Schalterstellung: Fenster öffnen. Bei Betätigung eines Wippschalters (S1, S2, S3, S4) wird Kl.d (+) mit Kl.b und Kl.v (–) mit Kl.a verbunden. Der Fensterantrieb senkt das jeweilige Fenster ab.

Schalterstellung: Fenster schließen. Soll das Fenster geschlossen werden, wird im Wippschalter Kl.d (+) mit Kl.a und Kl.e(–) mit Kl.b verbunden. Die Drehrichtung des Antriebsmotors wird umgekehrt, da die Klemmen a und b umgepolt werden. Das Fenster schließt.

Schließen der Fenster bei Zentralverriegelung.

Das Steuergerät für die Zentralverriegelung legt die Steuerspule des Steuerrelais Kl.85 an Masse. Dadurch werden im Relais die Kl.87 und die Kl.30 verbunden. Die Schalterklemme a wird über die Kl.c an Plus gelegt. Über Kl.b und Kl.e wird die Verbindung zur Masse hergestellt. Die Fenster

Kapitel 3 Neue Technologie // Chapter 3 New Technology

werden geschlossen.

Kombination von Fensterverstellung durch Wippschalter und Steuerelektronik. Dabei kann die Steuerelektronik zentral in einem Steuergerät untergebracht sein. Um den Kabelaufwand möglichst gering zu halten kann es im jeweiligen Fensterhebermotor integriert sein. Wird der jeweilige Bedienungsschalter des Fensterhebermotors kurz angetippt, veranlasst die Steuerelektronik, dass das Fenster geschlossen wird. Betätigt man den Testschalter länger, kann das Fenster in jede beliebige Position gefahren werden. Wird das Fahrzeug über die Zentralverriegelung abgeschlossen, schließen alle Fenster gleichzeitig bzw. werden sie in eine Lüftungsstellung gefahren.

Einklemmschutz. Um ein gefährliches Einklemmen von Körperteilen, wie z.B. Hände, Arme zu verhindern, darf die Schließkraft der Fenster einen bestimmten Höchstwert nicht überschreiten. Der Klemmschutz wirkt elektrisch, durch Abschalten des Elektromotors ab einer bestimmten Stromstärke oder mechanisch durch Lastkupplungen im Antrieb.

Neue Wörter

der	Fensterheber	车窗升降系统	der	Fahrschalter	主电路组合开关
das	Schiebedach	天窗	das	Hauptrelais	主继电器
der	Wippschalter	摇臂开关		umgepolt	颠倒极性
der	Tastschalter	按钮开关		ansteuern	移向……处控制
der	Seilzugantrieb	钢索传动系统	das	Steuergerät	控制单元
das	Schnekengetriebe	蜗杆机构	die	Steuerspur	控制线圈
	selbstsichernd	自锁	der	Kabelaufwand	电缆耗费
die	Bestätigung	按下，控制		antippen	触碰
die	Zentralverriegelung	中央控制门锁系统	die	Lüftungsstellung	通风位置
der	Schaltplan	电路图	das	Einklemmen	夹住
	Kl.= die Klemme	端子	die	Lastkupplung	载荷离合装置

Text 2 Comfort and convenience systems 舒适与便捷系统（英文）

Convertible roof actuation

The convertible roof actuation is of the electro-hydraulic type. A switch activates an electric motor which sets a rotary pump in motion. This generates pressure. Double-action hydraulic cylinders cause the roof to be opened or closed.

Hydraulic device

This consists of the following:

- Fluid reservoir.

- Electrically driven hydraulic rotary pump.
- Hydraulic control unit.
- Two double-action hydraulic cylinders.

Electrical device

This consists of the following main components:

- Convertible roof button (E137).
- Control unit (J256).
- Hydraulic pump motor (V82).
- Ignition/starter switch (D).
- Thermal cut-out (S68).
- Contacts for fitted convertible roof covering (F155, F156).

Principle of convertible roof operation

First, the convertible roof must be unlocked manually. Then, in the interests of safety, activation of the electro-hydraulic convertible roof is possible only with the ignition key inserted and the ignition switched off.

To do this, PIN S of ignition/starter switch D applies voltage to the convertible roof button E137. Once this is pressed, the control unit J256 receives voltage at PIN T1. It receives voltage in the same way from ignition/starter switch D via PIN P.

The working current supply for the system is via a thermal cut-out S68 from terminal 30 to PIN 30 of the control unit J256.

Since there is voltage at PIN T1 of control unit J256, the control unit controls direction of rotation the electric motor V82 for the hydraulic pump so the piston rod of the hydraulic cylinder retracts. The convertible roof is opened.

Closing the convertible roof

If the convertible roof is to be closed, the control unit J256 receives voltage from convertible roof button j E137 at PIN T2. It triggers the electric motor for hydraulic pump V82 to extend the hydraulic cylinder's piston rod. The convertible roof is closed.

To prevent the roof from being activated when the top cover is up, safely switches are installed. Switches F155 and F156 are reed contact switches that are switched without physical contact by magnets on the top cover studs. Switches F155 and F156 apply earth/GND to PIN S2 and PIN S1 of control unit J256 when a top cover stud is engaged. Control unit J256 now no longer actuates the electric motor V82.

New Words

convertible roof	敞篷	roof 天窗，车篷

Kapitel 3　Neue Technologie // Chapter 3　New Technology

hydraulic cylinder	液压缸	fluid reservoir	储液罐
actuation	驱动	thermal cut-out	热断流器，热熔保险器
electro-hydraulic	电液压的	piston rod	活塞杆
rotary pump	旋转泵	actuate	驱动

课文参考译文

电动车窗

电动车窗系统通过操纵摇臂开关（按钮）控制电动机打开或关闭车窗或天窗（如果有天窗）。

电动车窗系统通常使用钢缆传动系统驱动车窗玻璃的升降。驱动电动机通过蜗杆驱动钢缆使车窗打开或关闭。车窗的打开或关闭取决于电动机的转动方向。蜗杆机构的自锁效应可以防止车窗在外力的作用下打开。

电动车窗可以通过摇臂开关控制，也可以通过电子控制结合摇臂开关控制。通过摇臂开关控制时，开关控制相应的电动车窗电动机，可以使车窗打开或关闭。在中央控制门锁系统中，所有的车窗也可以同时关闭。

电动车窗的工作原理如图所示，当接通点火开关时，主继电器从端子15得到电源供给。当继电器触点闭合时，继电器端子30与端子87接通，并将电源电压提供到开关S1和S2的d端子。借助于与驾驶人车门开关S1集成在一起的开关S5后，后门开关S3和S4可以得到电源，或者电源供给能够被切断。

（1）打开车窗时的开关位置　打开车窗时，摇臂开关S1、S2、S3、S4的端子d(+)与端子b连接，端子c(-)与端子a连接。电动车窗驱动装置使相应的车窗玻璃下降。

（2）关闭车窗时的开关位置　如果要关闭车窗，摇臂开关的端子d (+)与端子b连接，端子e(-)与端子a连接。驱动电动机由于开关端子a和端子b的极性颠倒而反转，因此车窗关闭。

（3）中央控制门锁系统关闭车窗　中央控制门锁控制单元将控制线圈的端子85与接地连接，因此使继电器动作将继电器端子87与端子30连接。开关端子a通过开关端子c与电源正极连接，开关端子b和e与接地连接，因此车窗关闭。

（4）由摇臂开关和电子控制的电动车窗组合控制　电子控制装置可以安装在一个控制单元内。为了尽可能节省导线费用，利用电子控制装置将使车窗关闭。如是较长时间按动控制按钮，车窗就可以升降到希望的位置。如果汽车通过中央控制门锁系统锁止，所有车窗将同时关闭，或关闭至留有一定的通风间隙。

（5）防夹功能　为了防止身体的某一部位（例如手、臂）被车窗玻璃夹住，关闭车窗玻璃的力被限制在一个限定的大小。防止夹手功能通过电子控制装置实现，例如通过检测电动机的电流达到限定值，或在驱动系统中使用载荷离合装置实现防夹的功能。

Teil 8　Navigationssystem　导航系统
Part 8　Navigation system　导航系统

学习目标

【知识目标】
1. 掌握与汽车导航系统结构、分类、运行原理等相关的专业术语、单词和词汇。
2. 掌握汽车导航系统主要结构的德文、英文表达方法。

【能力目标】
1. 能对汽车导航系统总体结构的各部分细节进行中、德、英互译。
2. 能进行与汽车导航系统大体构造相关的德、英语资料阅读和翻译。
3. 能在汽车导航系统实物上标识出相应结构的德、英语单词和词汇。

Text 1　Navigationssystem 导航系统（德文）

Sie bieten Hilfe bei der Suche nach der richtigen Strecke zum Zielort und bei der Orientierung in unbekannten Gegenden. Navigationssystem können folgende Aufgaben übernehmen:

– Eigenpositionsbestimmung.

– Positionsübermittlung.

– Berechnung der optimalen Streckenführung unter Berücksichtigung der aktuellen Verkehrssituation.

– Zielführung durch Fahrtrichtungsempfehlungen.

In Bild sind alle beteiligten Komponenten und Teilsysteme dargestellt. Die Eingangssignale werden vom Navigationsrechner verarbeitet und auf dem Display in Form von Sprache und Bild ausgegeben.

新技术篇

Kapitel 3 Neue Technologie // Chapter 3 New Technology

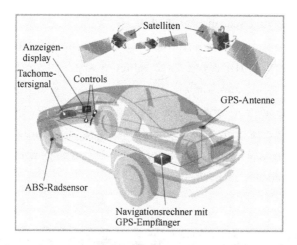

Bild: Komponenten eines Navigationssystems

Navigation computer with GPS receiver Navigationsrechner mit GPS-Empfänger

Eigenpositionsbestimmung. Sie bildet die Grundlage für die Berechnung einer Fahrtroute. Mit Hilfe von Global Positioning System (GPS) kann die aktuelle Position des Kraftfahrzeugs bestimmt werden. GPS besteht aus 24 militärischen US-Satelliten, die sich auf verschiedenen Umlaufbahnen um die Erde befinden. Diese senden in gleichen Zeitabständen Identifikations-, Zeit- und Positionssignale aus. Für die Bestimmung der eigenen Position durch den Navigationsrechner im Kraftfahrzeug sind die Signale von mindestens drei Satelliten, die über GPS-Antenne und GPS-Empfänger emfangen werden, erforderlich. Die Position kann mit den Daten von GPS auf etwa 30 bis 100 Meter genau bestimmt werden. Für den heutigen Verkehr auf den Straßen ist dies zu ungenau. Deshalb werden die Signale zusätzlicher Sensoren, wie z.B. Radsensoren, Tachosignal und G-Sensor im Navigationsrechner ausgewertet und verarbeitet. Eventuell erforderliche Korrekruren des Ortungsergebnisses, die durch äußere Einflüsse wie z.B. Fahrt durch einen Tunnel, Brücken usw. erforderlich sind, werden vom Navigationsrechner durchgeführt. Dadurch wird eine wesentliche Steigerung der Positions- und Zielgenauigkeit auf unter zwei Meter erreicht.

Positionsübermittlung. Sie dient dazu, um bei einem Notfall oder einem Fahrzeugdefekt den Rettungsdiensten oder Pannenhilfen den Standort des Kraftfahrzeugs zu übermitteln. Dadurch kann in kürzester Zeit Hilfe geleistet werden. Außerdem kann bei einem Fahrzeugdiebstahl das gestohlene Farzeug schneller gefunden werden.

Berechnung der optimalen Streckenführung.

Gibt der Fahrer über die Bedienungselemente oder durch Sprache ein Fahrziel ein, wird anhand der Daten des Straßenplanspeichers die optimale Streckenfürhung berechnet. Aktuelle Verkehrssituationen wie z.B. Stau, Baustellen, Straßensperren können durch Kommunikationseinrichtungen wie z.B. TIM (Traffic Information System), RDS (Radion Data System) oder über das Internet in der Streckenberechnung berücksichtigt werden.

Zielführung durch Fahrtrichtungsempfehlungen

Gibt der Fahrer über die Bedienungselemente einen Zielort ein, bestimmt die Navigationseinrichtung mit Hilfe von GPS seinen Standort. Von hier aus berechnet der Navigationsrechner die Route zum Zielort. Das Navigationssystem führt das Fahrzeug durch Fahrrichtungsempfehlung auf der berechneten Strecke zum Zielort. Radsensoren, meist die ABS-Sensoren an der nicht angetriebenen Achse, liefern Daten über die Fahzeugbewegung, wie z.B. die Anzahl der Radumdrehungen je Seite. So können z.B. Entfernungen gemessen werden und zwischen Geradeausfahrt und Kurvenfahrt unterschieden werden.

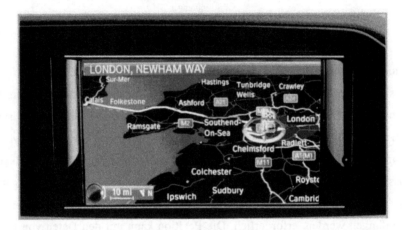

Bild: Anzeigendisplay

Bis neueren Systemen werden die Fahrzeugbewegungen durch das Tachosignal und den Signalen eines G-Sensors erfasst.

Tachometersignal. Es liefert Angaben über die zurückgelegte Wegstrecke.

G-Sensor (Drehratensensor, Gyroskop). Er erfasst die Drehbewegungen des Fahrzeugs um seine Hochachse (Gierbewegung) und registriert den Wert der Drehbewegung in Grad je Sekunde.

Mit den Werten von Tachometersignal und G-Sensor, können die Längen und die Krümmungswinkel von Kurvenabschnitten vom Navigationsrechner ermittelt werden.

Die von den Sensoren aufgenommenen Daten aus der gefahrenen Strecke werden mit den Daten der CD-Rom des Straßenplanspeichers verglichen und gegebenfalls korrigiert (Map-Matching). Dadurch kann die momentane Position des Fahrzeugs auf der eingeschlagenen Route genau bestimmt werden. Steht außerdem das GPS-Signal zu Verfügung, kann die Position zusätzlich geprüft werden. Fährt der Fahrer los, fürht ihn das Navigationssystem auf der vorgeschlagen Route durch Fahrtrichtungsanzeigen auf Anzeigendisplay (Bild) oder über Sprachausgabe zum Ziel. Falsche Richtungsänderungen werden sofort durch eine alternative Routenfürung korrigiert.

Kapitel 3　Neue Technologie // Chapter 3　New Technology

Neue Wörter

das	Navigationssystem	导航系统	der	Rettungsdienst	营救服务部门
die	Strecke	路段	die	Pannenhilfe	维修服务部门
die	Eigenpositionsbestimmung	定位	das	Bedienungselement	控制元件
die	Positionsübermittlung	定位数据传输	der	Straßenplanspeicher	地图存储器
die	Fahrtrichtungsempfehlung	路线建议	die	Kommunikationseinrichtung	通信装置
die	Komponente	部件		ABS(das Antiblockiersystem)	防抱死系统
das	Teilsystem	子系统			
das	Eingangssignal	输入信号	die	Achse	轴，轮轴
der	Navigationsrechner	导航计算机	die	Geradeausfahrt	直行
der	Satellit	卫星	die	Kurvenfahrt	转弯
die	Umlaufbahn	运行轨道	der	Drehratensensor, der Gyroskop	螺旋仪
der	Zeitanstand	时间间隔	die	Hochachse	垂直轴
das	Identifikationssignal	识别信号	die	Gierbewegung	偏离路线
die	Antenne	天线	die	Krümmungswinkel	转弯角度
der	Sensor	传感器	die	Zentralverriegelung	中央锁紧装置
der	Radsensor	车轮传感器	die	Funk-Fernbedienung	无线电遥控装置
der	Tachosignal=der Tachometersignal	速度传感器信号	das	Infrarot	红外线
die	Ortung	搜索	der	Transponder	发射机应答器

Text 2　Navigation system 导航系统（英文）

Navigation systems handle the following tasks:
- Vehicle positioning.
- Position data transfer.
- Calculation of optimum route based on current traffic conditions.
- Route guidance through turn-by-turn and lane change recommendations.
- Display of immediate surroundings as a 2D or 3D image (moving map) or photo.

Vehicle positioning.This forms the basis for calculation of a route. With the aid of the Global Positioning System (GPS), the actual position of the vehicle can be determined. GPS comprises roughly 24 satellites which follow different orbits around the earth. These emit identification, time and position signals at uniform intervals. For determination of the vehicle position using the vehicle's navigation computer, the signals from at least three satellites are required. The position can be calculated with the data from GPS to an accuracy of about 30 metres. In the case of integrated navigation systems, the vehicle's movements are also accounted for by the speedometer signal and the yaw rate sensor signals. This makes it possible to monitor distances while also distinguishing between straight-ahead driving and cornering. Any corrections to the positioning result that might be necessary due to external factors, such as tunnels, bridges, etc., are made by the navigation computer based on this information.

Position data transfer. This serves as a means of sending the location of the vehicle to rescue services in the event of an accident, or recovery services if the vehicle has broken down. Furthermore, the vehicle can be located more quickly in the event for the theft.

Optimal route calculation. When the driver enters the target destination using the control elements or voice input, the navigation equipment determines the vehicle's current location. From this point the navigation computer can calculated the best route to the target destination using data from the map memory. During the drive, the system constantly senses the current position and displays it on the map.

Dynamic route guidance. The latest traffic situations, e.g. congestion, road maintenance sites, road blocks, from communication sources such as TMC (Traffic Message Channel), RDS (Radio Data System) or the Internet can be included in the route calculation.

Route guidance through turn-by-turn recommendations. The navigation system guides the driver with recommendations on where to turn on the calculated route to the target destination. This is usually provided through voice output to prevent distracting the driver as much as possible. A route map or direction arrows on a display can also be shown for supplemental assistance.

Deviations from the specified route are corrected through alternative routing.

Integrated navigation systems. These offer the greatest vehicle positioning and route guidance accuracy, since they optimize this information using vehicle sensor data (radar sensors, yaw rate sensor, steering angle sensor). The controls and route display are provided via an LCD screen installed in the centre console area. This screen can be used for many other supporting systems and multimedia applications when navigation is not active.

Mobile navigation systems. The GPS receiver, computer, map storage and touchscreen (which serves as the input/output unit) are all in one compact housing.

Power is supplied via the vehicle electrical system receptacle in the centre console. A suction cup is used to secure the unit in a cradle on the windscreen.

The voice instructions can be output using the vehicle's audio system as long as both units have a bluetooth interface.

Smartphones. Smartphones can also be used for navigation. If they have the appropriate app installed, the can operate the same way as mobile navigation devices.

Additional functions. Features for navigation devices such as voice guidance, electronic driver log, retractable screens, touchscreen, or information about speed limits for the road the vehicle is on are available as options. In addition to route guidance, these devices also provide information such as the location of nearby filling stations, automotive workshops, hotels, restaurants, train stations, airports, points of interest (POIs), etc.

Mobile phone cradle with linked hands-free system

This makes calling with the mobile phone easier while driving. The mobile phone is inserted into a cradle specifically intended for the device type. This cradle supplies the device with power from the vehicle electrical system and establishes the connection to a hands-free system linked to the audio system.

When using hands-free systems, there is a risk of feedback if the echoes from the phone's electronic voice output are not suppressed. Therefore, complicated echo compensation technology has to be introduced that enables simultaneous talking and listening between people at each end of the line. This occurs on the basis of digital signal processors. In addition, measures are necessary to suppress the driving noise in the microphone signal. The mobile phone is also connected via the cradle to the mobile radio antenna in the vehicle in order to improve reception.

REVIEW QUESTIONS

1. Why is it necessary to install a pinch protection feature with electric power windows?
2. How are the windows closed with a central locking system?
3. What is the function of the seat occupant sensor?
4. How is the direction of rotation reversed on electronically controlled windscreen wipers?
5. What are the two operating modes for adaptive cruise control?
6. Describe the park distance control's operating principle.
7. What information does the driver receive from the operating and travel data display?
8. Explain the principle of operation of a navigation system.

New Words

navigation system	导航系统	orbit	运行轨道
route	路段	uniform intervals	时间间隔
vehicle positioning	定位	identification signal	识别信号
position data transfer	定位数据传输	antenna	天线
route guidance recommendations	路线建议	sensor	传感器
component	部件	speedometer	速度计，里程计
subsystem	子系统	yaw rate	横摆角速度
navigation computer	导航计算机	theft	盗窃
satellite	卫星	dynamic route guidance	动态路径导引

congestion	拥堵	hands-free system	免提系统
traffic message channel	交通信息频道	control element	控制元件
integrated navigation system	综合导航定位系统	map memory	地图存储器
steering angle sensor	转向角传感器	straight-ahead driving	直行
centre console area	中控台区域	cornering	转弯
suction cup	吸盘		

课文参考译文

导航系统

导航系统帮助驾驶人选择到达目的地的正确路线，以及在陌生环境下辨别方向。导航系统具有以下功能：

- 车辆定位。
- 传输定位数据。
- 根据当前交通状况的最佳路线计算。
- 给出到达目的地应选择的路线的建议。
- 输入信号由巡航计算机进行处理。输出信号通过图像显示或声音输出。

车辆定位

车辆定位是计算行驶路线的基础，借助于全球定位系统（GPS），可以确定汽车的实际位置。GPS由24颗在地球上不同轨道上运行的美国军用同步卫星构成，这些卫星以统一的间隔发射识别信号、位置信号和时间信号。汽车上的导航计算机要确定车辆的位置，至少需要从3颗卫星上通过GPS天线和GPS接收器接收信号。GPS确定的位置精度约为30~100m。这样的精度用于当今的道路交通还是不精确的。因此，额外将一些传感器的信号（如车轮传感器、车速信号和横摆角速度传感器信号）在导航计算机中进行评价及处理。这样不仅可以监测距离，而且可以识别是直线行驶还是转弯。由于外部原因，例如隧道、桥梁等可能需要由导航计算机对定位结果进行修正。由此将定位及目标精度实际提高到不足2m。

定位数据传输

定位数据传输用于当发生事故及汽车出现故障时，将车辆的位置信号发送至营救服务部门及事故救援部门，由此，可以在尽量短的时间内求得救援。另外，在车辆被盗时，可以迅速确定车辆位置。

最佳路线计算

当驾驶人使用控制元件或通过声音输入目的地时，根据导航计算机的数据计算到达目的地的最佳路线。实时的道路交通情况，如堵车、施工、道路封闭等情况可通过通信装置，例如TIM（交通信息系统）、RDS（道路数据系统）或者通过互联网在计算路段时加以考虑。

通过行驶路线建议的动态目标引导

当驾驶人使用控制元件输入目的地时,导航装置借助于GPS确定目的地。从这一点开始,导航计算机通过行驶路线建议将汽车在计算的路段上引导到目的地。车轮传感器,大多为安装在非传动轴上的ABS传感器通过车辆运动提供数据,例如每侧车轮的转数。由此可以测量距离并区分直行与弯道行驶之间的不同。

直至最新的系统汽车运动通过转速信号及G传感器信号采集。

里程表传感器。通过已驶过的路段提供数据。

G传感器(转速率传感器;陀螺仪)。在垂直轴向(横摆运动)采集汽车的旋转运动并将旋转运动的数值以每秒度数为单位进行记录。

导航计算机根据车速信号和横摆角度速度传感器信号能够计算弯曲道路的距离和角度。

传感器对行驶路途的详细记录与来自CD-ROM、DVD或地图存储器内的软件的数据进行比较,并根据需要进行调整(地图匹配)。通过这种方法,可以非常精确地确定车辆在设定路线的位置。如果能够得到GPS信号,车辆位置能够得到核实。导航系统可以在转弯处引导车辆按照建议的路线到达目的地。如果驾驶人在转弯处走错路线,系统会立即指示驾驶人更改路线到达目的地。

Teil 9　Zentralverriegelung　中央控制门锁系统
Part 9　Central locking system　中央控制门锁系统

【知识目标】
1. 掌握与中央控制门锁系统结构、分类、运行原理等相关的专业术语、单词和词汇。
2. 掌握中央控制门锁系统主要结构的德文、英文表达方法。

【能力目标】
1. 能对中央控制门锁系统总体结构的各部分细节进行中、德、英互译。
2. 能进行与中央控制门锁系统大体构造相关的德语、英语资料阅读和翻译。
3. 能在中央控制门锁系统实物上标识出相应结构的德语、英语单词和词汇。

Text 1　Zentralverriegelung中央控制门锁系统（德文）

Sie ermöglicht das Verriegeln, Entriegeln und Sichern aller Türen, der Heck- und Tankklappe eines Kraftfahrzeugs. Dies kann immer von einem Schließpunkt aus, z.B. der Fahrertür, Beifahrertür oder der Heckklappe erfolgen.

Je nach Komfort- und Sicherheitseinrichtungen am Kraftfarzeug ermöglicht die Zentralverriegelung z.B. automatische Schiebedach- und Fensterschließung, so dass auch nach abgezogenem Fahrzeugschlüssel die Funktion von Schiebedach und Fensterheber noch für einige Zeit, z.B. 60 Sekunden, erhalten bleibt.

Damit die Schlösser in den Türen, der Heck- und der Tankklappe verriegelt bzw. entriegelt werden können, sind Stellelemente notwendig.

Je nachdem wie die Stellelemente betätigt werden, unterscheidet man zwei Systeme
 – Elektische Zentralverriegelung.
 – Elekro-pneumatische Zentralverriegelung.
Elektrische Zentralverriegelung

Kapitel 3　Neue Technologie // Chapter 3　New Technology

Mit ihr werden die grundsätzlichen Funktionen wie Entriegeln und Verriegeln, z.B. der Fahrzeugtüren durch das Ansteuern von Stellmotoren in elektrisch betätigten Stellelementen durchgefürt. Die Ansteuerung erfolgt meist mit zwei Wechslern, wobei sich einer im Türschloss, der andere im Stellelement befindet.

Der vereinfachte Schaltplan in Bild zeigt das Zusammenwirken. Beim Drehen des Schlüssels werden das Schloss und der Wechsler S1 mechanisch betätigt. Er befindet sich an den jeweiligen Schließpunkten z.B. an Fahrer-, Beifahrertür. Dadurch können über das Steuergerät alle Stellmotoren, die Bestandteil der Zentralverriegelung sind, angesteuert werden. Der Wechsler S1 besitzt zwei Schaltstellungen: Verriegeln (V) und Entrigeln (E). Der Wechsler S2 ist meist im Stellelement integriert und wird über ein Schalgestänge oder ein Getriebe von Motor betätigt. Er schaltet als Endlagenschalter mit zwei Schaltstellungen den Stellmotor ein oder aus. Die Steuersignale werden über Verkabelung oder ein Bussystem (CAN-Bus, Multiplexer) an ein Steuergerät übertragen.

Wirkungsweise

Verriegeln. Durch eine Schlüsseldrehung werden im Wechsler S1 die Klemme (Kl.) 30 und die Kl. V verbunden. Dieser Steuerimpuls veranlasst das Steuergerät, Kl. 83a mit Spannung zu versorgen. Der Stellmotor M1 läuft. Im Wechsler S2 bleiben die Kl.83a und 83 solange verbunden, bis die Verriegelung ihre Endlage erreicht hat und die Verbingdung 83a und 83 durch den Stellmotor M1 unterbrochen wird. Der Motor bleibt stehen.

Entriegeln. Durch eine entgegengesetze Schlüsseldrehung werden im Wechsler S1 die Kl.30 und die Kl.E verbunden. Dieser Steuerimpuls veranlasst das Steuergerät, Kl.83b mit Spannung zu versorgen. Der Stellmotor M1 läuft jetzt in entgegengesetzter Richtung. Im Wechsler S2 bleiben die Klemmen 83b und 83 solange verbunden, bis die Entriegelung ihre Endlage erreicht hat und die Verbindung 83b und 83 durch den Stellmotor M1 unterbrochen wird. Der Motor bleibt stehen.

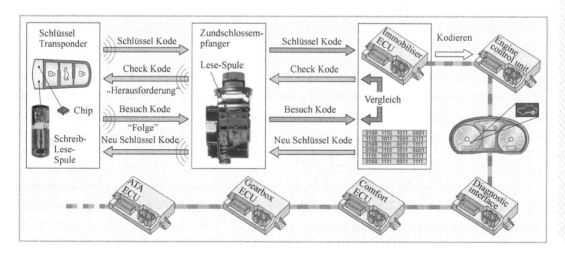

Bild:Vereinfachter Schaltplan eines Stellmotors mit zwei Wechslern

Elektrisch betätigtes Stellelement (Bild). Es betätigt die Verriegelung und Entriegelung. Das Ritzel des Stellmotors ist über ein Getriebe mit dem Antriebsritzel der Zahnstange mechanisch verbunden. Wird das Schloss im Schließpunkt einer ZV mit dem Schlüssel mechanisch betätigt, z.B. entriegelt, überträgt die Zug-Druckstange die Entriegelungsbewegung über Zahnstange und mehrere Zahnräder im Stellelement. Dabei wird der Wechselschalter (S2) mechanisch auf Endlage Entriegeln gestellt. Der Stellmotor bleibt stromlos.

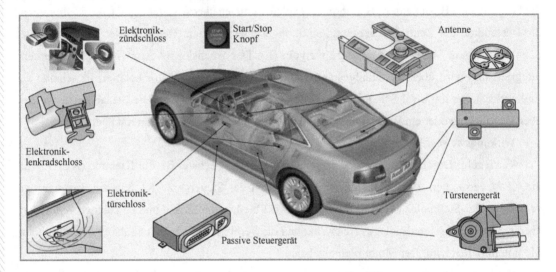

Bild. Elektrisch betätigtes Stellelement

Über die Stiftkontakte wird der Steuerimpuls Entriegeln an das Steuergerät weitergegeben. Die Stellmotoren aller übrigen Stellelemente werden mit Strom versorgt und führen den Entriegelungsvorgang aus.

Elektropneumatische Zentralverriegelung

Sie besteht aus einem elektrischen Steuerstromkreis und einem pneumatischen Einleitungs-Arbeitskreis (Bild).

Elektrischer Steuerstromkreis. Er steuert über Mikroschalter (Wechsler) in den Schlössern und den elektropneumatischen Stellelementen den pneumatischen Einleitungs-Arbeitskreis. Beim Drehen des Schlüssels im Türschloss wird ein Mikroschalter betätigt. Dieses elektrische Steuersignal wertet das Steuergerät aus. Es veranlasst die pneumatische Steuereinheit alle anderen Schlösser pneumatisch zu betätigen(Elektropneumatischer Arbeitskreis).

Pneumatischer Einleitungs-Arbeitskreis. Er betätigt die Stellelemnte durch Unterdruck oder Überdruck in einer Leitung. Wird z.B. das Fahrzeug entriegelt, herrscht in der Leitung Überdruck, wird das Fahrzeug verriegelt, herrscht Unterdruck.

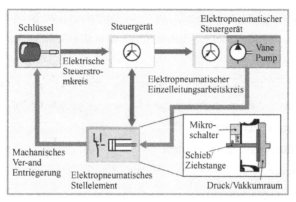

Bild:Schema Elektro-pneumatische Zentralverriegelung

Elektropneumatisches Stellelement (Bild). Es soll den Schließvorgang durchführen und ist an jeder zu schließenden Tür vorhanden. Wird von der pneumatischen Steuereinheit je nach Schließvorgang Unterdruck bzw. Überdruck erzeugt, wirkt dieser auf die Membrane in der Unter- bzw. Überdruckkammer des Stellelements. Die Membrane und das Schloss sind mit der Zug-Druckstange verbunden. Dadurch kann der Schließvorgang entweder mit dem Schlüssel direkt über das Gestänge oder pneumatisch durchgeführt werden.

Der Mikroschalter im Stellelement liefert bei verschlossenem Fahrzeug ein Massesignal an das Steuergerät. Bei einem Einbruchversuch wird über den entsprechenden Mikroschalter im Stellelement ein Plussignal zum Steuergerät geschaltet. Das Steuergerät reagiert. In der Safespule wird ein Magnetfeld aufgebaut und der Bolzen fährt in die Aussparung der Zug-Druckstange ein. Gleichzeitig wird in der pneumatischen Steuereinheit die Unterdruckförderung eingeschaltet. Das Schloss bleibt verriegelt.

Wirkungsweise (Bild)

Pneumatisch entriegeln. Der Überdruck wirkt auf die Membrane und drückt dadurch die Zug-Druckstange nach oben. Dadurch wird über ein Gestänge das Schloss mechanisch entriegelt.

Pneumatisch verriegeln. Der Unterdruck wirkt auf die Membrane und zieht die Zug-Druckstange nach unten. Das Schloss wird über das Gestänge mechanisch verriegelt.

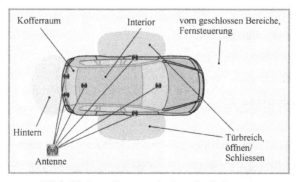

Bild: Elektro-Pneumatisches Stellelement

Pneumatische Steuereinheit. Sie besteht aus einer elektronischen Schaltung (Schnittstelle) und einer Bidruckpumpe. Die Elektronische Schaltung empfängt die Befehle des Steuergerätes und gibt sie an die Bidruckpumpe weiter.

Bidruckpumpe. Sie ist eine Flügelzellenpumpe, die Überdruck oder Unterdruck erzeugt. Dies wird dadurch erreicht, dass die Drehrichtung des Flügelrades geändert wird, z.B. bewirkt Linkslauf Überdruck und Rechtslauf Unterdruck.

Bedienung der Zentralverriegelungssysteme

Bei der Bedienung der Zentralverriegelung werden drei Systeme unterschieden:

– Mechanisches Schlüsselsystem.

– Infrarot-Fernbedienungssystem.

– Funk-Fernbedienungssystem.

Mechanisches Schlüsselsystem. Bei diesem System werden von einem oder mehreren Schließpunkten aus (meist die Vordertüren und die Heckklappe) durch Drehen des Schlüssels im Schließzylinder der jeweilige Schließpunkt mechanisch ver- bzw. entriegelt. Gleichzeitig wird durch einen elektrischen Schalter das Steuersignal für die Stellmotoren bzw. Pneumatischen Stellelemente erzeugt, die die Verriegelung bzw. Entriegelung an den anderen Fahrzeugöffnungsstellen durchführen.

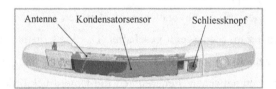

Bild: Infrarot Fernbedienungssystem

Infrarot-Fernbedienungssysstem (Bild). Neben der Möglichkeit, die vorderen Türen und die Heckklappe mechanisch zu ver- und entriegeln, ist es mit diesem System möglich, den Schließvorgang über ein Infrarotsignal aus einer Entfernung von ca.6 Metern einzuleiten.

Es kann aus flolgenden Komponenten bestehen:

– Sendeschlüssel.

– Infrarot-Steuergerät.

– Steuergerät mit Kombifunktionen.

– Relais für die Schließrückmeldung.

– Empfängereinheit z.B. im Innenspiegel.

– Pneumatische Steuereinheit.

– Stellelemente.

Wirkungsweise. Der Infrarotsender z.B. im Schlüssel sendet über Infrarotwellen Signale zur Empfängereinheit Infrarot-Fernbedienung. Der Empfänger ist mit dem Infrarot-Steuergerät verbunden. Es erkennt über das Relais Schließrückmeldung, ob die Fahrzeugtüren verriegelt oder

Kapitel 3　Neue Technologie // Chapter 3　New Technology

entriegelt sind. Wird das Fahrzeug verriegelt, wird dies dem Fahrer z.B. über einen Blinkcode mit den Blinkleuchten mitgeteilt.

　　Diese Informationen werden außerdem an das eigentliche Steuergerät mit Kombifunktionen weitergeleitet. Es ist über CAN-Bus mit der pneumatischen Steuereinheit verbunden. Sie erzeugt bei der elektro-pneumatischen Zentralverriegelung den erforderlichen Über- oder Unterdruck, um die Schließvorgänge zu ermöglichen.

　　Funk-Fernbedienungssystem. Zur Betätigung der Stellelemente kann auch ein Funkwellensystem eingesetzt werden. Funkwellen sind unempfindlicher in Hinsicht auf die Ausrichtung des Senders auf den Empfänger. Dies hat den Vorteil, dass z.B. die Einleitung des Schließvorgangs und Schärfen einer Alarmanlage verdeckt durchgeführt werden kann. Ein weiterer Vorteil besteht darin, dass bei Codierung des Schließsignals die Art der Codes wesentlich komplizierter sein kann und damit die Gefahr kleiner wird, dass Unbefugte diesen Code herausfinden können.

Neue Wörter

die	Zentralverriegelung	中央控制门锁系统		der	Unterdruck	真空
das	Verriegeln	锁止		der	Überdruck	高压
das	Entriegeln	脱开，开锁		die	Membrane	膜片
die	Heckklappe	汽车行李舱盖		das	Massesignal	接地信号
das	Schiebedach	汽车天窗		die	Safespule	安全线圈
der	Aktor	执行器		der	Bolzen	锁销
	pneumatisch	气压的		die	Aussparung	空白、空隙孔
der	Stellmotor	伺服电动机		die	Zweidruckpumpe	双压泵
das	Schalgestänge	杆件		die	Flügelzellenpumpe	叶片泵
das	Getriebe	齿轮机构		das	Flügelrad	叶轮
der	Endlagenschalter	终端开关		der	Linkslauf	逆时针转
die	Verkabelung	导线		der	Rechtslauf	顺时针转
die	Klemme	夹子，端子		das	Infrarot-Fernbedienungssystem	红外线遥控系统
der	Steuerimpuls	控制脉冲				
das	Ritzel	齿轮		das	Funk-Fernbedienungssystem	无线电频率遥控系统
die	Zahnstange	齿条				
die	Zug-Druckstange	推拉杆		der	Schließzylinder	锁芯
das	Gestänge	连动杆		die	Wagenfür	车门
der	Stiftkontakt	触点		das	Relais	继电器
der	Pneumatische Einleitungs-Arbeitskreis	单气动回路		der	Innenspiegel	车内后视镜
				der	Blinkmerker	闪烁信号
der	Mikroschalter	微动开关				

Text 2 Central locking system 中央控制门锁系统（英文）

A digital signal code is transmitted by a remote control via electromagnetic waves (infrared or radio) to a receiver in the vehicle. There, it is again converted into an electric, digital signal code and then decoded in ECU. The signal is transmitted at light speed (c_0=300,000 km/s).

Two different systems are available:
- Infrared remote control system.
- Radio-frequency remote control system.

Infrared remote control system

The signal is transmitted as a "light beam" at a frequency below the visible light spectrum (infra) and is thus invisible to the human eye. The disadvantages are as follows: shorter range (less than 6 metres), infrared remote control operation must be within line of sight of the receiver and the beam of light must not be obstructed. Radio-frequency remote control systems have been widely adopted as a result of these disadvantages.

Radio-frequency remote control system

The signals are transmitted in Europe via radio waves at a frequency of 433 MHz.

Advantages. Radio signal transmission provides the following advantages over infrared transmission:
- Greater range (up to 40 m).
- Line of sight with the vehicle is not necessary.
- Greater protection against decoding of the signal Function. The transmitter sends a digital numeric code to the receiver using a radio frequency. The numeric code comprises an identification code and the instruction for the locking system. The receiver decodes and checks the identification code. If the code matches, the tock command transmitted by the remote control is relayed to the central locking ECU.

Rolling code process. Part of the identification code is changed by the remote control according to a defined, secret algorithm. This renders unauthorised attempts to record the signal useless.

Passive access

The driver does not need to actively operate a key to lock or unlock the vehicle. The same goes for disabling the immobiliser and anti-theft alarmsystem as well as for starting the engine. All that is required is that the person carry the electronic key.

The operation and scope of this feature vary greatly among manufacturers. Passive access goes names such as keyless go, keyless entry, KESSV, comfort access, smart key, etc.

Design. In addition to the central locking components, the following are required:
- Receiver antennas with amplifiers.
- ECU.

Kapitel 3   Neue Technologie // Chapter 3   New Technology

- Electronic door handles.
- Electronic ignition lock.
- Electronic key.
- Start/stop feature.

Receiving antennas. These send radio signals with the identification number and coded identification request to the key transponder. They also receive the response and forward it to the passive access ECU. The antennas are on the inside and outside of the vehicle. The way the antennas are arranged makes it possible to determine in the ECU whether the key is inside or outside the vehicle.

Antennas, exterior. These are fitted in the doors or door handles and bumpers. The key can be positioned near a specific door or near the boot/trunk lid. This allows for selective access authorisation.

Antennas, interior. These are responsible for vehicle starting and operation as well as disabling of the anti-theft alarm system. They are typically installed in the centre console, rear shelf or roof.

Electronic door handle. This may include the following components:

- Door handle antenna. This is a coil which sends the coded transponder signals to the ECU for access authorisation.
- Sensor for access command detection. This is a capacitive sensor. The capacity of the sensor changes as a hand approaches the door. The ECU detects this change as an access command and begins to check access authorisation.
- Lock button. This forwards the lock command to the ECU for access authorisation.

Electronic ignition lock. This receives the key. To identify the electronic key and disable the immobiliser, the electronic ignition lock is fitted with a write/read coil for transponder interrogation. Some systems require only that the electronic key be inside the vehicle.

Electronic key. This consists of the remote control with transponder and supply of power. The key may take the form of a radio remote control or a cheque/credit card, for instance. A mechanical key is integrated for emergency unlocking should the power supply fail.

Emergency opening. Should the key battery fail, the vehicle can be opened using the emergency mechanical key. It may be possible to disable the immobiliser after the electronic key is inserted into the ignition lock. Power is supplied by the magnetic alternating field of the write/read coil in the ignition lock.

Start/stop feature. This works by pressing or turning the key in the electronic ignition lock or by pressing the start/stop button, depending on the vehicle. Pressing the start/stop button again or using a separate stop button switches off the engine, depending on the vehicle.

Automatic starting. The driver's start command is transmitted by the starting operation to the engine control unit. A key with the authorised transponder code must be inside the vehicle or in the electronic ignition lock. In vehicles with an automatic gearbox, the brake must be depressed and the selector lever must be in position P. Only then does the engine control unit release the fuel supply and the engine starts.

Passive unlocking (example). The sensor in the door handle recognises the access command and forwards it to the ECU for access authorisation (1a). The ECU simultaneously receives the status of the locking units (1b) and transmits an identification request (2) to the key via the exterior antennas. The key computes the access code and sends the result via the antennas and antenna amplifier back to the ECU (3) (challenge/response process). The access code is sent to the central ECU (4) via the data bus. The central ECU orders the door control unit (5) to forward the unlock instruction to the relevant lode motor (6).

Locking. Locking can be triggered automatically or by pressing a lock button on the door handle. Automatic locking is initiated when the transponder leaves the detection range of the exterior antennas.

The advantage of locking by pressing the button over automatic locking is that the driver consciously gives the command and hears the locking take place. Flashing of the warning lamps confirm the vehicle is locked.

Service key. The electronic key stores important vehicle information that is read out by a workshop information system when the vehicle enters the shop. Examples of the data stored include:

- service interval information.
- status of service fluid levels.
- status of coolant and engine oil temperatures.

New Words

infrared	红外线	ignition lock	点火锁
decode	解码	start/stop feature	起动/停止功能
ECU	电控单元	key transponder	应答器
light speed	光速	door handle	门把手
remote control system	遥控系统	bumper	保险杠
radio-frequency	射频	trunk lid	行李舱盖
light spectrum	光谱	authorisation	授权
beam	光束	capacitive sensor	电容传感器
numeric code	数字代码	automatic gearbox	自动变速器
algorithm	运算法则，计算程序	coolant	冷却液
amplifier	放大器		

新技术篇

Kapitel 3　Neue Technologie // Chapter 3　New Technology

课文参考译文

中央控制门锁系统

中央控制门锁系统可以保证所有车门、行李舱盖、加油口门可靠地锁止、开锁。

中央控制门锁系统可以由一个集中锁止点，例如驾驶人车门、前乘客车门或行李舱盖，控制所有车门的锁止。

根据汽车方便性和安全性设备的不同，有的汽车即使在点火钥匙拔下后，中央控制门锁系统仍可以允许天窗或电动车窗持续工作一段时间，例如60s。

为了能够将车门、行李舱和加油口门锁止或开锁，需要执行器或伺服电动机进行驱动。

根据执行器的不同，中央控制门锁系统可以分为：

1）电动中央控制门锁系统。

2）电控气动中央控制门锁系统。

1.电动中央控制门锁系统

在电动中央控制门锁系统中，车门的锁止和开锁功能由电控执行器，即伺服电动机实现。电动中央控制门锁系统通常通过两个转换开关工作，一个位于门锁，另一个位于执行器。

当转动钥匙时，锁芯被转动，转换开关S1被转换，转换开关S1一般位于相应的门锁，例如在驾驶人侧车门或前乘客侧车门。通过这种方法，中央控制门锁系统的所有伺服电动机都能够通过控制单元进行控制。转换开关S1有两个位置：锁止（V）和开锁（E）位置。转换开关S2通常集成在执行器上，由伺服电动机通过杆件或齿轮机构驱动。转换开关作为端点开关可以控制伺服电动机的开和关。控制信号通过导线或总线（CAN总线、多路传输），将控制信号传输到控制单元。

（1）锁止过程　转动钥匙，端子30与转换开关的端子V接通。由此产生的控制脉冲使控制单元给端子83a提供电压，伺服电动机M1转动。在转换开关S2中，端子83a和端子83保持接触，直至锁止行程达到其终点位置，端子83a和端子83由伺服电动机M1中断连接，伺服电动机停止工作。

（2）开锁过程　向相反方向转动钥匙，端子30与转换开关的端子E接通。由此产生的控制脉冲使控制单元给端子83b提供电压，伺服电动机M1向相反的方向转动。在转换开关S2中，端子83b和端子83保持接触，直至开锁行程达到其终点位置，端子83b和端子83由伺服电动机M1中断连接，伺服电动机停止工作。

（3）电动执行器　电动执行器控制锁止和开锁动作。伺服电动机通过齿轮机构驱动齿条移动。如果转动车门钥匙，例如开锁，伺服电动机就会转动，通过齿轮和齿条的传动使推/拉杆移动，实现开锁，并最终使两位开关S2到达开锁位置，伺服电动机停止转动。

开锁控制脉冲通过触点发送到控制单元，所有其他执行器的伺服电动机通电工作，执行开锁过程。

273

2. 电控气动中央控制门锁系统

（1）电控气动中央控制门锁系统的组成　电控气动中央控制门锁系统包括一个电控网路和一个单气动回路。

1）电控回路。电控回路控制单气动回路的工作。当转动门锁钥匙时，微动开关动作，控制单元接收微动开关信号，并控制所有其他单气动回路门锁的工作。

2）单气动回路。单气动回路利用管路中的真空或气压控制执行器的工作。例如当开锁时，管路中有气压；当锁止时，管路中是真空。

3）电控气动执行器。电控气动执行器如图所示。电控气动执行器用于每一个车门的锁止。当锁止或开锁时，气动控制单元产生压力或真空，作用于执行器的真空气室或压力气室的膜片，膜片和门锁与推/拉杆相连。通过这种方法，可以使用钥匙使联动杆动作，或通过气动方式将车门锁止。当车门锁止后，执行器内的微动开关提供一个接地信号到控制单元。如果有人试图破锁进入车内，执行器内的微动开关将发出一个正信号到控制单元。控制单元将对此做出反应，将在安全线内建立磁场，使锁销插入推/拉杆的孔中。同时，气动控制单元的真空源接通，保持门锁锁止。

（2）电控气动执行器的工作原理

1）气动开锁。作用于膜片的真空消失，推/拉杆向上运动，通过联动杆将锁打开。

2）气动锁止。真空作用于膜片，推/拉杆向下运动。通过联动杆使门锁锁止。

3）气动控制单元。气动控制单元由电路和双压泵组成。电路接收来自控制单元的指令，并将指令传送至双压泵。

4）双压泵。双压泵是一种叶片泵，通过改变叶轮的旋转方向，可以产生压力或真空。比如说叶轮逆时针方向旋转能够产生压力，顺时针旋转则会产生真空。

3. 中央控制门锁系统的工作过程

中央控制门锁系统有4种不同的类型：

① 机械钥匙系统。

② 红外线遥控系统。

③ 无线电频率遥控系统。

④ 具有自起动（无钥匙起动）功能的无线电频率遥控系统。

（1）机械钥匙系统　在机械钥匙系统中，通常需要将钥匙插入位于前车门或行李舱盖的锁芯中，然后转动钥匙柄实现锁止或开锁。同时，电开关为伺服电动机或气动执行器提供一个电信号，以实现其他车门的锁止或开锁。

（2）红外线遥控系统　在这种系统中，锁止或开锁可以通过红外线在约6m的距离之内实现。该系统由以下部件组成：

1）发射器钥匙。

2）红外线控制单元。

3）具有组合功能的控制单元。

4）锁止状态继电器。

5）接收单元，例如在车内后视镜。

6）气动控制单元。

7）执行器。

红外线发射器发射红外线频率范围内的光信号到接收器，接收器与红外线控制单元连接。红外线控制单元通过锁止应答继电器检测车门锁是否锁止或开锁。如果车门未锁止，可以通过转向信号灯的闪烁来提示驾驶人。

红外线信号也发送至具有组合功能的控制单元，该控制单元通过CAN总线与气动控制单位连接。在电动气控中央控制门锁系统中，气动控制单元产生压力或真空，以实现车门的锁止或开锁。

（3）无线电频率遥控系统　利用无线电信号也可以对门锁进行遥控。使用无线电信号发射器不需要正对着接收器。无线电频率遥控系统可以在隐秘的情况下实现车门的锁止和报警系统的激活。无线电波可以提供良好的保密性，防止盗贼破译信号密码。密码本身也能变换更复杂的组合。

（4）具有自起动（无钥匙起动）功能的无线电频率遥控系统　驾驶人进入车内不需要接触钥匙，只需要驾驶人身上带着电子钥匙，并接触任何一个车门把手就可以进入车内。车门把手的电容传感器检测到试图进入车内的信号，并授权控制单元，从而启动电子钥匙的发射应答器的感应问询信号，如果通过授权许可，车门就打开。车门的锁止通过按下锁钮实现。

Deutsch – English Kraftfahrzeugtechnik // German – English Automotive Engineering

Teil 10 Diebstahlschutzsystem 汽车防盗系统
Part 10 Anti-theft alarm system (ATA) 汽车防盗系统

学习目标

【知识目标】
1. 掌握与汽车防盗系统结构、分类、运行原理等相关的专业术语、单词和词汇。
2. 掌握汽车防盗系统主要结构的德文、英文表达方法。

【能力目标】
1. 能对汽车防盗系统总体结构的各部分细节进行中、德、英互译。
2. 能进行与汽车防盗系统大体构造相关的德语、英语资料阅读和翻译。
3. 能在汽车防盗系统实物上标识出相应结构的德语、英语单词和词汇。

Text 1 Diebstahlschutzsystem 汽车防盗系统（德文）

Es ist meitst in Verbindung mit der Zentralverriegelung in den Fahrzeugen eingebaut. Das Diebstahlschutzsystem hat folgende Aufgaben:

– Schutz vor Diebstahl des Fahrzeugs.

– Schutz vor Diebstahl von Fahrzeugteilen wie z.B. Radio, Airbag.

– Schutz vor Beschädigungen.

Das Diebstahlschutzsystem kann aus folgenden Komponenten bestehen:

– Wegfahrsperre.

– Alarmanlage.

– Innenraumüberwachung.

– Rad- und Abschleppschutz.

Die Aktivierung des Diebstahlschutzsystems kann wie bei der Zentralverriegelung erfolgen durch:

– Mechanisches Schlüsselsystem mit Türkontaktschalter.

Kapitel 3 Neue Technologie // Chapter 3 New Technology

- Infrarot-Fernbediegungssystem.
- Funkfernbedienungssystem.

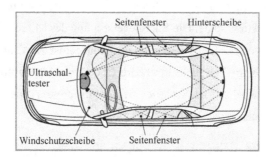

Bild: Aufbau eines Infrarot-Fernbedienungssystems

Wird das Fahrzeug mit dem Fahrzeugschlüssel verriegelt, erhält das Steuergerät über den Türkontaktschalter die Information zum Aktivieren des Diebstahlschutzsystems.

Wird das Farhrzeug über eine Infrarot- bzw. Funkfernbedienung verriegelt, wandelt der Infrarot-Empfänger das Infrarotsignal des Senders in ein elektrisches Signal um und leitet es an das Steuergerät weiter, welches das Diebstahlschutzsystem aktiviert.

Bild: Wegfahrsperre

Wegfahrsperre (Bild). Sie ist ein elektronisches System, das verhindert, dass unberechtigte Personen das Fahrzeug in Betrieb setzen können.

Die rechtliche Grundlage für die Sicherung des Fahrzeugs durch eine Wegfahrsperre ist u.a. in § 38a StVZO und der EU-Richtlinie ECE-R18 festgelegt. Danach gilt das Abziehen des Zündschlüssels und das Verschließen der Türen nicht als Sicherung des Fahrzeugs im Sinne des Gesetzes.

Die Wegfahrsperre besteht aus einem Steuergerät und je nach Hersteller entweder aus einem Handsender, mit elektronisch codiertem Zündschloss, einem Transponder oder einer Chipkarte.

Transponder (engl.Übertrager, Bild). Er besteht aus einem Mikrochip, der in einem Glaskörper gekapselt ist und einer Induktionsspule. Die Energieversorgung des Mikrochips erfolgt induktiv nach dem Transformatorprinzip von der Induktionsspule im Zündschloss zur Chipspule. Bei der Fertigung wird dem Mikrochip eine einmalige nicht löschbare Codenummer (Identifikationscode, ID-Code) zugewiesen. Gleichzeitig wird ein nachträglich programmierbarer Speicherbereich (EEPROM-Speicherbereich)für das Wechselcode-Verfahren reserviert.

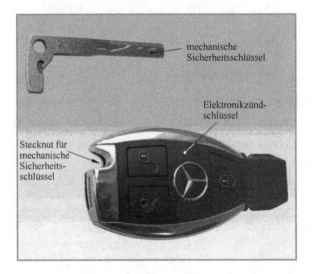

Bild: Tranponder

Wirkungsweise. Wird der Schlüssel im Zündschloss gedreht, überträgt die Induktionsspule Energie in den Mikrochip.

Diese Energie reicht aus, um den Code im Mikrochip abzufragen. Der Abfragevorgang wird vom Steuergerät Wegfahrsperre (Bild) eingeleitet. Der Transponder erkennt das Abfragesignal und übergibt seinen Identifikationscode. Dieser Code wird mit dem gespeicherten Code verglichen.

Ist der Code gültig, gibt das Steuergerät Wegfahrsperre z.B. über einen CAN-Bus an das Steuergerät Digitale Motorelektronik (DME) ein seinerseits codiertes digitales Signal weiter. Wird dieses Signal vom Steuergerät DME akzeptiert, kann der Motor gestartet werden.

Ist der Code ungültig, wird dies der DME mitgeteilt, der Motor startet nicht.

Gleichzeitig erzeugt das Steuergerät der Wegfahrsperre nach dem Zufallsprinzip einen neuen Code, der in den programmierbaren Teil des Transponderspeichers geschrieben wird (Wechselcode-Verfahren). Dadurch wird gewährleistet, dass bei jedem Startvorgang ein neuer gültiger Code im Schlüssel gespeichert ist, der alte Code ist ungültig.

Kapitel 3　Neue Technologie // Chapter 3　New Technology

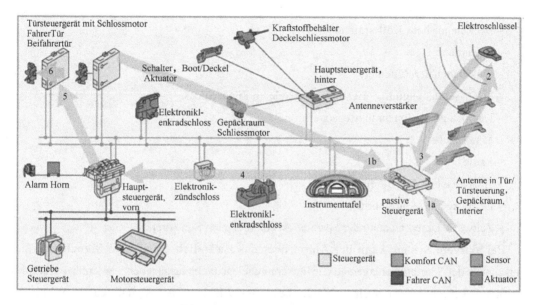

Bild: Systemübersicht Wegfahrsperre

Alarmanlage. Eine scharfgeschaltete Alarmanlage löst bei unbefugtem Eingriff oder Anstoß optische und akustische Warnsignale aus. Sie kann aus folgenden Komponenten bestehen:

- Fernbedienung.
- Steuergerät mit Spannungsversorgung.
- Ultraschall-Empfänger für Innenraumüberwachung.
- Türkontaktschalter.
- Kontaktschalter für z.B. Motorhaube, Heckklappe, Kofferraum, Handschuhfach.
- Lagesensor für Rad- und Abschleppschutz.
- Statusanzeige.
- Ultraschallsender für Innenraumüberwachung.
- Signalhorn.
- Startanlage.

Wirkungsweise. Ist die Alarmanlage aktiviert, überprüft das Steuergerät, ob Türen, Fenster, Schiebedach, Motorhaube und Heckklappe bzw. Kofferraumdeckel verschlossen sind. Die Verriegelung der Türen wird über die Türkontaktschalter, die von Heckklappe bzw. Kofferraumdeckel über deren Kontaktschalter festgestellt. Sind alle Voraussetzungen für den Verriegelungszustand erfüllt, können nach einer Zeitverzögerung von 10 bis 20 Sekunden alle Alarmeingänge Alarm auslösen. Die Alarmbereitschaft des Diebstahlalarmsystems wird über eine Statusanzeige z.B. blinkende LED angezeigt.

Folgende Komponenten können Alarm auslösen:

- Alle Türen.
- Heckklappe bzw. Kofferraumdeckel.
- Innenraum.
- Einschalten der Zündung.
- Schlüssel mit ungültigem Transpondercode im Zündschloss.
- Demontage des Innenraumsensors.
- Motorhaube.
- Radio.
- Ablagefach in der Mittelkonsole.
- Demotage des Alarmhorns.
- Zeitweise Unterbrechung der Spannungsversorgung am Steuergerät.

Bei aktivem System kann der Alarm über das zusätzlich eingebaute Signalhorn, über Blinksignale der Warnblinkanlage und der Innenraumbeleuchtung ausgegeben werden. Die Alarmzeit wird durch Vorgaben der einzelnen Länder bestimmt, z.B. kann das Signalhorn ein akustisches Signal von 30 Sekunden und die Blinkanlage mit dem Abblendlicht Blinksignale über 30 Sekunden erzeugen. Gleichzeitig verhindert die heute üblicherweise eingebaute Wegfahrsperre das Starten des Motors.

Das Diebstahlschutzsystem wird durch das Betätigen der Entriegelungstaste der Fernbedienung bzw. durch den Schließzylinder beim Entriegeln des Fahrzeugs abgeschaltet.

Innenraumüberwachung.

Es sind folgende Systeme möglich:

- Infrarot-Innenraumüberwachung.
- Ultraschall-Innenraumüberwachung.

Infrarot-Innenraumüberwachung. Bei ihr erfolgt die Überwachung des Innenraums durch einen Infrarot-Sensor. Mit dem Aktivieren der Alarmanlage, wird auch der Innenraum-Überwachungssensor aktiviert. Der Sensor führt innerhalb einer bestimmten Zeit, z.B. 10 Sekunden, einen Selbsttest durch und stellt anschließend durch Einmessen die räumlichen Gegebenheiten im Innenraum fest. Ändern sich diese Gegebenheiten mit einer Geschwindigkeit z.B. größer 0,1 Meter je Sekunde, löst das System Alarm aus.

Ultraschall-Innenraumüberwachung. Ein Ultraschallsender erzeugt im Innenraum des Fahrzeugs ein Ultraschallfeld mit einer Frequenz von ca. 20kHz. Ändert sich dieses Feld z.B. durch Hineingereifen oder Einschlagen einer Scheibe, so erkennt dies der Ultraschalldetektor anhand der Druckschwankungen im Feld. Die Auswerteelektronik lösst Alarm aus.

Kapitel 3　Neue Technologie // Chapter 3　New Technology

Neue Wörter

das	Diebstahlschutzsystem	防盗锁止系统
die	Zentralverriegelung	中控锁，中央闭锁装置
die	Wegfahrsperre	汽车防盗锁，防盗锁死装置
die	Innenraumüberwachung	内室防盗监测
der	Rad-und Abschleppschutz	车轮防盗和牵引保护
der	Türkontaktschalter	车门触点开关
das	Infrarot-Fernbedienungssystem	红外遥控系统
das	Funktfernbedienungssystem	无线电遥控系统
	verriegeln	闩上，关上
das	Steuergerät	控制器
der	Infrarot-Empfänger	红外线信号接收器
das	Infrarotsignal	红外信号
der	Zündschlüssel	点火开关钥匙
das	Zündschloss	点火开关
der	Transponder	发射应答器
die	Induktionsspule	感应线圈
das	Transformatorprinzip	变压器原理
die	Chipspule	芯片线圈
der	Transponderspeicher	转调存储器
der	Startvorgang	起动过程
	scharfgeschaltet	警报增强的
	unbefugt	擅自的，未经授权的
der	Ultraschall-Empfänger	超声波接收器
die	Motorhaube	发动机舱罩
die	Heckklappe	汽车后门
der	Kofferraum	行李舱
das	Handschuhfach	杂物箱
der	Lagesensor	位置传感器
die	Statusanzeige	状态指示器，状态指针
der	Ultraschallsender	超声波发送器，发射器
das	Signalhorn	喇叭
die	Startanlage	起动装置
die	Demontage	拆卸，解体
der	Innenraumsensor	车内传感器
das	Ablagefach	储物箱
die	Mittelkonsole	副仪表板
die	Spannungsversorgung	电压馈电
das	Blicksignal	闪光信号
die	Warnblinkanlage	警报闪光装置
die	Innenraumbeleuchtung	车内照明
das	Abblendlicht	近光灯
die	Entriegelungstaste	释放按钮，开锁触键
der	Schließzylinder	锁芯
die	Infrarot-Innenraumüberwachung	红外室内监控
die	Ultraschall-Innenraumüberwachung	超声波室内监控
der	Infrarot-Sensor	红外传感器
das	Ultraschallfeld	超声场
der	Ultraschalldetektor	超声检波器
die	Druckschwankung	压力波动
die	Auswerteelektronik	测量电子装置

Text 2 Anti-theft alarm system (ATA) 汽车防盗系统（英文）

This comprises the following components:

- ECUs, controllers and status indicator.
- Contact switches, for example for doors, bonnet/hood, boot/trunk lid, luggage or glove compartment.
- Infrared or ultrasonic interior monitoring system.
- Position sensor for wheel theft and tow-away protection.
- Signal horn with integrated power supply.
- Glass breakage sensors.

ATA activation. Activation can be automatic or can be set by the driver using the key. The alarm is issued after 10 to 20 seconds and is indicated via a flashing LED, for instance. Prior to the alarm, the control unit checks by way of the contact switches that the doors, windows, sliding sunroof, bonnet/hood and boot/trunk lid are closed.

Alarm trigger. The alarm is triggered by:

- unauthorised opening of doors, boot/trunk lid or bonnet/hood.
- intrusion into the interior.
- use of a key with an invalid transponder code.
- removal of the interior sensor/signal horn.
- removal of the radio.
- opening the glove or storage compartments.
- interruption of power supply to ATA ECU.
- change in vehicle position.
- pulling out the trailer hitch connector.

Alarm types. There are two types of alarm:

- Audible alarm via a separate alarm siren with integrated power supply.
- Visual alarm via the hazard warning system, the interior lighting or the dipped-beam headlamps.

Alarm duration. This is regulated by UN/ECE Regulation 97. In Europe, the audible alarm may sound for a max. of 30 seconds per event and must be silenced immediately after disarming.

Deactivation. This is done by pressing the unlock button on the remote control or inserting an authorised key into the electronic ignition lock.

Interior monitoring system. On activation of the alarm system, the motion sensors are also activated. A distinction is made between:

Infrared interior monitoring. With this system, monitoring of the interior is performed by an infrared sensor. It reacts to heat sources, such as people, and triggers the alarm.

Ultrasonic interior monitoring. A transmitter in the interior of the vehicle generates an ultrasonic field with a frequency of approx. 20kHz. The field changes, for instance in response to intrusion or a window being broken. The ultrasonic detector recognises the field change and triggers the alarm.

New Words

anti-theft alarm system	防盗报警系统	invalid	无效的
controller	控制器	transponder code	应答器编码
status indicator	状态指示	interior sensor	车内传感器
hood	发动机舱罩	trailer hitch connector	拖车连接器
ultrasonic	超声波	audible alarm	音响报警
interior monitoring system	内部监控系统	dipped-beam	近光灯
position sensor	位置传感器	deactivation	钝化，失活
tow-away	拖车	heat source	热源
glass breakage sensor	玻璃破裂传感器	transmitter	发射机
sliding sunroof	滑动天窗	detector	探测器
intrusion	干扰		

课文参考译文

汽车防盗系统

汽车防盗系统大多是与汽车中的中央控制门锁联系在一起安装的。汽车防盗系统具有以下任务：

- 防护整车被盗。
- 防护汽车部件被盗，例如：收音机，安全气囊等。
- 防护汽车伤害。

汽车防盗系统由以下部件构成：

- 防止他人开走的装置。
- 报警装置。
- 车内监控装置。
- 车轮及拖拽防护装置。

汽车防盗系统如同中央控制门锁一样通过以下方式激活：

- 利用车门接触开关的机械式车钥匙锁止系统。

——红外线遥控锁止系统。

——遥控系统。

当汽车用钥匙锁止时，控制单元通过车门接触开关获得激活防盗系统的信息。

当汽车用红外线以及无线电遥控锁止时，红外线接收器将从发射器接收到的信号或无线电信号转变成电信号，并转送至控制单元，控制单元激活防盗系统。

防盗锁止装置为一个电子系统，它防止未经许可的个人擅自操纵汽车。汽车安全保险的法律基础是德国道路交通法规的38a条款以及欧洲经济委员会的EU指令的规定。自该法规实施之日起，以往拔下点火钥匙及锁死车门即视为安全的规定不再适用。

防盗锁止系统由控制单元和手持式发射器或发射应答器组成。手持式发射器或发射应答器可以集成在电子钥匙或磁卡中。

发射应答器由一个封装在玻璃体内的微芯片和一个感应线圈组成。发射应答器由点火锁上的感应线圈提供电能，微芯片在生产过程中存入唯一的不可删除的密码（识别码），同时有一个可编程存储器（EEPROM）存储可改变的密码。

作用方式：当钥匙在点火锁中转动时，能量开始传输，汽车发动机防盗锁止系统控制单元开始问询过程。发射应答器检测问询信号并发送识别码，将识别码与存储在存储器内的密码进行比较。

如果密码正确，汽车发动机防盗锁止控制单元将通过CAN总线传递一组编码的数字信号至发动机管理控制单元。如果这一信号被控制单元认可，发动机就可以被起动。如果密码不正确，发动机将不能被起动。

同时汽车防盗锁止系统随意产生一组新的密码，并存储在发射应答器可编程的部分（密码变换过程）。通过这种方式可以确保每一次起动发动机都有一个新的正确的密码储存在钥匙内，以取代旧的作废的密码。

报警装置：当陌生人进入车内或冲击汽车时敏感的报警装置会激活声光警报系统。该系统由以下部件构成：

——遥控装置。

——具有供电功能的电控单元。

——车内监控用超声波接收器。

——车门接触开关。

——发动机舱罩、行李舱盖及杂物箱盖接触开关。

——车轮及防拖拽用位置传感器。

——状态显示装置。

——车内监控用超声波发射器。

——信号喇叭。

——起动装置。

作用方式：一旦警报装置激活，电控单元便开始检测，车门、车窗、天窗、发动机舱罩、行李舱盖是否关闭。通过车门接触开关确定车门以及行李舱盖是否锁止。如果满足锁止状态的所有前提条件，在10~20s的延迟时间后，所有报警装置均处于工作状态。防盗报警系统的警报随时准备通过状态显示器，例如闪光的LED显示。

以下部件可以激活警报：
- 所有车门。
- 行李舱盖。
- 进入车内。
- 起动。
- 将具有无效代码的钥匙插入点火锁。
- 拆卸车内传感器。
- 开启发动机舱罩。
- 打开收音机。
- 打开座间杂物盒盖。
- 拆卸警报喇叭。
- 电控单元有时供电中断。

当系统激活时警报可以通过额外安装的信号喇叭、闪光信号以及车内照明灯发出。警报时间根据不同国家的规定确定，例如：信号喇叭可以产生超过30s的声音信号，闪光灯装置可以产生超过30s的闪光信号。同时，当今在车上普遍安装的防盗锁也可阻止发动机的起动。

防盗系统可以通过按动遥控装置上的解除按钮以及通过汽车锁止装置的锁销切断。

车内监控通过红外线传感器来实现。用这一传感器激活警报装置，即利用车内监控传感器来激活。传感器在确定的时间内，例如10s进行自测，接着通过测量车内现况进行确认。如果现况以大于0.1m/s的速度改变则报警系统激活。

超声波车内监控利用超声波发射器在车内产生约20kHz频率的超声波场。如果这一超声波场有所变化，例如，有人进入车内或打碎玻璃，超声检测器便根据场内压力波动进行识别。评价后电子装置便激活警报。